ROYALS AND REBELS

PRIYA ATWAL

Royals and Rebels

The Rise and Fall of the Sikh Empire

HURST & COMPANY, LONDON

First published in the United Kingdom in 2020 by
C. Hurst & Co. (Publishers) Ltd.,
41 Great Russell Street, London, WC1B 3PL

Printed in the United Kingdom by Bell and Bain Ltd, Glasgow

A Cataloguing-in-Publication data record for this book is available from the British Library.

ISBN: 9781787383081

This book is printed using paper from registered sustainable and managed sources.

www.hurstpublishers.com

Every effort has been made to trace the collection currently holding Figure 9, the portrait of Maharani Mai Nakain, which is available on Wikimedia Commons under a Creative Commons licence. The publisher would be pleased to hear from the collection-holder to rectify any error or omission.

CONTENTS

Maps vi
List of Illustrations ix
Acknowledgements xi

Introduction 1
1. To Be a Sikh King 11
2. New Dynasty, New Empire 43
3. All the World's a Stage 85
4. After the Lion: Writing the Story of Ranjit Singh's Heirs 125
5. The Boy-King, the Rebel Queen and the British Empire 171
Conclusion 207
Appendices: Queens of the Sikh Empire 215

Notes 225
Bibliography 251
Index 263

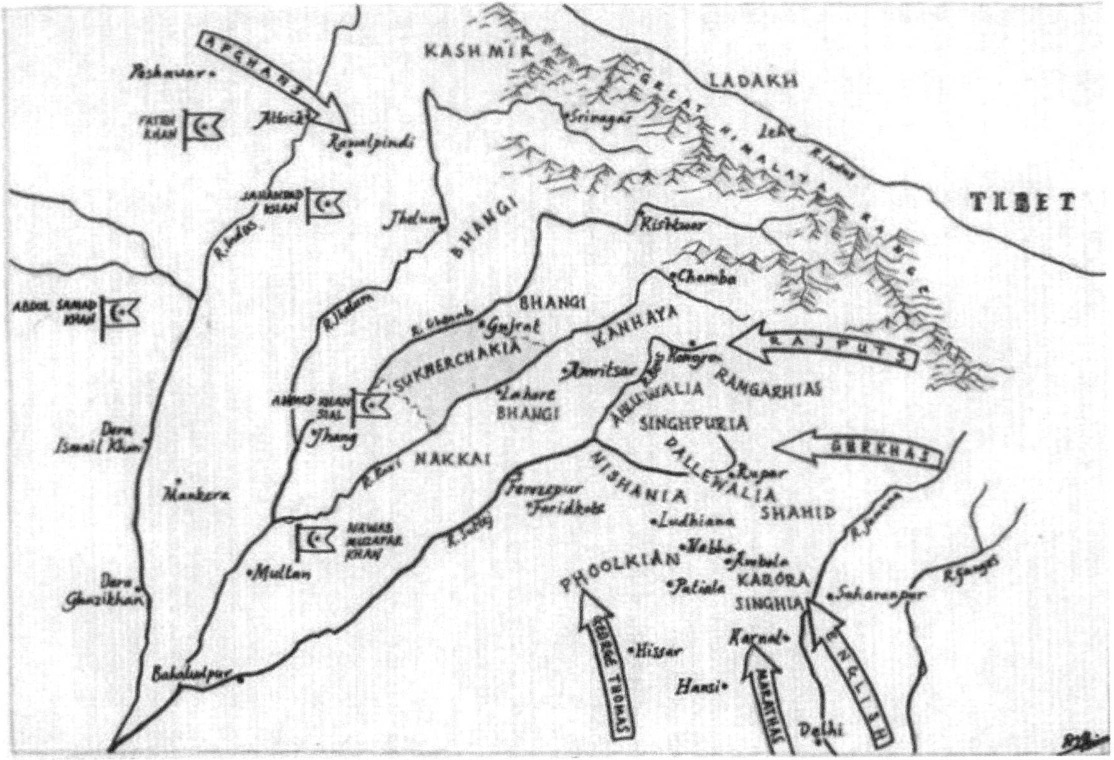

Map 1: The twelve Sikh *misls* or clans and surrounding powers, eighteenth century. © Navtej Heer.

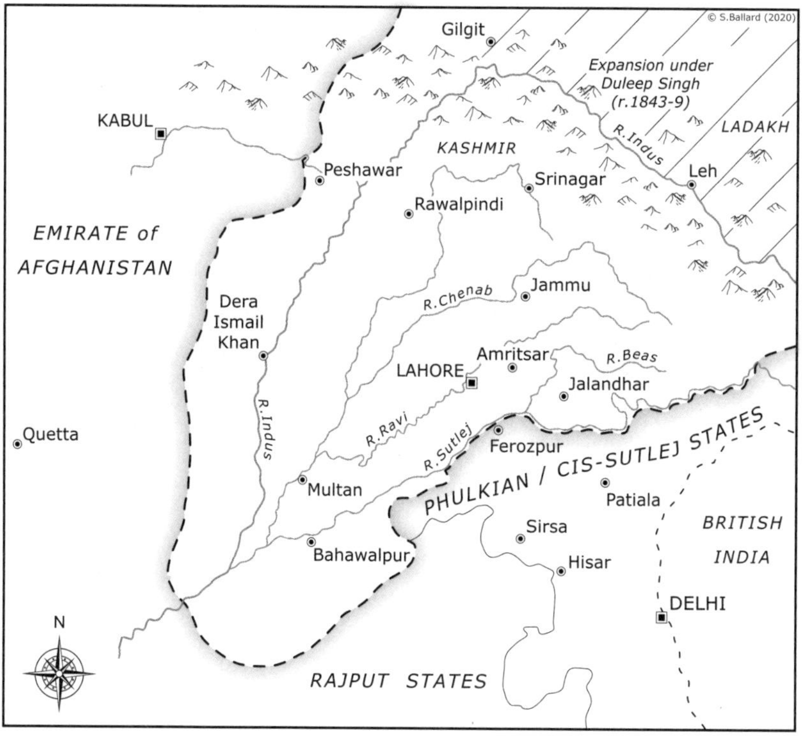

Map 2: The Sikh Empire and surrounding powers, first half of nineteenth century.

LIST OF ILLUSTRATIONS

The author and the publisher thank the following for their kind permission to reproduce illustrations in this book: Aown Ali (AA), the British Library (BL), the British Museum (BM), the Kapany Collection (KC), the Samrai Collection (SC) and the Victoria and Albert Museum, London (V&A).

1. Guru Nanak and Bhai Mardana in a landscape (SC).
2. Guru Arjan, seated portrait (SC).
3. Guru Gobind Singh, equestrian portrait mounted on a Mughal album page (SC).
4. Maharajah Ranjit Singh (© V&A).
5. Ranjit Singh's throne (© V&A).
6. Golden Temple, Amritsar (photograph by Kay v11, Creative Commons Attribution 4.0 International).
7. Scene from the Persian epic the *Shahnameh*: Rustem slaying a dragon with Guru Nanak and Guru Arjan depicted in the borders (SC).
8. Ranjit Singh and wives (Wellcome Collection, Creative Commons Attribution 4.0 International).
9. Maharani Mai Nakain (collection unknown, Wikimedia Commons/Creative Commons Attribution 4.0 International).
10. Mai Nakain's apartments, fresco of Guru Gobind Singh (photograph by AA).
11. Mai Nakain's apartments, ground-floor courtly fresco (photograph by AA).
12. Mai Nakain's apartments, courtyard (photograph by AA).
13. Ranjit Singh's wives committing *sati* at his funeral (© Trustees of the BM).
14. Maharajah Kharak Singh (SC).
15. Two men look through a telescope, Sanskrit astronomy manuscript (© BL Board. All Rights Reserved / Bridgeman Images).

16. Signs of the Zodiac, Sanskrit astronomy manuscript (© BL Board. All Rights Reserved / Bridgeman Images).
17. Maharajah Nau Nihal Singh (SC).
18. Nau Nihal Singh's haveli, western window (photograph by AA).
19. Nau Nihal Singh's haveli, lions around southeastern window (photograph by AA).
20. Nau Nihal Singh's haveli, interior (photograph by AA).
21. Maharani Chand Kaur (National Army Museum; public domain).
22. Maharajah Sher Singh (SC).
23. Maharani Jind Kaur (KC).
24. Maharajah Duleep Singh in *durbar* (SC).
25. Rajah Dhyan Singh, seated on a pavilion in the Lahore Fort (SC).
26. Rajah Gulab Singh, seated against a bolster (SC).
27. Sir Henry Lawrence (National Army Museum; public domain).
28. Duleep Singh signs the Treaty of Lahore (© Trustees of the BM).

ACKNOWLEDGEMENTS

This book has been a long time in the making and the list of people I wholeheartedly wish to thank is equally lengthy, so these acknowledgements will probably only scratch the surface. The very first people I have to thank are my old friends from the Oxford University Sikh Society. A talk they organised eleven years ago about Patwant Singh and Jyoti Rai's captivating *Empire of the Sikhs* was a remarkably fateful event in my life. Rupinder Ghatrora (the kind of friend who is also a bit like a big sister) told me strictly beforehand that, as I was the only History student in the group, I had better help out by asking the speaker a question, so that the Q&A wouldn't just be one big awkward silence. It wasn't a problem in the end: the talk captivated me to such an extent that I've not been able to stop asking questions ever since—sorry if it's got a bit much by now, guys!

I will never forget the strange and unexpected mixture of emotions that arose within me as I was listening to the speaker at that talk. Despite growing up in a Sikh family, and studying History at university, I had never otherwise learnt that a 'Sikh Empire' had once existed; nor that such fascinating characters as Ranjit Singh or Jind Kaur had once been its living, breathing, royal rulers. I was excited and fascinated by this sudden discovery of an overlooked aspect of my heritage, but also angry and disappointed that I had been ignorant about it for so long. These feelings drove me to sign up immediately as a volunteer with the Anglo-Sikh Heritage Trail, which had contributed the speaker who gave such a great talk, so that I could start learning more as soon as possible. My passion for this subject, and particularly my insatiable curiosity about the intriguing political career of Maharani Jind Kaur, kept me going long enough thereafter: first to write an undergraduate thesis, and then to undertake a PhD, so that I could research this history in as much depth and breadth as possible. It feels so exciting now to be sharing these findings with new readers in the form of a book, which I sincerely hope will ignite the spark of curiosity amongst more of us. There is so much more to learn about this fascinating period of history, and there are still so many important questions to be asked.

There are many people whose support and generosity have helped me to develop the ideas and research underpinning this book (all blame for any faults or mistakes of course lies with me). I wouldn't have been able to imagine and learn about Punjabi society in anywhere near as much depth had it not been for the support of Stephen Gucciardi and Mozghan Samadi in teaching me to read Punjabi and Persian; and also of Sahba Shayani and Zahra Shah, who translated and helped me to interpret passages of tricky Persian handwriting. I am also grateful for the help of staff at the Bodleian Library, the Royal Asiatic Society Library, the Royal Archives and the National Records of Scotland. I would like to offer particular thanks to the staff who work in the Asian & African Studies Room at the British Library, whose wit and good humour made my many visits there over the past eleven years extremely enjoyable.

My ideas on the Sikh Empire began to take formal shape under the wonderful guidance of Rosalind O'Hanlon, first as my undergraduate thesis supervisor and then as an examiner for my doctoral thesis. My work has been deeply enriched by her insightful comments and by learning from her invaluable expertise on early modern Indian history. I have equally to thank Peter Singh Bance for being so generous in sharing his incredible collection of Duleep Singh family artefacts and his own personal knowledge with me over the past ten years, since I first turned up at his office with a ton of questions about Sikh Empire history! I am also grateful to the incredibly generous colleagues and advisers who have read various thesis drafts for me over the years: Pritam Singh, Radha Kapuria, Amar Sohal, Nadhra Khan, Margret Frenz, James Belich and Miles Taylor. Each of you pushed me to think more deeply and creatively about my writing, and my work has benefitted immeasurably as a result. However, my biggest thank you in this regard has to go to my DPhil supervisor, Faisal Devji. Faisal has the most awe-inspiring intellect, combined with a quietly kind, generous nature—it was my immense good fortune to have the opportunity of working with him. It was also Faisal who encouraged me to be ambitious with the scope of this book, and not to shy away from tackling the entire rise and fall of the Sikh Empire, so I particularly hope he enjoys the result!

On that note, I also have to thank Michael Dwyer, for taking a chance on me as a first-time author. The time and encouragement that he personally gave me in the early stages of writing were incredibly kind, and I am delighted to have found such a happy home for my book, with Hurst. Thanks to Rhianna Louise for her publicity support, and to the two anonymous reviewers who kindly provided valuable, constructive feedback for the development of my manuscript. The biggest star is my editor, Lara Weisweiller-Wu. I feel like the luckiest writer in the world to have had Lara in my corner. She is incredibly smart, thoughtful and patient, and has been such a champion in helping me to say and achieve what I wanted to with the writing of this book. I have been deeply touched by the energy and care that she has dedicated to this volume, and cannot thank her enough.

Alongside the manuscript itself, I am delighted to be able to share a beautiful array of images in the pages of this book. I am honoured that the Samrai Collection has kindly agreed to let me print a number of previously unpublished paintings in its rare and wonderful collection of original artwork from Maharajah Ranjit Singh's court. Alongside these, I am equally grateful to Aown Ali for permitting me to print his photographs of the crumbling, but still fascinating, remains of Sikh royal architecture in Pakistan. Such visual sources have been immensely important in deepening my understanding of the lived dynamics of this period; helping me to uncover rich and sometimes forgotten perspectives that written sources perhaps only hint at. They are also treasures for the eye, and I hope that readers of this book enjoy studying them more closely. Another stunning image adorns the jacket of this volume: the fantastic cover illustration is by the extraordinarily talented Singh Twins. I am a huge fan of their work, and feel a thrill of excitement and gratitude every time I look at the cover.

Last but not least, I have to thank the dream team of loved ones who have supported me in my everyday life. My amazing colleagues and friends at King's College London have been a huge source of encouragement: especially Anna Maguire, Alana Harris, Bérénice

Guyot-Réchard, Abigail Woods; but, above all, my 'office buddy' Katharina Oke. Over the past two years, my wonderful friends have made me laugh, wiped away tears and kept me going during the personal highs and lows that have shaped this time. Simi Bansal, Arvinder Liddar, Lubna Ahmed, Steph Rowan, Amar Sohal, Aman Brar, Vicky McGuinness, Nisha Julka, Julia Heitmann and Sukh Sodhi—you have all lifted and inspired me in so many ways, and are the most amazing bunch of friends anyone could ask for. Thanks also to Jo Inskip for your patient, listening ear; and to Jan Marshall and Tim Charlton for letting me stay in your beautiful home, giving me the sanctuary I needed to see through a most difficult chapter.

For my family, a different message. To my siblings, Amrit, Lakshmi and Amar, I love you guys. Thank you to my Mum and Dad for being the kind of parents who gave me, their daughter, the opportunity to enjoy a great education, as well as the freedom and encouragement to pursue my own dreams and interests. For that I will be forever grateful. I dedicate this book to my grandfather, Avtar Singh Atwal. Much like Ranjit Singh himself, he never had the opportunity to get much of an education, but this didn't stop him from being an inquisitive and charming character. I lost my beloved grandfather last year, as I was nearing the end of the first draft of this book; but knowing that he was so proud and excited about it enabled me to keep going with writing, even on the most difficult days. And so, Baba, I hope you're happy that your name is now printed in a book, even if you didn't get to go to school as a little boy.

INTRODUCTION

Weddings are a big deal in many cultures around the world, but Punjabis are perhaps among the most notorious for their zeal in celebrating such occasions. Until 1947, the Punjab was one of the northernmost territories of undivided India, bordering Afghanistan, Nepal and Tibet. Like the rest of India, the region was partitioned in a hasty and rather thoughtless colonial exercise as the British made their exit, split between the new independent states of India and Pakistan—prompting a mass migration of millions of Punjabis in both directions across the new border. Even before that traumatic episode, many thousands of people of Punjabi heritage had scattered themselves around the world for a wide variety of reasons, forming an influential global diaspora from the late nineteenth century, if not earlier. Despite the dramatic social and cultural shifts that have accompanied these events in Punjabi history, marriages have consistently remained celebrations of huge importance for Punjabis. Today, recognition of this fact has spawned a fascination with the 'big fat Punjabi wedding' in Bollywood movies and academic studies alike. Punjabi weddings are known as joyful occasions, legendary for the boisterously fun ways in which they are celebrated—whilst also too often bearing a darker side, with a devastating socio-economic cost for the bride's family.[1]

Perhaps the ultimate wedding to end all weddings in Punjabi history was one held in 1837, to mark the first marriage of Prince Nau Nihal Singh. Nau Nihal Singh was the eldest grandson of the great Maharajah Ranjit Singh, a figure much valorised in Punjabi and even wider South Asian history as the *Sher-e-Punjab*—'the Lion of Punjab'. He is credited with having founded the rich and powerful Sikh Empire, which lasted from approximately 1799 to 1849. The guest list for his grandson's wedding would surely have read as a 'who's who' of the north Indian elite at the time, and at the top of this list were most certainly the representatives of the British East India Company, whose actions and opinions are recorded by history far more fully and faithfully than even those of the bridal family. Ranjit Singh spared no expense for such guests, wishing the pomp and glamour to make a lasting impression: the Maharajah sitting on a colourfully bedecked elephant, showering gold coins upon a crowd of local onlookers, was just one awe-inspiring spectacle among many others that he arranged for the month-long festivities.

> the Maharaja rode from the Shish Mahal, showered gold on the way and then went to the fort of Bhangian and felt greatly pleased with the performance of various ceremonies connected with the marriage of the *Kanwarji* [Nau Nihal Singh]. The mother of the glorious Prince, who was given to the veil behind the screen of chastity, came forward and the Maharaja said to her, 'This is the most auspicious and fortunate day I have been vouchsafed by God to see. I must thank the Almighty, for such a day was not vouchsafed even to my forefathers.[2]

The Maharajah certainly had a keen sense of the occasion. The lavish celebration of his grandson's marriage was not just another family party—like all royal weddings, it was a political and diplomatic performance, and a lasting reminder of the dynasty's spectacular rise. Ranjit Singh was for all intents and purposes a self-made Maharajah, who had built outwards and upwards from his clan's ancestral estate in Gujranwala, northwest Punjab. He conquered the former Mughal imperial capital of Lahore and eventually laid claim to almost the entire region of Punjab. At the time of Nau Nihal Singh's wedding, Ranjit Singh was at the height of his power. His burgeoning kingdom was making predatory inroads into Afghan and Tibetan territory, with particular success in the Himalayan passes around Ladakh. In the fluid and competitive world of eighteenth- and early-nineteenth-century India, following the decline of the great Mughal Empire, Ranjit Singh's kingdom was one of the subcontinent's most stellar success stories—rivalling for a time that other major player to emerge in the same era, the East India Company itself.

So the Maharajah had every reason in 1837 to exult with great joy amidst the glorious scenes at his grandson's wedding. He was the ruler of a fabulously wealthy kingdom, and the nuptials being celebrated marked a sense of hope that his newly established dynasty would hold sway in the Punjab for several more generations to come. Indeed, in the court records of the event, little mention is made of Nau Nihal Singh's bride or of her family, who are portrayed as being honoured even to have the Maharajah enter their home, let alone the even greater 'privilege' of having a daughter marry into his royal family. This wedding was really Ranjit Singh's story: both a proud day for him as a grandfather, and a triumph for the dynasty.

What particularly brings this home in the quote above is the Maharajah's recollection of his forefathers as he contemplates the celebrations. Neither Ranjit Singh's father nor his grandfather had lived long enough to see a grandchild of theirs come into the world. By contrast, the chronicles of Ranjit Singh's own court are full of records of his close relationship with his eldest grandson. Nau Nihal Singh doted on his grandfather as a child and young teenager. Now sixteen, the bridegroom was evidently a talented and dashing young prince, and the vaunted ideal heir to the throne—so of course his marriage was a special, even emotional moment for his grandfather to enjoy. But it was also a moment of enormous political importance.

Ranjit Singh spent his lifetime raising his family to dizzying new heights, not only in the reach of their territorial power but also in their social standing. As a young boy, he had inherited the charge of a *misl*: a Sikh warrior band that claimed to protect and control a particular swathe of Punjabi territory. From the early eighteenth century, twelve Sikh *misls* had emerged, they were originally intended to have equal status and to serve the wider Sikh community by protecting the land from external aggression, keeping the peace, and collecting revenue and resources for the support and betterment of Sikhs and Punjabis collectively. However, by the time Ranjit Singh came to power at the turn of the nineteenth century, a considerable gap had arisen between these egalitarian ideals that had once briefly motivated the *misls*, and the more opportunistic political actions of their leaders, the *sardars*. A deeply competitive rivalry broke out between the *sardars*, despite the strongly prevalent expectation that they honour the tenets of their Sikh faith and remain humble in their exercise of any temporal authority, rather than seeking to aggrandise their own fortunes at the expense of their own brethren. Within two or three generations, individual *sardars* had increasingly been turning the territories guarded by their *misls* into landed estates to be controlled in hereditary fashion by their sons or wider kin: many later developed them into their own small kingdoms.

This was the fiercely contested and changing elite world that Ranjit Singh entered when he became chief of the Sukerchakia *misl* in 1792, at the tender age of twelve. For much of the century, this had in fact been one of the smaller *misls*, but under Ranjit Singh's grandfather and father, Charat Singh and Maha Singh, it had emerged as the most competitive and ambitious. As we will see in the first chapters, the new young *sardar* continued to build on this strength, swallowing up the land of most other *misls* by the mid-1810s. Thus when Ranjit Singh, by then Maharajah, thanked God for allowing him to see a day 'not vouchsafed' even to his forefathers, I think we can rightly imagine him expressing delight in his family's standing, at a height that may have wildly exceeded the hopes and aspirations of those earlier generations.

How and why Ranjit Singh chose to embrace a monarchical style of rulership and to pass on the charge not just of a *misl* but an entire empire to his heirs, despite the potentially contradictory pulls of his Sikh heritage, is a topic that deserves much closer consideration than history has given it so far. This book endeavours to investigate these questions in a thoughtful fashion, and in no small part from an even more neglected perspective: the role played in the rise and fall of the 'Sikh Empire'[3] by the ruling women and young princes of Ranjit Singh's new royal house. These were key figures who, of course, would have played a prominent part in the wedding of Nau Nihal Singh, but who have been largely eclipsed in both contemporary and later written records of the event by the focus on the lionised Maharajah. From top to bottom, whether servants or queens, many other people contributed to the successes that led up to and enabled the staging of such a grand royal wedding—from those whose work went into the immediate organisation of its many glittering events, to those with a role in the military conquests, state-building and diplomacy that had created a kingdom vast and wealthy enough to fund and host such prestigious celebrations in the first place.

Whilst Ranjit Singh has received a great deal of attention from historians and biographers, these other people have remained mostly in the shadows. This book keeps to an elite perspective, focusing on the activities and destinies of the women and young princes among the Maharajah's immediate kin, and their role in shaping the fortunes of the nascent Sikh Empire. The idea for this book stemmed from my original desire to write a biography about Ranjit Singh's last wife and queen, Maharani Jind Kaur—who acted as regent for their young son, Duleep Singh, between 1843 and 1846. Jind Kaur had the responsibility of managing the kingdom thrust upon her whilst still in her early twenties, and under deeply treacherous circumstances: her five-year-old son was made the new Maharajah after his older half-brothers had been killed in the bloody power struggles following Ranjit Singh's death in 1839. When Duleep Singh and Jindan (as she was popularly known) were enthroned in 1843, the expectation of the governing Punjabi ministers and British political officers who engineered their accession was that the little boy and his young mother would be pliant puppet rulers, who would stand by and watch whilst the new prime minister, Rajah Hira Singh, entrenched his own power as the de facto leader. However, to their dismay, Jind Kaur was not a woman to be overlooked lightly. The more I learnt about the Maharani's political career, the more it emerged that—although she was evidently not always the most shrewd or mature politician (especially at the outset of her reign)—she made up for these weaknesses with her sheer determination and fierce commitment to maintaining the independence of her son's position as Maharajah.

I was intrigued by the 'saint/sinner' reputation that had settled around Jindan from the late 1840s onwards, after she was forcibly separated from her nine-year-old son and banished from Lahore on the orders of Henry Montgomery Lawrence, the then Political Resident and Jindan's main rival for control over the Lahore government. Lawrence had succeeded in ousting the Maharani after weakening her reputation as much as he could by exploiting her unpopularity amongst several of the key male Punjabi figures in the Lahore *durbar* (court). He had drawn on specious evidence of her complicity in a plot to assassinate both Lawrence himself and one of the former generals of the Sikh army, in order to accuse of her treason; and he had lent credence to rumours that Jindan spent her nights in the company of multiple lovers, such 'debauchery' rendering her an unfit mother and example to the Maharajah. Jind Kaur fought back hard against Lawrence and his gendered manipulation of her image and political freedom, but without success. Yet, while under house arrest at Sheikhupura Fort, she took to discreetly plotting an anti-British rebellion, which was subsequently known as the Second Anglo-Sikh War. Today, the Maharani is almost as valorised within Sikh history as Ranjit Singh himself, but for different qualities: if he was the Lion of Punjab, then Jind Kaur was the heroic rebel queen, who courageously fought to protect her husband's and son's empire, and ultimately the freedom of the Sikhs and Punjab as a whole.

As an undergraduate and later as a PhD student, I was keen to explore the interesting dichotomy in Jind Kaur's 'heroine'/'whore' reputation among past commentators and biographers, and to examine her apparently outlying status as a female leader in Punjab amongst a swathe of powerful Sikh and British men. As I began delving into the records of the era, it became clear to me that Jindan was not such an exception after all. The story of female power in the Sikh Empire, and even the power of their sons—the young princes of Punjab—is much richer and more significant than historians have acknowledged. The very place where Jind Kaur was first imprisoned, Sheikhupura Fort, is itself redolent with the historical legacy of the Punjabi royal women who came before her. The fort and its neighbouring lands had been the landed estate of Mai Nakain, the second wife of Ranjit Singh and grandmother to Prince Nau Nihal Singh. A close reading of the courtly chronicles from Lahore and neighbouring Sikh states reveals tantalising fragments and snippets about this Maharani's activities in the early nineteenth century, during the making of the Sikh Empire. I discovered just how active Mai Nakain was not only in the local administration of her estate, but also in diplomatic relations, military campaigns and the education of her son, Kharak Singh, who was Ranjit Singh's eldest son and the first heir to the new Lahore throne.

Mai Nakain was the queen to whom Ranjit Singh was expressing his delight at the royal wedding, though her name was covered in that account with a literary 'veil of chastity' by its author, Sohan Lal Suri, the conservative chronicler of events at the Lahore court. Suri is just one of a long line of commentators on the history of the Sikh Empire to have relegated the Maharani and many of her contemporaries to a marginal role, if they are mentioned at all. Yet even the small fragments of evidence that remain about women such as Mai Nakain give us a vivid glimpse of the integral role that they played in building the famed empire and dynasty that emerged in nineteenth-century Punjab. This is the culture that should frame our view of Jind Kaur's part in the desperate battle to keep the dynasty's power alive and out of British hands in the late 1840s. Making these links allows us to appreciate at a deeper level how Punjabi political culture worked, and to understand—finally—how critically important women were within it. Only by looking at how the nature of royal women's agency changed over time can we understand the arguably fateful consequences of these shifts, for royal Punjabi culture and for the Sikh Empire as a whole.[4]

The young Duleep Singh also saw his own position—the very role and status of the Sikh Maharajah—evolve significantly in the 1840s, amid conflicting and changing expectations. Just as his mother's queenly predecessors inform our view of Jind Kaur's own actions, we can see both the legacy Duleep inherited and how it was disrupted during his reign by looking back: the training and lifestyles of not only his illustrious father, but equally importantly his older fellow princes, reveal the culture that emerged around elite Punjabi boys and young men. Their duties and education were designed to prepare them for their future responsibilities, and were just as important in the formation of the Sikh Empire as the personality of Ranjit Singh.

Historians have so far paid little attention to these aspects of the Empire, which has really limited our understanding not only of how this kingdom came into being and how it operated, but also how and why it fell after just fifty years of existence. This oversight is partly down to who was controlling the narrative in the crucial decade between Ranjit Singh's death in 1839 and the East India Company's annexation of the Sikh Empire in 1849. Accounts of this period have been dominated by the voices of British imperial officers and political commentators, many of whom were highly dismissive of the Maharajah's successors, heaping blame on them for the unruly state of affairs at Lahore after his death and the subsequent fallout in Anglo-Sikh relations, which eventually led to wars between the Empire and the Company in 1845–9. Subsequent generations of historians and biographers have not been critical enough in their analyses of these early British accounts, many of which were written by Company officers who were increasingly keen to establish direct British sway over the Punjab, in order to bring that wealthy and vital geopolitical region under tighter control for the benefit of the Company's financial health and security.

If we take these colonial texts in the order in which they were written and published, and look more closely at how they discussed the activities of Ranjit Singh and his family, what we find is that these British narratives had their own internal tensions and debates, which clearly evolved over time and actually presented a set of very mixed views about the Maharajah's dynasty. As the later chapters of this book will show, the more negative narratives about Ranjit Singh's heirs were more highly favoured by senior Company officials, and only gained prominence over time—particularly after the British had been to war with the Sikhs and eventually conquered their kingdom. Such controversial acts of imperial and military fiat of course had to be justified: to support a liberal view of British policy in India, and to guard against accusations of bad faith or even stirrings of rebellion elsewhere. Ranjit Singh had been a much-loved ruler, and he had remained faithful to his friendship pact with the East India Company until his last breath. It is not surprising therefore to find many British accounts of the late Sikh Empire period which celebrate Ranjit Singh, whilst discrediting the political acumen and even right to rule of his heirs after his death—paying little heed to the role those queens and princes had played in supporting the Maharajah's rise to power during his lifetime. This simplistic categorisation of Ranjit Singh as a good ruler and his successors as bad ones has gone unquestioned, apart from the exceptionally intent fascination with the kingdom's final rulers, Jind Kaur and Duleep Singh.

In this, the history of the Sikh Empire and its royal family has something strongly in common with that of the Mughals. The style of nineteenth-century British writing about the bloody and treacherous battles for the Lahore throne that took place between 1839 and 1844 echo colonial narrative tropes about the earlier Mughal Empire, particularly the supposedly disastrous impact of princely succession struggles on weakening that state. These arguments have been used to explain the 'inherent' flaws in the governing style and structure of 'Oriental Despotism', thereby justifying or paving the way for the more 'enlightened' form of rulership that Europeans claimed provide to the East. Munis Faruqui and Ruby Lal are two scholars who have done much to confront and overturn these long-standing narratives about Mughal princes and royal women, which were spread by British colonial writers and later developed by Indian historians.[5] Instead, they have provided a much more nuanced and insightful understanding of the dynamic and integral roles played by such figures in the making and sustaining of sociopolitical networks and the cultural representation of their dynasty. This book takes inspiration from these new perspectives and approaches pioneered by historians of the Mughal dynasty. It also builds on the important work of earlier scholars in the field of Sikh and Punjabi history, including J.S. Grewal, Louis Fenech and Purnima Dhavan, who have been at the forefront of revising our understanding of the nature and culture of the Sikh rulers who emerged in this period.[6]

Royals and Rebels is therefore written in the hope of inspiring a new kind of conversation about the Sikh Empire and the worldview of its ruling elite, particularly by weaving gendered and cultural perspectives more tightly into the way we look at this period of history, and by offering a far bigger cast of characters than the central figure of Ranjit Singh. Past historians of the Sikh Empire have made ample use of many contemporary historical accounts, both Punjabi and British, but this book challenges those sources in new ways. It also pays close attention to the material remains of the royal Punjabi world, in order to bring more vividly to life some perhaps forgotten aspects of the kingdom. Remarkable artefacts such as Ranjit Singh's gilded throne or the fading paintings of Mai Nakain's private apartments can tell us deeply valuable things about the lives and thoughts of their former owners. This mixture of new material and new questions hopefully makes for a richer and more detailed history of the rise and fall of the Sikh Empire, but there is still so much research to be done.[7] I hope that this book can spark a renewed interest in such endeavours—with a view to enhancing our knowledge not only of this particular Sikh kingdom, but equally of what it meant to become and to be an Indian king.

In many ways, this retelling of the Sikh Empire—from the perspectives of the new men, women and children who were in charge of ruling over it—enables us to tap into and better appreciate something else too: the significant amount of change, competition and opportunity that characterised the eighteenth and early nineteenth centuries on the Indian subcontinent. In this period, when the Mughal Empire was crumbling away, power and territory were very much available for the taking right across South Asia. This enabled a diverse range of enterprising new elites to take hold—an eclectic mix that included Tipu Sultan, Begum Samru and of course the East India Company, to name but a few better-known examples. The Sikhs of the Punjab were another key group that benefited from this situation, fighting tooth and nail to establish control over as much of northern India as possible. But how did one royal family come to achieve pre-eminence over this entire community? And how and why did Ranjit Singh's dynasty then seek to project itself as a competitive player on the regional and even global stage, by moving to engage with the British powers that would ultimately be its downfall?

If we are to truly understand why Ranjit Singh felt so thankful on that wedding day to have exceeded the great successes of his forefathers, it is only right that we look back at the world his ancestors had lived in and helped to shape, in order to appreciate the tremendous changes that the Maharajah and his growing dynasty wrought as they built a new, imperial kingdom. This novel royal culture, painstakingly built by the royal family of the Sikh Empire, was a fascinating and cunning mix of ideas inherited and adapted from both historical and contemporary societies—the culture of the Empire's Mughal predecessors in India; newer, European notions of royal presentation; as well as Sikh traditions and values. Eighteenth-century Punjab was a crucible for all of these ideas and practices, out of which the Sikh Empire was forged. It is to that rough and ready environment that we shall now turn, leaving for the time being the spectacle and drama of royal weddings in the glittering heyday of Ranjit Singh's imperial court.

1

TO BE A SIKH KING

The early decades of the eighteenth century were a time of great hardship and precarity for Ranjit Singh's ancestors and their fellow Sikhs. In 1708, the last of their ten Gurus, Guru Gobind Singh, died of wounds inflicted on him by a pair of Pathan assassins who had infiltrated his camp. It is believed within Sikh tradition that these assassins were sent to kill the Guru on the orders of the local Mughal governor, whose authority over the territory and resources of the Punjab—a key province of the Mughal Empire—was starting to evaporate, due to the growing popularity and influence of the Sikh Gurus.

These Gurus were the spiritual leaders of a new, young religious community ('Sikh' means 'disciple' or 'learner'), which had been founded in the Punjab by the first 'teacher', Nanak (1469–1539). Guru Nanak was born into a Hindu family, but, as a child, he rejected many of the ritualistic practices that he was urged to follow, practices which had come to be associated with the Hindu religion. Though he was interested in aspects of Hindu religious thought as well as Sufi Islam, the young Nanak would shape his own ideas on spiritual philosophy, divinity and religion into a new body of beliefs, which became known as *Sikhi* (or Sikhism in modern English parlance). The Guru's teachings rejected notions of social division and hierarchy along the lines of class, creed, caste or gender, which had predominated within fifteenth century Punjabi society. He preached and wrote poetic verses about how every man, woman and child shared an equal connection with—and indeed, were a part of—the divine being of God. The figure of God is given a number of names in the *Guru Granth Sahib* (the compiled verses and teachings of the Gurus), but was essentially conceived as all-pervasive throughout the universe, both creating and destroying everything in it—a being without gender or concrete form, present in every individual and every object.

The Gurus emphasised meditation on the name of the Divine as the ultimate form of worship, as well as rejecting all kinds of hermetic and ritualistic behaviour. They encouraged Sikhs to live and work as part of the world, but said that they should aim to remain unaffected by its illusionary temptations. The inclusive, egalitarian ethos of the Sikh faith made it and the Gurus hugely popular among a wide cross-section of Punjabi society. It was supposedly Guru Har Rai, the fifth master, who first inspired Ranjit Singh's great-great-grandfather to embrace the Sikh faith.[1] The Gurus themselves placed all the credit for their inspiring ideas at the feet of the Divine, whom they referred to as the *Sacha Padishah* or 'True Emperor'. However, over time, their followers increasingly began to regard them as more than just spiritual guides, seeing them as their worldly protectors and even rulers. This gradually came to complicate the relationship between the Gurus and the political elites of their day: Hindu kings who ran small but significant states within the hills of that region, as well as later Afghan invaders, but mainly the Mughal imperial dynasty and their governors in the Punjab.

This chapter looks at the increasingly complex Sikh-Mughal relationship, during and beyond the time of the Gurus, and at the new relationships that emerged in the post-Mughal power vacuum of the eighteenth century. All of these evolving political and cultural dynamics shaped the nature of Sikh ideas of kingship in the period leading up to Maharajah Ranjit Singh's dynasty. Given the fact that several Gurus and many Sikhs were tortured and killed as a result of the Mughal state's persecutory impulses, it is unsurprising that the Mughals and their ruling culture should have taken on painful and negative associations within Sikh popular memory. However, despite this, as many contemporary historical sources show, the overall picture of the Sikh-Mughal relationship was never wholly or straightforwardly antagonistic. This will be an important fact to remember as we explore the nature of the new kingdom established by Ranjit Singh and his family at the start of the nineteenth century. We can see this clearly by entering the world of the Sikh Gurus themselves. Those ten founding masters inspired many with their influential ideas about power and leadership, forged through their exchanges and clashes with the rulers of their day—encounters that ranged from the friendly to the deadly.

Gurus and Kings

The Gurus were around at a time when monarchy was most definitely the political norm. However, we must recognise that new 'kingdoms' were still being created around the globe even into the nineteenth century, and royal elites in Ranjit Singh's day were continually trying to assert themselves in a multitude of ways—a fact that perhaps conflicts with modern, popular understandings of that century as an era in which nation-states and democracy were becoming the order of the day. Take Europe, where new states headed by royal dynasties were created throughout the nineteenth century, even as demands for constitutional reforms of monarchies were growing louder and revolutions were taking place. Examples include the kingdoms of Greece, Belgium, Bulgaria and unified Italy. This period also saw monarchical rule extended into other parts of the world now controlled by European empires. In 1815, Brazil was created as a kingdom ruled over by the Portuguese royal family; perhaps most intriguingly, in 1822, Mexicans asked for the Spanish king to remain as their head of state, despite having just defeated the Spanish imperial army in a bid to secure independence.

The same was true of India, where from the seventeenth century onwards, a vast number of new 'kingdoms' both big and small emerged on independent terms out of the ashes of the Mughal Empire—many of them would live on as 'princely states' until a short while after the end of the British Raj in 1947. In 1858, the British Crown replaced the East India Company at the head of the Indian Empire, itself laying claim to the mantle of the last Mughal Emperor. Royalty would continue to occupy an important place in the governance and rituals of South Asian political life well into the twentieth century, despite the disruptive impact of British colonialism and the rise of Indian nationalism, which largely came to favour democratic, republican rule.

As I have argued elsewhere, all of this shows that monarchies and royal cultures remained an important part of society and politics well beyond the time of the Sikh Gurus.[2] It is high time that we set Ranjit Singh and his predecessors among the Gurus and *misls* within this context. The Sikhs were clearly not the only people in India who overthrew their erstwhile rulers and charted their own path to power, and admittedly the 'Sikh Empire' was relatively short-lived by comparison with many of the other 'kingdoms' mentioned earlier, lasting for only fifty years. Yet the fact that Sikhs, too, were deeply interested in ideas of kingship shines a light not only on Sikh politics, but also to an extent on an exciting regional or even global era, filled with people trying to do new and intriguing things with royal culture. What Ranjit Singh's family did so successfully in the Punjab, and the partial origins of those ideas within Sikh culture and history, are elements of a much broader story of empire-building, experimentation and public image-shaping, as rulers sought to justify or entrench their hold on power in a competitive and changing world.

Within the Indian subcontinent alone, the Sikhs have been witness (and partly contributors) to the passing of three empires created by external conquerors: the Lodis, the Mughals and the British. The experiences of the Gurus and their people during the making and breaking of the first two not only shaped their political ideas of kingship, but also helped create an important sense of confidence within Sikh philosophy more generally: that worldly power could always be subject to challenge and resistance, if called for. This became a compelling factor that arguably empowered eighteenth-century Sikh *sardars*, including Ranjit Singh's forefathers, allowing them to aspire to royalty in their own right. This is why, to understand the rise and fall of the Sikh Empire, we must first turn to the Gurus, and the new sort of society that took shape from their ideas in early modern Punjab.

Although the Sikh Gurus criticised emperors and other ruling elites repeatedly in their writings and throughout their lifetimes, it is significant that they did not directly advocate the abolition of the monarchy at any time.[3] It was accepted as the contemporary political idiom and the institutional form of local rulership. Nevertheless, the Gurus took monarchy as a trope, along with the trappings of royal culture, as useful symbols for a creative and subversive critique of the successive rulers that the Sikhs were exposed to over the course of ten guruships and approximately two-and-a-half centuries. From these writings one gets the sense that the role of the king in and of itself is the most morally testing position a human can ever find themselves in. With such absolute power comes the greatest opportunity of all to indulge in the five core temptations and ego-centric failings that the Gurus warned against: lust, greed, attachment, anger and pride. To judge by the Gurus, then, it would seem that more was expected of a king than of anyone else, in terms of upright conduct within the world of the everyday.

This moral (or immoral) conduct of kings was clearly something that the Gurus observed up close and reflected on deeply. During the 1520s, Guru Nanak himself witnessed first-hand the invasion of Punjab and Hindustan by the army of the first Mughal Emperor, Babur, and the overthrow of the former Lodi dynasty. He wrote about these events in his moving *Baburvani* verses, which subsequently became a part of the Sikh holy teachings, the *Guru Granth Sahib*. This poetry powerfully brings to life the trauma that the conquering soldiers unleashed on the people of Punjab—rich and poor alike. From his verses, we can see that the first Guru felt the suffering and plight of women most keenly: he focuses repeatedly on describing, in explicit terms, how they are brutally attacked within their own homes. His stanzas about the shocking treatment meted out to royal women are especially evocative in illuminating how the social order of the Punjab had been completely overturned. No one could now be saved from insult or harm:

jin siri sohani patia mangi pai sandhur,
se sir kati munian gal vicu avai dhur
mahala andari hodia hun bahani na milani hadur.
(*Guru Granth Sahib*, 417)

Who once had luxuriant braids,
Adorned with auspicious vermilion,
Their hair lies hacked off with scissors;
... Their throats choke with dust.
Who once enjoyed the sanctum of palaces,
Cannot even find a spot in public...[4]

The fate of these women echoes that of their princes, as the Guru narrates how the Lodi rulers are themselves 'trampled in dust' after losing in battle to the Mughals. He touches repeatedly on the fact that tragedy befalls the lives of everyone in the region, whether Hindu or Muslim, yet the Mughals remain miraculously uninjured. He concludes that such is the 'sport' of the Creator, who enables such events to take place in the world. Guru Nanak's words thereby contain a universal warning for earthly kings like the fallen Lodis: one can be 'consumed by wealth and ultimately wasted by wealth', but even the greatest of riches will not save you when the Divine decides it is time for your demise.[5] As the first Guru tells it, the Creator is the 'True Sovereign', for whom it is a matter of play to bring down kings and make new ones; the power of a worldly ruler can do nothing to stop this, no matter how much pride they might have in their treasure chests, armies or personal strength.

We can see in the *Baburvani* verses that this '*sahib*' or 'lord' evoked both awe and anger in Guru Nanak: for being able to make such momentous events happen, but equally because he felt that the Creator had been unjust in wreaking havoc upon the lives of innocent, defenceless people, rather than simply between two equally strong armies. Interestingly, it is not Emperor Babur that the Guru tries to call to account, but the Sovereign Creator—declaring that the Divine, like any king, should not neglect treating all of his subjects with fairness.[6] The Guru was in a complex position, however: the narrative triangulation between him, Babur and God varies if we look at different accounts of Sikh history.

One later Sikh scholar called Rattan Singh Bhangu, writing long after Guru Nanak's time in the early years of Ranjit Singh's reign, suggested that the first Guru and Babur had a personal meeting, in which the Guru actually agreed to bless the invading Mughal with sovereignty (*padshahi*) over Hindustan. According to this account, which blends mythology with history, Guru Nanak had far-reaching spiritual (and political) power, acting as a blessed representative of the Creator on Earth. Bhangu portrays his Guru as the supreme spiritual sovereign of Hindustan, over and above the Prophet Muhammad:

Babur pleaded to be blessed with sovereignty over India,
So that his writ might run over the twenty-two Indian provinces.
Instantly did Prophet Muhammad reject Babur's plea with a remark,

> That He had no divine sanction for granting sovereignty over India. (76)
> ... [This] being the sole prerogative of Guru Nanak,
> Babur should have no expectations from his prophet about it. (77)[7]

Bhangu, writing in the nineteenth century, casts Guru Nanak himself as a 'prophet': not only with the power to sanctify Mughal rule over India, but equally with sufficient mystic foresight to be able to predict that, within seven generations, Babur's descendants would arrogantly turn against the Guru's own successors and proclaim themselves as 'sovereign'. In other words, sovereignty for Babur's house was not for the conqueror to take, but for Guru Nanak to grant, and his decision was an informed one, with a time-limit attached. Through this apocryphal account of the Nanak–Babur encounter, Bhangu attributes the Mughal decline to the fact that Babur's descendants broke his promise of loyalty to Guru Nanak, beginning to stray from the path of fidelity and humility, from the reign of the fourth Emperor, Jahangir (1605–27) onwards. Indeed, later generations of Mughal rulers began actively persecuting the Gurus and the Sikhs: Jahangir initiated this acrimonious shift when he ordered the torture and execution of the fifth Sikh master, Guru Arjan (of which more later). Bhangu concludes that it was Aurangzeb—the sixth and last 'Great' Mughal Emperor—who ultimately sounded the death knell of his own dynasty, by allowing Guru Tegh Bahadur to be executed and then the sons of Guru Gobind Singh to be mercilessly killed.[8]

This matters because it completely subverts Mughal-centric eighteenth-century perspectives of the relationship between the imperial state and the Sikh people. Here the Gurus and the *misls* are not deviant upstarts who threatened Mughal sovereignty; instead, Guru Nanak is the original, legitimate fount of honour for Mughal rulership. In Bhangu's telling, as soon as Babur's dynasty turned against the house of the Guru, only Sikh rule could rightfully replace Mughal political hegemony in the Punjab—specifically the Khalsa, created by Guru Gobind Singh to inherit the royal standing wrenched back from the unworthy Mughals. Bhangu offered this narrative in the nineteenth century as a corrective to British political agents who were actively seeking to gain intelligence on the Sikhs, both for themselves and for the Mughal court in Delhi, which the East India Company was continuing to prop up. Bhangu was specifically responding to a version of Sikh history by a Muslim writer in British employ, who he was concerned would only produce an account favourable to the Mughals.[9]

It is not entirely clear whether Bhangu's meeting between Guru Nanak and Babur ever took place, let alone whether the Guru actually gave the invading emperor his blessing. What is important about his version of events is its reflection of the fact that, over time, Sikhs increasingly came to perceive their Gurus as sovereign figures in their own right, and as challengers to the Mughal and other ruling elites in the Punjab. This understanding of Sikh rulers' power was at a considerable remove from the humble manner in which Guru Nanak and his successors tried to represent themselves, as the devoted 'slaves' of the Creator.[10] But it was still a belief that had become well entrenched by the time of Bhangu—which was also the time of Ranjit Singh.

* * *

In actuality, this was a shift that had its origins during the lives of the Gurus themselves. Three of the nine Sikh masters who came after Guru Nanak were particularly pivotal thinkers in developing the ideas of Sikh kingship that would later influence Ranjit Singh's conception of his own rule: Guru Arjan (1563–1606), Guru Hargobind (1595–1644) and Guru Gobind Singh (1666–1708). Beginning with Guru Nanak himself, the Gurus began establishing their own towns, wherein they could hospitably accommodate a growing congregation. The first Guru founded the settlement of Kartarpur Sahib, and Amritsar itself was created by Guru Ram Das (as Ramdaspur) and Guru Arjan. Guru Arjan also founded another town, Hargobindpur, named after his son, to celebrate the birth—recognisably 'kingly' behaviour—and the last Guru, Guru Gobind Singh, even founded a fortified town, Anandpur Sahib. The Gurus assumed central leadership over the shaping and managing of these 'pilgrimage centres', which attracted a wide variety of new residents and migrants, and quickly became flourishing socio-economic hubs in their own right, situated as they often were on key trade routes within Mughal Punjab.[11] It was not surprising that Sikhs and their neighbours would soon come to see the Gurus as the local rulers of these important towns, since their leadership over them was not only generally respected, but also integral to their functioning.

The fifth Guru, Arjan, was arguably the first to espouse a 'Sikh' philosophy of rulership, and was a key thinker on this question. He was the youngest of the four sons of the fourth Guru, Ram Das, and grew up during a period of developing confidence amongst the nascent Sikh community. As a boy, Arjan was given a rich and varied education, not only in religious matters, but equally in political philosophy and ethics—much like the training provided to a young prince of Mughal India or Renaissance Europe. After becoming Guru in 1563, he became especially scholarly, building up a library of knowledge at what would become the pre-eminent Sikh city of Amritsar. The most important of Guru Arjan's learned endeavours was his devoted effort to compile the collected works of his predecessors into a unified volume, forming the beginnings of the *Guru Granth Sahib*—to which the guruship would eventually pass according to the wishes of the last personal leader of the Sikhs, Guru Gobind Singh.

The period of Arjan's guruship was one in which the Sikh community was consolidating and really beginning to flourish. In the holy city of Amritsar, Guru Arjan worked side-by-side with his followers to construct the Harmandir Sahib (or the Golden Temple, as it is popularly known today), the most famous of all Sikh gurdwaras or shrines, on the foundation of Ramdaspur, the town constructed by his father. It is evident that the Guru actively tried to welcome as many people as possible into his community. One of the verses that he penned, which later became part of the *Guru Granth Sahib*, is striking in the way that it inverts the traditional relationship between a king and his followers, and instead depicts the Guru acting as the devoted servant of his Sikhs: 'I have established the *dharamsal* [here 'Sikh place of worship'] of Truth. I have assembled the loyal Sikhs of the Guru [*Gursikh*] after locating them assiduously from far off places. I wash their feet, wave the fan over them, and humbly touch their feet.'[12]

The mention of the fan being 'waved' over the 'loyal Sikhs' is telling. This was not just indicative of the Guru's hospitality, but was also symbolic of ancient Indic courtly practice. The *chauri* was a type of fan or whisk (often made out of a yak's tail hair) traditionally waved over a king to prevent any dust or dirt from settling on them. To this day, in gurdwaras around the world a *chauri* is continually waved over the *Guru Granth Sahib* while it is being read from, to keep it continually pristine—the words of the Gurus are thus treated as the embodiment of the wisdom of the *Sacha Padishah* ('The True Emperor', or God), and their royal, sovereign nature suitably revered.

It is clear that Guru Arjan thought deeply about the nature of his power. In his poetry and in his actions, he advanced his ideas about the concept of *halemi raj* ('just and humble rule'), which he rejoiced had been established in Amritsar: 'The merciful Lord has now ordained a commandment that none shall be domineering over others. All shall abide in peace, prosperity and justice. Thus is established the rule of justice and humility on earth.'[13] Indeed, during the Guru's lifetime, the physical complex of the Harmandir Sahib soon came to be known as the *Darbar Sahib* (roughly understood as the 'court of God'). The building at the centre of the complex, the gurdwara (a Sikh temple, but literally translating as 'the abode of the Guru') housed the compiled teachings of the five Sikh masters, which ordinary Sikhs were encouraged to revere as the Gurus themselves. The gurdwara was then constructed with doors on all four sides, to symbolise how people from all backgrounds and walks of life are welcome in the earthly abode of the Divine. The fact that this shrine was built by the collective labour of Guru Arjan and his followers echoes the idealised nature of the new kind of just, egalitarian and harmonious society that the Sikh Gurus were seeking to create.

Interestingly, the gurdwara was positioned on an island-like plinth in the middle of a large water tank, with a walkway around it on all four sides. This is no accident of design. The plinth was kept at a slightly lower level than the walkway, pointing again to Guru Arjan's wish to 'symbolise the virtue of humility'.[14] The architectural design of the overall Harmandir Sahib complex, particularly its construction within a pool of water, thus gives physical form to the core ideas of the Gurus: 'As the lotus flower remained dry in the water, so [the] Harimandir gave the message of living creatively in the world without being affected by its temptations.' The lotus flower has long held connotations of humility and purity within medieval Indic traditions, and its central usage in the Guru's building plans highlights how well-versed Guru Arjan was in the ideas and symbols of ancient Indo-Persian philosophy, which informed the worldview of royal courts leading up to his day.

It was perhaps this learned nature, coupled with the spiritual wisdom that the Guru evinced, that impressed the relatively like-minded Akbar, the third Emperor of the Mughal dynasty. From Mughal court records, we have direct testimony that Akbar (1542–1605) met with Guru Arjan, and noted with great pleasure that the Sikh leader was a man who possessed 'a great store of love'.[15] Akbar was a relatively liberal Emperor, who was extremely curious about other religious communities, and rather pluralist in his own beliefs and practices. Not only did he abolish the *jizya* tax on non-Muslims during his reign, but it is further believed that he waived state demands for other taxes on towns under the care of Guru Arjan—apparently because the Guru made a request along these lines following a famine in the region. Akbar was also impressed by and respectful of the Guru's ideas and his activities at Amritsar; even if Guru Arjan's ideas were about just and humble rule, he clearly understood just as well as a Renaissance prince—or a Mughal one—how to use buildings and monuments to create an image of leadership.

However, this warm and friendly relationship between the Sikhs and Mughals would not continue for much longer. In his memoirs, the next Emperor, Jahangir, derided Akbar's relationship with Guru Arjan, writing that 'my father was very submissive to dervishes'. As a prince, Jahangir had been particularly suspicious of Guru Arjan's growing popularity, and noted with alarm how he had witnessed the conversion of 'some ignorant and stupid Muslims' to the Sikh faith. Equally perturbed by the Guru's increasing following were several of the Hindu kings in Punjab, who had held control over the region's hill states for generations. A number of lower-caste groups, particularly Jatt migrants, were flocking to Amritsar and other Sikh towns in greater numbers; they were attracted by the Sikhs' egalitarian, anti-caste ideas, but their arrival and conversion disquieted the local governing elites, with growing complaints to the Mughal authorities about the activities of the Sikh movement.[16] Alongside this, the bards of Guru Arjan's court had been actively composing popular hymns that celebrated the Gurus, representing them as reincarnations of the legendary Hindu king Rajah Janak—a favourite figure from Hindu epics, who was fabled as a model ruler.[17] Increasing numbers of Sikhs directly perceived and venerated the Gurus as kingly figures, something that no doubt would have irked the feelings of both local rajahs and the Mughal Emperor himself.

The entire ideology of the Sikh Gurus about rulership certainly constituted a considerable challenge to their contemporary political elites: perhaps particularly the Mughals, who had actively claimed to be 'sacred kings' and 'Caliphs of the Age' in their own right—a mode of spiritual self-representation that had started with Akbar, but took on stronger connotations under his son and grandson, Jahangir and Shah Jahan.[18] The latent criticisms made by the Gurus about the worldly rulers of their day implied that far too many such kings had either historically or recently proven themselves to be but vain individuals, neglecting to humbly submit themselves to the Almighty and, as such, falling far short of their claims to be 'perfect men'. To add insult to injury in the short term, Jahangir was particularly affronted by Guru Arjan's support of his own rebellious son, Prince Khusrau, who was challenging his position on the Mughal throne.[19] It was in this context of growing mistrust and jealousy towards the Sikh leader that Jahangir ordered that Guru Arjan be executed in May 1606.

* * *

The torture and killing of Guru Arjan was undoubtedly an act of brutal violence, marking a major break in the relatively amicable Sikh-Mughal relationship that had gone before it within just eight months of Akbar's death. In Sikh tradition, Guru Arjan's murder is considered to be a critical watershed moment and the Guru is popularly thought of as a martyr, who laid down his life in the name of the Sikh faith. It is also seen as a serious turning point for the Sikh community, its politics and its notions of a ruler. Guru Arjan's successor was Hargobind, his only son. The sixth Guru (1595–1644) was a game-changer when it came to Sikh notions of sovereignty, with a dramatically new way of building on his father's endeavours: by embracing the lifestyle and appearance of a spiritual warrior prince. According to Sikh legend, this new direction began on the very day of Guru Hargobind's accession.

The story has a pivotal place within Sikh popular tradition. On the day of his coronation, the new Guru proclaimed that he would wear two swords, one on each hip: representing how, in future, he would act as a sovereign wielding both worldly power (*miri*) and spiritual authority (*piri*). This was a novel concept, and Guru Hargobind sought to entrench it by moving to establish an army and 'militarise' a section of his followers. He is popularly thought of as an avenger of his father's martyrdom. His accession was equally significant for another reason: it marked the first time in Sikh history that a Guru had been succeeded directly by his eldest son. Before Guru Arjan, the first four Gurus had shown little regard for primogeniture when selecting their replacements, basing the choice on the individual's merit as a student/disciple. Guru Nanak overlooked his own sons and hand-picked one of his most devoted servants, Bhai Lehna, to succeed him, re-naming him Angad ('my own limb'). Guru Angad (1504–52) followed the same method when appointing Amar Das as the third Guru (1479–1574).

The fourth master, Guru Ram Das, was the first to appoint a family member as his successor—Guru Arjan was his third and youngest son—but the martyred Guru went further than his predecessor. Hargobind was not just his son, but his first-born son; and when he became Guru at the tender age of eleven, he was the first Sikh to directly inherit the estates of a previous Guru. And this wasn't just any Guru leaving his legacy to his son: Guru Arjan had devoted himself to building up a number of prosperous Sikh towns, the ultimate prize of course being Amritsar itself. This crucial wealth of resources enabled Guru Hargobind to actively embrace a kingly demeanour, even going so far as recruiting his own small army, 'crowning' himself with a jewel-studded turban, and constructing the new Akal Takht (Throne of the Timeless One) immediately behind the Harmandir Sahib at Amritsar.

There was certainly unease and concern within the *panth* (Sikh people) at Guru Hargobind's sudden dramatic change in the style of the guruship. His 'reign' also saw a cleavage forming within the community. The sons of his father's eldest brother, Prithi Chand, attempted to challenge his succession, portraying themselves as the 'true' Gurus and more authentic representatives of the philosophy of Guru Nanak. This rival Guru lineage vigorously critiqued the kingly and martial demeanour adopted by Guru Hargobind as indicative of the very slide to vanity and self-aggrandisement that past Gurus had criticised for so long, and as a betrayal of Guru Nanak's ideas of good leadership, which they identified as pacifism and renunciation. As such, they may also have been better placed than Guru Hargobind to continue enjoying support from the Mughal dynasty, as their pacifism will have made them seem much less of a threat than the new 'warrior Guru'. Ultimately, these 'pretenders' to the guruship were sidelined—their objections never managed to draw sufficient followers from the *panth*—but their dissension shows the magnitude of Guru Hargobind's re-imagining of what it meant to be Sikh and to rule.

Nevertheless, despite the obvious departures from past practices and ideas of Sikh leadership, and despite the alarm with which these were met in some quarters of the Punjab, Guru Hargobind's relations with the Mughals were not inherently antagonistic—that would be far too one-dimensional an assessment. Even though the relationship entered a much darker phase after the execution of Guru Arjan, the Mughals clearly continued to show an interest in patronising the Sikh community—choosing to support one 'Guru lineage' over the other, in order to try and shape the development of the *panth* in ways that did not clash with imperial interests in Punjab.[20] Additionally, Emperor Jahangir's attitudes towards Guru Hargobind were subject to continual shifts. He left the young Guru undisturbed for some time after his father's execution, but on hearing how the Sikhs' new leader had begun building up an army, Jahangir issued a summons for him to be brought to the imperial court for an inquisition. Sikh tradition suggests that the Emperor was then rather impressed by Guru Hargobind's noble bearing and moral rectitude, with some popular stories even recounting how the two went on hunting trips together, the Guru heroically saving the Emperor from a tiger. Jahangir would eventually lock up Guru Hargobind at Gwalior Fort—only to free him again some time later. These twists and turns highlight the contingent nature of relations between the Sikh and Mughal leaders: there was an admittedly unequal balance in terms of hard power, but also an increasingly close and tense conflict over which ruler could wield the greater charismatic influence on their own people. This contest seems to have been rooted in somewhat overlapping or shared cultural norms of courtliness, ethics and masculine honour.

Indeed, no matter how inhumane and oppressive Jahangir's actions may of course look to Sikhs, the Mughal Emperor too was committed to upholding a vision of himself as a 'sacred king', whose reign was just as wise and noble as the *halemi raj* model espoused by the Gurus. The Mughal court was constructed in such a way as to project not only the invincible power of the men who ran it, but also its superior cultural and moral refinement. As the historian Louis Fenech puts it, 'In the context of traditional Indian courtliness, such apparent juxtapositions are, in fact, displays of balance and speak to the highly cultivated virtues of the monarch or courtiers in question: power and eminence on the one hand, beside which are lodged humility and self-effacement on the other.'[21]

In other words, Jahangir would have been insulted whether he was perceived as a brutal, cruel king or a weak and ineffectual man. The Gurus clearly understood very well this power/virtue balancing act, taking a similar interest in Indo-Persian politics, ethics and philosophy, and being educated on these subjects with the same kinds of literature as abounded in the libraries and homes of Mughal servants and courtiers—this would also be the case with Ranjit Singh in the nineteenth century.[22] By fashioning himself as a sacred warrior king, Guru Hargobind was actively taking on the mode of masculinity and princely conduct that had long been at the centre of Mughal self-representation.[23] His exact aims in so doing are hard to ascertain, since unfortunately we have little written record of the sixth Guru's own thoughts.[24] But what we can be sure of is that his legacy of the warrior prince model was alive in Ranjit Singh's day; the Maharajah, known as the Lion of Punjab, was a celebrated conqueror who brought most of the region under his kingdom's control through raid and battle; but, like Guru Hargobind, he also never lost sight of the need to display princely virtue.

* * *

The Guru who seemed most of all like an 'Indo-Timurid prince' was Guru Gobind Singh (1666–1708), and we have better records of his style of rulership, clearly documenting the subversive and bold nature of his revisionist royalism. In his own court, the tenth and last Sikh master appears to have acted as the most regal Guru of all, heir to the innovations of both the 'scholar prince' Guru Arjan and the 'warrior king' Guru Hargobind. Guru Gobind Singh surrounded himself with an eminent circle of poets and thinkers, collected a library of intellectual riches, and worked to finish Guru Arjan's compilation of the *Guru Granth Sahib*. He also embraced the martial outlook that Guru Hargobind had championed after the execution of his father, fortifying the city of Anandpur Sahib and, above all, establishing an armed corps of Sikh warriors, which he famously formalised with the creation of the military–religious brotherhood of the Khalsa.

Guru Gobind Singh also clashed with the Mughal Emperor, Aurangzeb (reigned 1658–1707). Never before had the cultural and political tensions of the entangled Sikh–Mughal connection been so evident. Much of the Guru's childhood echoes the experience of his ancestor, Guru Hargobind: the young Gobind inherited the *gurgaddi* (the Guru's throne) at an even younger age than the sixth Guru had, following the brutal torture and murder of his own father, Guru Tegh Bahadur, on Aurangzeb's orders. In his adulthood, acrimony between the Sikhs and the Empire intensified even beyond this, wreaking unrelenting devastation on Guru Gobind Singh's personal life, which he bore with an incredible amount of inner strength. The Guru's court was scattered in 1704–5 after being attacked by the combined forces of the local Mughal administration and rival Hindu kings whose states bordered Anandpur Sahib. This coalition laid siege to the Guru's citadel, forcing him and his embattled entourage into the wilderness of northern India's jungles.

On surrendering his beloved fort of Anandpur, Guru Gobind Singh was given a promise in Aurangzeb's name that he, together with his family and the remnants of his army, would be allowed to evacuate the town in peace and safety. However, as the Guru's retinue departed, they were treacherously attacked by the Mughal forces; large numbers of the Guru's devoted soldiers were killed, including his two eldest sons. Thereafter, his mother and two youngest sons were also kidnapped and killed on the orders of the then Mughal governor of Punjab, Nawab Wazir Khan. Yet despite this, like

Guru Hargobind before him, the last Guru never turned against the entire Mughal dynasty nor sought to advocate its overthrow—he even ultimately extended support to one of Aurangzeb's sons, Prince Muazzam, to help this formerly liberal overlord of Punjab in his struggle to take over the imperial throne.

Despite his forced flight from the citadel, and despite his continued engagement with or support for the Mughal regime, it would be wrong to infer that Guru Gobind Singh felt forced to submit to the imperial power of his day. On the contrary, his personally rebellious and subversive stance is strikingly obvious in the *Zafarnamah*, a letter that he apparently wrote as a direct rebuke to Aurangzeb after the fall of Anandpur. This is his description of the Emperor: 'The *shāhanshāh* [king of kings] of all things on earth; the ornament of the throne (*aurang-zeb*) who [possesses] the wealth of the age, but is [nevertheless] far from faith.'[25] In this letter, the last Guru draws powerfully upon his deep engagement with Indo-Persian classical literature to construct a trenchant critique of Aurangzeb's credentials as a ruler and a Muslim, calling out the treachery of the attack on the Guru and his retinue as they retreated. Guru Gobind Singh lays out in detail the moral failings of Aurangzeb in not keeping his word by dispensing justice fairly to the Sikhs, instead allowing them to be attacked in a dishonourable and cowardly fashion.

If Aurangzeb ever read this letter, which heavily evokes the moralising language and imagery of the Iranian epic, the *Shahnameh*, it would not have failed to have an impact on him; those Persian tales of the glorious battles and dramatic misfortunes of past kings were a treasured favourite of the Mughal court, and had long provided a cultural template for their self-fashioning as model rulers. Here Guru Gobind Singh engages with the Mughal political elite on their own terms, having been equally well-educated in their cultural and literary forms.[26] The *Zafarnamah* was the literary equivalent of a huge slap in the face, condemning the regime by its own standards.

The last Guru worked to give life to the scholar Guru Arjan's concept of *halemi raj* in his own way: through his creation of the Khalsa on the Vaisakhi festival of 1699, and by proclaiming that, after him, there would be no further human Gurus. The Khalsa was a new militarised brotherhood for Sikh men and women. A leading factor in Guru Gobind Singh's decision to shape the growing Sikh community in such a martial mould was the fact that he and his people were increasingly subjected to attacks by the forces of both the Mughals and the rajahs of the Hindu hill states, with whom they would continue to fight battles for the next few decades. In 1708, during his final days, the last Guru went one step further and declared that thenceforth there would be no more human Gurus after his death; instead, the guruship would be vested jointly within the body of the Sikh people (the *Guru Panth*) and the holy writings of the Gurus (the *Guru Granth*).

As we have clearly seen, Sikhs had looked to the Gurus as their leaders for nearly 250 years; with these landmark decisions, Guru Gobind Singh now affirmed that both spiritual and worldly sovereignty should be understood as being diffused amongst the Sikh people as a whole, rather than embodied by any one human figure. Sikh tradition tells us that, when he created the Khalsa, the Guru anointed five of his bravest and most loyal disciples as the first initiates of the brotherhood—they subsequently became known as the *Panj Pyare* (the Five Beloved Ones). He then requested that these five induct him into the Khalsa order too, on an equal footing. This effectively mutual 'coronation' between master and disciples, in a simultaneous ceremony, diffused the ruling authority amongst them collectively.[27] Those Sikhs newly 'baptised' into the Khalsa were empowered to take new surnames—'Singh' for men and 'Kaur' for women—shedding their old family names, which were typically rooted in caste lineages. It was at this point too that the Guru himself took on the name 'Singh'—he had formerly been known as Gobind Rai.

The 'Lost Sikh Republic'

Out of these final deeds and decrees of Guru Gobind Singh rises an uncomfortable concern for those looking at the rule of Ranjit Singh: several of his most recent Sikh biographers seem to be preoccupied with the idea that the 'Sikh Empire' should really have been governed in a 'republican' fashion. Khushwant Singh and Patwant Singh have been two of the Maharajah's most popular biographers. Their works greatly champion the achievements of their illustrious compatriot, the Lion of the Punjab, and are generally positive—even celebratory—about the gritty guerrilla warfare waged by revolutionary Sikhs in the eighteenth century to uproot the powerful Mughal and Hindu dynasties in the Punjab. Yet, at the same time, both biographers are of the opinion that Sikhism and monarchy are a bad fit. From this viewpoint, the hierarchical nature of dynastic rule actually goes against the egalitarian principles advocated by the ten Gurus. Given everything we have just learnt about the monarchical habits of the Gurus, what makes commentators see things in this republican light? And if that really is the true nature of Sikh society, then why, upon unifying the divided Sikh war-bands into a powerful and independent polity, did Ranjit Singh choose to establish a hereditary monarchy and to govern the Punjab as an empire?

For these scholars, the true intention of Guru Gobind Singh in declaring the end of individual guruship and founding the Khalsa warriors was that this powerful brotherhood would ultimately root out the traditional royal and imperial elites of the Punjab to rule in an entirely new and radical mode, self-governed by a righteous code of personal and spiritual ethics, in a democratic and republican manner. In other words, they see what happened after the last Guru's death—and what Ranjit Singh ultimately disrupted with his hereditary imperial dynasty—as a major break away from India's prevailing styles of rule, which had centred around a monarch, in favour of an ideal Sikh polity that would be its opposite. Somewhat paradoxically held up as proof of this 'natural' Sikh inclination toward republicanism, there is a popular idea that the Maharajah humbly saw his court as ruling on behalf of the *Sarkar-i-Khalsa*, the 'government of the Khalsa'.[28] To support it, both Patwant Singh and Khushwant Singh point out the ways in which Ranjit Singh deviated from accepted styles of Indo-Persian royal and kingly culture. He refused to sit on the Mughal throne at Lahore after capturing the Mughals' former royal fort; and he minted coins bearing not his own name and image, as Mughal emperors' had done, but those of the Gurus, declining that opportunity to proclaim his personal sovereignty.[29]

Khushwant Singh, one of the most renowned Sikh writers of the twentieth century, also highlights his assumption that Ranjit Singh only felt pushed to take on the title of 'Maharajah' after the birth of his first son, Kharak Singh, in 1801. He is at pains to emphasise that, amongst Sikhs, the ruler was keen to be referred to as the plainer

'Singh Sahib'. Patwant Singh is much more critical of what he sees as Ranjit Singh's deviation from the earlier, more democratic forms of Sikh self-governance. By this he means the early eighteenth-century, post-Guru institution of the *gurmata*, a term that can be approximately translated from the Punjabi as 'the decision of the Guru'. It was understood to be a binding decision made by and for the Sikh congregation following discussions held in open meetings, always in the presence of the *Guru Granth Sahib* and in consultation with its wisdom. This style of collective decision-making was of an improvised nature. For Patwant Singh, this was the last Guru's reforms in action, and therefore Ranjit Singh's assumption of control over policy marked a departure from this 'republican' model of 'joint sovereignty'. Patwant Singh does characterise the Maharajah as something of an enlightened despot, and portrays him as having been a 'secular', fair-minded and talented ruler of a diverse Punjabi population. However, he ultimately concludes that the failure of the 'Sikh Empire' was due to his misguided imposition of a system of hereditary monarchy on the Sikhs—one that went against their 'psyche' and thus was doomed to fail.[30]

But was Ranjit Singh really so heavy-handed a ruler, or so deaf to his people's political spirit? Let us look at a little more closely at the *gurmata*. It appears to have emerged in the months following the death of Guru Gobind Singh in 1708, as a local, day-to-day way for Sikhs to debate and make decisions on pressing issues, as they sought to preserve and strengthen their community without the guidance of a new Guru. To tackle the most urgent and complex problems facing the entire *panth* (Sikh people), large *gurmata* meetings were held in Amritsar, the most important Sikh city. Among the foremost were questions 'regarding defence against a common enemy, infringement of the Khalsa code of behaviour by an individual, and other important matters'.[31] The Sikhs had to decide how to protect their community against internal collapse; persecution by antagonistic Mughal or Hindu rulers in Punjab; and attack by a newer external danger, the invading armies of neighbouring Afghan warlords.

However, if we actually consider the history of the *gurmata*, it becomes clear that the tradition was actually quite short-lived, lasting for only a few decades. As more recent research has clearly shown, there was a significant decline in the inclusive and democratic nature of the *panth*'s decision-making assemblies as early as the lifetime of Ranjit Singh's grandfather, Charat Singh, in the middle of the eighteenth century.[32] By then, the *gurmata* assemblies were co-existing with another form of politics: the power-sharing arrangement between the twelve Sikh *misls*, the bands of Sikh warriors who had earlier been part of Guru Gobind Singh's army. Upon his death, the *misls* had taken on the responsibility of protecting the Khalsa brotherhood from repression by regional political elites, as well as fighting to seize direct control over the lands in which Sikhs lived. The *gurmata*'s importance and prevalence seems to have evolved as the nature of the *misls* themselves shifted.

These twelve warrior groupings that emerged across the Punjab from the early 1700s are generally thought to have been of similar size and status, as well as being egalitarian in the way in which its members treated and related to one another. The chief of a *misl* was initially known as a *misldar* and later as a *sardar* (male) or *sardarni* (female). In the beginning, these chiefs were appointed on a meritocratic basis, with all *misls* participating in *gurmata* gatherings on equal terms. Charat Singh was the *sardar* of the Sukerchakias: a relatively small *misl* that took its name from his family's ancestral village of Sukerchak in Gujranwala. But the Sukerchakia *misl* punched above its weight: despite its size and humble origins, it achieved great prominence due to its success in safeguarding much of northwestern Punjab from repeated Afghan incursions.

As the century progressed, the focus—or rather the ambition—of the *misls* gradually shifted from self-preservation to aggression or expansion: capturing territory from other regional powers and consolidating Sikh control over it. If neighbouring groups or elites were considered to be hostile to the *misl* or to collective Sikh interests, their lands were the most likely to be raided. Since Sikhs were a relative minority within the larger population of the Punjab, the *misls* also began charging what they called *rakhi* (protection money/tribute) from all the inhabitants of their newly conquered territories. Between this Sikh activity, the equally disruptive effects of repeated Afghan invasions of northern India, and the uprisings of other Punjabi communities, the old Mughal imperial system was decimated, and the dynasty lost its hold over one of its richest provinces.[33] The Sikhs were only partially successful (or even interested) in forming alliances with other such rebellious groups, and so in times of critical danger, the *misls* would unite together to form a single army, known as the Dal Khalsa; this enabled the Sikhs to fight multiple battles against invading Afghans in particular.

With their growing stronghold in northwestern Punjab, where the majority of Sikh–Afghan battles first ensued, Charat Singh and then his son Maha Singh (Ranjit Singh's father) were perfectly poised to command a leading position within the ranks and leadership of the Dal Khalsa. As a result, their voices would come to carry greater weight within the *gurmata* assemblies at Amritsar too—as a whole, the *sardars* became increasingly dominant figures in these gatherings, effectively assuming the authority to make decisions on behalf of the people and only consulting within a much smaller number of 'elite' figures. In other words, even if Ranjit Singh was rather autocratic in the way that he put a stop to the *gurmata* assemblies, it is fair to say that was he only following in the footsteps of these earlier *sardars*. His own power was built upward and outward from the *misl* controlled by his family; his father and grandfather had not been the only Sikh chiefs of their generations to concentrate a great deal of power and territory in their own hands. This power was then passed down to their kin through a shift to hereditary succession. By the end of the eighteenth century, many such *sardars* had transformed themselves into kings, long before Ranjit Singh entered the scene—though he would of course go on to act even more ambitiously than any of these predecessors.

What's more, even before the *misl* chiefs became hereditary *sardars*, even in the time of the Gurus, there were nuances within Sikh ideas of royalty and courtliness—these have been highlighted by recent research on the period, as have the overall complexities of the *panth*'s engagement with the ruling powers of their day, and the evolving ways in which the Gurus and later *sardars* were themselves represented as royal figures.[34] Indeed, as we'll see, even among scholars presenting a trenchant dichotomy between Ranjit Singh's self-centred 'monarchy' and the 'republican' ideal of the sovereign, democratic Khalsa, some seem to believe that Guru Gobind Singh wished the members of his Khalsa to form a new kind of 'aristocracy': one that was 'dedicated and consciously trained' and whose members should be chosen not 'by right of birth' but by dint of their noble conduct, 'grounded in virtue, in talent and in the self-imposed code of service and sacrifice'.[35] The new brotherhood may not have been based on inherited superiority, but was still to be composed of a 'select few' deemed to be of merit.

Working within binaries of 'monarchical rule' versus 'republicanism', or even 'Sikhs' versus 'Mughals', is clearly far too simplistic an approach to the nature of Sikh political thought. Why, then, has a group of modern Sikh scholars been so convinced that Ranjit Singh broke with the 'Sikh republic'? For one thing, it is important to recognise that the scholars who have argued that kingship is anathema to the 'republican ideals' of Sikhism are typically anti-monarchy themselves. The writer and politician Kapur Singh (1909–86) is perhaps the ultimate example of this. He directly asserted that Ranjit Singh's assumption of the title of 'Maharajah' was thoroughly 'un-Sikh'.[36] Unlike many other Sikh and Punjabi scholars, Kapur Singh—who is clearly the core influence behind Patwant Singh's critique—was no fan of the Maharajah. He even argued that Ranjit Singh's government was of an entirely oppressive and backward nature, and that it drew inspiration from a 'Hindu theory of monarchy';[37] one that made the Maharajah out to be a 'god-king', who could not be challenged by anyone on earth. Kapur Singh even went as far as asserting that Ranjit Singh had been happy to let the Sikh people revert back into the 'pale of Hinduism', so as to enhance his own despotic power.[38]

These debates about the correct or most appropriate models of 'Sikh sovereignty' continue to be important issues today—above all for those within the community who are committed to keeping Sikh institutions alive, to promote the strength, integrity and in some cases, orthodoxy of the *panth* or people. The fierce arguments about what constitutes a natural or ideal form of Sikh power are perhaps especially fraught amongst those fighting to establish a new *Khalsa Raj*, particularly those involved since the 1940s with the movement for 'Khalistan', a self-governing Sikh state in South Asia. Seen in this light, it is easier to understand the strong positions taken by Sikh scholars focused on their history, not only to make sense of it for themselves, but also to seek out political models to empower their people in the here and now. For Kapur Singh's mid-century generation of scholars, the 1940s and 1950s weren't all that different from the post-Mughal period of the *misls*. With the end of the British Raj in 1947, the map of the Indian subcontinent was once again subjected to a whole series of deeply contested re-imaginings of its territorial form and internal borders; this turmoil, too, gave rise to fervent new debates about how political authority should operate in a changing world.[39]

In other words, Sikh attitudes and ideas towards royal culture, the institution of 'kingship' and the idea of sovereignty were as deeply nuanced in Ranjit Singh's day as they are in the twenty-first century, drawing on a wide array of cultural perspectives. The Maharajah's embrace of dynastic rule in the early nineteenth century marked the emergence of a whole new kind of 'royal' people, but he didn't take this step out of a vacuum and he was not solely responsible for it. He was building on the conquests and changes wrought by his forefathers, but also on the legacy of the Gurus—including the reforms of Guru Gobind Singh. We've seen the arguments that the last Guru had intended the Khalsa to represent a Sikh republic quite different from Ranjit Singh's style of leadership. But we can see the flaws in this logic just by looking at these new words that the Guru introduced to Sikh politics.

'Khalsa' originates from the Persian term *khalisa*, which at the time usually referred to the property—typically land or territory—of the Emperor.[40] The Guru may have had his disciples induct him into their brotherhood, but his status clearly still has a distinctly kingly echo: perhaps as the first among equals. 'Singh' and 'Kaur' were equally regal titles to take on: Singh was a common name utilised by Rajputs, the Hindu ruling or warrior caste, and Kaur was a vernacularisation of the princely title *kanwar*. So the new Khalsa initiates were indeed being raised up from their respective caste backgrounds and as social subordinates of their erstwhile rulers, but the equality they now enjoyed was that of royal individuals in their own right—as long as they remained adherents of the strict ethical code of the *Guru Granth Sahib*. This was not a republic set in motion, nor was it an absolute rejection of monarchy as an idea or model. Instead, royal authority, while still recognised, was now diffused and spread in a radically new form throughout the entire Sikh *panth*, just as the light of God was thought to be present within every human being (*joti jot*). Guru Gobind Singh had taken the old Mughal ideal of 'sacred kings' and shaped it into an entirely novel vision of his own.

* * *

This was the revolutionary new set of ideas that gradually emerged through the lifetimes of the ten Sikh Gurus, which empowered the Sikh *panth* to rebel against the prevailing social and political order of their day. However, there are two key issues with over-simplification of this story: firstly, the Gurus of course were not there to comment upon the development of Sikh society after Guru Gobind Singh's death, making it really quite hard to say with absolute certainty what kind of political model they would have deemed best or most appropriate. It was for their followers to turn the vision of self-rulership into an everyday reality. Secondly, we cannot overlook the fact that the nature of the Sikh *panth* itself continued to evolve as the eighteenth century unfolded. This in turn meant that the way in which rulership and sovereignty operated within Sikh society also remained in flux throughout this pivotal period before Ranjit Singh came to power.

One of these important changes came with the significant numbers of migrant Jatts who were initiated into the Sikh faith, and then the Khalsa, from the seventeenth century onwards. They were attracted by the egalitarian ethos of the Gurus and the Sikh *panth*'s promise of social mobility on respectable terms, as well as the opportunity to join the increasingly affluent *misl* warrior bands, who openly flouted and disturbed the authority of local Mughal and Afghan overlords. Indeed, another transformation taking place in the period between Guru Gobind Singh's death and the reign of Ranjit Singh was the transition of the *misl sardars* from leaders within a largely meritocratic and martial society to the kings of small, refined and relatively elitist royal courts and territorial states. As the Khalsa grew and attempted to assert itself more as a body, greater efforts had to be made to codify its ethos and ensure the consolidation of the *panth*—taking into account the tensions emerging between ideological notions of Sikh egalitarianism and a developing sense of hierarchy amongst the *sardars* and the rest of the Sikh people.

Of course, then as now, the *Guru Granth Sahib* itself was the 'go-to source' for Sikhs (or modern historians!) looking for guidance on how the Gurus wanted the *panth*'s members to conduct themselves. Additionally, Sikhs of the eighteenth century produced new 'codes of conduct' for their community, known as *rahitnameh*. A passage from one such text dating from the late eighteenth century is illustrative of common admonishments from this period: 'The Raja should show affection to the poor Khalsa. Give him money or a horse, for thus his attachment will become stronger ... Keep only Singhs as your servants ... A Singh must never wield a weapon against another Singh. See him as the Guru. Fear the Khalsa.'[41] As we have already seen, the verses of the *Guru Granth Sahib* are often steeped in allegorical references to a courtly modus operandi; in this *rahitnama*, too, it was perfectly acceptable for a Sikh to be a 'Rajah'. Altogether, this again gives the lie to the pro-republican arguments of scholars such as Kapur Singh, since it appears that eighteenth-century Sikhs had no real qualms about their co-religionists being royal.

What such Sikh manuals for conduct do show us is a determined effort being made to ensure that these new Sikh kings stayed grounded in their community. As Purnima Dhavan has highlighted, this particular text promotes the concept of *dharamyudh* (holy war) against Muslims, in order to discourage *sardars* from recruiting peasant soldiers from other communities, or forming alliances with Mughals or Afghans. This is telling evidence of a considerable gap emerging between the Sikh *sardar*/rajah and the Khalsa peasant soldier, one that was testing the former's 'fidelity to notions of a shared Khalsa *dharam*', or religious ethics.[42] The practicalities of building and protecting their *misls*' sovereignty over their newly-conquered lands often drew the *sardars* into actions that conflicted with the strictures and values of the emerging Khalsa *rahit* (code of conduct). They had to negotiate diplomatic settlements to protect themselves and their lands from invading Afghans; or actively fight other Sikh *misls* in order to annex or consolidate territory, or secure revenues and control armies. As we'll see more closely in the next chapter, this was repeatedly the case for Ranjit Singh's ancestors, the heads of the Sukerchakia *misl*.

Dhavan's important findings have highlighted how these tensions between the conflicting concerns of 'emerging Khalsa conventions' and the changing demands of heading a *misl* led to a shift in notions of Sikh sovereignty. As they transformed themselves into rajahs, the erstwhile *sardars* were evidently keen to use their influence within the community to move away from an idealised model of joint, equal sovereignty vested across and within the Khalsa (if such an ideal ever fully existed); instead, they sought to encourage acknowledgement of their autonomy as rulers over nascent kingdoms. This is why, by the middle of the eighteenth century, although *gurmata* assemblies were still open to all Sikhs, it was increasingly *sardars*/rajahs like Ranjit Singh's grandfather who would lead conversations and take the lion's share of decision-making over key strategic matters facing the *panth* as a whole.

Even more intriguingly, the *gurmata* assemblies are not even mentioned in one earlier and particularly fascinating source: the *Prem Sumarag Granth* (The Book of the True Path of Love). This text is of especial importance in the debate around ideas of Sikh kingship, since it assumes that a Maharajah and a royal court would be the basis of a future centralised Sikh government. The *Prem Sumarag Granth* is a richly detailed and instructive code of conduct that also acts as something of a treatise on the ideal Sikh state, according to its (unfortunately unknown) author. There has been some conjecture that it may have been a *granth* written by Guru Gobind Singh himself, but this is highly debatable; it seems more likely that it was produced by a well-educated Sikh, perhaps of a Khatri background.[43] The dating has also been subject to a great deal of discussion, but there is a growing consensus that the first manuscript was likely written around the early eighteenth century, in the years immediately following the death of the last Guru if it is not a direct product of his own court.[44]

The eighth chapter, on the 'patterns of political conduct', is the most detailed and insightful for outlining how the governing infrastructure of a Sikh state should be organised and managed. Its recommendations are so thorough that the imagined Maharajah is even advised to employ dancing girls in his court, so as to be able to 'expose to temptation' anyone who has adopted the 'garb of ascetic renunciation'.[45] What emerges powerfully throughout this chapter is that the Maharajah is expected to be an entirely exemplary ruler in his moral conduct: whose core responsibilities lay in upholding justice and promoting the happiness and welfare of the people. Interestingly, a hereditary monarchy does seem to be given as the preferred/assumed model, since roles and responsibilities are even described for the sons, brothers and wives of the Maharajah, as well as notes on how to handle fraternal conflicts over succession.[46] However, no indication is given as to whether the Maharajah should come from a particular lineage or section of society.

The implication seems to be that anyone could occupy the position of ruler, but that they would then be held to a very high standard of accountability. In repeated refrains throughout the text, the actions and *karma* of Maharajah and subject are represented as being intertwined:

> Whenever any individual commits either an evil deed or a virtuous one, causing thereby either grief or joy, the responsibility is shared equally by the ruler and his subject. Whenever anyone living under his authority causes happiness, the ruler receives a share of the merit earned thereby; and likewise a share of the demerit whenever any subject causes suffering. He partakes of both the vice and the virtue of his subjects. In the court of Sri Guru Nirankar Akal Purakh [God] a ruler will be interrogated on issues of justice. He will be asked about these and nothing else.[47]

The Maharajah is thus set up as both the servant and role model of his people. He is bound to ensure that their every need is met, just as a caring parent would; he must be an authoritative figure, commanding respect by acting as a strong and fair dispenser of justice, who submits himself to the same rules and principles applied to his people. All are enjoined to adhere without complaint to this system of societal justice, which is suggested as being the supreme authority in the land, at least until one reaches the 'court of Akal Purakh', the Timeless Being or Immortal One—the ultimate arbiter of everyone's fate.

But how can we know what readers thought of these arguments, or how extensively the *Prem Sumarag* manuscripts were even circulated? We can't be certain about how far, if at all, the text represents a consensus about ideas of Sikh kingship. What we can see, however, from the very existence of a work on this subject, is that it was being thought about and discussed in Sikh society at this time. With the end of the Gurus, the emergence of the Khalsa and the *gurmata* assemblies and the transformation of the *misls* and their rulers, it is obvious that Sikh political ideas and practices were in considerable flux during the eighteenth century. This is surely understandable, given the relative youth of the Sikh *panth* as a whole, and the extremely challenging circumstances in which the fledgling community was living and developing in 'post-Mughal' Punjab. At best we can guess that the Sikhs of the early 1700s were experimenting with a variety of different ways to govern themselves, seeking to adapt to both the loss of Guru Gobind Singh and the gradual crumbling of imperial rule in the Punjab; as they were doing this, they will have been responding to the wide array of contending powers and notions of authority that rose up to fill that vacuum.

Seen from this angle, it is also perhaps unsurprising that ideas about monarchy would have been in the mix, since it was a form of political authority that generations of Punjabis had become thoroughly accustomed to. It is important to remember that this confrontation with royalty and its different possible forms was not just happening in the Punjab, but across the Indian subcontinent, as the entire edifice of the Mughal Empire was forced to give way piecemeal to a whole host of new challengers, from martial peasants akin to the Khalsa Sikhs to formerly loyal Mughal governors—many of whom recognised that it would be in their best interests to re-invent themselves as kings, rather than continuing to serve a dynasty in decline.[48] And if we accept this complex landscape of rupture, contestation and innovation, it is hopefully easier to understand why Ranjit Singh took on the grandiose title of Maharajah, at the same time as humbly labelling his government the *Sarkar-i-Khalsa*.

The Making of a Maharajah

We do not know how directly or extensively Ranjit Singh himself engaged with the kinds of ideas and writings that have been discussed in the past few pages. The Maharajah is believed to have been largely illiterate, but that does not mean that he was not interested in the written word, and certainly not that he was unconcerned with what past or contemporary thinkers had to say about the philosophy of kingship. There is ample evidence to show that he had his own *kitab-khana* or library at his capital of Lahore, filled with many of the kinds of works that the Gurus and Mughal princes before him would have studied. From extant copies of such books—which are today scattered in libraries throughout Indian and Pakistani Punjab, as well as in the UK and elsewhere around the world—we can see that Ranjit Singh collected many original works from these earlier periods, as well as ordering his own scribes and artists to reproduce other key texts on courtly ethics, political philosophy and many subjects besides.

Passages from these volumes were read out to the Maharajah and debated in his courtly gatherings on several occasions; and, as we shall see in the coming chapters, he would himself draw upon stories from such literature in conversation with his courtiers from time to time, in ways that shine a light on how he understood his own and his family's status as a new royal elite. We know this because, by the latter stages of his reign, Ranjit Singh had a courtly chronicler in his employ, to record and memorialise the events of his court. His name was Sohan Lal Suri, and he captured the Maharajah's activities in his five-volume *Umdat-ut-tawarikh*: a diary-like history of the kingdom of Ranjit Singh's family, beginning with his great-great-grandfather's embrace of *Sikhi* and ending with the exile of his youngest son, Duleep Singh, after the East India Company's annexation of the Sikh Empire in 1849. We will return to Suri's very helpful record, as well as learning a bit more about the court historian himself, throughout this book.

That Ranjit Singh commissioned such a history to be written, as well as the fact that he tried to learn in his own way about philosophies of kingship, clearly shows that he was neither an ignorant simpleton, nor a man purely interested in war and conquest. He was acting as a literary and artistic patron, just as any other Indian prince before him would have done, and it is hard to doubt that at least some of the ideas he absorbed from such literature had an influence on the shaping of his ruling style. On the other hand, we should not see this as mere mimicry of older Indo-Persian royal culture, and especially not as the new Sikh kings 'copycatting' the Mughals. Not only did the Maharajah refuse a Mughal throne and coins bearing his name, he and the other Sikh rajahs never attempted to claim spiritual authority nor to sacralise themselves in any way, unlike Akbar, Jahangir or Shah Jahan. The Sikh chiefs equally neglected Mughal forms of strict hierarchy, namely the *mansabdari* system in which courtiers and servants of the imperial household were ordered according to a given military rank, which reflected personal allowances or privileges, and the number of cavalry retainers they were expected to provide.[49] Rather, the first Sikh 'kings' carved out a superior position for themselves within a new, alternative hierarchy, developing their power as this was unfolding within eighteenth- and early-nineteenth-century Punjab.

To an extent, therefore, it seems fair to agree with the idea that Ranjit Singh embraced Guru Arjan's notions of *halemi raj* on his own terms.[50] I would like to suggest that there is even a compelling stylistic connection between the Harmandir Sahib in Amritsar and the golden throne that Ranjit Singh commissioned for himself to use, as an alternative to sitting on the grand Mughal one in the Lahore Fort. The Maharajah donated large sums of money for the gurdwara in the Harmandir Sahib complex to be decorated with sheets of gold, in order to pay respects to the central Sikh shrine in his own way. It is for this reason that we know this gurdwara as the Golden Temple today. His new throne (described as a small, 'bath-tub-like chair' by Khushwant Singh!)[51] was similarly covered with gold, and had subtle floral patterns carved into it by an expert craftsman. As a movable seat, it was not quite as grandiose as the great thrones on which past rulers had sat at Lahore, but it was a throne nevertheless. And, just as we saw with the design of the Harmandir Sahib devised by Guru Arjan, the base of the Maharajah's throne is composed of two tiers of lotus petals—again alluding to the humble style of rulership long associated with ancient Indian courtly culture, but most urgently expected of Sikh kings.[52]

Ranjit Singh's golden throne thus shows us something of the careful balance that he attempted to strike in the way he presented himself as a monarch: somewhere between showcasing his personal power and demonstrating his obeisance and piety with respect to the legacy and ideals of the Gurus. But a monarch he was—in all of this, we cannot overlook the fact that *halemi raj*, though emphasising humility, still 'regards rule or Raj' as central to its construction. As

Louis Fenech says, 'rule, whether exercised with humility or not, requires strategies to ensure order and to guarantee that such rule continues'.[53] So just how did Ranjit Singh go about building his empire? We have seen in this chapter the complex ideas from Punjabi and Sikh history that he will have drawn on, but now we have to turn to Ranjit Singh's own lifetime: in more immediate, practical ways, the Maharajah's reign was built with the help of his family—his queens and his princes. Together, they would become the Punjab's newest imperial dynasty.

2

NEW DYNASTY, NEW EMPIRE

By the time Ranjit Singh was born in November 1780, the Sukerchakia *misl*, headed by his grandfather Charat Singh and then his father, Maha Singh, had moved outwards from its estate of a few villages in Gujranwala, to conquer a swathe of land across north-western Punjab. By the time the young Ranjit began walking, he had already been provided with a significant powerbase from which to launch his career and build the foundations for a new, dynastic empire. Yet the eminent Sikh historian Professor J.S. Grewal noted in 1981, '[T]he obvious fact that Ranjit Singh was a ruler of the third generation in the Sukerchakia family has not been properly appreciated by his historians'.[1]

This line reads a little bit like a rebuke to generations of Ranjit Singh's biographers, who have often been all too quick to treat him as something of a 'superman'. In his own work, Grewal certainly does not detract from the many talents of the Sikh Maharajah; but here he is also clearly making an important point, urging readers to reflect upon the considerable boon that the young Ranjit Singh was granted as the heir, rather than the founder, of an increasingly powerful war band. When we look at these early expansionist activities of the Sukerchakia *misl*, it becomes clear that it was not just the amount of territory captured that smoothed the path for Ranjit Singh's future, but also the immensely valuable resources that his grandfather and father had brought under their family's power. Sites such as Kotli Loharan and Pind Dadan Khan yielded control over matchlock manufacturers and salt mines, which strengthened the fighting power of the *misl*'s warriors and enriched its *sardars*.[2]

In a more worrisome manner, as we saw in the previous chapter, the location of Sukerchakia territories also brought them into close contact with often hostile Afghans and Pathans. Nevertheless, the steadfast manner with which Ranjit Singh's father and grandfather faced up to repeated incursions and threats from such foes had led to them being respected as strong leaders by their fellow Sikhs. This in turn excited a mixture of admiration, fear and jealousy amongst their neighbouring chiefs, whether Afghan, Pathan or Sikh—demonstrating that the Sukerchakia *misl*, though originally one of the smallest, was definitely in its ascendancy by the time of Ranjit Singh's birth, in terms of power, authority and wealth. To consolidate their growing military and territorial strength, Charat Singh and Maha Singh quickly established a basic but effective administrative system to collect revenue and maintain law and order in their new domain. This meant that by the end of the eighteenth century there was already at least a rudimentary bureaucracy in place, bringing in a steady flow of money, which the young Ranjit Singh would later use to fuel his more ambitious campaigns.[3]

Thus, as Grewal points out, there was a 'remarkable degree of continuity [between] the political activities of Maha Singh and the early activity of Ranjit Singh'—reminding us that, although very talented and determined, the most famous Sukerchakia *sardar* was much less of an innovator or solitary genius than has hitherto been claimed. Instead, we can see that, even before Ranjit Singh took over the *misl* after his father's death in 1790, something like a dynastic project was already emerging with the Sukerchakias; one that Ranjit Singh did not create, but would certainly take forward to dizzying new heights.

As we explore the making of the Sikh Empire in this and the next chapter, instead of focusing solely on the role of the 'great man' himself, we will look more closely at the 'family' behind the Sukerchakia *misl*. The Punjab's new Maharajah did not just benefit from the helpful inheritance of his male warlord ancestors. During his own lifetime and reign, Ranjit Singh's empire-building was supported and enhanced by other members of his family, especially as it grew in size. This included a large number of female relatives, whose involvement has rarely been discussed seriously by historians of the Ranjit Singh period, but whose contributions were fundamental to the Sikh Empire project. During the future Maharajah's adolescence, alongside certain maternal uncles, his mother, Raj Kaur, and his first mother-in-law, Sada Kaur, were highly important figures. During his adulthood and later life, several of his wives, as well as their sons and heirs, were increasingly on the frontlines of empire construction, serving as principal agents in state-formation and diplomatic roles of a markedly royal style.

With this in mind, it is arguably more appropriate to describe this family as a 'dynasty'. They were not explicitly spoken of in their own time as 'the Sukerchakia dynasty', but this book will use that term to refer to the royal family—partly for clarity and convenience, but also because there can really be no doubt that Ranjit Singh and his family did act as a dynasty. Despite the new Maharajah's government being represented in his own day as the *Sarkar-i-Khalsa*, or his kingdom being popularly known today as 'the Sikh Empire', power was actively concentrated in the hands of Ranjit Singh and his kin, both male and female; and their authority was meant to be passed down in hereditary fashion over the generations.

It is also not a stretch to say that, in their shift from *misl* to empire, Ranjit Singh and his royal family engaged in a form of 'dynastic colonialism'.[4] The nature of Sukerchakia military conquests, marital alliances and royal patronage of arts and architecture shows how the self-made Maharajah and his closest relatives successfully laid claim to both land and power throughout the Punjab, whilst also gradually increasing their cultural 'soft power' over a wider geographical span in northern India and its border with Afghanistan. In doing so, the dynasty of the Sikh Empire became the dominant political players in the region by the 1830s, with only the East India Company to rival them.

Not Just a Wedding

It is not without reason that the first pages of this book opened with a description of the lavish and extravagant spectacle of a Punjabi royal wedding. Marriage was a central mechanism through which the Sukerchakias were able to build social and kinship connections, enabling the power of the *misl* to be embedded across its growing expanse of territory in northwestern Punjab and beyond. The nature of Sukerchakia marriages would change considerably over time; they moved from being contained within roughly the same class of Sikh *misl* families to a more wide-ranging set of unions with women of varying classes and communities, as well as embracing concubinage. Polygamy was a common practice amongst Punjabi elites of all faiths in this period, and until the turn of the nineteenth century, it was also practically the norm for all ruling dynasties globally apart from Christian European royal houses.[5] The style of nuptial celebrations conducted by Ranjit Singh's family would also be transformed over generations, becoming more conspicuously royal and spectacular, as we shall see in a later chapter. These changes reflect the general shifts taking place in the political world of the Punjab in the Sikh Empire period—not least the move from warrior bands generally led by men, to an inherited imperial dynasty in which, of course, women were as vital as men.

Matrimonial alliances were crucially important for the early Sukerchakia *misl* in gaining strong, protective friends, partly because of the difficult personal circumstances that core members of the Sukerchakia family had to overcome during the 1770s and 1780s. Both Maha Singh and Ranjit Singh inherited the charge of the *misl* unexpectedly as young boys, due to the sudden and untimely deaths of their fathers. Charat Singh was killed in a freak accident in 1774 when his matchlock exploded in his hands and left him mortally wounded, leaving his 15-year-old son Maha Singh at the head of the *misl*. His mother, Mai Desan, ran affairs for a while on his behalf. Later on, Maha Singh himself succumbed to disease and passed away in 1790, when Ranjit Singh was just ten. Thus, like his father before him, during Ranjit Singh's early years as a newly anointed *sardar*, the task of managing *misl* matters actually fell heavily on the shoulders of his mother, Raj Kaur, who acted as regent.

In the competitive world of late-eighteenth-century Punjab, such regencies could render a *misl* vulnerable, and a deceased *sardar*'s family evidently relied on support from extended or collateral relations in order to avoid being attacked or subsumed by rivals. Nevertheless, Sikh women acting as regents of a *misl* were vitally important in providing stability and continuity in the handling of wider political and social relations. In several cases, betrothals with other *misls* had been settled on during the sardar's lifetime, but were only formalised into marriage in the more challenging circumstances after his death, under the watchful eye of the widowed regent. For example, in 1765, Ranjit Singh's grandfather had reached a major agreement with the Bhangi *misl* over disputed territories in northwestern Punjab and Kashmir. This new accord, which amicably divided the contested lands between the two *misls*, was cemented by the betrothal of his young daughter to Gujar Singh Bhangi's second son, binding the families to one another. This enabled them to collaborate on further expansionist campaigns against Afghan-ruled territory.[6] Yet the marriage was not officially celebrated until after Charat Singh's death, when it was settled by Mai Desan and her adviser, Dya Ram; thus Ranjit Singh's grandmother ensured that the Bhangis didn't exploit the situation, but kept to their word.[7] His own mother, Raj Kaur, oversaw his marriage to Mehtab Kaur (daughter of the Kanhaiya *misl*) after his father's death: she had agreed the match with Sada Kaur, another widowed regent, who had rather exceptionally managed to take hold of the Kanhaiya *misl* despite the presence of her husband's brothers. Raj Kaur's feat of diplomacy was all the more remarkable given that her departed husband had had a hand in the death of Sada Kaur's own spouse.[8]

All of this makes clear that senior and extended relations, both male and female, were deeply involved in the management of *misl* affairs during the late 1700s. At the turn of the century, as Ranjit Singh was trying to find his way as a young *sardar* replacing a more experienced one, this form of support was crucial for safeguarding the clan's interests during the transitional phase, giving Ranjit Singh time and space to be prepared for the responsibilities of leadership. In such a rough and ready world, familial elders were the people who would train the young *sardar* in political and military strategy. In his first mother-in-law, Sada Kaur, Ranjit Singh gained an exceptionally powerful ally and mentor: after his marriage to her daughter, she seems to have been much more active and prominent in his life than his own mother was. In his late teens, the young *sardar* collaborated with Sada Kaur in raids and in the expansion of his territories. Her role in the conquest of Lahore, the former Mughal capital of Punjab—a key foundational moment in all histories of the Sikh Empire—has often been overlooked by Ranjit Singh's biographers, an oversight detrimental to our understanding of the cultural politics involved in expanding the *misl*'s territorial domains, as well as of the core influences at work within the schooling of a young *sardar*.

By the end of the century, the Sukerchakia chief was increasingly able to embark on aggressive campaigns and to take on more powerful rival *misls*. According to the court historian Sohan Lal Suri, Ranjit Singh received a summons from several influential Muslim citizens of Lahore, asking him to wrest the city from the control of the Bhangi *sardars*.[9] In accordance with the customary assistance owed to a son-in-law and ally, Sada Kaur took her own forces to join his. In addition to this solid backing from Sada Kaur and the Kanhaiyas, the capture of Lahore was also thanks to a new alliance with the neighbouring Nakai *misl*, following Ranjit Singh's second marriage to Mai Nakain in 1798.[10] As we can see in Map 3 (Appendix), the territory collectively controlled by the Sukerchakia, Kanhaiya and Nakai *misls* encircled the city, which was being tightly grasped by the Bhangis as a lucrative stronghold. The Kanhaiya domain lay to the north-east in the countryside between Amritsar and the Kangra hills; whilst the Nakai lands were to the south-east, between the Ravi and Sutlej rivers, bordering but not subsuming the other powerful Punjabi city of Multan. Ranjit Singh could not have contemplated taking Lahore without these allies.

Sukerchakia–Bhangi relations had become increasingly fraught and competitive since the days of Charat Singh and Gujar Singh, which apparently led Ranjit Singh to consider Lahore as fair game despite the marriage alliance between the two clans that his grandmother had sealed. That match had been overtaken by Ranjit Singh's own: military assistance from his two sets of marital kin enabled him to bring a combined force of 25,000 cavalry and infantry to the gates of the Lahore Fort, where the Bhangis were entrenched, in 1799. The invaders managed to enter the city with ease, and took the incumbent chiefs, Chet and Mohar Singh Bhangi, completely by surprise. Yet while Ranjit Singh celebrated his victory by parading through the city and paying his respects at the Badshahi Masjid, it was Sada Kaur who set about establishing political control over its conquered inhabitants:

> The said lady busied herself in the management of political and financial affairs. The people of the city petitioned against the chiefs

> of the troops who had resorted to looting. Since the protection of the helpless and the prosperity of the subjects is an attribute of good government, it was declared in the city with the beating of the drums and peace and order was established. The people felt satisfied with this commendable action. They, therefore, wished for the raising up of the banners and increase of the glory of the exalted one [Ranjit Singh]. The glorious one wished to attack and arrest Chet Singh, the evil doer. But the said lady, out of her sagacity and wisdom, suggested that by [such a] siege and battle the whole city would be laid waste. The Sardars of the neighbourhood would join by way of supporting the opponent. The best course, therefore, was to satisfy the said person [Chet Singh] by every possible means, to turn him out of the fort and [for Ranjit Singh] to establish himself over there. To that end the said lady after considerable consultation sent for Mohar Singh and sent a word to Chet Singh through him. It was to the effect that, if he wished for the safety of life and property ... he should remove all his things from the fort. He would be granted the town of Vainiki by the Sardar for his maintenance ... On those terms the said lady brought about an agreement. Chet Singh left in the early hours of the morning for Vainiki with all his goods, grains, etc. The victorious monarch of the world entered the fort on the 3rd of Safar (1214 A.H.) [7 July 1799].[11]

Despite the presentation here of Ranjit Singh as the 'victorious monarch of the world', the main actor in this narrative is Sada Kaur, and the manner in which she tutored her young warrior son-in-law to act as a gracious conqueror. He was essentially being initiated into the forms of diplomacy that Sikh elites had developed as the political culture of the *misls* evolved throughout the eighteenth century, enabling the increasingly powerful *sardars* to negotiate political relations with one another. This was a complex and sensitive undertaking, for the *sardars* had to balance projecting their growing power against being somewhat careful to preserve the *izzat* or 'honour' of their rivals, who were still nominally equal members of the Khalsa brotherhood. This was why the *sardarni* took on the heavy responsibility of tactfully ensuring the peaceful surrender of the Bhangi chiefs and that the city's inhabitants would be won over by generous treatment. If she hadn't intervened to counteract further bloodshed and a protracted struggle in this way, it could have given cause for other local *sardars* (presumably either kin or feudatories of the Bhangis) to turn against Ranjit Singh's party, if they felt that the fight had not been fairly won.

The protocol followed in this instance for staging victory and defeat between fellow Sikh *sardars*—'satisfying the said sardar', by allowing him to make a safe and honourable surrender, and granting him an alternative portion of land and means of subsistence—was the typical manner in which any defeated Sikh chief was treated. In many ways, this custom in turn followed older, Rajput codes of martial honour, in which a warrior secured authority and legitimacy by recognising a worthy foe in his opponent, and the defeated individual acknowledged the victorious ruler's supremacy by accepting the grant of a piece of land (and in the Mughal case, also a *khi'lat* or robe of honour).[12] Throughout Ranjit Singh's later career, this protocol was followed fairly consistently, but it is interesting to see here how the rash nineteen-year-old *sardar* had to be reined in by his mother-in-law and instructed on the proper mode of handling a vanquished opponent, in order to avoid jeopardising a major victory.

Sada Kaur would come to the young *sardar*'s aid like this repeatedly over the next few years. The taking of Lahore was not the end of the Sukerchakia *misl*'s struggle with the Bhangis. A fresh and hotly contested battle was waged soon after, and once again Sada Kaur's Kanhaiya *misl* joined forces with the Sukerchakias and Nakais against the Bhangis, the Ramgarhias and their local Afghan allies. When this battle was eventually won after eight months, Sada Kaur came to the rescue once again, this time after problems suddenly cropped up in another quarter: Ranjit Singh's maternal uncle, Dal Singh, became perturbed about the increasing power of the Sukerchakias and joined forces with Sahib Singh Bhangi of Gujrat (the Bhangi son who was married to Ranjit's paternal aunt). To make matters worse, Dal Singh's wife, Dharam Kaur, refused to give up their fort of Akalgarh to Ranjit Singh without a fight. Sada Kaur once more managed to negotiate a resolution, this time supported by Kesra Singh Sodhi (a well-respected descendant of the Sikh Gurus). Soon after this, she even had to shore up Ranjit Singh's finances, when his troops demanded their pay following the busy season of campaigning. Even here Sada Kaur was able to smooth over matters for her temporarily cash-strapped son-in-law, handing over her own gold bangles to the commander of the men to 'defray the expenditure'.[13]

We can see from such recurring fracas how deeply kinship relations were implicated in the politics of the competing Sikh *misls*. The marriages arranged for the young Ranjit Singh during his minority were crucial to protecting his interests during a vulnerable stage, and then enabled the Sukerchakias to go on to a more aggressive footing. In time, Ranjit Singh learnt how to shift his use of these kin relations, apparently without a great deal of remorse, depending on his changing needs and priorities as *sardar*. Though his ties to Sada Kaur's and Mai Nakain's people served him well, he also set about constructing a wider network of kinship ties, through a larger number of alternative marriages (See Map 3 in the Appendix). Historians have not probed this trend deeply enough, but—together with the training and deployment of the princes as administrators—this series of strategic marriage alliances was key in allowing Ranjit Singh to break away from a dependency on Sikh elites of the *sardar/misldar* class, projecting himself and his descendants into a newer, superior league of royalty. This implicitly involved a rejection of 'horizontal' social and political parity between the twelve *misls*; instead the boundaries of Ranjit Singh's newly emerging dynasty shifted, to incorporate and privilege only those individuals immediately beneath him in a patriarchal hierarchy: his growing number of wives, and the new royal lineage created with the birth of his sons.

Sada Kaur was one of the first to fall victim to this shift in her son-in-law's dynastic allegiances: this is one significant break that is discussed commonly enough by Punjabi historians, perhaps due to its remarkably ruthless nature. This change was the direct result of the birth of a son, Kharak Singh, to Ranjit Singh and his second wife, Mai Nakain, in 1800. The arrival of a baby boy meant that there was a new heir to continue the Sukerchakia line, but it also signified that, in the ranking of Ranjit Singh's allies and wives, Sada Kaur and her daughter Mehtab would have to take a step down. It is widely agreed upon that Ranjit Singh deliberately sidelined his senior mother-in-law, who was known to pose a threat to his ambitions to cement his clan as the leading political players in the Punjab.

To continue the bond with Sada Kaur's *misl* whilst undercutting her personal authority, the infant Kharak was engaged to Chand

Kaur, the daughter of a junior branch of the *misl*. The Kanhaiyas could not now directly oppose the Sukerchakia heir-apparent, even though he and his mother stood as rivals to Mehtab Kaur's interests.[14] The exact date on which this engagement was formalised is not known, but in all likelihood, it took place close to the time when Ranjit Singh had himself declared as Maharajah of Punjab in 1801, through the grace of Baba Sahib Singh Bedi—a revered Sikh religious leader, descended from Guru Nanak. Over the next ten years, the newly created Maharajah would use his son as something of a political weapon more than once; especially to assert himself against his other main in-laws, the Nakais.

The break with Sada Kaur, and the subjugation of both the Kanhaiyas and the Nakais, should not be seen as a standalone event. Instead, the later marriages of the Maharajah and his sons should be scrutinised more closely, and recognised as being part of a larger, concerted dynastic project. Although the exact total of wives taken by Ranjit Singh and his principal heirs is not known, they numbered at least forty-three women for the period between 1795 and 1842.[15] These women hailed from diverse locations across the Punjab, reaching out to its fringes (see Map 3 in the Appendix). The network created by the widespread range of Sukerchakia marriages closely reflects the expanding empire that was built during the Maharajah's lifetime. His first two marriages in the 1790s, to Sada Kaur's daughter and to Mai Nakain, were certainly designed to provide his *misl* with powerful and supportive allies of an equal political and social standing. Thereafter, during the 1810s and 1820s, the Maharajah contracted a series of marriages for the sake of territorial gain. The first two of these unions, to the widows of a Sikh landowner, were particularly important in his empire-building enterprise, and they were formed simultaneously.

After the death in 1811 of Sahib Singh Bhangi, Ranjit Singh took charge of two of the deceased *sardar*'s wives, the sisters Rattan Kaur and Daya Kaur. This was done through the rite of *chadar dalni*, which literally translates from Punjabi to mean 'throwing a sheet over someone'. This metaphorical phrase relates to the custom of a man taking a widowed, vulnerable or otherwise willing woman under his protection, in the role of a wife. Widowed women who entered the Lahore *zenana* (harem) by this custom were considered in a somewhat separate and secondary category to those who had only been married to Ranjit Singh, and these 'weddings' were not celebrated with the full matrimonial rites of either the Maharajah's or the woman's religion. But Ranjit Singh's marriage to these two sisters was an absolutely crucial step in his early efforts to cement his expanding power and territorial reach, both symbolically and practically.

The gesture had two political purposes. Firstly, the provision of shelter and care for the kin-women of a deceased rival *sardar* demonstrated Ranjit Singh's adherence to the codes of *izzat* (honour) in Sikh elite culture, in which women were never to be harmed or treated discourteously. It was also for this reason that the Maharajah formally made lifetime provision for the care of Sahib Singh's mother, Mai Lachmi, and older wife, Raj Kaur, who was after all also Ranjit Singh's paternal aunt.[16] Secondly, although respect for a worthy foe was thus signalled, so was their subjugation—an obvious demonstration that the foe was no longer capable of adequately protecting his female relations. Beyond this symbolic power of the marriage, there was also a concrete purpose to the Maharajah taking up the Bhangi women as his own. It finally allowed him, once and for all, to take a firm hold of Amritsar: another city held by the Bhangis, but also of course one of unparalleled importance to the Sikhs and to the Punjab as a whole.

The gendered nature of Ranjit Singh's political strategy cannot be ignored. Increasingly, the capture of forts and fields from their original owners, or the settling of agreements with new tributaries, would go hand in hand with the incorporation of local women into the dynasty.

We see this strategy unfolding further for another twenty years (up until 1832), during which time Ranjit Singh married seven women who were all the daughters of Sikh Jatt *zamindars*. These *zamindars* (landowners) were much lower down in the ranking of Punjabi society than a *sardar* or *misldar*, but union with their families was still useful for the Maharajah. They entrenched his ties with potentially influential *biradari* (kinship) networks in the localities that he was seeking to penetrate and bring directly under Sukerchakia control. These families were concentrated within a line that roughly sliced through the centre of the Punjab.[17]

The main courtly chronicle for the reign of Ranjit Singh and his successors, Suri's *Umdat-ut-tawarikh*, contains scattered references to several of these hastily arranged marriages, which took place on tours, during which the Maharajah would typically inspect the works of his *kardars* (local revenue officers) or collect tribute.[18] Ranjit Singh was increasingly resorting to marriage across class boundaries as a means of cultivating the loyalty and collaboration of local elites, and cementing his sovereign claim to the ownership and control of the land. But this was not a one-way street. In a couple of cases, including that of Jind Kaur—who would later rule the Empire as her boy Duleep Singh's regent—there is credible evidence that the women's own parents initially suggested the match. Jind Kaur's father was the Maharajah's kennel-keeper at the Lahore Fort, so it is obvious how forging a kin connection with the ruling dynasty would have been an attractive means of social advancement or 'protection' for lower or middling families.[19]

The greater portion of the marriages of the Sikh princes also took place from the 1810s. Suri's courtly chronicles point to Ranjit Singh himself largely assuming the responsibility for arranging and organising the weddings of his first-born son and grandson, and suggest that he used these occasions as opportunities to further develop and optimise dynastic ties and power relations. As we will see in Chapter 4, the two most important of these weddings were orchestrated to proclaim the power, wealth and grandeur of the self-made Sukerchakia dynasty as the rulers of the Punjab, not only within the region itself, but also, increasingly, in the world beyond their Empire. But beyond the spectacle of the wedding itself, and beyond the major unions, there was continuation of Ranjit Singh's own marital projects. Going by the chronicles and the pension lists, the vast majority of princely marriages were with the daughters of prominent Sikh *sardars*, reinforcing ties with the class from which the Maharajah himself had emerged. As the Appendix map shows, the princes' marriage alliances also furthered the gendered strategy of incorporating women from the fringes of the Sikh Empire—reaching into the domains of the Punjabi states not under Ranjit Singh's control through the marriages of Princes Nau Nihal Singh and Sher Singh. Rather than form a political or military alliance with one of the major dynasties there, the Maharajah accepted a proposal from the Bhadaur *sardar*, marrying his eldest grandson, Nau Nihal Singh, to the *sardar*'s daughter. This created a new connection with and influence over an area that, by treaty, Ranjit Singh was supposed to leave untouched—and so the marriage also entailed the nominal recognition of his supremacy.[20]

While Ranjit Singh's dynasty was expanding and changing the nature of its alliances with other Sikh powers, the Maharajah and his sons also married Hindu and Muslim women, again from a variety of class and caste backgrounds. The Maharajah's most famous 'love marriages' were with Muslim dancing girls: Moran (1802) and Gul Begum (1832). Several Hindu princesses were also taken as brides by Ranjit Singh, Nau Nihal Singh and Sher Singh. Women such as Ranis Katochan and Raj Banso were daughters of the Punjabi hill rajahs, whose dynasties had been ruling over small and wealthy principalities for centuries, but who would be made into vassals by Ranjit Singh by the 1830s. Lastly, several Pathan women also entered the Lahore *zenana* during this period, as the Sikh Empire expanded to take over Kashmir and prise away sections of Afghan territory. One, Jind Kulan of Mankera, was presented to the Maharajah by her father in 1824; while another girl, Zebo, was sent as a concubine by the Governor of Kashmir in 1832 (who may have been Prince Sher Singh), after she had been given to him by her father.[21]

By the last years of Ranjit Singh's reign in the 1830s, a formidable number of very different women were incorporated into the Sukerchakia house. Collectively they would be referred to using the term *sarkarat*.[22] This was a plural reference for those queens who took the title Sarkar after their name following their marriage to the Maharajah. This was certainly an enhancement on the title *sardarni* or the more general term *musammat*, which were both applied to earlier generations of elite women within Sikh *misls*, such as Sada Kaur or Raj Kaur.[23] In the writings of the Sikh Empire's court historians, titles such as Maharani/Rani Sahiba or Sarkar, or the description of a woman as *purdahnashin*, are used to mark a class difference between a royal lady and other women who frequented the court in various capacities, such as servants, dancers, courtesans and slaves. The wearing of a veil (*purdah*) over the face, or sitting behind a screen, was observed by the most elite women of the court as a means of symbolically protecting their honour; but it also effectively altered their behaviour and the connotations of the space they occupied, demarcating both their bodies and surroundings as superior and exclusive in nature.

This hierarchy was never a fixed one, however, and it shifted continually throughout the first half of the nineteenth century. One account of Ranjit Singh's marriage to the dancer Gul Begum, is a case in point. At the age of eleven, a talented young writer called Amar Nath was able to capture the dramatic moment when the Maharajah fell head over heels for Gul Begum whilst watching her dance at a lavish evening party held at Amritsar. Ranjit Singh decided almost immediately that he had to marry her and did so with great pomp and pageantry. He brought his new bride back to Lahore seated on his own elephant and radically enhanced her status by giving her the exalted new name of Maharani Gul Bahar Begum. Amar Nath stated that, in gifting her this new *khitab* (title), Ranjit Singh had elevated her to a position even above that of the *purdehdar* (veiled/courtly) women, who were now set to the task of massaging Gul Begum's feet![24]

On occasion, the status of the Punjabi queens could be extended to incorporate their relations too. Amar Nath records that Gul Begum's brothers were granted a *jagir* (a landed estate) and given a *nawabi* title.[25] As we shall see in Chapter 5, Jind Kaur's brothers, Jawahir Singh and Hira Singh, also had *jagirs*, and the former became *vazir* when the Maharani became regent of the Empire. An alternative, though equally inclusive, approach was followed in the case of Maharani Roop Kaur's family. Her father was the *lambardar* (headman) of Kot Said Mehmood village, near Amritsar. To this day, Roop Kaur's descendants preserve her memory in a small museum that they have constructed in their renamed ancestral village, Kot Khalsa. They have carried the surname 'Sarkaria' ('of the *sarkar*') for several generations, which they claim was given to them as a royal gift by Ranjit Singh, after he 'adopted' Khushal Singh, Roop Kaur's nephew, who was a talented soldier.[26]

Through the rich diversity of these marriages and their purposes, we are looking at a vivid picture of one of the great strengths of Ranjit Singh's dynasty: its thoroughly inclusive and adaptable nature. This was a major shift away from the practices of preceding generations: Ranjit Singh's father and grandfather seem only to have taken one or two wives, and exclusively married women from similarly elite Sikh backgrounds. As Maharajah, Ranjit Singh actively sought to widen his kinship ties and attach to himself a greater variety of marital partners, ranging across the regions and communities of the Punjab. This flexible approach in building connections across newly-assimilated territories altered the very composition of the royal family at the head of the former Sukerchakia *misl*, enabling it to at least partially reflect the diversity of the population over which it ruled. Ties of this nature, which linked the dynasty intimately to different parts of its growing empire, surely contributed to the Maharajah's ability to undercut the local authority of rival *misldars*, and to break free from his earlier dependence on such senior collateral relations as Sada Kaur.

In some ways, you could even say that Ranjit Singh's rather open-ended 'marriage policy' bore parallels with that of the Mughal emperor, Akbar. As Ruby Lal has argued, Akbar's massive number of marriages (potentially up to 5,000 women) was a way of 'symbolically demonstrating that the world was under the emperor's protection'.[27] Although Ranjit Singh and his sons did not go to such extreme lengths, we can certainly see a similar principle at work through the conduct of *chadar dalni* 'protection' marriages, or by their acceptance into their *zenanas* of women offered by their own parents. It was also an 'index of power' for a king or emperor to be able to exert such patriarchal authority over a far-flung kin network, one that reached into territories whose ownership was claimed or contested by other rulers, from rival *misldars* in central Punjab and Afghans to the west, or the Cis-Sutlej Rajahs in the east. However, such a marriage strategy was certainly not without its problems. For one thing, developing as it did over around thirty years, the overall impact of this network may well have been cumulative, and patchy in different regions, rather than facilitating an overnight transformation in the dynamics of elite Punjabi politics.

On a more day-to-day level, the *zenana*'s combination of women from very different backgrounds, with competing ambitions or outlooks, could prove extremely troublesome. This was partially caused by competing notions of *izzat*, which proved tragically disastrous for one Maharani. On occasion, Ranjit Singh used to hold special *durbars* or courts with his wives. At one such event, he teasingly asked a dancing girl, Allah Jowai, to tell him which of his queens she thought was the most beautiful—a question the dancer wisely hesitated to answer. On further prompting by the Maharajah, Allah Jowai pointed to the Rajput princess Raj Banso and said, 'This Maharani is the moon and the others the stars of your harem.' Ranjit Singh apparently disagreed with this response, as he asked the dancer whether she was sure that Moran, one of his Muslim brides, was not more beautiful. To be compared unfavourably with a former dancing girl by her husband reputedly offended Raj Banso so deeply that she took a lethal dose of opium that same night and died in her sleep. The Maharajah was forced to perform her cremation with a deep sense of remorse and, according to the records of the Fakir family (who were senior Lahore courtiers), no similar gatherings of Punjabi queens were held by him again.[28]

This was not the first time that Ranjit Singh's marriage to Moran landed him in serious trouble. In openly flaunting his happiness at having wed the beautiful dancing girl, the young Maharajah had managed to upset the sentiments and beliefs of a strictly orthodox sect of Sikhs. The Akalis acted as the keepers of the Harmandir Sahib and Akal Takht in Amritsar—the two core sites of spiritual decision-making for the Sikh community. During what was essentially their honeymoon period, Ranjit Singh had been parading with Moran on elephant-back through the streets of Lahore, enjoying a drink or two along the way. The result of the Akalis' displeasure was a summons for the newly betrothed king to report directly to the Akal Takht to receive a punishment. He was invited to apologise and humble himself before the collected Sikh spiritual leaders, before being sentenced to a punishment of 100 lashes on the back, to be carried out in public, as well as the payment of a fine. Different accounts of the episode clash over whether or not the Maharajah was made to suffer at least one symbolic strike before being pardoned, but all agree that he readily paid the fine of Rs. 125,000.[29]

One interesting thing about this episode is its timing: it appears to have taken place at some point in 1802, only about a year after Ranjit Singh had been anointed as Maharajah of the Punjab. It is possible to infer from the Akalis' disapproval of the new young Maharajah's actions, and his own readiness to meekly accept the punishment meted out to him, that, in this early stage of his reign, Ranjit Singh still needed to be mindful of and to abide by the presiding social conventions imposed by more established Sikh authorities.

It is noticeable that the Maharajah faced no such opposition following his similar marriage to the dancing girl Gul Begum in 1832, despite the fact that this wedding too was celebrated with much public jubilation, as well as proving somewhat disruptive to the internal hierarchy of the Punjabi royal *zenana* with the foot-washing incident recorded by Amar Nath.

In other words, the style in which the Maharajah established his own brand of 'dynastic colonialism' could cause considerable tension. It involved significant cultural and political change, which was not easily accepted or conformed with by all groups or individuals within the Punjab and therefore had to be introduced and handled carefully. It is fair to say that the abovementioned episodes were rare and exceptional events, and also that Ranjit Singh's wives otherwise largely entered into the spirit of his dynastic project. In this regard, it pays to give more attention to the queens themselves, by piecing together the fragments of evidence in contemporary sources to break through the all-too-common Orientalist stereotypes that abound when it comes to Punjabi royal women.

The World of the Maharanis

First of all, despite the repeated reference to the queens being *purdahnashin* (observing the veil or *purdah*), these women were not secluded and were certainly not all restricted to the confines of a royal *zenana*. Amongst the droll, unpublished letters of a British *memsahib*, Isabella Fane, we actually find evidence to suggest that the Lahore *zenana* was not a fixed, institutionalised space in Ranjit Singh's kingdom, but perhaps only acted as temporary accommodation for royal women:

> Runjeet had assembled his wives together in a tent in a flower garden. It appears that they don't all put up together in a zanana, but were thus congregated for our accommodation ... We found him bundled up on a chair, surrounded on each side and behind with these loves. There were ten of them, and each had a female attendant with a punkah, to drive away the flies.[30]

Several of the queens may have lived within the Lahore Fort, but many of them also had a *haveli* (mansion) of their own, within or outside of the city. On the occasion Isabella Fane describes here, in

March 1837, the queens were gathered to receive her as an important guest: she was the daughter of the East India Company's Commander-in-Chief, Sir Henry Fane. Fane was heading a British delegation to the spectacular wedding of Prince Nau Nihal Singh, and as we shall see later, this meeting between Isabella and the Punjabi queens was an important opportunity to strengthen the bonds of diplomatic friendship between the British and the Punjabi rulers, through their mutual participation in this major dynastic event for the Sukerchakias. This was a relatively special and rare occurrence for the Maharanis, but can nevertheless be seen as an extension of the active role played by at least a few of them in the cultural and political affairs of their kingdom.

In a way, looking for 'gender equality' as we understand it in today's terms is perhaps not a good fit, considering the circumstances of nineteenth-century Punjab. Anyone who sought to overshadow or rival the dominance of Ranjit Singh—man or woman—would sooner or later face the threat of being subsumed with the tightening grasp of his power throughout the region. But within his dynastic and imperial project, there was certainly a role for women to play. The queens were in receipt of large pensions, mostly likely derived from their ownership of *jagirs* or estates: their possible engagement with these tracts of land, and more generally their utilisation of any personal wealth, influence or ability, are matters that cry out for greater inspection in histories of the Sikh Empire. The Maharajah's first two wives, Mehtab Kaur and Mai Nakain, evidently chose to live on their *jagirs* of Batala and Sheikhupura, rather than at court in Lahore. In Mehtab Kaur's case, this would seem to have been partly due to the fact that she did not get on well with Ranjit Singh, and perhaps also because she shared the competitive instincts of her mother Sada Kaur and the Kanhaiya *misl*.[31] At any rate, this Rani died in 1813, so she was unable to extensively participate in or shape the developing royal culture during her lifetime.

On the other hand, Mai Nakain was a dynamic agent in this project—perhaps understandably so, since she was the mother of the heir-apparent. She lived a relatively independent and regal life in Sheikhupura from 1811, after her young son, Kharak Singh, captured the fort there. Like any other *jagirdar*, the Maharani was expected to provide tribute for the Lahore treasury from her land revenues, and to furnish troops and other military resources, which she did very effectively during the campaign to annex Multan. This city, the most powerful in Punjab after Lahore, was on the border of Nakai lands, and it was Kharak Singh who was entrusted with its conquest.

Mai Nakain appears to have made considerable efforts to restore the *haveli* and fort of Sheikhupura, which had originally been commissioned by the Mughal Emperor Jahangir when he was a prince, to act as a 'recreational complex' for himself and his entourage on their hunting parties in the region. It would appear that the initial design of the royal accommodation was split into a *divankhana* and a *zenankhana* (male and female living quarters); however, recent research suggests that the former men's apartments were taken over by Mai Nakain herself, whilst her staff were accommodated in the attached quadrangle which had housed the old women's quarters. The Maharani apparently restored the brickwork and strengthened the foundations of the building, but most interestingly of all, she commissioned talented Pahari artists to decorate the interior apartments.[32]

Sheikhupura was the home of the Maharani for much of her adult life, until her death in 1838. It does not seem as though she left any kind of written records behind her, and only a handful of (deeply valuable) mentions are made of her in contemporary manuscript sources. This makes the paintings that she had commissioned for the walls of her *haveli* the only real evidence that we have left to give us a sense of her as a person, as well as an idea of her lifestyle and status within the Empire. Even more sadly, Sheikhupura Fort is no longer open to visitors, as the building is in such a dilapidated state that the local authorities have deemed it unsafe for tourists or researchers to go inside—no one has yet come forward to carry out conservation works on its internal structure either, which is most frustrating. Fortunately, however, an extremely kind Pakistani-heritage photojournalist, Aown Ali, has shared with me the extensive set of photographs that he was able to take of the fort's interior some years ago—a few of which are included as plates in this book. From these images, we can get a glimpse of the former Maharani's home, where some of the beautiful artwork that once adorned her living quarters has not yet peeled off or faded out completely.

Though there are only a few, scattered references in Suri's chronicle about Ranjit Singh's visits to the region (predominantly on hunting trips), it would certainly seem from the paintings in Mai Nakain's apartments that the Maharani was keen to mark the space as one in which lovers could meet and enjoy the beauties of nature. The figures of colourfully attired dancing girls and guards bearing spears or hunting equipment are painted around or near doors and entrances, demarcating the rooms as spaces for entertainment, but of an exclusive nature. Intermingled with this imagery are *ras-lila* scenes with Krishna and various *gopi* (his devotees, lovingly performing a classical dance around him), as well as depictions of other lovers meeting or parting. However, this was not just an inward-looking space for bearing witness to the Maharani's relationship with her husband. We also see numerous indications of Mai Nakain's desire to celebrate and glorify the future of the dynasty, for which she herself had provided hope by delivering an heir.

One alcove by a window captures a poignant moment between a lady and a prince, perhaps meant to depict the Maharani and her son Kharak Singh. She holds on to his shield and sword, while he stands with arms out-stretched next to a steed on which he was obviously meant to gallop away. Garden imagery particularly abounds amid the artistic designs of Mai Nakain's apartments, with delicately painted flowers and birds covering the upper and lower panels of most of the walls. This vividly connects the royal living quarters with the rich, luxuriant countryside in which they were situated; whilst the recurring presence of bowls or bushes laden with fruit would tend to point to the Maharani's own fertility, connecting her continuation of the Sukerchakia dynasty with the prosperity of the land over which she ruled.[33] Such imagery is mirrored in the poetry of Suri, who documented the events of the Sikh Empire in his Persian courtly chronicle, the *Umdat-ut-tawarikh*—for example, when he describes the happiness of the Maharajah's subjects at the marriage of Prince Kharak Singh to Chand Kaur in 1811. Suri equates the people of Punjab with the flowers of a prosperous garden ('*hadiqeh-ye daulat va iqbal*'), whilst presenting Ranjit Singh and his family as 'clouds of goodness' who showered riches and joy among their subjects, thereby causing the 'buds of their hearts' to be 'set aflame with happiness.'[34]

We have seen how Sikh rulers of the post-Guru period had to find a way to incorporate the ten masters' legacy into their own claim to power, and Mai Nakain was no different in this respect. Two panels in the Maharani's rooms, again above doorways, depict Guru Nanak and Guru Gobind Singh in a rather regal style. The first Guru is painted seated on a cushion, in an easily recognisable pose: leaning to one side with one leg over the other, listening to his friend Bhai Mardana playing the *rabab*. A tree covers his head, effectively resembling a royal canopy. Warriors are paying homage to him with bowed heads and clasped hands. Overall the impression is of the Guru holding court, receiving his devoted followers in the open. The painting of the last Guru takes this regality even further and depicts him as the ideal noble warrior prince, riding on a powerful horse with a royal retinue around him. The master is surrounded by retainers carrying typically royal insignia, such as an *aftabgir* (sun shield) and *morchal* (fly-whisk), while another bearer walks ahead of the party carrying the Guru's standards. Guru Gobind Singh has a classically royal eagle perched on his arm (again a fairly common representation of the last Guru), while a dog, possibly a greyhound, runs alongside his horse, suggesting that this scene might have been intended to portray the Guru himself on a hunting trip.

With this artwork in the former Mughal fort, Mai Nakain presents the Sikh Gurus as the successors to the Mughal royal style. Their invocation in this context would not only demonstrate the Maharani's personal piety, but also the blessings of the Gurus upon the royal house of which she was a part.[35] This was yet another instance of the continual balance of power with humility that characterised the Sukerchakia raj. We can see this juggling act carefully emphasised in a later portrait of Ranjit Singh. Like Guru Gobind Singh, the Maharajah is depicted on horseback, and his head is surrounded by a halo and covered by a *chattri* (parasol); but Ranjit Singh does not seek to directly emulate the Guru by wearing a *kalgi* ornament on his own turban.[36] Instead, the Maharajah's wealth is conspicuously spread throughout the scene: it is displayed through the rich apparel of his attendants, and particularly the ornamentation of his steed, which wears a plume and is bedecked in jewels. He holds lightly on to a rose, as he moves through verdant countryside that seems to blossom with his very presence. Although Ranjit Singh does not bear arms himself, his power is nevertheless represented through his soldierly attendants, who carry weapons covered in cloth speckled with gold. Thus a representation that could seem quite feminine on the surface was actually a conjoined mode of self-representation that the Maharajah shared with his wife, to subtly demonstrate their wealth and power. The gendered boundaries of rule and control of the countryside were essentially extinguished, since for the most part Mai Nakain was the royal representative who supervised and managed affairs in Sheikhupura, acting as a proxy for the Maharajah.

This late painting of Ranjit Singh is equally reminiscent of earlier Mughal works that featured Akbar in hunting scenes and imperial progresses through the countryside, which were meant to demonstrate how the Emperor's travels enabled him to connect more with the people and land under his rule—to which, according to his own court chronicler Abu'l Fazl, he was destined to bring order and prosperity. In a similar manner, Sohan Lal Suri narrates how, during a visit to Sheikhupura, Ranjit Singh upbraided and imprisoned the local *thanedar* (superintendent) appointed by Mai Nakain, when he failed to give a satisfactory account of his work.[37] Such episodes in Suri's rather hagiographic work were generally meant to demonstrate the sagacity and fairness of the Maharajah's rule, and to confirm his fatherly care for his subjects all over his empire, and the artwork decorating Mai Nakain's apartments show that she understood just as well as her husband how to fuse and refashion idealised visions of the Mughal and Sikh past, to proclaim the virtues of a new imperial age for the Punjab.

Back in the capital Lahore, the Muslim queens, Moran and Gul Begum, also used culture to make their mark in the developing power structures of the court. As we have seen, both these women were elevated from the *tawaif* class of dancing girls and courtesans. They were both intelligent women, who used their newfound wealth to further enhance both their individual elite standing and the dynasty's reputation for royal largesse. Moran commissioned a mosque to be built in the city, as well as a madrasa to house scholars interested in Islamic and Persian studies who could not afford to make the long journey to Iran.[38] Gul Begum built a pavilion, which was later converted to a *samadhi* (mausoleum) to house her remains after her death. This was situated within a beautiful new garden, through which the Maharani was known to take walks. Again, the pavilion/mosque was embellished with intricate horticultural paintings, which may also have matched the Rani's apartments in her own Lahore *haveli*.[39] This 'soft power' exercised by Gul Begum seems to have been matched by some 'hard power' too. Like Mai Nakain, the dancing-girl-turned-queen saw personally to the affairs of her *jagir*: a royal order from the official records of the court suggests that she dismissed the revenue officer managing her estate so that she could take direct charge—even calling on royal troops to prevent further interference from such local officials.[40]

These projects of the Muslim queens show that, despite the significant emphasis on elite Sikh representations of power in spaces associated with the dynasty, this was not necessarily the dominant mode; there was still room for royal women of other faiths and backgrounds to engage in the cultural project of celebrating Sukerchakia rule. In fact, their activities perhaps better enabled the dynasty to appeal to the diverse population over which they ruled, and could certainly be seen as fitting closely with the manner in which Ranjit Singh was himself keen to support and engage with religious scholars and institutions of all faiths in the Punjab. The Maharajah's court lavishly celebrated many of the key festivals observed (often jointly) by Sikhs, Muslims and Hindus throughout the year. Particularly in the precolonial period, and at least until the mid-nineteenth century, the religious boundaries of Punjabi society were quite fluid; this facilitated overlapping participation at one another's religious celebrations, and even—to some extent—shared veneration of the religions' leaders and practices.[41]

Taken together, these artworks and monuments of Ranjit Singh's queens show how the new royal family was able to set up a significant cultural and political shift in the Punjab, all with the purpose of cementing their dynasty firmly at the helm of regional society. The extensive range of marriages entered into by Ranjit Singh and his sons may have created a web of useful local alliances, but they also brought forth, in time, young women who were themselves interested and skilful in supporting and enhancing the dynastic project—in their own ways and for their own purposes.

Princes in Training

If we see the role of Maharanis as one face of the Sikh Empire coin, on the other side would certainly be the princes: the sons and grandsons of Ranjit Singh and his Sikh wives.

It is important to note from the outset that much of what we know about the Sikh princes has been coloured by the largely negative debates and accounts regarding their reigns as Maharajah: Kharak Singh, Nau Nihal Singh, Sher Singh and Duleep Singh ruled in the decade between Ranjit Singh's death in 1839 and the eventual fall of the Empire in 1849. A lot of blame for the kingdom's demise has been laid at the doors of Ranjit Singh's first three successors in particular (Duleep Singh is usually excused because he was only four when he was placed on the throne in 1843). Kharak Singh, Nau Nihal Singh and Sher Singh have often been regarded as entirely inferior rulers and characters compared with their illustrious father and grandfather. Yet the politics behind such accounts of the princes' reigns and personalities have rarely been probed or thought about with much criticality.

As a result, the history of the rise and fall of the Sikh Empire has all too frequently been reduced to the story of Ranjit Singh and his career, with an unquestioning assumption that he above all else was responsible (rightly or wrongly) for building and holding together the pan-Punjabi kingdom, and that therefore its collapse after his death was inevitable, since there was no one who could equal his skill or verve as a political leader. Of course, as we have already seen, it's simply untrue that the 'solitary genius' of Ranjit Singh led to the rise of a new dynastic empire in the Punjab. In Chapters 4 and 5, we will look more closely at the reigns of the last four Maharajahs and the eventual collapse of the Sikh Empire, but for now, I want to focus on a different question. Historians of the period have been so focused on the princes' supposed role in the kingdom's downfall that they've almost entirely neglected another question: what was the princes' role, as boys and young adults, in the making of their family's new kingdom?

I think it is of vital importance for us to ask this question, if we really want to understand just how the Sikh Empire emerged and, moreover, how it actually worked. Whatever we may come to think of the failings of Kharak Singh, Nau Nihal Singh and Sher Singh as Maharajahs, we should not let the politics of hindsight blind us to the valuable roles that they were made to play during their father's reign. So, just as we have been trying to tease out a sense of the world in which the Empire's queens moved and acted, let us now add the lives and careers of the princes into the mix.

What exactly did it mean to be a Sikh prince? In thinking about this, we have to remind ourselves again that Ranjit Singh himself only assumed the title of 'Maharajah' in 1801. The role and status of his sons were thus just as much 'under construction' as they were for the Maharajah himself and the women of their family. As we've just seen, the 'royal' and 'imperial' nature of the transformed Sukerchakia *misl* first took its new shape through the expansive marital network forged by Ranjit Singh, and through the ways his wives interpreted their queenship. But just as important were the education and early careers of the princes, which formed a pivotal part of the dynasty's overall political development and managing the expansion and representation of its emerging empire, as well as a way to prepare the princes for their own political futures, whatever those might turn out to be.

We can notice the rising power and pretensions of Ranjit Singh's dynasty in the changing nature of the titles given to these young boys as the nineteenth century progressed. Glancing through Suri's eminently useful chronicle, we see that the eldest sons, Kharak Singh and Sher Singh, are mentioned using the title *sahibzadah* in the first few years of their life. This is a Persian title, which refers to the 'son of a gentleman' or similarly elite figure, but certainly not someone whose father was a Rajah or Maharajah. It was only as the princes grew older, and as Ranjit Singh's stature rose beyond that of a *sardar* running a *misl*, that the boys were accorded more princely, regal ranks, referred to as *kanwar* or *shahzada*. At the same time, though, there are also plenty of instances in which their names are given as 'Khalsa Kharak Singh' or 'Khalsa Sher Singh', dropping their princely designations—alongside their increasingly royal or imperial self-representation, then, the new Punjabi ruling dynasty consistently remained careful about tempering its monarchical standing with deference to the body of the Khalsa as a whole, even if it was only in a symbolic sense.

Kharak Singh was the first of Ranjit Singh's two 'legitimate' children, born to the Maharajah's second wife, Mai Nakain. As the oldest son, he was recognised as the heir apparent in 1816. Whether Ranjit Singh also had daughters, and what may have happened to them, is something of a mystery. Intriguingly, in a later account book kept by Maharajah Duleep Singh, we find a number of female children mentioned in a list of pensions being paid to the remaining members of the boy king's extended family. These payments were given to the late Maharajahs' widows, and through them to their children or households.[42] The name of the queen is given in one column, then in the next one we see listed the numbers of 'sons' and 'daughters' that she had. However, no names are given for any of the daughters; and, in the case of Ranjit Singh's wives, it is not made explicitly clear whether these girls were fathered by the Maharajah himself. Unfortunately, the records of Ranjit Singh's own day are equally silent about the existence of any daughters, and so thus far it has not been possible to uncover more information about who these young girls were or what role, if any, they played in the world of the Sikh Empire.

Adoption of both male and female children was nevertheless a relatively common practice amongst Indian ruling elites during this period and was carried out by several of Ranjit Singh's wives—an act that could have significant political consequences. Most infamously, Sher Singh and Tara Singh were recognised as the sons of the Maharajah's first wife, Maharani Mehtab Kaur, but it was widely held that they were 'illegitimate' and not actually fathered by Ranjit Singh. Many popular oral sources suggest that the redoubtable Sada Kaur had encouraged her daughter Mehtab to pass off her slave-girls' children as her own, in order to contest the superior position Mai Nakain had been able to assume after giving birth to Kharak Singh. By all accounts this was a very unsuccessful ruse, but nevertheless, as we shall see a little later, the presence of such princely contenders would quickly become crucial for bigger political games than the rivalries between Ranjit Singh's queens—young Sher Singh in particular would be increasingly co-opted into Sukerchakia empire-building goals.

Suri's *Umdat-ut-tawarikh* is very useful in several ways for understanding how lines were drawn between the statuses of these different royal sons. We've already looked at this chronicle a few times in the past few pages, but it is worth dwelling for a second on what we know about the chronicler himself and the nature of his historical writings. Sohan Lal Suri was a *vakil* (clerk/agent) working in the Lahore royal court (*durbar*). He was a diarist who regularly recorded the events of Ranjit Singh's *durbar*; but it appears that he also built on the work of his father, Ganpat Rai, who had earlier documented the events of Charat Singh and Maha Singh's careers, to compile a complete history of the Maharajah's family.[43] It is not clear whether Ganpat Rai was ever formally employed by the earlier Sukerchakia *sardars* to keep a record of their *misl*'s history, and it certainly seems that Ranjit Singh himself only came to be aware of Suri's writings in the later years of his reign, when he finally began paying the *vakil* to act as his official court historian. Suri's combined text, the *Umdat-ut-tawarikh*, is perhaps the most detailed and insightful source available for understanding the inner world of Ranjit Singh's royal family, since the chronicler was present for many of the key courtly events that he describes, and otherwise apparently took painstaking care to find out from others what had happened, so that he could record everything with as much detail as possible.

Yet we have to bear in mind that Suri himself would have had his own biases and interests, which certainly coloured the nature and content of his writings. I have already called attention to the almost propagandistic way in which he wrote about his master Ranjit Singh, whom he evidently revered, and we have seen how conservatively he viewed the queens—never speaking of them by name, instead typically referring to them with modest epithets such as the lady 'given to the veil of chastity'. Nevertheless, his comments on the princes and their lives are most fascinating. The first mentions of them appear when he documents the kinds of celebrations that were held to mark their births, and the differences between these occasions formed a critical starting point for the increasingly fierce competition between the princes during their lifetimes.

For example, Suri tells us of the great deal of money and effort expended by Ranjit Singh to promote Kharak Singh's birth in 1800, through his widespread distribution of alms—a significant move to garner popular support in and around Lahore, which he had only just conquered. The historian enthusiastically characterises the baby prince's arrival as a blessing to the local population:

> There was general pleasure and merry-making. The dust of distress and suffering was removed from the minds of the people. The persons who had been blinded with adversity procured the *kohl* of sight on account of abundant charities and alms. The oppressed ones derived great pleasure.[44]

By contrast, in his later comments regarding the birth of an heir to Maharani Mehtab Kaur, Suri only mentions one child, Sher Singh (despite the fact that he was reputedly a twin), and his account is much more muted. He notes that 'varieties of comforts and dainties were provided' by the Maharajah to his wife, and that he seemed to have 'derived great pleasure and satisfaction from the auspicious news'.[45] However, there is no allusion to alms-giving or any public celebrations that remotely resembled the events around Kharak Singh's birth. Thereafter in his chronicle, Suri only ever refers to the brothers, Sher Singh and Tara Singh, as the 'grandsons of Sada Kaur'.

Suri combined his interest in the history of the Sukerchakias with his keen personal appreciation for the sciences of astronomy and astrology. He drew detailed horoscopes to go with his accounts of the births of Ranjit Singh and Kharak Singh, which he either produced himself, or had copied from the ones drawn by the appointed court astrologers.[46] Alongside these drawings, he provided extensive commentaries on how to interpret them as indicators of the future character and capabilities of the heir in question. This kind of practice was popularly associated with notions of 'sacred kingship' connected with Mughal and Safavid (Persian) rule, the cultural cross-currents of which met in the region of the Punjab. Of course, as we have seen, the Sikh royals of this period did not aspire to be religious leaders. Nevertheless, both they and their courtiers were aware of how, within much older practices of Indo-Persian kingship, 'history and astrology were sister disciplines'. In such a world, 'astrology was as "political" a science as history', and 'kings and their enemies used astrology to ascertain the health of the realm and the lifespan of the present dispensation.'[47] The horoscope of a newly born prince could therefore be a valuable indicator of the kind of man and ruler he would become as a fully-grown adult, giving a glimpse of how he would himself 'make history' in the future.

Suri's astrological drawings are also critically important in another sense, as a major distinguishing factor between Ranjit

Singh's sons: whether or not the individual child was considered important enough for a horoscope to be commissioned after their birth. Not only could Kharak Singh's horoscope be used to try and predict his future as a king and a man, but it was also a marker of his status in the present, as a leading prince. On the other hand, the absence of a horoscope in Suri's text is equally of interest, suggesting that the birth of that child was not considered as significant as others within elite courtly circles. We could therefore make a judgement about the relatively inferior status (at birth, at any rate) of Sher Singh, Tara Singh, Multana Singh, Peshaura Singh and Kashmira Singh, as none of these princes have horoscopes featured or alluded to in Suri's writings—indeed, aside from Sher Singh, their births are not even mentioned in the history itself.[48]

Having said that, was this understanding of the 'legitimacy' or 'illegitimacy' of a princely birth a widely shared one, or did Suri's own personal opinions and ideas influence his portrayal and ranking of the Sikh princes in his chronicle? We can see that Suri understood and privileged the blood link as the main determinant of who could be considered a rightful heir in his pointed reference to Sher Singh and Tara Singh as the 'grandsons of Sada Kaur', as well as in the following quote, where he mourns the untimely deaths of both Maharajah Kharak Singh and his son, Nau Nihal Singh, in 1840:

> At that sad moment there was not a single eye which had not become fraught with disgust and sorrow. The ashes of the father and son were made to depart by the way leading out of the gate under the city wall ... and such a huge crowd of the people residing in Lahore was witnessed there at that time that the people, having closed the shops in the town, were weeping and crying, which showed that it was the last day of the death and demise of the dynasty of the Noble Sarkar [Ranjit Singh] ... In seventeen months [after the Maharajah's death], not a single trace was left of his dynasty, which was a decoration for the kingdom ... [and] an imparter of comfort and convenience to the world and its people...[49]

Even if Suri felt that Ranjit Singh's 'dynasty' had died out with his first-born son and grandson, however, throughout his chronicle he still recognised as princes those sons whom he otherwise viewed as illegitimate or outside of his constructed lineage of the Sukerchakia 'house'. The term used for 'dynasty' in Suri's text is the shared Persian and Punjabi word *khandan*: a word that can refer to a 'household' or 'family', but equally to a more elite form of kinship unit or ancestral lineage, linked with the root word *khan*, relating to a Central Asian noble/lord. Certainly the word *khandan* describes a much more regal and dynastic entity than any eighteenth-century references to the 'Sukerchakia *misl*', a clear sign of the social and political mobility of Ranjit Singh's immediate kin.[50] No matter what Suri thought of the wider family members beyond Kharak Singh's direct line, Suri could hardly neglect to mention these lesser princes, since they also formed a major part of the workings of the Sikh Empire. Indeed, he continued to document events after the demise of Kharak Singh and Nau Nihal Singh, right through to the last Maharajah Duleep Singh's final departure from Lahore in 1850 after the British annexation of his territories.

In the early volumes of Suri's chronicle, the junior princes are presented in a somewhat tense narrative relationship within the historian's upholding of the Sukerchakia bloodline as pre-eminent. This trend rises to a peak in Suri's account of Sher Singh's reign (1841–3), in which he is not afraid to criticise the fourth Maharajah's unchivalrous treatment of the widows of Kharak Singh and Nau Nihal Singh (see Chapter 4). The fact that junior sons perhaps not even fathered by Ranjit Singh were recognised as princes, despite Suri's judgement, points to the relatively inclusive manner in which his wives' children were absorbed into the dynastic fold, rather like his flexible approach to marriage. One reason for this was perhaps the Maharajah's wish to ascertain that he would have sufficient heirs to follow him, but I would suggest that a more pressing concern was the need to ensure the firm establishment of the dynasty's supremacy during his own lifetime. Like several of his wives, Ranjit Singh's sons were regularly deployed to act as representatives of his royal house, in Punjabi society and before the wider world.

Princes as Weapons, Princes at Work

We have already seen how Kharak Singh's birth and betrothal were significant political events in themselves, enabling Ranjit Singh to distance himself from his mother-in-law Sada Kaur. The two young princes Kharak Singh and Sher Singh would essentially be weaponised as they grew older, allowing the Maharajah to further subordinate his marital kin. In 1811, at the age of ten, the apparently very precocious Kharak asked his father to give him control over the estates of the Nakai *misl* (his mother's clan), promising that he would provide a much greater tribute than they did if his request was favoured. Whether or not the prince actually said this, he was put in charge of a body of troops by his father and sent away to the district of Kasur. Together with the experienced general Mohkam Chand, the prince was (nominally) charged with taking in hand the Nakai villages and forts of Chunian, Dipalpur and Satgarha. When Kahan Singh Nakai received the news that his property in Kasur had been signed over to his nephew, he had been quite innocently engaged in military service, in accordance with the Maharajah's orders. Suri describes how the 'perturbed' *sardar* immediately dispatched his advisor, Diwan Hakim Rai, to Lahore as fast as possible, to dispute the unjust assumption of his territory. However, the Maharajah's reply was simply that Kahan Singh 'could not go against royal orders' and that, after all, 'the Prince was the grandson of the Nakais.'[51]

The Persian word *navoseh* was used here to refer to Kharak Singh: specifically meaning a grandchild born of a daughter.[52] Kinship ties were clearly being manipulated in this incident to overturn the hierarchy of relations between the Maharajah and his in-laws. Kharak Singh, though younger in age, was made to displace his uncle as the head of his maternal family, thereby superseding him as heir and owner of the Nakais' property, without reference to any male heirs that Kahan Singh might have had—there might not be any more direct example of 'dynastic colonialism' than this. The move of course brought the Nakai territories indirectly under the control of Ranjit Singh, who had the ultimate say over his sons' *jagirs* or estates; he could (and did) switch them around at will. This was a bold act of interference, rewriting norms of *misl* succession; Ranjit Singh was effectively claiming that the female line now attached to his dynasty should be deemed superior to the Nakais' male line, and replacing the traditional mode of landed succession—through which property and wealth had passed from father to sons, and only after the death of the father—with the inheritance of all property by the son of the clan's daughter.

Kahan Singh vigorously protested against this arbitrary reduction of his own claims to his ancestral lands, arguing that the Maharajah's demands went against all recognised tradition and laws. He abandoned his post and went in person to Lahore to protest, whilst his relations and dependants (*vabastegan*) rallied to strengthen their forts against the arrival of the prince's troops.[53] Ranjit Singh was furious when he heard about this resistance, and initially refused his brother-in-law an audience, humiliating him further by keeping him shut out of the Lahore Fort for the best part of a day. Eventually, however, the Maharajah met with Kahan Singh privately and reached an agreement, whereby the *sardar* would be allowed to keep the fort of Baherwal, with a *jagir*-based maintenance of Rs. 20,000, as long as he agreed to cede the rest of his property to Kharak Singh.

In the midst of all of this, Baba Sahib Singh Bedi—the descendant of Guru Nanak who had anointed Ranjit Singh as Maharajah—had somehow caught wind of the oppression of the Nakais and sent 200 of his own men to the bank of the Sutlej River, to provide them with support against the prince's forces. The involvement of this revered Sikh elder was most likely an important influence in persuading Ranjit Singh to handle the matter with caution. We can see evidence of his deference to Sahib Singh in the fact that he swiftly issued a letter to his son, warning him not to interfere with the Baba's men. Nevertheless, when Kahan Singh returned to Kasur after his meeting with Ranjit, his royal nephew's advisers initially paid little heed to the Maharajah's instructions, overstepping the mark by immediately arresting the *sardar* and stripping him of all his property. Ranjit Singh cracked down on this independent policy very quickly, ordering that Kahan Singh be released and presented with a horse, a shawl and a golden bangle by the young prince.[54] Thus although the Maharajah was clearly unafraid to tamper with established Sikh modes of landed succession, knowing that he was powerful enough to enforce such changes, he still recognised that his actions against other Sikh *sardar*s could easily backfire on him if they appeared too harsh. As he had learnt the rules of the game from Sada Kaur, so he now ensured that his son in turn learnt to respect and adhere to such conventions for his own benefit.

This new policy of altered landed succession would be deployed against Sada Kaur herself soon after. Following the death of

Maharani Mehtab Kaur in 1813, she pushed Ranjit Singh to recognise the 'twins' Sher Singh and Tara Singh as his sons and as princes, in addition to granting them their own *jagirs*. The Maharajah seized this as an opportunity to begin reducing his mother-in-law's territorial power, and retorted that she should give over her property as Kanhaiya *sardarni* to her grandsons, so that they could begin to learn about the running of an estate.[55] He willingly took the young Sher Singh into his favour, and encouraged him to make further demands for land from his grandmother—all with the long-term ambition of gradually nullifying her longstanding influence.

It was in this context that Sher Singh appears to have been given his mother's former east Punjabi estate of Mukerian to live on, and it was after this point that he too was increasingly given administrative and diplomatic duties to perform. These were similar to the princely responsibilities that Kharak Singh had been given from the age of seven, before he took over his uncle's estate: the young prince had begun with capturing the fort of Sheikhupura and was soon after tasked with handling revenue collection at Sahiwal, which was given to him as his first *jagir*.[56] As we know, his mother, Mai Nakain, was personally installed as the stewardess of Sheikhupura Fort from 1811. By the end of the 1810s, Ranjit Singh had established his nearest kin and heirs prominently at the forefront of a new imperial administration in the Punjabi countryside, flanking Lahore to its east and west. This enabled the Maharajah to focus on entrenching his control of the capital city, whilst also consolidating the Sukerchakia hold on the territories formerly controlled by rival *misls*.

Over time, as both they and the Empire grew, the lives of the Sikh princes would grow increasingly busy. They were awarded *jagirs* through which to finance their households and lifestyles, but they had to balance the management of these estates with other duties: leading military campaigns or engaging in administrative work across far-flung imperial territories; providing hospitality to important dignitaries; maintaining quality troops and ensuring the payment of revenue to the royal treasury; and making regular appearances at the Lahore *durbar*. The several volumes of Suri's chronicle include numerous references to letters written by the princes to the Maharajah (apparently in Persian), informing him of the progress and completion of royal orders, or asking for advice and assistance.

With every task, the princes were supposed to meet a high standard in representing their royal house before both their own subjects and any foreign visitors to the Punjab. They were expected to work towards the consolidation and expansion of Sukerchakia rule, and as such were often given commanding posts at the peripheries of the Empire. For example, as he grew into adulthood in the 1820s, Kharak Singh spent much of his time in western Punjab, settling Multan and the areas bordering Sindh. In the early 1830s, Sher Singh was the *nazim* (governor) of Kashmir. As a young teen at the very end of Ranjit Singh's rule, his grandson Nau Nihal Singh was sent to earn his stripes at Peshawar in the face of Afghan opposition, with the support of his equally young half-uncles, Peshaura Singh and Kashmira Singh, who were instructed to protect his supply of foodstuffs and arms from nearby Attock.

For much of the early lives of these young men, such postings were nominal commands. They formed a large part of elite education, through which a prince could gain direct practical experience of leading troops into battle, maintaining law and order, and administering revenue matters. The nature of this training bears very close resemblance to the Mughal model of princely education. History-writing on the Mughal Empire raises a similar issue to that on Ranjit Singh's dynasty and the Sikh Empire: both British accounts and Indian nationalist/earlier postcolonial historians drawing on them often lay blame for the decline of the Mughal Empire on the supposedly destabilising and destructive nature of Mughal princely rivalry and succession crises after the death of Aurangzeb. However, recent research has shown that the weaknesses of the late Mughals and the nature of eighteenth-century princely conflict had specific causes and characteristics, and were not of a timeless or 'typically Oriental' nature; colonial readings of such events overinflate the harmfulness of interdynastic rivalries.

In other words, the negativity of colonial narratives about Mughal succession struggles do not accurately reflect the experiences of princes and imperial society; they were simply useful as a basis for critiquing Mughal rule and legitimising the growing encroachment of British authority through the governors of the East India Company. In fact, it is increasingly coming to light that the early modern period, particularly the century from the reign of Akbar

(1556–1605) to the accession of Aurangzeb (1658), was a time when this princely competition and self-assertion were factors that strengthened Mughal rule. It helped to expand the territorial reach of the Empire as princes sought to make a name for themselves by adding more land to the Mughal domain; whilst additionally ensuring that the focus of debate or contention remained exclusively upon the members of the Mughal dynasty, rather than giving encouragement to alternative pretenders.[57]

To me, there are clear parallels in this matter between the Mughal dynasty and the Sikh royals of the early nineteenth century. It is certain that Ranjit Singh didn't seek to copy wholesale the ruling style of the Mughals, yet the manner in which the princes were trained to act as soldier-administrators and diplomats, and were deployed across northern India to expand and represent the Empire, carries unmistakable parallels to the Mughal style of princely education established under Akbar. The Maharajah's embrace of such an approach for the training of his own sons was implicitly connected with his ambition to create his own dynastic empire in the Punjab, building on the successes of his forefathers. We can see that he approved of the practices of Mughal fatherhood, and admired the kind of brave heir that such parenting could produce, in this sample of one of his many conversations about the Mughal past:

> the Maharaja further added, 'Emperor Shah Jahan had four sons. While they were yet in their younger years a mad elephant appeared at the gate of the fort. The elephant driver said that it had become disobedient and the Emperor ordered his sons to fight it. All the four princes got ready to oppose it separately, according to the order. When they went before the elephant, one by one, the driver of the elephant told them that the elephant was out of control and they returned on hearing that it was so. When the turn of Aurangzeb came he rushed forward with great daring and courage and stood right opposite the elephant. The elephant driver cried that it was out of control. Aurangzeb said that he too was a prince, who had never known obedience to or control under any master, and went straight towards the elephant and inflicted upon it two or three strokes of the sword with the result that the elephant fled away. The Emperor heard this account and remarked that Aurangzeb was fit to occupy the throne of sovereignty...[58]

Ranjit Singh shared this tale after an incident in which he himself had narrowly survived being trampled by a *mast* (wild, deranged) elephant. Suri describes with much literary flourish how the Maharajah, on seeing the rampaging beast, remained seated in his carriage with 'perfect firmness of mind', whilst others scattered to save their own lives. Supposedly, the 'kingly terror' exuding from the Maharajah struck the elephant with 'awe', causing it to run away in a different direction, which enabled the Lahore gatekeepers to ensnare it more easily. Though in this quote Ranjit Singh attributes the power to Aurangzeb, the ability to subdue and overawe wild elephants was held to be a particular talent of Akbar's, demonstrating his God-given right to assert supremacy over man and beast alike.[59] In many ways, the Maharajah's chroniclers adopted a very similar style to the Mughal court historian Abu'l Fazl's *Akbarnama*, which portrays Akbar as the perfect man and emperor, and it is equally apparent that Ranjit and several of his courtiers were deeply interested in and respectful of Akbar's ideas. It is known that a beautiful manuscript copy of the *Ain-i-Akbari* was produced at Lahore during his reign, as well as several reprints of the *Akbarnama*. The Maharajah's copy of the *Ain-i-Akbari*, a collection of imperial administrative reports from Akbar's reign, even opens with illustrations of his and Akbar's courts, depicting the two rulers in almost identical poses and settings in an effort to highlight the idealised parallel between them.[60]

Suri establishes Ranjit Singh himself as the perfect princely model from his early years within the Sukerchakia *misl*. In an account of the period immediately before Ranjit Singh's accession, Suri records how Maha Singh had sent his 10-year-old son to lay siege to Sohadara fort in 1790. The *sardar* had been orchestrating the campaign personally, in an attempt to oust his great rivals, the Bhangis, but fell dangerously ill during the course of the proceedings and,

> on account of his illness, withdrew to Gujranwala and engaged master physicians for his treatment ... There, according to the wish of God on the 5th of Baisakh, Sambat 1847 Bikrami [19 April 1790] he breathed his last. The exalted one [Ranjit Singh], while at Kot Maharaj, expressed great sorrow and grief on receipt of the news, but he made himself steadfast by dint of God-given courage. He engaged himself in

> battle. After the expiry of the fixed number of days he came to Gujranwala and attended to necessary [funeral] rites.[61]

In this passage, Ranjit Singh comes across as the perfect heir: despite feeling a tangible sense of loss at the death of his father, he continues to honour his memory and upholds the duty of a warrior prince in the most exemplary manner, by staying on the battlefield to protect his patrimony. Throughout his account of the Maharajah's childhood, Suri emphasises his subject's martial qualities above all else, turning even negative consequences into auspicious signs that the boy would one day grow up to become a great conqueror. This rather hagiographical style is nowhere better exemplified than when he describes how a near-fatal attack of smallpox robbed Ranjit Singh of the sight in his right eye during his early childhood. Traditionally across the Mughal, Afghan and Ottoman kingdoms, blind princes were considered unfit to rule, and in the case of feuds over dynastic successions, a victorious prince would often have the sight of his rival sons or brothers put out, to ensure that he would not face further challenges from them. Luckily in Ranjit Singh's case, the boy still retained one good eye, and Suri highlighted this mark of fortune by relating Maha Singh's response on receiving the sad news of his son's grave illness:

> He clapped his hands and said in the presence of Bahar Singh Man and others that the prince of high pedigree [Ranjit Singh] would resemble Sardar Gujar Singh in a very good manner. That was to say that the said son too [Gujar Singh], was one eyed and showed combative intentions.[62]

This was essentially the ideal against which the Sikh princes, as well as other young elite Punjabi men, were held up during Ranjit Singh's reign. Given this social context, it is not so surprising to see Kharak Singh being sent out to capture a fort at the age of seven—it would have seemed the norm, or even a necessity, for a son of the imperial house to engage in such military ventures. If they were to be considered fit to rule and if the power of their *misl* or family were to survive and grow, martial skills were vital for young Sikh *sardars* or princes to learn and excel at. On the surface, this would suggest that martial prowess was prized above all else in the making of a young man's character in early-nineteenth-century Punjab or northern India.

Certainly, from the late seventeenth century onwards, Mughal models of 'martial masculinity' set by Akbar were increasingly challenged by the alternative cultural and political ideals of the 'peasant brotherhoods in arms' that were emerging as rivals to this imperial dynasty, including the Marathas, invading Afghans, and the Sikh Khalsa.[63] In the changing world of the Indian subcontinent, the prince of a new warrior kingdom was ideally a simple man, devoted more to his arms than to jewels, and above all an active and brave leader, not afraid to personally lead his band of loyal followers into battle. To an extent we can see parallels between this image and aspects of Ranjit Singh's own style, particularly the Maharajah's general simplicity of personal dress, and his valorisation of martial abilities in himself and other Punjabi men. This would imply a split developing between a martial-masculine ethos of independent warriorship, and the more 'feminised' arena of the court, occupied by 'dandified men' and *zenana*-bound women.[64]

However, as we saw in Chapter 1, it is difficult to argue for a firm binary between Mughal and Khalsa attitudes to courtly culture; the egalitarian, martial ethos of the Khalsa was softened during the course of the eighteenth century, to enable Sikh *sardars* to establish a hybrid form of courtly culture and raise themselves above the Jatt peasant class from which they had originated. And, as we've seen here, in finding models to guide his moulding and presentation of his kin, Ranjit Singh chose (initially at least) to look beyond the history of the Khalsa in favour of a deep engagement with the Mughal past. Like the Sikh Gurus and other prominent *sardar*s before him, the Maharajah adapted and reshaped earlier literary, artistic and practical ideas of Indo-Persian royal culture to fit comfortably with the political and cultural circumstances of his day, and to meet his own interests. The way he chose to raise his sons was no exception.

There is also evidence to suggest that this intellectual engagement was taken further and in new directions by his eldest son, Kharak Singh, who appears to have commissioned the production of an original illuminated Sanskrit manuscript: the *Sarvasiddhantattvacudamani*, or 'The Crest-Jewel of the Essence of all Systems of Astronomy'. This act of princely patronage on Kharak Singh's part somewhat confounds the view offered by many contemporary British sources claiming that the prince was widely considered to be a man of 'weak intellect', and something of an 'imbecile' (see Chapter 5). The manuscript, which was most likely begun in the 1830s and was produced in Benares, included a treatise and accompanying diagrams comparing Indian, Islamic and European ideas on astronomy. The first portion of the book included folios bearing delicately painted and richly coloured portraits of Ranjit Singh, together with depictions of the Sikh Gurus and various Hindu deities.[65]

The existence of this work, which is of exquisite quality, complicates in important and necessary ways the conflicting, but largely one-dimensional, portrayals of the Maharajah and his family members that have long been floating around, either from a colonially inflected British perspective—characterising the Punjabi royals as unrefined people with a predominant interest in land-grabbing and military aggression—or from a modern, idealised perspective of Khalsa history, which holds up Ranjit Singh and many of his famous generals as model Sikh warriors, who took on a particular form of humble yet martial and masculine identity, whilst abjuring the more dandifying and self-aggrandising tendencies of the late Mughal emperors. This simplistic and Orientalist binary has also coloured perceptions of the Sikh princes, likened to those weak late Mughals and considered unable to live up to their father's example. But rather than being some 'inherent' characteristic of a barbaric people, it's clear when looking closely at Ranjit Singh's dynasty that the use of martial imagery was a deliberate, intellectual strategy for the construction of their social and political authority, skilfully balanced with their newly created courtly world and their cultural connoisseurship. Nowhere is this more evident than in Kharak Singh's astronomy manuscript.

It is also imperative to recognise that the supposed gender boundaries between courtliness and martial masculinity, and between women and men more generally, were actually rather blurred in Ranjit Singh's Punjab. We have already seen how elite Sikh women from the *misl* period could act relatively independently in military and administrative affairs, as well as working as the instructors and guardians of young *sardar*s, including Ranjit Singh himself. Under the Maharajah, this would evolve into women's participation in princely training. In December 1816, Ranjit Singh dismissed the adolescent Kharak Singh's tutor and companion, Bhaya Ram Singh, after it was found that he had been embezzling funds from the territories he had been appointed to administer jointly with the prince. In his stead, Mai Nakain was made to take over the supervision of her son's affairs, for about eighteenth months. Mother and son would together play a leading role in the conquest of Multan, a major strategic post in western Punjab. Mai Nakain set up camp with her own troops at Kot Kamalia during this campaign, where she was also responsible for organising supplies of grain, cannonballs, gunpowder and *ghubara* (mortars) to be sent to the front at Multan.[66] Her involvement in his mission challenges the assumptions that women were 'unmartial', as well as completely overturning later Orientalist stereotypes of passive, secluded Indian royal women, who supposedly controlled and corrupted their sons' minds through 'nefarious *zenana* intrigues'. Such worldly interests and pursuits sit equally awkwardly with Punjabi literary representations of royal women, which sought to emphasise their modesty and seclusion, symbolised through references to them as *purdahnashin*—likely an attempt by the courtly chroniclers to fit their own understanding of regional gender conventions into their portrayal of the queens, even though these did not necessarily cohere with their lived reality.

These activities of the Maharanis were not exactly indicative of 'gender equality' in a straightforward sense, however. Mai Nakain was only allowed to wield such powers under the auspices of the Maharajah, in order to serve the interests of the dynasty by tutoring their son to be a more effective ruler. Of course, this did enable her to exert a considerable amount of authority, but unfortunately we are unable to discover directly her own views on the dynamics of her kinship relations and the power struggles within them. We get the sense that Mai Nakain was deeply invested in promoting the future of her son and supporting him in becoming the next Maharajah of Punjab—but could she also have been happy about him taking control of the territories of her ancestral kin, the Nakais? Or would she instead have felt pain at the loss and humiliation inflicted on her brother, Kahan Singh?

As for Sada Kaur, we know that the once matriarch fell victim to her desire to push forward the claims of her grandsons, Sher Singh

Fig. 1: Guru Nanak (1469–1539), the first Sikh Guru (right). Provincial Mughal, early eighteenth century.

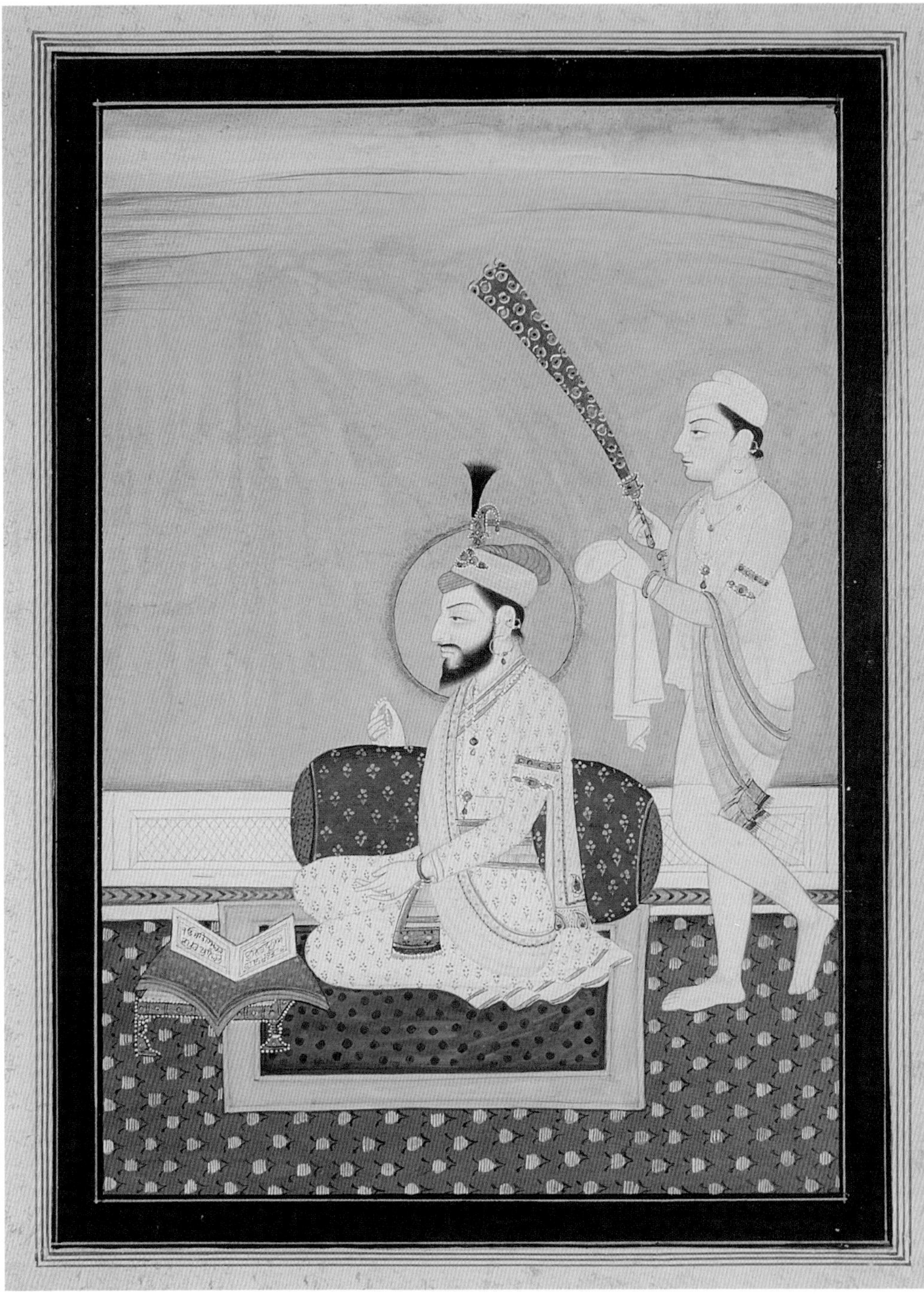

Fig. 2: Guru Arjan (1563–1606), the 'scholar Guru', with the *Guru Granth Sahib*—which he first compiled. Pahari, from the family workshop of Nainsukh of Guler, c. 1810–20.

Fig. 3: Guru Gobind Singh (1666–1708), tenth and last Sikh Guru and founder of the Khalsa. Pahari, attributed to Nainsukh of Guler and his family workshop, second half eighteenth century.

Fig. 4: Maharajah Ranjit Singh (r. 1801–39), the 'Lion of Punjab' and founder of the Sikh Empire. Opaque watercolour on paper, c. 1835–40.

Fig. 5: Ranjit Singh's gilded throne at Lahore. The Maharajah refused to use the Mughal throne there after his conquest, commissioning this one in c. 1805–10.

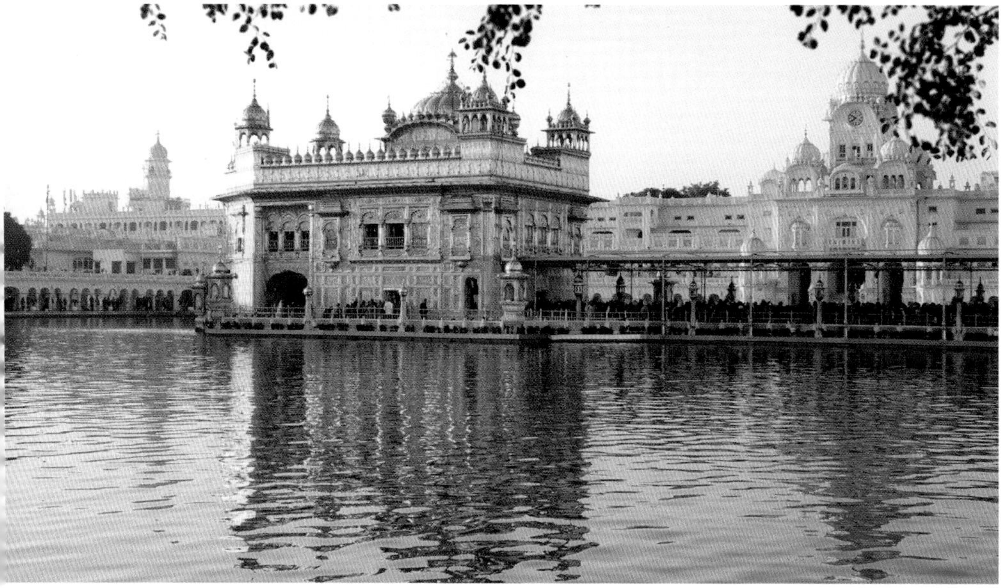

Fig. 6: The Golden Temple at Amritsar, jewel of Sikhism, built by Guru Arjan and his followers in the 1580s.

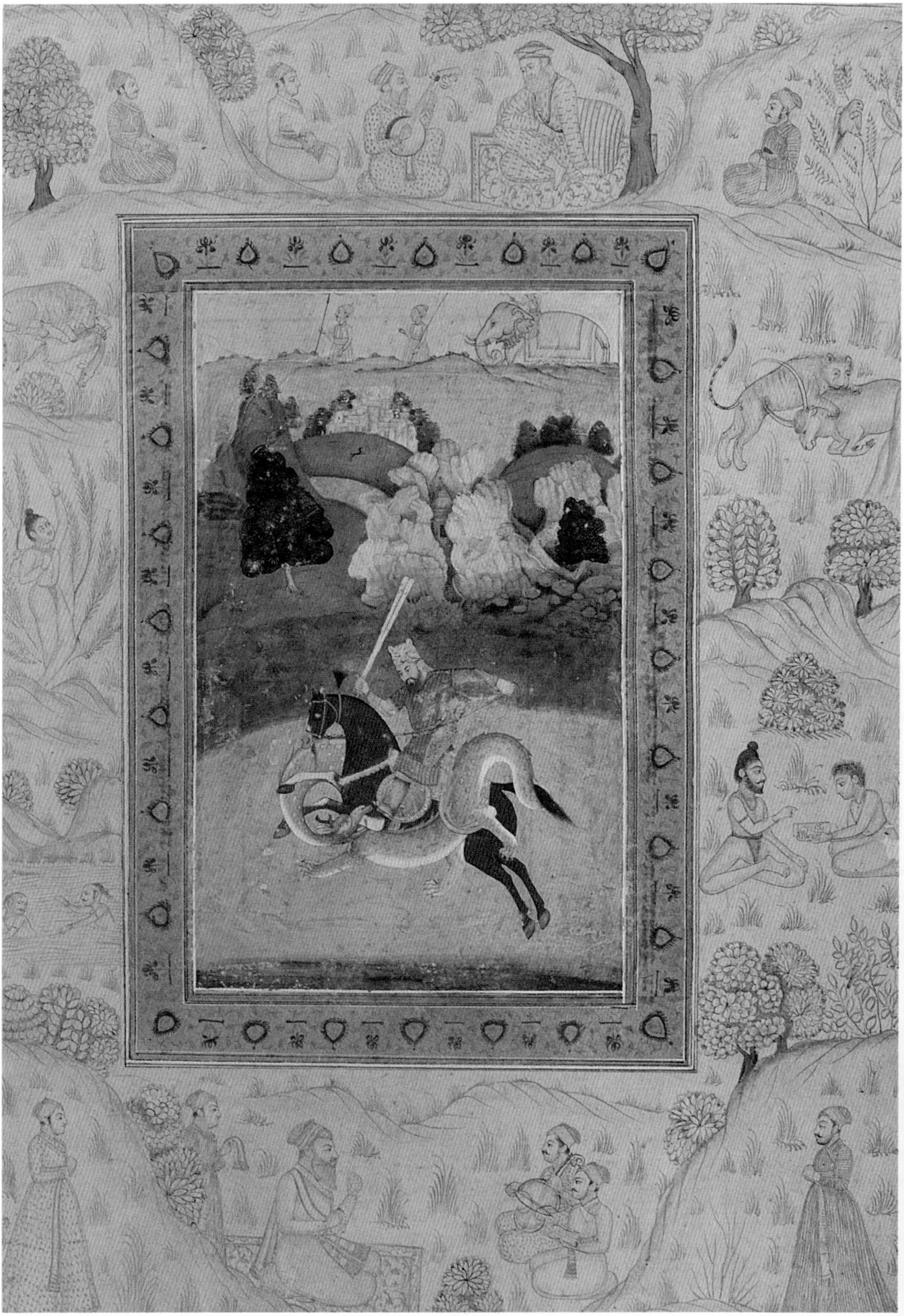

Fig. 7: A scene from the *Shahnameh*, the Persian epic that inspired both Mughals and Maharajahs with its legends of glorious rulers: here King Rustem slays a dragon. Note in the border Guru Nanak (top) and Guru Arjan (bottom), both attended by musicians. Lucknow or Patna, c. 1780.

Fig. 8: *Ranjit Singh, Maharaja of the Punjab, with his wife and child accompanied by his secondary wives*. This is East India Company artwork, but it is the only painting I know of showing the Maharajah with his queens. Gouache with oxidised gold, page 140.

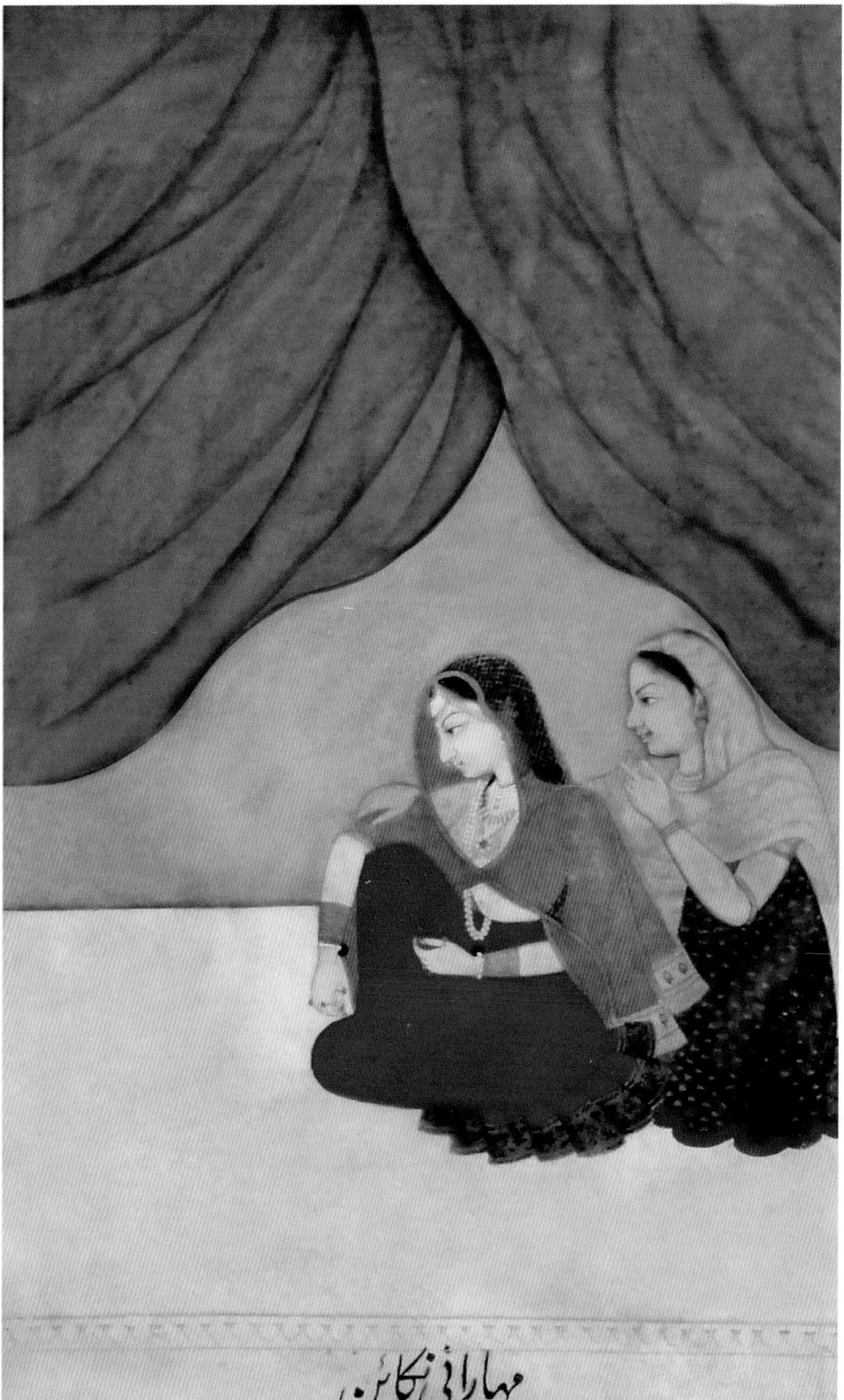

Fig. 9: Mai Nakain, formally Maharani Datar Kaur (m. 1798, d. 1818), the powerful mother of Ranjit Singh's heir. c. 1810–30.

Fig. 10: Fresco of Guru Gobind Singh on a stairway door transom in Mai Nakain's lavishly restored apartments, Sheikhupura Fort.

Fig. 11: Courtly scene in a ground-floor chamber of Mai Nakain's apartments, Sheikhupura Fort.

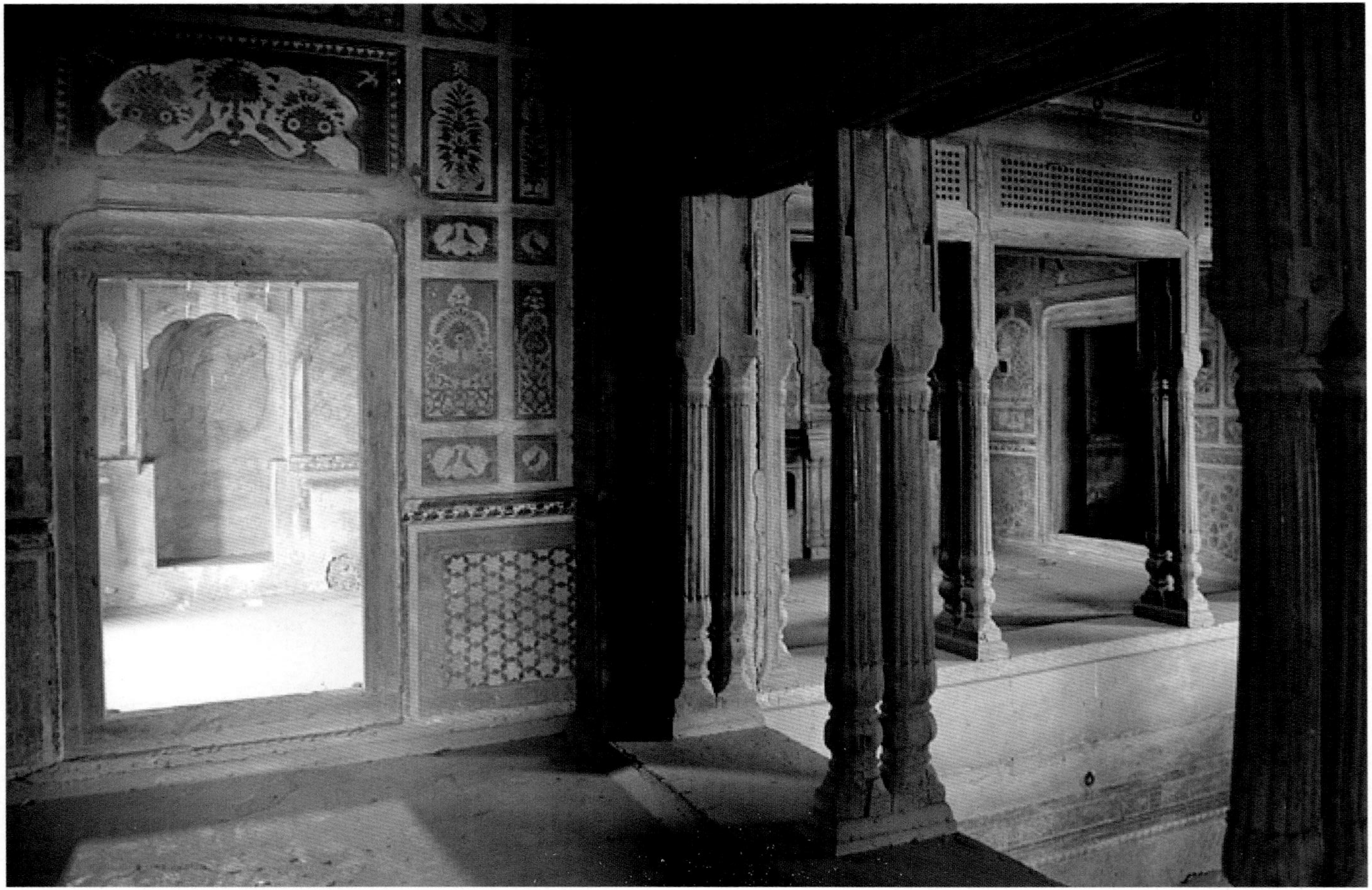

Fig. 12: Wooden columns in the courtyard of Mai Nakain's apartments, Sheikhupura Fort. These pairs of columns are typical of Sikh Empire architecture.

Fig. 13: *The funeral of Ranjit Singh*. Some of the Maharajah's wives are beside him on the pyre, ready to commit *sati*. 1840, painted on paper.

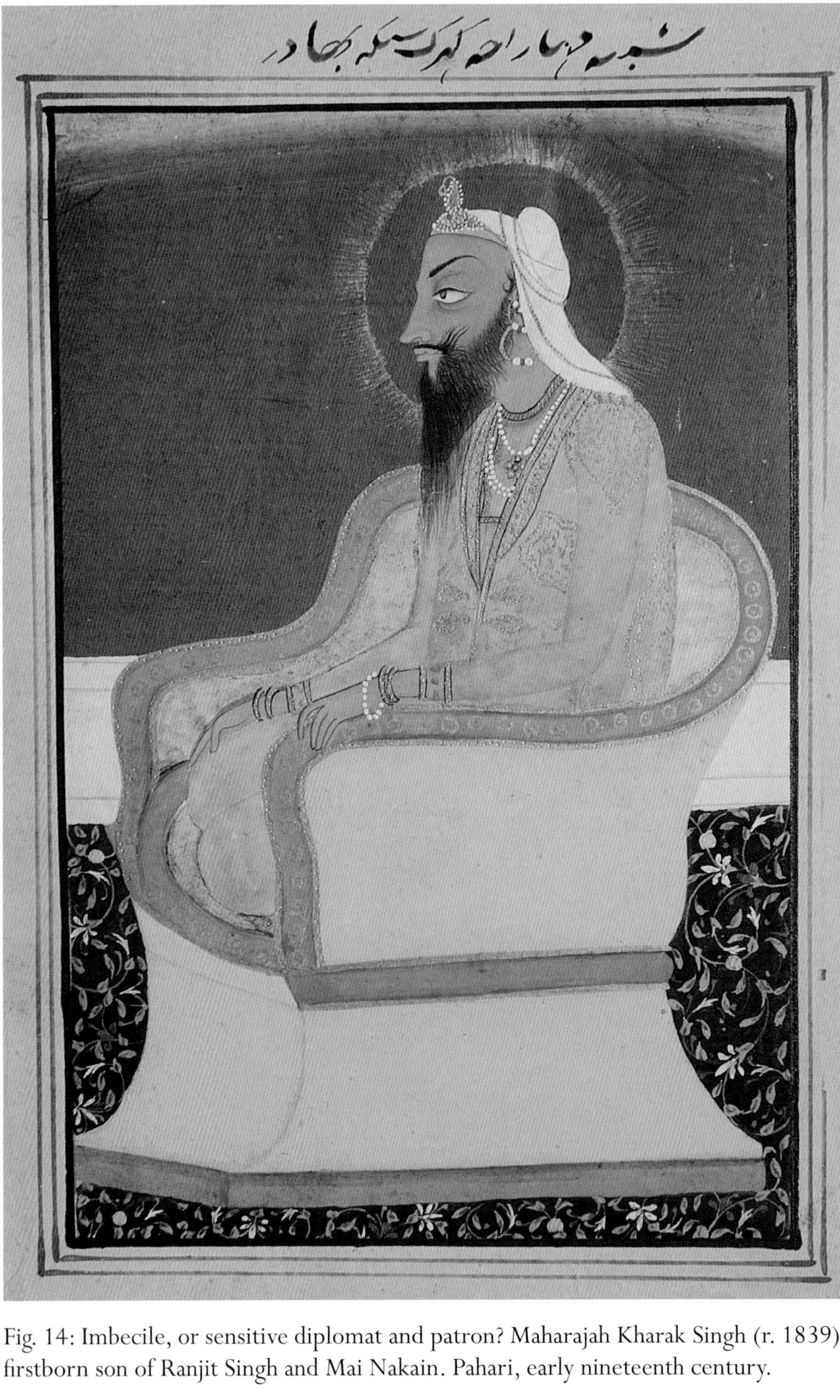

Fig. 14: Imbecile, or sensitive diplomat and patron? Maharajah Kharak Singh (r. 1839), firstborn son of Ranjit Singh and Mai Nakain. Pahari, early nineteenth century.

and Tara Singh, to partake in the spoils of their father's growing kingdom. In fact, her ambitions really went far beyond this, since the *sardarni* was equally keen to establish her own kingdom under Kanhaiya rule, separate to that ruled over by her Sukerchakia allies. From this point of view, it is not surprising that she put up a fierce resistance to her son-in-law's endeavours to push through the cession of Kanhaiya estates to Sher Singh or Tara Singh. Indeed, the feud between Sada Kaur and the Maharajah grew so intense that she even tried to court the support of the British in order to strengthen her hand against him. Ranjit Singh managed to stop her in her tracks after several months of bitter conflict, eventually taking control of her territory and relegating her to effective house arrest for the remainder of her life.

Yet, if the rumours mentioned in a poem written by a Chattha clansman are true, Sada Kaur's fate was perhaps fortunate in the grand scheme of things. In his epic about the clashes between the Sukerchakia *misl* and the Chattha clan (the occupants of areas such as Rasulnagar on the border between the Punjab and Afghan lands), Pir Muhammad pours scorn over the character of Maha Singh, Ranjit Singh's father, suggesting that he was so intoxicated by a youthful lust for power that he 'burnt' his own mother (alluding to matricide) in order to push her aside and take charge of the Sukerchakia *misl* earlier than nature itself would allow him to.[67] Courtly sources from the Maharajah's *durbar* are again silent on such violent tales and, interestingly, do not even discuss the deaths of any of the royal women apart from Mai Nakain. Yet this murky narrative was seized upon by British colonial commentators, who even accused Ranjit Singh himself of having murdered his own mother, Raj Kaur, when he was an up-and-coming young *sardar*—adding a further salacious tale that he had been driven to do so out of rage at finding her having an illicit affair with her chief adviser.[68]

Putting this gossipy storytelling to one side, what really comes out of all this is the clear fact that—however male writers both then and subsequently might have felt about it—female political activity was not eliminated altogether within the Punjab. Rather, it was harnessed and channelled in such a way as to ensure that it would strengthen and not challenge the rule of the Sukerchakia males. Women were rarely allowed to rule in their own right as independent figures, but the combined force of the queens and princes was the very foundation of the Sikh Empire's rise. Ranjit Singh's flexible incorporation and deployment of both royal women and his sons for the purposes of empire-building were major strengthening factors in the expansionist campaign of his former *misl*. Together, the leading members of this newcomer dynasty became experts in reading, and turning to their advantage, the political and sociocultural landscape of the region.

What really enabled this ambitious strategy to work well was the fluidity of political relations in this period. In the next chapter, we will turn to the royal family's engagement with its foreign neighbours. The Sukerchakias were certainly not the first elite to take an interest in re-inventing older forms of courtly culture and adapting the institution of monarchy; and they were not the only ones playing this game. Soon it would become a concern that they shared, or even competed over, with senior East India Company officials and even British royalty, who were increasingly becoming a part of the refashioning and connecting of British and Indian monarchy.

3

ALL THE WORLD'S A STAGE

In early August 1838, Colonel Claude Martin Wade set out for Lahore from the British outpost of Ludhiana. This was a journey that he had made many times in his career as the East India Company's 'man on the spot' or 'Agent for the Governor-General', responsible for handling affairs with the Sikh states and other countries beyond the Company's 'North-Western Frontier'. Wade had held that post for nearly fifteen years by the summer of 1838 and had become a well-known figure amongst the Punjabi ruling elite in that time. On this occasion, however, he was carrying with him a particularly important set of documents. He needed to ensure that they were signed by none other than Ranjit Singh, who had been reigning as Maharajah for almost forty years.

These were the papers for the Tripartite Treaty: a formal alliance between the Sikh Empire, the East India Company and the toppled Afghan monarch Shah Shuja-ul-Mulk. It brought the three sides together in a military and political pact, with the aim of making war on Afghanistan and wresting the reins of this kingdom away from the formidable chieftain Dost Muhammad Khan. For the British, 'No policy would be perhaps wiser, than to maintain Sikh influence between India and Cabool, and to place the Punjab in the balance against that country.'[1] As for the view at Lahore, from the outset of discussions over this proposal Ranjit Singh had recognised that such a war could provide a valuable opportunity for him to achieve his long-held goals of annexing a number of Afghan strongholds, particularly cementing his hold on border towns such as Peshawar or Jamrud. However, he also had a number of worries about the endeavour. He was sceptical about the wisdom of restoring Shah Shuja to his lost throne. Moreover, despite having been consistently faithful in his 'friendship' with the Company, he was wary of becoming entangled with them in such a strategically risky region, and especially of facilitating the expansion of British influence into Central Asia, at a potential cost to the security of his own kingdom. Formal and informal discussions had therefore been going on for some eighteen months to bring the Maharajah round to the idea of an Afghan war.

As the Company's agent for the Sikh states, Wade had been an integral figure in the negotiations and relationship-building that had eventually brokered the Maharajah's agreement to a deeper alliance, and coming to get the treaty papers signed at long last was certainly a major moment not only for his career, but also for Anglo-Punjabi relations as a whole. Wade arrived at the Punjabi capital with the documents on 14 August. What historians have hitherto overlooked, however, is the fact that he was only able to ask the Maharajah to ratify the treaty on the second day of his visit—for he had actually been summoned to Lahore by Ranjit Singh's ministers for a very different reason.

On 20 July, Mai Nakain, Ranjit Singh's senior Sikh wife, had passed away. The Lahore court was in mourning. On receiving this news, Wade had immediately dispatched a letter of condolence to the Maharajah. A *vakil* (diplomatic agent) had been promptly sent back to him, stating that custom demanded he travel to Lahore as soon as possible, to pay respects to Ranjit Singh on behalf of the British government. It is not clear whether there had already been a prior agreement to finalise the Afghan treaty at this time, but evidently the concerns of the mourning royal family eclipsed everything else, and it was primarily for this reason that Wade had had to set out for Lahore. The death of a senior rani, the mother of the heir-apparent, was no small event in early-nineteenth-century Punjabi society, even though it has subsequently escaped the notice of historians interested in this period.

Although Mai Nakain had spent many years managing her own *jagir* and fort at Sheikhupura, her body was brought to Lahore to receive its last rites, in what can only be described as a state funeral:

> The glorious bier of the one taking the way to the stages of the everlasting world began to proceed with indescribable glory and pomp and large sums of money were showered from over it.

> Such a huge crowd of people gathered together that all the male and female inhabitants of the town of Lahore and its suburbs came up for the sacred sight of that angelic personality ... that not a single place could be seen devoid of the crowd. When two or three hours of the day were left the corpse of that one, who had led a very good life, was burnt in the garden near the dome of Anarkali and a thousand kinds of sorrow and grief raised the dust of sadness about the hearts of the people.[2]

The funeral seems to have particularly united the people of Lahore in grief with the bereft prince, Kharak Singh, at the loss of his mother. Although senior figures of the Lahore *durbar* played leading roles in the funeral, the description in Suri's history suggests that the event was much more about the participation of the public in collective mourning with the dynasty. Elite figures from within and outside the kingdom didn't begin coming to see the Maharajah and Kharak Singh to formally offer condolences in more a ritualised style until after both the Maharani's funeral and then her son's observation of a two week-long period of secluded mourning. Once this had passed, customary visits of condolence were paid to the Maharajah, but more especially to Kharak Singh, by the representatives of neighbouring Sikh rulers and collateral relatives of the Sukerchakia house.[3]

On the occasion of a death in the family of a prominent rajah or *sardar*, it was always a member of the leading clan of a Sikh *misl* or kingdom, rather than a *vakil* or even a senior courtier, who would be sent to pay respects to the bereaved. Mai Nakain had herself carried out such duties during her lifetime, travelling more than once to Una (the ancestral home of the Bedis, descendants of Guru Nanak) to offer condolences to Baba Sahib Singh Bedi (who had officiated at Ranjit Singh's 'coronation' as Maharajah) after the deaths of his wife and son.[4] Such visits were critically sensitive acts of diplomacy, which re-affirmed bonds of kinship or friendly alliance between different Sikh clans, through a show of reverence for the departed and care for the bereaved.[5]

In this milieu, the presence of the East India Company and its political agents was rather anomalous. Wade had no kinship ties with either his superiors in the Company or any of the Punjab's ruling dynasties, and it was also far from clear which if any foreign royals he could represent, for the position of the Company in relation to both the British and Mughal Crowns was a contradictory and complicated issue. Technically, the Company was meant to be subordinate to both dynasties, but it largely pursued an independent policy of trading and empire-building in India.[6]

It would appear, however, that Ranjit Singh went to considerable efforts to mitigate this ambiguous situation, by inducting Wade and other senior representatives of the Company into regional modes of courtly and interdynastic diplomacy—not only on the occasion of his queen's death, but also during many other encounters. Claude Martin Wade had gained a particularly rich experience of the Punjab's local cultural politics during his long career at Ludhiana and, as we shall see, he had become personally friendly with the Maharajah.

On his arrival at the Lahore Fort on 14 August 1838, Wade was ushered into the *durbar* by Fakir Azizuddin, the top diplomatic adviser at Lahore, to meet with the Maharajah. The British officer, finely attuned to the need to pay appropriate respects on such an occasion, began by condoling with Ranjit Singh on behalf of 'the Nawab Sahib, the Governor-General' (of India, Lord Auckland), and then spent some time discussing with him in rather philosophical terms how 'everyone had to traverse that high road' at some stage in their life. The conversation turned to the Maharajah formally asking after the health of Lord Auckland, and only then moved on to political matters, particularly the pressing issue of preparations being made in Hyderabad for the onset of war with Dost Muhammad, as well as the Maharajah's concerns over who exactly would be footing the bill for restoring Shah Shuja to his old throne.[7] Ranjit Singh and Wade had another meeting on the following day to further these discussions, at which the British agent was finally given the opportunity to present the Maharajah with his copy of the treaty document. It was at this point that Ranjit Singh 'decorated it with his own seal', thereby finally and officially setting the Punjab on a war footing alongside the British.

This was certainly a point of serious historic significance in the Sikh Empire's relationship with the British. Yet the circumstances in which the ratification took place were kept very subdued, given the fact that Wade was at Lahore first and foremost on a condolence visit. At that same meeting, immediately after Ranjit Singh had placed his seal on the treaty papers, the Maharajah took the time to give his British guest detailed instructions on how and when he should go to visit Prince Kharak Singh in order to pay respects for the loss of his mother. The visit was arranged for that very day, at a time appointed by the *durbar*, and Wade was conducted to the prince's Lahore *haveli* by Bhai Ram Singh, a leading Sikh minister and religious scholar attached to Ranjit Singh's court, and part of another religious family much revered by the Maharajah.[8] Suri briefly describes the meeting between Wade and the grieving heir to the throne as follows:

> At about the third quarter of the day, Captain Sahib went to the glorious Prince, apologised in condolence to him, gave him the presents which had been entrusted to him for him and expressed great sorrow on account of the death of the venerable mother of the Prince. After that for a few hours they kept on talking with a view to strengthening the foundations of unity and friendship.[9]

What is unmistakable here is the way in which important personal contact between Company representatives and members of Ranjit Singh's closest family was closely interwoven with the development and growing intimacy of Anglo-Punjabi relations in this late stage of Ranjit Singh's reign. Diplomatic discussions were brokered through both the evolving components of the Punjabi state and its royal dynasty. Though the latter perhaps carried a softer, more ceremonial sort of power than the former, it could certainly not be overlooked by Company officers seeking to influence Punjabi affairs; at least, not without causing severe complications in their relationship with the region's ruling elite.

In this chapter, we will delve much more deeply into the role played by the Punjab's ruling dynasty in such diplomatic encounters, as well as exploring the nature of the political culture driving all of these activities. We won't necessarily go into detailed 'terms and conditions' of the various treaty negotiations that went on between the Punjabis and the British, or reflect on who the 'winners' and 'losers' of such diplomatic battles were. This kind of political history has already received a great deal of attention in studies of the Sikh Empire, with certain scholars judging Ranjit Singh quite negatively for agreeing to the Tripartite Treaty, viewing this as an indication of his weakness and mistaken compliance in the face of an increasingly assertive Company elite.[10] This seems a rather harsh judgement, as there is considerable evidence to suggest that the Maharajah thoughtfully evaluated the worth and wisdom of his relationship with the British on multiple occasions and took active steps to counter the growing power of the Company wherever he could. It is significant that Ranjit Singh concluded repeatedly throughout his reign that a renewed and increasingly deep commitment to friendship with both the Company and the British Crown was in the best interests of his kingdom and dynasty.

What we will discover in this chapter is that the long-term development of the Anglo-Punjabi 'friendship' formed another key aspect of the political strategy behind the making of the Sikh Empire. Ranjit Singh sought to bind senior British officials in a close friendship with his immediate family, to ensure that the strategic alliance he had formed with the East India Company and the British Crown would remain steadfast for the future. I say the Company and the British Crown because, as this chapter will reveal, the Maharajah was not content merely to treat with Company officials—he was eager to achieve an equal status to that of foreign royals like George IV (r. 1820–30) and the young Queen Victoria, who came to the throne in 1837 in the twilight of Ranjit Singh's reign. The true scope of the Maharajah's ambition went far beyond the desire to supersede his Sikh counterparts, or even becoming one of the leading political figures of northern India. The goal Ranjit Singh had in mind as he shaped the Sikh Empire's foreign policy was nothing short of projecting the name and fame of his kingdom onto a global royal stage, and securing its position there for generations to come. This was the loftiest dimension of the dynastic project embraced by the Punjabi royal family, and the ultimate culmination of the original Sukerchakia *misl*'s empire-building.

Since the mid-eighteenth century, when the *sardars* began transitioning into rajahs, a whole system of inter-*misl* and intercourtly relations had come into being in the Punjab. The Sikh rulers balanced the projections and representations of their growing power and wealth with a shared commitment to new notions of elite Sikh courtliness, which gave 'a nod to the egalitarian claims of the Khalsa brotherhood',[11] leading to the development of creative new forms of diplomacy and courtly culture both within and between the immediate circles of these *sardar-rajahs*, as they blended together older traditions of Indo-Persian royal culture with the ideals espoused in Sikh political thought.[12] While 'none of these ceremonies did away with the rivalries and violence generated by the growing competition among chiefs,' as the historian Purnima Dhavan points out, 'the expectations of good conduct and shows of public solidarity by the Sikh chiefs were important in crafting a common courtly culture throughout the Punjab.'[13]

The new Sikh kings were bound together by a shifting mixture of *biradari* (kinship relations forged through blood and marriage) and religious ties, marked through increasingly lavish public celebrations of births, marriages and deaths; this culture also connected individual rulers to subordinate groups within Punjabi society, such as Jatt peasants who could provide military support.[14] Adapted Mughal, Rajput and local Hindu elite social protocols included the practice of giving a *khi'lat* (a gift signifying honour bestowed) to bind somebody to the ruler; the exchanging of turbans between equals to mark a brotherly relationship (and the converse act of stripping a man of his turban, the worst form of insult and dishonour for a Sikh *sardar*); and the adoption of signs and symbols marking out *misl* heads as increasingly kingly figures: well-known royal insignia such as kettle drums, elephants or parasols.

The dynastic ambitions of Ranjit Singh and his rivals had to play out their struggles within this cultural and political context, which demanded respect for ties of *izzat* (honour) and a 'culture of relatedness'. Historians looking at early modern political culture in India more broadly have used this concept to explain the often very closely intertwined notions of 'the family' and 'the state' in precolonial Indian kingdoms: rather than being separate or even 'antithetical' entities, the state and the ruling family mutually constituted one another.[15] This certainly applies to social and political relations within the early Sukerchakia kingdom, particularly Ranjit Singh's method of expanding his imperial authority through a large number of strategic marriage alliances across conquered territories. As we have seen, this conjoined style of alliance-making and empire-building enabled local political groups to become directly connected with the dynasty ruling the newly emergent Empire, and allowed the royal family to bolster its own legitimacy and ensure the stability of the new government it was seeking to impose over newly absorbed territories. Whether marriage alliances or condolence visits, all of this activity in the early Sikh Empire was an integral part of diplomatic culture, just as important as the more obviously state-centred events, like meetings between kings and ambassadors or the signing of treaty documents.

As we know from Chapter 1, in the Punjab this 'culture of relatedness' was not only about literal kinship, but also went hand-in-hand with the need to honour a more spiritual or imagined form of 'kinship', due to the expectations that a Sikh *sardar* or rajah should show respect towards their 'Khalsa brethren'. We know that, as the *misls* became more internally competitive over their territorial expansion in Punjab, their relationships became more complex and even combative. However, even as the Sukerchakia dynasty and court became more ambitiously outward-looking and cosmopolitan, the vestiges of these older Sikh traditions and social norms from the time of the Gurus didn't vanish entirely. Instead, they became one strand among many in the evolving politics of the region. Begum Samru of Sardhana was another emerging Indian leader who regularly 'deployed familial language to describe a variety of her relationships' with the Mughal Emperor and a wide range of European officials. Her career would become a source of inspiration to Jind Kaur, Ranjit Singh's last wife and future Queen-Regent of the Sikh Empire, who would declare a wish to rule the Punjab independently in the style of the Begum; Jind Kaur too was adept at manipulating both familial and gendered rhetoric for her own political ends (see Chapter 5).[16]

This commonly established 'culture of relatedness' or 'dynastic diplomacy' was creatively adapted and manifested in a number of ways during Ranjit Singh's day, enabling the new elites of the Punjab and South Asia as a whole to build connections with a variety of valuable allies. This was how they effectively projected power and cemented their own authority within a competitive political world. In other words, these new dynamics to Sikh and Punjabi politics and society considerably shaped the diplomatic culture that Wade and his colleagues had to learn to navigate as Ranjit Singh's reign progressed. The early nineteenth century in particular was a pivotal point for the making of both the Sikh and British Empires in India, and at this crucial juncture these two rising powers saw an alliance, rather than a conflict, as a useful vehicle to achieve their goals. As we look at the experiences of Ranjit Singh's heirs in the following two chapters, we will see more closely the changing British views on this matter; but here we will focus predominantly on the perspective of the Sukerchakia dynasty. What was in it for them?

The Making of the Anglo-Punjabi Alliance

Ranjit Singh first came into contact with the East India Company quite early on his imperial career: in 1806, just five years after he took on the title of Maharajah. In these initial interactions with the British, there are some noticeable and significant parallels with his reliance, as a new young *sardar* in his teens, on his older extended kin in handling relations with rival or neighbouring Sikh elites. Similarly to the way his mother-in-law Sada Kaur had carried out negotiations for him when he ventured to capture Lahore in 1799, for example, when it came to handling relations with the British a few years later, the young Maharajah turned to his uncle, Rajah Bhag Singh of Jind. This half-brother of Ranjit Singh's mother was a king in his own right, in the southern part of Punjab not under the Sikh Empire's control. He was the ideal 'middle man' to connect his nephew with the British.

Bhag Singh's kingdom was located in the lands between Ranjit Singh's territory and the northern reaches of the East India Company's dominion. Since the mid-eighteenth century, the rulers of Jind and the other independent Sikh states between the Sutlej and Jumna rivers had been in communication with the British residency at Delhi, where Company officers were presiding over the declining Mughal court at the old imperial capital. Bhag Singh put Ranjit Singh in touch with them. The initial reason for establishing contact was a rather simple and pacific one: obtaining sanction for passage to Hardwar, in British-controlled territory, to fulfil the Maharajah's wish to bathe in the Ganges during the Kumbh Mela pilgrimage festival. However, the nascent dialogue established between Lahore and Delhi would quickly take a much more serious turn.

Within that same year, a new threat to the British emerged. Yashwant Rao Holkar was a leading rajah and military commander of the Maratha Empire, the other great rival to the Mughals and the British during this period of Indian history. In 1806 he went on a hunt through the subcontinent looking for allies to support him in his struggle for supremacy against the Company. Holkar travelled to the Punjab in person to negotiate with its new Maharajah and the other leading *sardars*—leaving Ranjit Singh in a quandary as to whether he should side with the British or the Marathas. This dilemma points to the contingencies that abounded in the early days of the Anglo-Punjabi alliance, particularly the nebulous and contested balance of power in South Asia in this period. Had Ranjit Singh chosen to ally with Holkar against the Company, the political complexion of nineteenth-century northern India might have turned out very differently. Instead, Bhag Singh would emerge as a crucial figure in setting his nephew, the face of the Punjabis, against the Marathas.

The Rajah was a figure of importance in both camps, and Lord Lake, the then Governor-General of Punjab, and Sir Charles Metcalfe (the Company's special envoy for handling relations with the Sikh states) were relying upon him to convince Ranjit Singh that it would be better to side with the Company in the event of an Anglo-Maratha War. The Maharajah did indeed agree to a treaty, co-signed also by his friend and ally, the neighbouring Rajah of Kapurthala, Fateh Singh Ahluwalia, formally renouncing any ambitions to support the Maratha confederacy and vowing to remove any of Holkar's troops from the Punjab, in return for a promise that the British could not enter the region.[17] By way of reward for his mediation, the Company gave Bhag Singh a *jagir* in the environs of Shahjahanabad, or 'Old Delhi'.

As can be seen from Suri's chronicle, the Rajah continued most diligently and wilfully to make certain that relations between the Sikh Empire and the Company remained on friendly terms at least up until 1811, by acting as a mentor to Ranjit Singh as Sada Kaur had done in his earliest years as ruler. Bhag Singh ensured that his nephew did not lapse into reconsidering an alliance with Holkar and took care to reassure the very wary Metcalfe that the Maharajah would remain faithful to the 1806 treaty.[18] His travels to and from his newly acquired lands enabled him to act somewhat like an ambassador between the Lahore court and the Company's Delhi residency. Throughout these early encounters, the Rajah's influence was crucial in teaching Ranjit Singh how to work well with the British, and in setting Anglo-Punjabi relations on an even, relatively amicable footing.

Unsurprisingly, however, the Rajah also utilised his favourable standing with the British to protect the concerns of his own small kingdom, Jind. Bhag Singh and several of the other former Phulkian chiefs ruling over the Sikh states south of the River Sutlej—most especially the Rajahs of Nabha and Patiala—had competitive, expansionist visions of their own, and were becoming increasingly wary of the growing power and territorial reach of Ranjit Singh, which had thrown the old *misl* system out of kilter. Caught between the 'great power' empires of the Sukerchakias and the Company, by 1808, these Cis-Sutlej Rajahs concluded that striking their own deal with the British would be the only way to safeguard their independence in the Punjab. Much like Ranjit Singh himself, and contrary to historians' depictions of precolonial rulers as naïve 'natives' in awe of the British newcomers, the independent Sikh kings viewed a pact with the Company as akin to 'consumption', which could sap their strength and potentially involve the 'eating up of vital parts'; they nevertheless decided that this would be preferable to 'sudden death' at the hands of Maharajah Ranjit Singh, who they feared would strike with the force of 'scarlet fever'.[19] Having weighed up the risks, a British protectorate was agreed.

It was in this context that Sir Charles Metcalfe ventured to Lahore to open up a formal dialogue with Ranjit Singh. The British envoy needed to secure the Maharajah's acknowledgement of this prior arrangement with the Cis-Sutlej states, but he was also charged with the goal of strengthening ties with the Maharajah sufficiently to prevent him ever siding with the French or Russians against the British—a worry that had begun to animate sections of the Company's governing elite. There is little evidence to suggest that Ranjit Singh ever showed much inclination towards courting a formal alliance with the French or the Russians. However, the political intelligence and the correspondence of the Company authorities does highlight the significant obstacles that they faced in dealing with the Maharajah and his advisers at this time, since the protectorate set up with the Cis-Sutlej kingdoms had caused considerable resentment at Lahore.[20] Ranjit Singh had long hoped to bring the Phulkian Rajahs under his own sway, and to secure the Jumna River as a boundary between his kingdom and the rest of India, but this dream had now been dashed. During Metcalfe's stay in Punjab, the Maharajah showed his displeasure by prevaricating in his negotiations and even ditching his guest to make some predatory forays around the Cis-Sutlej region. However, when the British envoy lost his patience and began making hostile remarks about the likelihood of a future rupture with the *Sarkar-i-Khalsa*, Ranjit Singh realised that it would be a safer bet to keep the British on side.[21]

The result was a 'friendship treaty' signed in 1809, which set the River Sutlej as the southern border between the Sikh Empire and that of the Company, and allowed the Maharajah free rein to expand as far northwards as he wished into Afghan and Central Asian territory, without any interference from the British. In addition to this, and most likely as a partial form of retaliation for the separate treaty agreed by the Cis-Sutlej states, Ranjit Singh also demanded to be recognised as the Company's primary ally in the Punjab.[22] This unsurprisingly led to a significant shift in the nature of his relationship with his uncle, the Rajah of Jind. After the signing of these Anglo-Sikh treaties, Bhag Singh continued to work towards keeping relations between Lahore and Delhi on a smooth plane, but his ability to continue claiming seniority over his nephew was increasingly subject to challenge. Despite the new restraints he faced on his territorial ambitions for direct control over the south, Ranjit Singh was still able to exert a cultural and social supremacy over his uncle, through the recognition he had gained from the British.

The tension this caused in the relationship between Ranjit Singh and Bhag Singh was in ample evidence during a visit paid by the Rajah to the Lahore *durbar* in 1817. On this occasion, he was accompanied by his son and four councillors, all of whom were presented on their arrival with highly valuable *khi'lats* (robes of honour). Bhag Singh's own *khi'lat* consisted not only of fine clothing, but also jewels and an elephant. The Maharajah did not stop there, in addition he awarded his uncle a *jagir* worth Rs. 7,000. These lavish gifts placed Bhag Singh in a quandary. By accepting them, he would be acknowledging his nephew's supremacy over him—since such items could only be granted by a superior ruler to a subordinate. According to Suri, the Rajah deliberately projected an air of indifference to the gifts and tried to avoid giving any impression of accepting them. However, standing as he was within the court of Lahore, he really had no other option but to take what he was being given, as otherwise it would appear as though he wished to insult or oppose the Maharajah. This was an impression that he could not afford to make, incurring as it would serious problems between his state and the larger empire under Ranjit's control. Indeed, although Ranjit Singh himself seemed generosity itself in this episode, Suri notes that the Maharajah's unnamed courtiers effectively pushed the Rajah (discreetly, but forcefully) to accept the gifts, or else—in the process, cementing his relegated status with the social hierarchy of Punjabi elites.[23]

This formalisation of the boundaries between and relative ranking of the new Sikh kingdoms shaped the foundations of Anglo-Punjabi relations. By 1809, a fluid mixture of intradynastic collaboration and more formal, interstate treaty negotiations had come to define their new relationships with the East India Company. Although a settlement had been reached on paper, with Ranjit Singh clearly established at the top of the political pile in northern India, these treaties would not quite put an end to the competition between the Sikh states north and south of the River Sutlej, nor curtail the importance of dynasty in the framing of their interactions. Instead, the agreements with the British simply introduced a new player into this rapidly evolving political world. As this episode has shown, Governor-General Lake and the envoy Metcalfe had quickly learnt how to leverage the relationships between Sikh rulers to bring the young Maharajah round to the British side—setting the stage for the kind of work that Claude Wade would have to do more intensively into the 1830s.

After the 1809 friendship treaty was signed, Ranjit Singh moved away from reliance on his uncle in handling relations with the British and took matters into his own hands, with the support of a talented set of advisers attached to his *durbar*. Initial contact between Delhi and Lahore seems largely to have been channelled through the appointment of *vakils* (diplomatic agents), Indian intermediaries acted as the bearers of gifts and correspondence. The visit of a *vakil* to either the Lahore *durbar* or the Delhi residency in this early period of the Anglo-Punjabi 'friendship' was usually quite formal, and typically entailed the following ceremonial activities as standard protocol:

> For some time Munshi Abdul Nabi Khan, Vakil of the English, had arrived at Lahore with fine presents for the strengthening of mutual friendship. The Sarkar [Ranjit Singh] sent for the Vakil in private and asked him what the Hon'ble Company thought of the friendship and goodwill of the Sarkar. The said Vakil replied that the bond of unity was very strong and it always tended to increase goodwill. In future it should be strengthened and it would result in the welfare of the people ... The Sarkar granted the Vakil a shawl, a sheet of silk, a sheet of flowered cloth, a fine horse and some cash.[24]

Such activity represented a temporary shift away from the more dynastic mode of diplomacy we saw at the start of this chapter. The *vakils* were professional men of scribal backgrounds with the ability to write and speak in Persian, the language of diplomacy and courtly administration in India. They were hired to work ostensibly in the mode of a civil servant: formally representing one government to another, and gathering news and intelligence from their posting to be passed back to more senior officers for decision-making or relaying to the Maharajah or British Resident. Such figures remained in service throughout the lifetime of the Sikh Empire, and were generally recognised as holding an intermediate rank in the diplomatic hierarchy that would emerge within Anglo-Punjabi relations by the 1830s.

However, as diplomacy between the Company and the Punjab became more involved and complex, there arose a greater need for deeper and more regular contact between senior officials from both governments. British political agents were posted at Ludhiana from 1809/10 (after the town was ceded to the Company by Bhag Singh) and were gradually tasked with handling relations with the 'Northwest Frontier': the Sikh states, Afghanistan, Nepal and beyond. Talented soldier-administrators such as David Ochterlony, Claude Martin Wade, George Clerk and others were appointed to this office. At the same time, the emerging class of senior, semi-professional courtiers grew at Lahore, and became increasingly important in the handling of diplomatic relations with foreign powers.

At Ranjit Singh's *durbar*, the leading man in external affairs was Fakir Azizuddin, though other figures were also recognised for their talents in this field, including the *vakil*, Rai Gobind Jas, and the *sardar* and general, Lehna Singh Majithia. The names of such men are mentioned with much respect time and again throughout contemporary Punjabi and European sources. These senior courtiers were highly valued by the Maharajah himself, and when it came to dealing with complex matters of war, trade and alliance-making, Ranjit Singh relied upon their specialist knowledge of neighbouring states, as well as their tactful, intelligent style of negotiating. Fakir Azizuddin was particularly renowned for his ability to smooth over a difficult situation. This talent meant that his standing at the Lahore *durbar* only grew more influential under the next Maharajahs, Kharak Singh and Sher Singh, when his experience and skills were heavily depended upon to keep relations with the Company on the even keel established by the late Ranjit Singh.[25]

Nevertheless, during the first Maharajah's lifetime, Azizuddin and others remained well aware of their position within the social ranking of Punjabi society, which entailed limitations on their roles and actions. Even the most senior courtiers could only act on specific orders or speak in an advisory capacity, and ultimately had to abide by Ranjit Singh's decisions. Their primary duty was to serve the interests of the Maharajah, by ensuring that he and his dynasty appeared in the best possible light in all encounters and transactions with foreign rulers. Although the likes of Azizuddin may have supplied much of the intelligence that shaped and underpinned Punjabi relations with their neighbours, the diplomatic role of the 'statesman' was rendered subordinate to that of Punjabi royalty. By the 1830s especially, much greater emphasis was being laid on the visibility of the imperial dynasty in foreign affairs, and particularly on encouraging intimacy between the Sikh princes and senior representatives of the Company.

This shift in approach was an integral part of the Sukerchakia house's project to consolidate its hold on its pan-Punjabi territories. Projecting an image of a dynasty that was powerful and authoritative, yet willing to engage with the outside world, seems to have become an important concern for Ranjit Singh by the second half of his reign. As the princes came of age, it became easier to use them just as much in diplomatic activity as in the administration and martial expansion of the Empire. Crucially, too, this formed another important aspect of their education, a fact that has hitherto been overlooked by historians of this period. The Sikh princes were being inducted into this wider dynastic project at the same time as Wade and other British officials, as they prepared for their future roles as rulers of an influential and increasingly cosmopolitan kingdom.

A Dynasty on Display

For the earliest visits of British political agents to the Punjab, a key protocol had been that they would be received by the most senior courtiers and *sardars*, who would bring them to the court or camp of the Maharajah. By the middle of Ranjit Singh's reign, however, his sons were gradually made to shoulder this responsibility wherever possible. As young boys, they were accompanied and assisted in these meet-and-greets by a leading *sardar* or by Fakir Azizuddin, the Maharajah's chief diplomat; but, as they grew older and more experienced, they were expected to host receptions for foreign dignitaries independently, and to cover all expenses from their own income on behalf of the *durbar*. The earliest known example of a Sikh prince receiving a British guest was Colonel Wade's first official visit to Lahore in 1826/7. Wade, the East India Company's agent in the Punjab, was received by Prince Sher Singh and Fakir Azizuddin, some 4 or 5 miles outside of Amritsar. Ranjit Singh himself was occupied with supervising preparations for the visit at Ram Bagh, where he had ordered all of the *sardars* to be in attendance, bedecked in 'costly yellow garments', ceremonial swords and jewels. He received a report from the prince and Azizuddin as soon as they had settled Wade in his apartments, allowing the Maharajah to begin forming his own impressions about the British representative before their meeting.[26]

By the 1830s, the last decade of Ranjit Singh's reign, a clear hierarchy had emerged regulating who would be appointed as ceremonial representatives to welcome visiting dignitaries. At its apex, of course, was the Maharajah himself, at the centre of a circle surrounded by his sons; Sher Singh was only ever deputed to entertain political agents like Wade, whereas Kharak Singh and Nau Nihal Singh—the princes in the direct line of succession—were given the responsibility of attending to the Governor-General. There was also a role for the 'lesser' Sikh elite of *sardars* and rajahs outside the imperial dynasty. We can see this hierarchy in operation through the management of a Wade state visit in May 1831: five discrete stages of entertainment and reception were laid on for him as he progressed from Ludhiana to Adinanagar, where he was meant to be meeting the Maharajah. The hospitality accorded to the agent was exceedingly generous.

Wade was first to be received at the fort of Phillaur, where he was given Rs. 1,100 to cover his personal expenses, as well as 'lambs, milk, butter, curd, sweets, straw, wood-fuel and charpoys' with which to feed and take care of his camp. Thereafter, he was to halt at Phagwara in the domains of Fateh Singh Ahluwalia, who was effectively a feudal subject of the Sikh Empire by this time; then Wade was to travel on to the Sodhis of Kartarpur, before again being looked after by the Ahluwalia Rajah's representatives at the village of Tanda. At each of these stages, the British agent was to be supplied with more food and cash. The fifth halt, immediately before his being formally received by the Maharajah, took place at Prince Sher Singh's *jagir* of Mukerian.[27] On this occasion the sources do not mention the prince being assisted by Fakir Azizuddin or anybody else. Sher Singh was by now in his mid-twenties and was evidently deemed responsible and experienced enough to be able to manage affairs on his own.

For Ranjit Singh, the hospitality provided on such an occasion was evidently a matter deserving of the greatest care, seeking to ensure that any valued guests could not fail to leave the Punjab with a favourable impression of its society and rulers. Suri, along with numerous contemporary European writers, commented on the elaborate preparations and lavish attention that marked the reception of European travellers within the Sikh Empire. Whenever a new foreign visitor was to be welcomed, the Maharajah and his advisors spent much time and energy considering issues such as the gifts to be presented, the attire and presentation of courtiers and troops, and the individuals to be appointed to receive guests or accompany them on their departure. The responsibility of taking care of one of the Governor-General's representatives was by no means a light task, and the individual chosen was considered to be acting as a proxy for Ranjit Singh himself.

Despite his wariness of growing British power in India, the Maharajah remained remarkably faithful and scrupulous in his adherence to the 1809 friendship treaty with the Company. As well as the Maratha advances, he also rejected overtures from the Gurkhas to join them in an anti-British alliance, having decided that the Anglo-Punjabi partnership was most likely to act as a powerful source of stability for his rule.[28] This consistency, coupled equally with his impressively rapid advances in empire-building across a very difficult region, made Ranjit Singh an attractive strategic ally to the British, especially at a time when many Company officials were concerned (or stirring up concern) about a potential threat from Afghanistan, Russia and Persia against their position in South Asia. The 1830s marked the pinnacle of friendly relations between the Sikh Empire and the Company, during which time the mature Maharajah and his now-established dynasty met and became close to two successive British Governors-General: Lord Bentinck and Lord Auckland.

Aside from Wade's regular visits, Ranjit Singh hosted two spectacular *durbars* in 1831 and 1838, to welcome Bentinck and Auckland respectively to his kingdom. The 1831 Rupar *durbar*, conducted on a far higher level of grandeur compared to Wade's receptions, has been likened by some historians to the meeting of the English and French kings, Henry VIII and Francis I, at the Field of the Cloth of Gold.[29] In terms of high politics, the major outcome of these two top-level encounters was the Tripartite Treaty of 1838 that Wade brought for signature to Mai Nakain's funeral: the military and political alliance formed between the British and Sikh Empires to collectively further their strategic interests in Afghanistan and Central Asia. As we know, some Punjabi historians have focused on charting the development of the negotiations between Ranjit Singh and the Company, and particularly on debating the extent of the Maharajah's astuteness in handling his dangerously ambitious ally. However, such narratives and debates leave us with a relatively narrow picture of the cultural and social dynamics of these important courtly events. They also limit our understanding of what Ranjit Singh's goals could have been on such occasions—in particular by overlooking the considerable effort made by the Maharajah to put his nearest relations on display in the best possible fashion, and to construct and celebrate what he clearly hoped would be lasting diplomatic ties, based on personal and dynastic friendship. This chapter in the making of the Sikh Empire can only be fully understood or brought to life through the events at court in Lahore.

A month prior to the 1831 Rupar *durbar*, for example, Prince Kharak Singh was introduced formally to Wade and another famous Company ambassador, Alexander Burnes. Going by Suri's account, it appears that this prince, by now 30 years old, had not had the opportunity to meet the Governor-General's agent prior to this occasion, but it couldn't wait any longer—partly because Kharak Singh was heir to the throne, but also more pressingly because he and his ten year-old son, Nau Nihal, had been assigned the responsibility of attending to Lord Bentinck during his visit to the Punjab. When Kharak Singh came to meet them, Wade and Burnes were guests of the Maharajah at a private *durbar* held in the *baradari* of the Hazuri Bagh, the beautiful pavilion and gardens newly laid by Ranjit Singh just outside the Lahore Fort. It is likely that the men would have conversed in a mixture of languages used in the region, Punjabi, Hindustani and Persian; Burnes in particular was a renowned linguist. The meeting was very significant, as Burnes had been appointed to officially present Ranjit Singh with gifts from the British King and Prime Minister. These consisted of four large dray horses, the like of which had not been seen by the Maharajah before, and a carriage, all sent directly from England. In the words of Wade (as noted by Suri at least), it was a 'blessed day because the representative of the king of London had reached the court of the Maharaja.'[30]

Seen from the perspective of Ranjit Singh and his courtly circle, this occasion marked an opportunity for the Punjabi *durbar* and dynasty to become more closely connected with its British royal counterpart, through the medium of the Company. The introduction of Kharak Singh, especially the very personal manner in which he was encouraged to greet Wade, becomes all the more interesting in this context: 'the glorious Prince Khalsa Kharak Singh appeared with his chieftains clad in yellow garments and decorated with bejeweled ornaments ... The Maharaja said that the Captain Sahib [Wade] should be hugged and the prince, according to the orders, embraced the Sahib...'[31]

In this instance, the order given to the Sikh heir-apparent to 'hug' representatives of the British Crown unambiguously demonstrated that the Punjabi dynasty was keen to reciprocate the apparent friendliness exhibited by the British monarch. An embrace between a Punjabi royal and a senior British dignitary would become a symbolic marker of the growing intimacy between the two powers, demonstrating the development of a deeper sense of closeness and friendship different from or perhaps going beyond the act of ritual incorporation involved in the bestowing of a *khi'lat*. Such gestures involving a personal touch would only be repeated on very special diplomatic occasions, and were exclusively restricted to the most elite Punjabi and British figures, thereby projecting them as a unified and intimate class of their own. In the *durbar* held for Lord Auckland in November–December 1838, there was a noticeable increase in the physicality of the interactions between Ranjit Singh and the British officials:

> The Sarkar put a pearl necklace around the neck of Clerk Sahib and said to the Nawab Sahib [Governor-General Auckland] that thereafter Clerk Sahib had become the agent at Ludhiana [replacing Wade]. He should ask him to manage all the affairs according to the rules of the glorious governments. [Auckland] put the hand of Clerk Sahib into that of the Sarkar. Misr Beli Ram [the royal treasurer] brought scent in a gold flask. The Sarkar rubbed it on the clothes of [the Governor-General] and the military Lat Sahib [the Company's Commander-in-Chief] with his own blessed hands. The Sarkar took the Nawab Sahib by the hand and showed him the horses. Then he took him into his *Bechoba* [a tent without poles] and showed him his bejewelled bedding.[32]

Despite the friendliness of such interactions between the British and Punjabi elites, power politics were at work still, particularly within the very nature of the gifts being exchanged. Dray horses had been chosen by Company authorities for presentation to the

Maharajah for two reasons. Wade and other British officials involved with Punjabi affairs were aware of how much Ranjit Singh loved horses and that he was an avid collector of rare and high-quality breeds; so to present him with such large beasts all the way from England would be a surefire way to impress him. The other reason was less innocent. The need to carefully transport such large horses (together with a carriage) to Lahore provided the ideal excuse for Company officials to secure permission from the local rulers of Sindh and the Punjab for placing British-owned boats on the rivers that ran through those regions. This enabled Burnes and Wade to make notes on their navigation and trading capabilities, and to share this valuable knowledge with British merchants for the first time.[33]

It does not seem that Ranjit Singh ever realised the true intent behind these novelty presents, but he was equally adept himself at experimenting with gifts as political weapons. Around the same time that the river plan was hatched by Company officers, the Maharajah had begun designing a new honorific order and medal with which to reward his most senior and loyal officials and generals. The Order of the Bright Star of the Punjab (*Kaukab-i-Iqbal-i-Punjab*) was the resulting decorative order, the design and inspiration of which is thought to have been based largely on the Napoleonic *Légion d'honneur*. To the surprise of the visiting British officials, one day the Maharajah produced this medal for bestowal on Lord Auckland and Agent Wade. This was a problematic gift for a number of reasons—firstly due to the fact that Company officers were technically only supposed to accept chivalric orders and titles from the British Crown. However, above all, the gift of such a medal would likely have been particularly galling for Auckland—all parties involved were aware that he had been held as a prisoner of war by the French earlier in his military career. While on the surface Ranjit Singh's award of this medal to the Governor-General seemed like a marker of great preferential treatment, it was equally something of a warning signal. It symbolised the Maharajah's courtly connections with Auckland's French rivals, as well as his mastery of cultural forms of power play—highlighting overall that Ranjit Singh was not a man to be trifled with.[34]

From Suri's words on the appointment of George Clerk—'Clerk Sahib' in the quote above—we can also see that at the Lahore *dur-*

bar, the Governor-General was referred to using the titles of 'Nawab Sahib' or the more informal 'Lat Sahib' (*Lat* being the Punjabi rendering of the word 'Lord'). The Company's position in India in the first half of the nineteenth century was indeed complex, as we have seen, and the status of the Governor-General in relation to the British Crown and Punjabi royalty remained a point of confusion for the Maharajah and his courtiers—one that had to be resolved carefully in order to preserve Ranjit Singh's own prestige and standing. Referring to Auckland as a 'Nawab' when he came to visit in 1838 was most likely an acknowledgment of the Company's position as the governor of Bengal, following the granting of that province to Clive by the Mughal Emperor in 1765. Yet it would seem that British officials were recognised by the Sikh Empire as being representatives of the British Crown, rather than the Mughal one, as is evident from Wade's speech about the 'blessed' nature of the meeting between the representatives of the British monarch and the Punjab's rulers.

A year before Auckland's visit, Suri's chronicle records the details of a conversation between the Maharajah and a European doctor (possibly W.L. McGregor) who was travelling through the Sikh Empire. Among the many questions he put to his guest, Ranjit Singh asked 'which of the Sahibs had the greater rank in the eyes of the King of London'; to which the doctor replied that the Governor-General was regarded as the superior of all other officers.[35] This exchange satisfied some of the Maharajah's curiosity, but apparently did not ease all apprehension about rank. Even in the midst of the celebrations held for Lord Auckland in December 1838, the question of the Governor-General's political standing continued to perplex Ranjit Singh:

> The Jamadar [Khushal Singh, doorkeeper to the Lahore Fort] wished to find out which of the chieftains was to be deputed for the reception of the Nawab Sahib on the following day. The Sarkar observed that he could hardly understand the matter. The Sarkar would go himself. Subsequently the Sarkar ordered that Kanwar Kharak Singh would go.[36]

The appointment of his eldest son and heir for this reception was a significant change of mind. The decision reiterated that the Maharajah was of a higher status than the Governor-General; despite the great deal of importance, even deference, accorded to Bentinck and Auckland in direct conversation and correspondence. In sending Kharak Singh rather than attending to the Governor-General himself, Ranjit Singh was aligning himself more with the British Crown than with its highest representative, and ambitiously claiming parity in social and diplomatic standing with that foreign dynasty.

Unlike inter-Punjabi or inter-European relations, within Anglo-Punjabi exchanges there was never any intention of uniting the two dynasties through marriage or other forms of kinship bonding—although Ranjit Singh is on record having once expressed a wish for an English wife, and even having joked, on seeing a portrait of Queen Victoria, that she would 'make a very decent Nautch [dancing] girl'![37] In a more formal sense, however, the increasingly intimate and personal contact we've seen between the British officials and Punjabi royalty can be interpreted as standing in for the creation of such interfamilial alliances. Although several Punjabi royal men had the opportunity to be introduced to and converse with the most powerful British officials, on major diplomatic occasions it was generally the princes who would accompany the highest-ranking British guests to meet the Maharajah, wherever his court was being held. Through the establishment of such a protocol, Ranjit Singh sought to represent himself as both the apex of Punjabi society and the central, most important figure in the encounter between his dynasty and the Company. He would certainly act, or endeavour to be recognised, as a generous and attentive host; but his imperial dignity had to be maintained above all else in courtly encounters, whether they involved Punjabi or foreign guests.

Watering the Garden of Friendship

The locations of these Anglo-Punjabi diplomatic encounters are also worth considering. The meetings often took place within the formal setting of either a regular or a more grand *durbar*, but primary sources are equally full of other occasions when British officials were welcomed into more relaxed spaces. Many British accounts of the Sikh Empire have fixated on the court's *nautch* parties, in which entertainment supposedly centred on performances by Ranjit Singh's dancing girls, as well as the Maharajah's attempts to ply all of his guests with extraordinarily powerful cocktails.[38] W.G. Osborne's published diary is one of the most widely cited of such accounts. He was a key member of Lord Auckland's entourage during the Governor-General's 1838 tour of the Punjab, and was therefore invited to all the celebratory events put on by the Maharajah. However, in his writings, he passes on more rumour about the nature of Ranjit Singh's parties than insight based on his own experiences:

> [The Maharajah] said, 'You have never been at one of my drinking parties; it is bad work drinking now the weather is so hot; but as soon as we have a good rainy day, we will have one.' I sincerely trust it will not rain at all during our stay, for, from all accounts, nothing can be such a nuisance as one of these parties. His wine is extracted from raisins, with a quantity of pearls ground to powder, and mixed with it, for no other reason (that I hear) than to add to the expense of it ... It is as strong as aquafortis, and as at his parties he always helps you himself, it is no easy matter to avoid excess. He generally, on these occasions, has two or three Hebes in the shape of the prettiest of his Cachemirian [Kashmiri] girls to attend upon himself and guests, and gives way to every species of licentious debauchery.[39]

Fortunately for Osborne, the rain never came before the end of his stay at Lahore, so he was never forced to be Ranjit Singh's drinking buddy. However, he did get to see several performances of the Maharajah's dancing girls and admitted to finding them impressive as artists, not just for their striking physical beauty. The internal contradictions of Osborne's writings reveal their problematic nature, highlighting their rather reductive view of elite Punjabi culture and socialisation, unless read with a more critical eye. Osborne and many of his colleagues often reiterated stereotypes about Oriental decadence and debauchery when describing courtly life within the Sikh Empire.

Fortunately, however, they also sometimes mixed such gossipy tales with mentions of other interesting types of hospitality provided for them by the Maharajah or his sons and courtiers.[40] Let us return to the 1831 *durbar* put on for Governor-General Bentinck, and more specifically the meeting with Wade and Burnes at Hazuri

Bagh, the newly constructed pavilion and garden outside the Lahore Fort. The location of this gathering was discussed a great deal by both Ranjit Singh and Wade, as the Maharajah was evidently very proud of hosting his guests at his beautiful new gardens:

> The Maharaja said that … Hazuri Bagh had been built by him and that before him, beginning from Delhi Gate up to Shalabagh, the whole area was very well-populated and was covered by fine buildings; and that there were very many gardens and orchards which attracted the heart and excited the envy of paradise. Captain Sahib [Wade] said that by the grace of the glory of the Maharaja once again fine buildings would be set up in that area.[41]

Wade had already been to see Ranjit Singh four days prior to this meeting. On that day, he had been entertained in the Shalabagh—the Maharajah's name for the Shalimar Gardens, originally commissioned by the Mughal Emperor Shah Jahan, where beautifully decorated canopies and flooring had been laid out amidst the plants and fountains. No doubt Ranjit Singh's decision to entertain Wade and Burnes in the Hazuri Bagh on Wade's next visit was influenced by the admiration he had expressed for the Shalabagh:

> The Captain Sahib felt very happy and pleased at the attractive sight of the happily laid out garden, the setting up of the tents and the decoration of floors … and the flow of fountains and the waterfall, which made the whole thing an enviable copy of the early spring in Persia.[42]

This description was penned by Suri, Ranjit Singh's official court historian; his evocation of 'early spring in Persia' shows the Maharajah's desire to portray his reign as restoring Lahore to the glory and beauty of its Mughal days, or even enhancing it with new buildings and decorations—mirrored of course by Mai Nakain's activities at Sheikhupura. This involved a particularly keen engagement with older, Indo-Persian literary and artistic culture. At some point during their conversations about landscaping gardens, the Maharajah even gifted Wade with a copy of a manuscript text from his royal library entitled *Hamishah Bahar* ('Forever Spring').[43] This book was a treatise on maintaining gardens and fine outdoor buildings, written in Persian apparently by the Maharajah's head gardener, Muhammad Fazil. Ranjit Singh was illiterate, but this never stopped him from having a fascination with books, which he collected extensively and often had read to him. Wade later presented his copy of this text to the Royal Asiatic Society in London, and in his accompanying letter he noted that the Maharajah had given it to him in the hope that it would act as a source of inspiration for the gardens that the political agent was planning for Ludhiana, where he hoped to transplant and cultivate the rare flowers and plants of Kabul and Kashmir. As we have already seen, the cultivation of gardens and the utilisation of natural imagery in art came to be well associated with Ranjit Singh and his queens, forming a key part of the ways in which they sought to shape a positive image of the power and nature of their dynasty. Here we now see the Maharajah's keen desire to integrate his British friend within this wide-ranging dynastic project, by affecting to instruct Wade in the best way to lay out a garden for the British residency at Ludhiana—widening the display of his munificence and connoisseurship beyond the boundaries of his own empire, and endeavouring to mark the green spaces of British India with the stamp of his cultural influence and authority.

This little incident again indicates the shifting dynamics of Anglo-Punjabi courtly exchanges, as Punjabi and British elites moved beyond the ritualised and formal practices of presenting *khi'lat*s or *nazarana* (tributes to a royal), and increasingly made an effort to make both the diplomatic encounter and the gifts exchanged more personalised and familiar. Although Ranjit Singh was perhaps 'showing off' by drawing Wade's attention to his beautiful royal gardens or his connoisseurship of nature, his gift of the horticultural manuscript does seem notably less politically charged than the earlier gifting of the horses and medals. It suggests that a relative sense of intimacy had developed between the two men during the course of their conversations—which, we must remember, unfolded gradually over nearly sixteen years, while Wade was serving at Ludhiana.

In fact, Wade briefly gave his own impressions of the Maharajah in his letter to the Royal Asiatic Society, describing how 'in every thing but effeminacy of character there were many points of resemblance between Shah Jahan and Runjeet Singh, & in none more so than in their Horticultural pursuits, the gratification of which was one of Runjeet Singh's constant sources of occupation & delight.'[44] This 'green-fingered' and artistic side of Ranjit Singh's character is rarely mentioned by his other European contemporaries or by his subsequent biographers, but nevertheless was a side of his personality that he felt willing to share with a British political officer with whom he had become somewhat intimately acquainted. Certainly, it seems fair to assume that such exchanges had developed a mutual understanding of character between the Maharajah and the British Political Agent, as well as of their respective personal and political interests—all of which are likely to have facilitated the growing closeness in Anglo-Punjabi relations overall.

Gardens were also often employed as literary metaphors within the Persian correspondence between the British and the Punjabis, to symbolise the world in which their alliance was based. This in itself directly echoed the kind of imagery that had abounded throughout Mughal courtly poetry and political treatises for generations: the imperial garden was often invoked symbolically to represent 'paradise on Earth'.[45] It is another reminder of how steeped Ranjit Singh and his courtiers were in the cultural heritage of the former Mughal rulers of Lahore, and how they tried to make this their own. Take the letter sent by the Governor-General to the Maharajah following the presentation of the British King's gifts. This was personally delivered by Wade to the Lahore *durbar*, and was read out by Azizuddin to the assembly: 'It stated that the strengthening of the foundation of unity and friendship was making progress every day and the garden of friendship and affection was being well watered by the raining of clouds of communion'.[46] Hence the union of elites, whether featuring Punjabis or their neighbours, was idealistically claimed to result in the betterment of the condition of the people (though we know little of what ordinary Punjabis actually thought about all this). The use of such flowery phraseology should not be dismissed as a sort of generic artifice employed within official correspondence. Even if this was propaganda, it was propaganda within a consistent courtly theme that coloured the image the royal family sought to project for themselves; this imagery then became thoroughly infused into many Anglo-Punjabi courtly encounters during the 1830s.

The royal gardens of Lahore became quite renowned amongst Europeans, and Claude Wade was certainly not the Maharajah's only foreign guest to enjoy the honour of being entertained in the Shalimar or the Hazuri Bagh. During Auckland's state visit to the Punjab in December 1838, Prince Kharak Singh gave Emily Eden (the Governor-General's sister) a personal tour of the gardens and pavilions, whilst his father received Auckland for talks in another outdoor *durbar*, followed by a spectacular evening party enlivened by music and fireworks.[47] Additionally, tours for Wade were even extended to include viewings of what might otherwise be considered the more 'private'—or certainly exclusive—areas of the royal household. One week after his meeting with Burnes and Kharak Singh, Wade requested to see the interior of the Lahore Fort, and was accordingly shown the Takhtgah (the throne room/main audience hall), the Musumman Burj and the Khwabgah (the royal apartments and sleeping chambers).[48] All areas of Ranjit Singh's dynastic, courtly life seemed open for display to his most favoured guests, to dazzle them as much as possible with carefully orchestrated grandeur.

In some ways, this readiness to invite elite British representatives into the domestic areas of the royal household disturbs standard, often gendered, understandings of the separation of 'private' versus 'public' areas in royal courts. In Chapter 2, we already saw from the diary of Isabella Fane that a formal and secluded women's sphere—an institutionalised zenana or harem—simply did not exist at Lahore. Alongside the princes, Punjabi queens could also be requested to participate in diplomatic activities. This happened at least twice during the reign of Ranjit Singh: firstly with Isabella Fane in March 1837, during Nau Nihal Singh's wedding; and again when the queens met with the Eden sisters in December 1838.

Of course, there were some significant gendered and cultural differences with encounters involving Punjabi royal women. For example, their meetings with Europeans could only be with other women, and always took place essentially behind closed doors. This was entirely unlike meetings between Punjabi men and British men or women, which could be carried out in a variety of either open or more exclusive spaces, in different places within the capital or around the Punjab. However, these few restrictions of protocol do not detract from an overarching point: that Punjabi royalty did not concern themselves too deeply with efforts to preserve the 'sanctity' of their dynasty or their domestic spaces, in the manner that other Indian royal houses had done in the past, particularly the Mughals. Although Ranjit Singh and his family were careful about observing and enforcing their dynasty's supreme status in relation to other Sikh and Punjabi rivals, the Maharajah was unabashed about actively using his sons and wives as ambassadors, and his court and household as a platform for building new connections with the wider, transnational world of royalty.

Royal Weddings: Putting on a Show

Of all the events organised by Ranjit Singh and his *durbar* servants, the royal weddings of his first-born son and grandson were the most crucial in melding an ambitious and spectacular dynastic exhibition, together with the pursuit of core diplomatic goals. Of course these two princes each married several times, but two key royal weddings stood head and shoulders above the rest: the 1811 marriage of Kharak Singh to Chand Kaur of Sada Kaur's Kanhaiya *misl*, and the 1837 union of their son Nau Nihal Singh and Sahib Kaur, daughter of the highly respected veteran *sardar* Sham Singh Attariwala. The alliances forged by these weddings were somewhat similar to Ranjit Singh's first couple of marriages, in that they followed the pattern of forming closer bonds between the Sukerchakia house and other powerful Sikh *misl* chiefs. However, I would suggest that a subtly shifting difference is visible in the aims behind the Maharajah's own weddings and those of his immediate heirs. The 1811 and 1837 princes' weddings marked a dramatic increase in the level of royal symbolism used, projecting the establishment of a new social hierarchy in the Punjab. Additionally, whereas Ranjit Singh's early marriages (and to an extent, Kharak Singh's marriage to Chand Kaur) were essentially concerned with embedding the Maharajah within local *biradari* (kinship) networks or securing other *sardars* as allies, the marriages of his son and grandson were increasingly about celebrating the power and eminence of their royal dynasty on a broader stage, by inviting and prominently co-opting other powerful rulers from across and around the Punjab within the lavish festivities.

Wedding celebrations would begin with the dispatching from Lahore of sweetmeats to all neighbouring courts via *vakils* (intermediaries), to announce the engagement of a prince, presumably together with wedding invitations. It was customary for each visiting dignitary to give a substantial gift to the family, known as *tambol* in Punjabi (the ceremony itself is typically known by the name of *neundra*). Suri's chronicle helpfully provides a record of the *tambol* gifts presented at Kharak Singh's wedding to Chand Kaur, showing who attended and how much they chose (or may have been expected) to give.[49] Perhaps unsurprisingly, given his earlier prominent involvement in the diplomatic affairs of Lahore, Ranjit Singh's uncle, Rajah Bhag Singh of Jind, gave one of the largest offerings: Rs. 11,000 and an elephant. This was closely followed by Rajah Jaswant Singh of Nabha, who gave the same amount of cash, minus the elephant. The large gifts of these southern Punjabi kings were indicators of their friendliness with the Sikh Empire's royal family, as well as their command of great wealth. But the sums given by the Cis-Sutlej Rajahs were nearly matched by some of the contributions from the Maharajah's senior courtiers, including Fakir Azizuddin, who gave Rs. 9,000—highlighting that wealth could perhaps be accumulated just as well in Ranjit Singh's service as outside of it.

Colonel David Ochterlony was sent to the wedding as the East India Company's representative by Charles Metcalfe, the British envoy to the Punjab, and he personally presented a gift of Rs. 5,000. This sum was more in line with the contribution of the minor Punjabi hill Rajahs, including the Rajahs of Jasrota or Nurpur, who gave Rs. 4,000 each. Yet, although Ochterlony's gift was only a quarter of the amount presented by the largest contributor, the Nawab of Multan, Suri's account of the wedding shows how the groom's party gave the British official disproportionately special treatment. Only the receptions accorded to Ochterlony and the Cis-Sutlej Rajahs are described in any detail. The court historian praises Ochterlony as 'the wisest man of the age', and is warmly appreciative of the General's generosity in giving *tambol* out of his own pocket, separately to the offering of the Company.[50]

Suri also unequivocally conveys that the entirety of the wedding was meant to astound and impress the assembled guests. He records the Maharajah's orders for all of his attendants and vassal *sardars* to don 'graceful garments and distinctive clothing', so that when the groom's party proceeded to Amritsar the next day, they would 'create wonder among the onlookers'. The united wedding procession that took place thereafter, between Amritsar and Fatehgarh, must have been an incredible sight:

> Fireworks of all kinds were displayed. A moving throne and 'Shalabagh' which were adorned and decorated with various kinds of flowers ... were carried over the shoulders of about 100 men ... After this glorious tents and well equipped canopies and shamianas were sent towards Fatehgarh, and the glorious Prince [Kharak Singh, the groom] was made to sit upon an elephant, and that light of the garden of kindness, that woman accustomed to observe veil behind the screens of chastity, the mother of the Prince [Mai Nakain] was made to sit in a chariot that was set with jewellery and had a crown over it. Thus they were made to proceed to Fatehgarh.[51]

This procession was undoubtedly designed to be an explicitly royal occasion. The prince travelled on an elephant, the traditional transport of Indian monarchs or those honoured by royalty. No fewer than twenty-nine further elephants followed Kharak Singh, each carrying the prominent courtiers and 'near-attendants' of the Maharajah. The Persian copy of Suri's history held by the Royal Asiatic Society Library provides us with a few additional details to those given in the above translation. From this text we can tell that, despite Suri's emphasis on Mai Nakain's personal modesty, the Maharani's chariot would have stood out dramatically amid the crowd. It was made from gold, and the term Suri used for 'chariot' was actually the Sanskrit word *ratha*.[52] This word could have evoked associations with Subhadra, wife of Arjuna and one of the three Hindu deities worshipped at the Jagannath temple, who rides a *ratha* in the annual Rathayatra festival. Going by Ranjit Singh's prominent alms-giving to the temple, most famously in his death-bed wish to give the *Koh-i-Noor* diamond to its priests, I might hazard to speculate that this was an attempt to cast Mai Nakain in the image of Subhadra.[53]

It would appear, however, that at this relatively early stage in his reign, just ten years after being declared Maharajah in 1801, Ranjit Singh's income was insufficient to support such extravagant grand-standing. A day or so after the wedding, the Maharajah's 'wise coun-sellors' advised him to avoid further 'large expenses' and to encourage his guests to go home as soon as possible. As a result, Fakir Azizuddin was sent to Ochterlony to give him permission to leave the Maharajah's presence, delicately taking care not to betray the fact that his early departure was required for the sake of economy.[54]

* * *

Kharak Singh and Chand Kaur's wedding can evidently be viewed as an ambitious attempt at staking an aspirational claim to royal status. It marked a transitional phase for Ranjit Singh and the Sukerchakia *misl*, as he sought to move away from being regarded as just another *sardar*, and instead to represent his son as the heir to a new royal lineage. The Maharajah's revenue base limited his ability to indulge in a great deal of largesse in 1811, but this would completely change by 1837, when he arranged the marriage of his eldest grandson. The festivities lasted for just over a week, beginning around 2 March 1837. Furthermore, unlike Ochterlony's trip to Kharak Singh's wedding, a much larger British delegation was invited to his grand son's nuptials, and it would stay in the Punjab until the end of the month. On this occasion, the British party would be headed by the more senior figure of Sir Henry Fane, the Company's Commander-in-Chief of India. The elaborate and longer-lasting hospitality for Nau Nihal Singh's wedding took many months of careful planning and no expense appears to have been spared.

It is important to note here that, while we can get a detailed understanding of the wedding preparations and festivities from the *Umdat-ut-tawarikh*, we also have to recognise that Suri's account was written somewhat in the mode of an official souvenir for the occasion. Immediately after the departure of the British from Lahore, Suri was issued with a letter by the Maharajah, ordering him to 'give a full account of the marriage of Kanwar Nau Nihal Singh, the visit of the Lat Sahib (Sir Henry Fane) and of the Rajas of the Cis-Sutlej territory.' The command also bade the historian to include details in his narrative of the 'total expenditure' for the wedding, as well as describing 'the friendly and jovial gatherings at Shalabagh and the Octagonal Tower [the Mussumun Burj]'. The account was to be included within his history as a lasting record of the grand occasion, but had to be read out to the Maharajah first.[55]

This is one of a handful of examples in which Suri mentions that an event was specifically ordered to be included in his text by Ranjit Singh. Up until 1831, the Maharajah had not even been aware that Suri, a *vakil* working at the Lahore *durbar*, had been compiling a chronicle of his kingdom's history since 1812.[56] The work was brought to his attention when Wade requested permission to read Suri's book, after having heard about it from Fakir Azizuddin. Only after assessing the veracity and positivity of Suri's account of his reign did Ranjit Singh give permission for the writer to visit Wade and share the work with him—for which occasion he ordered Suri to wear 'fine clothes and gold bangles'.[57] This also provides another significant point for comparison with Kharak Singh's 1811 wedding. It emerges from the *Umdat-ut-tawarikh* itself that Ranjit Singh and his successors would periodically have Suri read out portions of his chronicle in the *durbar*, apparently as a form of entertainment for the Maharajah and his courtiers, to reminisce over or perhaps celebrate achievements in the kingdom's recent history. We do not know whether Ranjit Singh ever heard or checked the early portion of Suri's work documenting his son's marriage; but by the time of Nau Nihal Singh's wedding, it's clear that Ranjit Singh wished his dynasty and reign to be represented in a specific style, both for posterity and for the wider world of his own day.

To begin with, Suri's account provides details of the daily progress made on preparations in advance of the big event, showing us how the festivities were organised and, most interestingly, how deeply involved key royal figures were in these activities. Around 10 February, Kharak Singh and Nau Nihal Singh were ordered to Amritsar to get the wedding venue ready. Both princes had been supervising important strategic posts before this, with the groom managing his first mission at Peshawar and his father based at Multan, but wedding preparations had evidently shot to the top of the list of imperial priorities. Around the same time, Ranjit Singh's minister Bhai Ram Singh was sent from Lahore to Attari to instruct Sham Singh Attariwala, the father of the bride, in 'all the details of the preparations ... for the entertainment of the glorious Sahibs [the British delegation] and to see to the dowry'.[58] The Maharajah also personally and minutely inspected every single detail of the hospitality and gifts to be provided, from the wine to the jewellery.[59]

Punjabi royal men and women were all involved in this occasion, which provided a valuable opportunity to enact and proclaim unity across the dynasty's various branches. There was something of a gendered split in the assigning of responsibilities for various parts of the festivities. It would seem that Ranjit Singh and the princes managed the logistical side of arrangements for the reception of all the important guests, whereas the queens conducted many of the customs of the wedding itself. Through Suri's narration of the *vatna* ceremony, we get a rare insight into an occasion when many of the Maharajah's closest family were gathered together in one place. This ceremony is a customary part of pre-wedding celebrations in Punjab, at which the bride and groom have their limbs and faces massaged by their close relatives, with a turmeric paste blended with oil. The paste, known as *haldi* or *vatna*, is considered to make the skin shine with a healthy glow, and is applied to make the couple look more attractive on their wedding day.

Although Nau Nihal Singh was the son of Kharak Singh and Chand Kaur, his parents largely took a secondary role to his grandparents, Ranjit Singh and Mai Nakain, who appear to have entirely supervised the arrangements for his marriage. At the *vatna* ceremony, we see the senior Maharani directing the activities, welcoming her husband, the Maharajah, with a *sarwarna* gift (*sarwarna* literally means to wave something—usually cash—over somebody else's head as a form of blessing), and then instructing her son Kharak Singh to do the same. Mai Nakain and Ranjit Singh were also the first to rub the *vatna* paste on the face of the young bridegroom. It was obviously a joyful occasion, as the Maharani's sister was even able to get away with playfully rubbing paste and oil into Ranjit Singh's beard. Instead of getting annoyed, the Maharajah merely chuckled and presented her with a gift of money, which she audaciously managed to get converted into a *jagir*![60] From Suri's 1837 *tambol* accounts, we can see that a number of Punjabi queens were also involved in the gift-giving ceremony.[61] Nineteen women are included in Suri's list, and with the exception of Mai Nakain, who matched Fane's gift of Rs. 15,000, they presented individual gifts of Rs. 50–500.[62] This was a chance for the lower-ranking queens, many of whom did not have children of their own, to be incorporated into the celebrations and thereby bind themselves with young Nau Nihal

Singh and his future family, who would one day succeed as heirs to the throne.

Noticeably, apart from the *tambol* ceremony, most of the festivities featuring the royal women were carried out before the arrival of the British guests on 6 March. There was evidently a subtle step-change in the ceremonies at that point: from the more relaxed family events allowing the dynasty to come together and celebrate, to a new stage that was more about carefully staging a grand display for the visiting dignitaries, to give a very particular image of Punjabi courtly life. Suri tells us:

> All the victorious troops were standing drawn in lines on both sides and none dared heave a sigh out of the awe of the kingly presence. The elephant drivers stopped in the middle of the road, according to the order of the Maharaja. The glorious Sahibs stood up from their seats on the elephant according to their custom, to offer salutation first. After that the Maharaja shook hands [with Commander-in-Chief Fane] and enquired after his health. As desired by the Sarkar, Kanwar Kharak Singh rode his elephant. The Lat Sahib [Fane] got up from his elephant and went over to the *howdah* occupied by the Maharaja. It appeared as if two most auspicious planets had joined together in one zodiacal [conjunction].[63]

The first line of this quotation points to the precision and intense scrutiny that Ranjit Singh had enforced in the orchestration of this scene to welcome the British delegation. Such rigour would be continued throughout the events of the whole month, as the concern to impress the British officials and other prominent onlookers was obviously paramount—in fact, Sir Henry Fane is mentioned far more substantially in Suri's account than the bride herself, Nanki Kaur, who is not directly referred to even once by the court historian. Instead, the whole scenario was clearly about celebrating the success and glory of the ruling dynasty, and of entrenching further its ties with other emerging powers in the region.

We can see this attitude at work in Suri's brief description of the actual marriage ceremony. The father of the bride is presented as being the recipient of a great honour when the groom's party arrive at his village: the Maharajah supposedly 'imparted light to the house of Sardar Sham Singh', who welcomed him and 'thanked God on account of his visit'. Thus, although Sham Singh Attariwala was a distinguished and eminent Sikh *sardar*, Suri suggests that the marriage of his daughter to Prince Nau Nihal Singh was not an equal match, as the dynasty of the Maharajah was far more exalted. Nevertheless, he emphasises Ranjit Singh's piety and humility, quoting him on several occasions as he utters his own thanks to God during the festivities. We have already encountered one of them in the opening paragraphs of this book: 'This day is a most blessed day. Even my forefathers were not blessed with such a day. I thank God a thousand times and yet find my tongue incapable of rendering him due praise.'[64]

Both the Maharajah's father and grandfather had died young, leaving their wives and young sons to manage their *misl* in a vulnerable state. Ranjit Singh, however, had managed to survive such challenges; by the time of Nau Nihal Singh's wedding in 1837, he had lived a comparatively long life of almost sixty years, breaking with precedent and enjoying the opportunity to witness the marriage of his beloved grandson and future heir. A sense of optimism and the expectancy of continued future glory pervades Suri's descriptions of the wedding, particularly as he narrates the prince's excellent presentation in his conversations with British representatives both during and after the festivities. A number of military reviews were carried out after the wedding, at which the drill and firing capabilities of the Maharajah's best troops were exhibited to Fane and his colleagues. On one of the last days of the British visit, the young bridegroom was also asked to display both his own troops and his personal martial skills—a task that he managed to perform with great éclat:

> Kanwar Nau Nihal Singh was ordered to equip most fittingly the triumphant troops with all sorts of equipment, ornaments, bejewelled gold saddles and so to show their parade to the Lat Sahib in such a fine style that it may strike astonishment in the eyes of onlookers, and others who might come to hear of it. As the respectable Kanwar was blessed by the sunshine of glory and the shadow of the favour of God, he showed great smartness and form in the display of spear from horseback...

Such showcases of martial prowess, coupled with military reviews, were commonplace features of northern Indian diplomacy in this period: they were integral to the construction of masculine identities, and the making and breaking of friendships and alliances between male rulers.[65] The prince's skill in the saddle, combined with the impressive performance of his infantry and cavalry soldiers on parade, must have created the desired effect, since Fane was apparently moved to offer his congratulations to the Maharajah on having such a talented grandson and worthy heir to his kingdom.[66]

Cementing the Alliance

As Ranjit Singh would have been well aware, his British guests did not just treat their invitation to his grandson's wedding as an excuse for a holiday. The Company delegation's month-long stay in the Punjab was utilised by Sir Henry and his assistants to assess the strength and prowess of the Maharajah's armed forces. Henry Edward Fane—nephew of the Commander-in-Chief—was one such assistant present for both Nau Nihal Singh's wedding and the later tour of the Punjab carried out by Lord Auckland in 1838–9. The younger Fane's published diaries demonstrate the visiting British dignitaries' keen observations of the Maharajah's troops at both events, recording how quietly impressed they were by the considerable improvement shown in the quality of the Sikh army by 1839. Most interestingly, though, he notes that this development was clearly a result of the Maharajah having paid close personal attention to the performance of the Company sepoys, which he had been able to witness at reviews of the British-Indian regiments held alongside those of the Khalsa Army during the post-wedding diplomatic events. The Maharajah was apparently assiduous in noting any discrepancies in the strength of his own men as compared to the Company troops, and then in taking care to work on these issues before the next review took place, which would then be taken as a fresh learning opportunity.

Early on in his career, Ranjit Singh had become aware of the superiority of the style of troop formations and technology utilised by European military leaders in India, and was wary of the potential threat that this posed to the independence of his kingdom. He reached these conclusions on the basis of knowledge gathered through his extensive intelligence network, which kept him informed of the Company's widespread conquests throughout the rest of India during the early nineteenth century. Concerns about protecting his own power against British colonial expansion certainly contributed to his decision to side with the Company against the Marathas when Yashwant Rao Holkar asked him for help in 1806, but it equally inspired him to learn from British military prowess so as to achieve parity with it. This led Ranjit Singh to extensively remodel the Khalsa Army into a much more European style after becoming established in his Lahore capital. He went to considerable lengths to achieve this throughout his 38-year reign as Maharajah: hiring European mercenary generals to train his new infantry and artillery regiments; scrutinising the manoeuvres of British-Indian troops at reviews held in the Punjab; and famously peppering British officials with questions about their army in order to soak up as much information as he could with which to shape his military goals.[67] In the process, the old military system of the *misl* era was completely overturned, and the Khalsa Army was reformed into a centralised body of infantry and cavalry troops, subordinated as much as possible to the personal authority of the Maharajah and his government at Lahore.[68]

The British military authorities were well aware of the Maharajah's military and imperial ambitions, and their wariness of the Khalsa Army's increasing size and centralised efficiency equally convinced them of the need to keep the Punjabis on side and to use Ranjit Singh as a buffer-like ally, rather than to excite him as a foe. Sir Henry Fane reported back fully on the thought-provoking observations that he had made at the 1837 wedding, and recommended that the Governor-General recognise the need to bind the Sikh Empire more closely to the Company if an Anglo-Afghan war was to be attempted.[69] The idea of restoring Shah Shuja to the Afghan throne also appears to have been suggested to Fakir Azizuddin and Rai Gobind Jas by Claude Wade and his colleagues during the last week of their trip, along with other proposals to open up commercial navigation on the River Indus and to establish a cantonment at Shikarpur.[70] Azizuddin and Gobind Jas shared these proposals with the Maharajah and his other advisers after the last of the guests had departed; and, as we know, they would be negotiated and debated for nearly two years before being resolved with the signature of the Tripartite Treaty.

This brings us full circle in our exploration of the royal family's role in the negotiation of Ranjit Singh's strategic alliance with the British: discussions were apparently initiated at the wedding of Nau Nihal Singh, and the treaty was signed during Wade's condolence visit on the death of his grandmother Mai Nakain. In 1837 particularly, the invitation of the British delegation to the weeks-long royal wedding provided the opportunity for prolonged and close contact between Punjabi and British elites, which increased the confidence and cohesion of the relationship and enabled major strategic plans for further, more intensive collaboration to be laid on the table. The rapturous praise that the Maharajah received from the departing Fane gives explicit evidence to support this idea, and may well have contributed to Ranjit Singh's desire for the events of the wedding to be recorded by his court historian:

> The *Lat* Sahib said that he would describe in London his praiseworthy virtues, his courteousness, his equipment of troops, the prosperity of his country and the devotion of his subjects to him ... and that he would not forget all that as long as he lived, and finally that he would for ever cherish the memory of the Maharaja as a King of great virtues. He further said that the Sahibs, who were the greatest travellers of the time and had reached all the corners of the globe, had never come across any other ruler like him in wisdom, intelligence, good sense, gentleness, generosity, and kindness ... it went without saying that that the treaty and agreement between them would remain firm and strong from generation to generation, and that the marriage and their visit will remain for ever a memorable event.[71]

Seen from Ranjit Singh's perspective, such flattering words were probably the most gratifying form of recognition that he could have asked for, as Fane's statements could not have accorded more positively with the Maharajah's ambitions to achieve a reputation rivalling that of the world's other ruling monarchs of his age. The Commander-in-Chief's promise to write about the wedding to his superiors in London gave Ranjit Singh the pleasure of believing that his kingdom and dynasty would be spoken of in admiring terms at the capital of another great empire. It also reassured him that the grand dynastic exhibitions that he had orchestrated with such painstaking attention had succeeded in binding British rulers in lasting friendly ties with his royal house for generations to come. Exactly how this relationship would be viewed from the British perspective, and the terms on which it would evolve both within the Punjab and beyond after Ranjit Singh's demise, are the subjects to which we will now turn.

4

AFTER THE LION

WRITING THE STORY OF RANJIT SINGH'S HEIRS

In the British Library in London, there lies a spectacular yet curious manuscript about astronomy. Written in Sanskrit, the book's title is *Sarvasiddhantattvacudamani*, which translates as 'The Crest-Jewel of the Essence of All Systems of Astronomy'. It was put together in nineteenth-century Benares (Varanasi), the great centre of learning for Sanskrit scholars in India, and its author was a renowned astronomer, Durgashankar Pathak. In the book, Pathak ambitiously aims to compile all existing knowledge about astronomy from India, Europe and the Islamic world. His work was clearly intended for a Sikh patron, however: alongside its exceptionally fine illustrations of constellations or signs of the zodiac, there are beautiful portraits of the first and last Sikh Gurus, Guru Nanak and Guru Gobind Singh.[1] There is even a caption within the book suggesting that it once included a portrait of Maharajah Ranjit Singh, though this is now oddly missing.

As we saw in Chapter 2, this manuscript is thought to have been commissioned by none other than Ranjit Singh's eldest son, Prince Kharak Singh, sometime between 1833 and late 1839. This tells us that Kharak Singh, who reigned from 27 June 1839 to 5 November 1840, was potentially something of a cultural connoisseur. To have commissioned such an intellectual piece of work, as well as to have ordered its production at such a distance from the Punjab, would suggest that the second Maharajah of the Sikh Empire had at least some experience in dealing with expert scholars and artists, perhaps combined with a special interest in astronomy.

It was clearly a bespoke piece of work too, since the manuscript originally contained a detailed copy of a horoscope for his boy, Nau Nihal Singh. We have seen how integral such horoscopes were for marking the legitimacy and relative importance of a princely birth, and equally for gaining an understanding of how a prince's future character and prospects could be expected to turn out. If the story of its origin is really correct, then this old book has an added touch of poignancy to it, since we may be able to see it as a special gift that was intended to be shared between father and son.

Somewhat tragically, however, the book was not very kindly received by Nau Nihal Singh when it arrived in Lahore in 1840. Pathak brought the book to the Sikh imperial capital in person, but was apparently driven out of the city by the 'enmity' of the prince, then 19 years old, and the astronomer was only able to return to his home in Benares 'with great difficulty'. Subsequently, major adjustments had to be made to the book's contents, presumably to allow Pathak to quickly find a new patron for his work and recoup any losses he might have incurred from its production. All mention of the prince's horoscope was removed from the book, and instead a tribute and new portraits of the prominent *sardar* Lehna Singh Majithia were added.[2] Majithia was known to have been a very learned man, with extensive interests in engineering and science. He himself spent a considerable amount of time in Benares, and apparently was at some stage even a student of Pathak's: one of the book's illustrations shows him and his son being given an astronomy tutorial by the scholar. The *sardar* would thus have been the ideal person for the out-of-pocket Pathak to approach as a replacement buyer; today, on the British Library's own website, Majithia is even credited as being the original patron—the more messy history with Kharak Singh and Nau Nihal Singh being somehow overlooked.[3] This throws up questions of how and why would the prince reject such a special item commissioned by his father, and why could Kharak Singh himself be so easily dismissed as the work's patron.

At the heart of all this lies a conundrum: how do we untangle the deeply complicated history of the succession struggles that developed after the death of Ranjit Singh in June 1839? A sense of difference and disagreement between Kharak Singh and Nau Nihal

Singh certainly emerges from this particular episode and indeed, from all accounts of Kharak's very brief reign as Maharajah, we know that a terrible rift occurred in the relationship. This led Nau Nihal Singh to almost entirely usurp his father's powers during the latter's lifetime, becoming an exceedingly domineering prince regent; the most conspiratorial account even claims that the prince was entirely indifferent to his father's death in November 1840 and that he instead regarded it as a day for 'rejoicing'.[4] It is also widely thought that between Kharak Singh and his son, the latter was the more able and favoured heir of Ranjit Singh—mostly because he was supposedly most alike to 'the great Maharajah' in character and attitude.[5] As we shall see in this and the next chapter, after his death Ranjit Singh—or a particular image and characterisation of him—was made the gold standard for measuring achievement in all matters of rulership, a standard against which his heirs and successors were (usually unfavourably) compared by both contemporaries and later historians.

Certainly during his own lifetime, Ranjit Singh had doted on his eldest grandson with great affection, as is clear from what we've learnt about the Maharajah's jubilations during Nau Nihal Singh's lavish first wedding. On the other hand, Kharak Singh had occasionally felt compelled to complain to the Maharajah that he was over-indulging the young prince, giving him lucrative estates despite his refusal to do what he was told or accept the administrative tasks assigned to him, simply because he did not like where he was being sent.[6] Yet again, this does not explain why Nau Nihal Singh would have turned on his father so sharply—especially considering how, coupled with this paternal discipline, Kharak Singh was also apparently prepared to honour his son with such beautiful gifts as the astronomy manuscript, which has never before been considered in accounts of the struggle between them. Unfortunately, we simply do not have enough reliable evidence to help us decisively understand what caused this father–son relationship to become so very bitter and murky.

As for whether Kharak Singh himself was really responsible for commissioning the astronomy book, there too lies a deeper kind of political competition—one that is actually easier for us to unravel and delve into more closely. There has been a longstanding assumption made about Kharak Singh's character, which has not only been used by some to justify the manner in which he was politically sidelined by his son, but perhaps may have also contributed to him being overlooked by history as the possible patron of such an exquisite work of art and scholarship. This view was raised predominantly by British commentators who were the second Maharajah's contemporaries: that he was 'of weak mind' and something of an 'imbecile'. Kharak Singh's character is represented in this manner repeatedly in a number of British accounts by individuals who had formerly been guests of Ranjit Singh at Lahore, or who had been involved in working with the Sikh government on behalf of the Company. This description of the heir to the throne by Alexander Burnes, dating from the last years of Ranjit Singh's reign, is a particularly good example:

> Our first visit after alighting at the Baghi Wazeer, which was assigned as our residence, was to the Prince Kurruck Sing. His imbecility is such that he can scarcely return an answer to the most simple question; he was, however, extremely obliging; invited us to visit the new fort of Sumungur, which he is now building on the ruins of the Bala Hissar, and promises to be, when finished, a place of considerable strength. He also paraded his forces for our inspection, both infantry and cavalry: the first consisted of twelve battalions and twenty guns, and went through its brigade-exercise well. The sight, however, of 12,000 cavalry was much more imposing as they passed in review order before us in the fine plain of Peshawur. The only drawback to the enjoyment of these scenes was the weakness of the poor prince, which was really distressing: he could neither put a question, nor answer one, without being prompted. [As a mocking parallel, a] Peshawuree told us an amusing anecdote of a half-witted king of Balkh, who was ruled by his minister. On one occasion, when a foreign ambassador was to be presented, the vizier, fearful that his master would commit himself, prevailed on him to allow a string to be tied to his foot, and passed under the carpet in such a manner that the minister might hold the other end; and it was arranged between them that, whenever the vizier pulled, the king was either to speak or to desist from any inappropriate speech. The audience took place: the ambassador spoke; and the king replied; but, alas,

> the reply was only "Kush mu koonud!!" (he pulls). Again the ambassador spoke, and even more deferentially than before; but again the poor king shouted out "Kush mu koonud! Kush mu koonud!" to the unspeakable grief and dismay of his prime minister. "Now," added the Peshawuree, "our prince [Kharak Singh] wants a guide-string as much as the king of Balkh."[7]

This passage is one of the most detailed among the few direct descriptions of Kharak Singh available to us. It offers some valuable, if contradictory, insights into his character and abilities. On one hand, we see through the Company ambassador's eyes how the prince was extremely socially inept and evidently relied on the support of his courtiers in managing diplomatic conversations. Yet on the other, 'the extremely obliging' Kharak Singh clearly understood very well what the responsibilities of a good host should be; beyond that, he is noted here as being the master of an impressive military and administrative centre of imperial rule—built, no less, in Peshawar, a city with key strategic fortresses and valuable trading opportunities, which had long been fought over between the Sikhs and Afghans.

Burnes' use of the term 'imbecility' to describe the 'weakness of the poor prince' is crucial to understanding the conflicting representation here. In early nineteenth-century English, the word 'imbecile' could be used to refer to someone who was 'stupid', but in a medical sense, could be also be interchanged with the term 'idiot', which then denoted someone who was afflicted with varying degrees of 'permanent cognitive disability'.[8] By comparison, in the contemporary Punjabi sources, little mention is made of the prince's potential 'disability' or even any of any significant 'weakness'. There are certainly records of incidents when, as a youth, Kharak Singh was rebuked by his father for mistakes he made with the various leadership responsibilities assigned to him—including for overstepping the mark with his uncle Kahan Singh Nakai, as we saw in Chapter 2. But the Punjabi histories never touch upon any difficulties with speech or social interactions, and if anything, his alleged patronage of the astronomy manuscript complicates even further the picture of his intellectual capabilities.

Whatever its truth or falsehood, had the Sukerchakias been aware of this account by Burnes it would have undoubtedly struck a hard blow to Ranjit Singh's endeavours to present a favourable and impressive picture of his family, and particularly of his immediate heir. In the hypermasculinised world of both Punjab and British imperial society, any such form of cognitive disability would likely have been judged harshly, especially when the individual concerned was succeeding to the throne of a powerful empire, where expectations of their ability would run extremely high. We could perhaps contemplate the thought that the Maharajah's court historians were involved in 'covering up' Kharak Singh's perceived weaknesses, but that seems a rather simplistic way of looking at the situation. Even Burnes' account still has an element of nuance in its characterisation of the prince, echoing the details given in Suri's chronicles about his evident capability in handling important strategic and governing duties.

Burnes extrapolated a broader and more controversial political argument from his assessment of Kharak Singh's character, apparently suggesting that, amongst other concerns, it was an indication of the instability of Sikh power, which he believed would likely implode after the death of Ranjit Singh, its territories 'over-run, and perhaps dismembered into small states'. Burnes disliked the idea of an Afghan war pact with the Maharajah for this reason, finding it short-sighted. He predicted that the collapse of the Sikh Empire after Ranjit Singh's demise would leave the Company bereft of an ally: 'it would be imprudent to reckon on tranquillity' in the Punjab at that point, he warned his superiors in the Company government, for it was only 'the single mind' of Ranjit Singh that was able to control the different political 'factions' of the region's elite. With his loss, 'the disappearance of one man shall have ceased to bridle zeal' among 'the Affghan', who 'admits no sovereignty of the Sikh'.[9]

As we will see throughout this chapter and the next, a number of leading British officials also put the first Maharajah on something of a pedestal in this manner, claiming that he was the only man whose authority was worth respecting in the Punjab.[10] As Burnes and these others saw it, contrary to all we have seen of the queens, princes and courtiers building and strengthening the Sikh Empire, 'the supreme power of each nation depends upon the individual who wields it'.[11] By 1838–9, as it became more evident that Ranjit Singh's health was in fatal decline, speculation increased amongst

Company ranks about what would happen with his heirs. Some British officers were even inclined to advocate sidelining the next generation of Punjabi royals altogether, in favour of a more assertive, if not downright interventionist or imperialist, policy towards the Punjab, so as to strengthen the Company's sway in the region of India's northwestern frontier.[12]

However, this is not to say that all British officials were necessarily in agreement with such views or plans. As we saw in the last chapter, Wade and other senior Company men had worked hard to bring Ranjit Singh to the table for the Tripartite Treaty; Burnes' report arguing against the alliance was dramatically at odds with their views. The Political Agent Claude Martin Wade was very closely acquainted with the Sukerchakia royal family, and arguably had the greatest first-hand knowledge of regional political affairs of all the leading Company officials involved with the Sikh Empire. Drawing on this insight, Wade sought to directly counter the influential arguments of his rival, Burnes, who had become increasingly keen to ditch the Sikh alliance in favour of an Afghan one. Wade set out an opposing view of Prince Kharak Singh in a dispatch to their immediate superior, Sir William Macnaghten (Secretary to Governor-General Auckland), in January 1838:

> Kanwar Kharak Singh … wants energy and his manners are not in his favor nor is his mind brightened by those beams of intelligence which appear both in the conduct and the observations of his young and active son, but I am not inclined to consider him so utterly destitute of intellect as is generally supposed. The studious manner in which he has avoided for many years taking any prominent part in the affairs of his father's Government beyond what he may be charged to do is the result of reflection and does not arise from indifference to his situation. He has a just perception of Ranjit Singh's distrustful character and considers it good policy to follow the course which he has adopted [staying out of things] … He had at one time a large force under his command and paid by himself of which he has been dispossessed more perhaps from the Maharaja's distrust than the Kanwar's alleged incapacity to manage his affairs. At present he has only a small establishment but still retains about ten Lakhs of Rupees of territory while his son is charged with the government of the recent conquests of the Sikhs

> in the direction of Dera Ismail Khan. Kanwar Kharak Singh is of a mild and humane disposition and though not much feared he is loved by his dependants while no one in the country bears ill-will to him for he has injured no one.[13]

In his rather long letter, Wade went into significant detail weighing up the varying cases for Kharak Singh, Sher Singh and Nau Nihal Singh's claims to the throne, as well as considering the other key players who could pose a threat to their family's standing as the rulers of the empire—figures whom the Company could have supported had they wanted to find alternative 'allies' in the Punjab. The letter shows the success of the royal family's dynastic diplomacy: Wade had been sufficiently convinced by it to support their ongoing rule and the perpetuation of the Anglo-Punjabi alliance, rather than seeking to switch to a more warlike or imperialist footing after Ranjit Singh's expected death. It highlights too that Wade had reached this conclusion on the most valuable contender to back after the Maharajah's demise through his own thorough and independent assessment of the characters and positions of each leading member of the royal family, as well as the other courtly elites at Lahore. It is therefore significant that Wade decided that Kharak Singh's succession would be in the best interests of the Company, arguing that the prince would be a safe pair of hands who could keep Punjabi society secure enough for it to continue as a reliable buffer state on the Company's northwestern frontier. Wade acknowledged that Kharak Singh may not have been the sharpest man around, yet was happy enough to assert that the rumours about his deficiencies were rather misleading.[14]

Set against Burnes' writings, this brings to light an important yet overlooked fact: that there was internal debate and inconsistency within Company circles about how the next generation of Punjabi royals should be perceived and treated. The implications of this were hugely significant in shaping the opinions and policy decisions of high-ranking British officials, but it is equally important for us to recognise how such accounts have come to powerfully influence our view of Ranjit Singh's successors today. This is not to say that the narratives presented by men such as Burnes or Wade should be perceived as entirely misleading or untruthful; but simply that, altogether, British narratives about Punjabi elite figures should not be taken entirely at face value. We must instead recognise how they influenced one another, and how their nature and perspectives were continually shifting and being re-evaluated in the face of fresh or changing strategic considerations.

An added issue that cannot be omitted is the fact that British commentators from the Sikh Empire period were extensively influenced by Orientalist understandings of India: they may well have viewed Indian people, culture and society as being of scholarly, political or even romantic interest, but many nevertheless saw 'Indian civilisation' as inherently inferior and 'backward' compared to Europe and the West. Company officers of this mindset only valorised those Indians perceived to be most like them, and so it is unsurprising that they championed Ranjit Singh, the 'Lion of Punjab', for his strong rulership and active embrace of a military alliance with the British, while largely deriding his heirs for their supposed weaknesses. In the language of Orientalism, the first Maharajah had the merit of having overcome the traits 'typical' of Asian men—decadence and effeminacy, key tropes in the opposition set up between 'rational' Western civilisation and the 'sensual' civilisation of 'Eastern' peoples. His sons and grandsons, on the other hand, were not seen as having escaped their 'nature' in this way.

It is vital to recognise these issues when exploring the history of Ranjit Singh's successors as Maharajah, because we are much more dependent in this period on British or European writings. For the years between Ranjit Singh's death in 1839 and the overthrow of the last Maharajah in 1849, the colonial sources remaining to us outnumber the Punjabi ones; and the Punjabi texts we do have are far fewer in number than the more plentiful internal records for the lifetime of the first Maharajah.[15] For instance, although Suri's chronicle covers the history up until 1850, his writing on the events and immediate aftermath of the first Anglo-Sikh War (1845–6) is missing from the versions of the text we have today, because he never got them back after lending them to a British officer to read. By contrast, British and European writing on the Punjab seemed to grow rapidly from the late 1830s: not only private Company correspondence and intelligence records, but also the emergence of widespread media coverage and published diaries, novels and travelogues, produced for growing British-Indian audiences by European individuals who claimed to have been witness to the events that unfolded in this crucial decade. This makes the messy tale of the astronomy manuscript all the more intriguing and eye-opening, not least because, according to many such British accounts, it would have been unthinkable for Kharak Singh to have the intellectual wherewithal or education to even come up with such an idea.

As a combined result of their greater prevalence and influence over time, these colonial narratives about the 'weak characters', 'bitter divides' and 'chaos' of Ranjit Singh's surviving family have become increasingly entrenched, and have come to be more or less accepted as truisms within modern biographical and historical works on this period of Sikh and Punjabi history. This is most definitely a far cry from the manner in which the Maharajah himself had hoped his kin and kingdom would be perceived or remembered. In almost all narratives about the ruling Sukerchakia dynasty, with growing regularity after Ranjit Singh's death but even during his reign, the Maharajah's male and female heirs were represented as unequal to the task of running his vast and powerful empire. Take, for example, these comments:

> Khurak [sic] Singh, the eldest, is an imbecile, and affects the *religieux*. Sher Singh, the second, is far from clever, but he is prudent; he is fond of imitating the military and Europeans. Tara Singh, the third, is a dissolute vagabond, leading the most reckless life in the common *bazārs*. None of them appear much at *durbār*, and the two latter are known not to be really sons of the Māharājah, who, perhaps, keeps quiet the mystery of their birth, as a check against any possible designs of his acknowledged son.[16]

As well as these, about the last ruler of the Sikh Empire, the boy-king Duleep Singh:

> The education of princes is at all times a difficult matter; more especially in a court so rude as that of the Punjab. Runjeet Sing, 'the great Maharajah', could neither write nor read; and he left few behind him much more accomplished than himself. It is perhaps expecting too much therefore that Maharajah Duleep Singh should care to be a scholar; but it will be something if he makes himself independent of others in reading a petition, or affixing his signature to a Purwannuh [royal permit].[17]

In the first account, we see again the idea of Kharak Singh as some kind of 'idiot', suggesting that this was becoming a shared opinion in British circles. From the second quote about the 'rude' nature of the court established by the 'uneducated' Ranjit Singh, it would appear that the writer clearly had no understanding or appreciation of the kind of courtly and administrative training that the Sikh princes had been made to undertake from a very young age—let alone acknowledging that they or any other members of the Maharajah's family could have been patrons of art, culture or scholarship.

These two passages were written by Henry Montgomery Lawrence: a Company officer who was a contemporary of Claude Martin Wade, but who would supersede him in the post-Ranjit Singh 1840s as the key influential British figure in relations with the Punjabis. The first quote comes from Lawrence's popular historical fiction series, *The Adventures of an Officer in the Service of Runjeet Singh*, which was written in 1840 and originally published in instalments in the *Delhi Gazette*, before being edited and printed as a novel in London in 1845. It would go on to become a widely cited source for later European and South Asian writers on Sikh and Punjabi history, despite being a work of fiction, because Lawrence claimed to have based it on first-hand knowledge and research into the recent history and political life of Ranjit Singh's kingdom.[18] Significantly, the books of Alexander Burnes are mentioned as being among the key works used by Lawrence to produce his account—we can certainly see the link between the two men's understanding with the echoed reference to Kharak Singh as an 'imbecile' here, which is all the more interesting since there is little evidence to suggest that Lawrence ever met him in person. We can nevertheless see how quickly one man's personal opinion might become received historical wisdom when it came to colonial accounts.

On the other hand, the second passage is from a private letter written by Lawrence in 1847 to the Secretary of the Governor-General. By that point in time, the Punjabi monarchy and government had lost a great deal of its independence, following the defeat of the Khalsa Army during the First Anglo-Sikh War of 1845–6 (see Chapter 5). Henry Lawrence had become a figure of immense influence in Anglo-Punjabi politics after that disaster as the Company's first ever Political Resident at Lahore, with the power to administer the Sikh government on behalf of the young Maharajah Duleep Singh. This marked a massive shift away from the earlier dynamic that had existed between Ranjit Singh and the British elite of his day, when much of the Sikh Empire's dealings had been with mere 'agents'—who represented the Company but did not claim to rule. Lawrence's appointment to the new office of Resident also meant that his earlier pronouncements about the recent history of the royal family began to carry greater weight than those of any British officer before him; as we shall see in the next chapter, his views of the dynasty would have a direct impact on reshaping the very nature of the Punjabi monarchy—down to the day-to-day life of Ranjit Singh's last son and heir, Duleep Singh.

All of this shows that there are clearly some significant issues and challenges facing us when piecing together the history of the characters and reigns of Ranjit Singh's successors, as well as their changing relationships with their regional neighbours. This must have been an immensely tumultuous period: little over five years after the Maharajah's death, his kingdom was at war with its foremost ally and his three eldest heirs had all died. By 1849, the entire Sikh Empire would be formally taken over by the Company, and the ruling power of the Punjabi royal dynasty completely extinguished. A lot of ink has already been spilt in trying to get to the bottom of what exactly precipitated the fall of the Empire, and who or what might have been to blame—issues that many commentators have been rather too fixated on. Despite this obsession, there has never been any real agreement about who the 'real villains' were, or whether larger, more impersonal forces like economics or ideology had a greater role to play.

This interest in the reasons for the demise of the Sikh Empire, or the controversies of the Anglo-Sikh Wars, has been driven in no small part by the fact that the annexation of 1849 is a hugely important event for Sikhs and Punjabis, widely considered to mark the end of the region's 'national independence'. Within the broader politics of nineteenth-century South Asia, the takeover of the Sikh Empire by the Company also represented the fall of the last major independent kingdom on the Indian subcontinent. The Punjabi lands would thereafter be governed as part of the British Raj until August 1947, when they were split asunder by the Radcliffe Line drawn throughout the Punjab to partition it between India and

Pakistan. The story of the fall of the Sikh Empire therefore cuts across interlocking agendas about the history of sovereignty, nationalism and imperialism on a number of levels. It is a topic that can arouse considerable passion and which can be represented in a number of different ways to support different cultural or political agendas. This starts perhaps with debates between men such as Burnes and Wade, and continues today, from romanticised Bollywood-style film and TV productions about Ranjit Singh and Duleep Singh to the radical, sometimes violent demands for a sovereign Sikh state that we saw in Chapter 1.[19]

However, by occupying ourselves too heavily in a search for straightforward answers explaining the kingdom's fall, or by fixating on uncovering the 'truth' about the many scandals that emerged around the power struggle over the Lahore throne, we have too often missed or glossed over fragments of evidence that tell us something far more interesting about the lived experiences of the key figures involved in these pivotal events, both Punjabi and British. What we lose in all of this is an understanding of what happened after 1839 to the royal, dynastic culture that Ranjit Singh and his family had built with such creativity and ambition in the earlier decades of their rule. Up until now in this book, we have been engaged in teasing out and examining the evidence of the hitherto overlooked dynamism of the ruling house, and the ways they collectively built a new kind of kingdom and royal culture to cement their power and influence in the face of numerous challenges. These dynastic ways of being and working that emerged from the days of the expanding Sukerchakia *misl* would surely not have vanished overnight with the death of Ranjit Singh on 27 June 1839. As talented and ambitious a man that Ranjit Singh might have been, and as powerful a blow his death surely was to those who had come to depend upon him, we have to question whether his passing really was the crucial turning point that it has since been made out to be.

This bigger picture is about situating not just Ranjit Singh himself, but the entire Punjabi monarchy within a broader view—one of changing fortunes for new and old ruling elites, in a world where the position of monarchy was beginning to evolve in important ways. We saw in Chapter 1 how the rise to power of Ranjit Singh and the Sukerchakia *misl* was partly supported by and partly a product of new ideas about kingship that emerged in the eighteenth century, amidst the decline of Mughal power in South Asia. We now also need to think about what the 'decline' in the fortunes of the Punjabi dynasty itself can tell us about the continually shifting standing of royal power, as our focus heads towards the middle of the nineteenth century, when British colonialism and ideas about Indian royal culture were increasingly having an impact in the region.

These questions have not yet been much asked about the Sikh Empire—mostly because many people, from Ranjit Singh's day to ours, have been guilty of reducing its history to that of the story of the 'great Maharajah', or particularly of succumbing a little too heavily to the nostalgic lionising of his character. This tendency was arguably started with the hagiographical writings of his loyal chronicler, Sohan Lal Suri, and the view of Ranjit Singh as the sole foundation and guiding light holding the Empire together became an increasingly useful stick for Company officials to beat his heirs with in the period after his death. However, if we are now ready to discard that old narrative, then it is worthwhile considering just how and why this version of events came into being, and what it potentially blurs about the inner life of the former Sikh Empire.

This is not to say that Ranjit Singh was 'actually' a 'bad' ruler, nor that his successors were necessarily 'better' than him; nor even that we should disregard any historical criticism of their natures. I am not seeking to champion or denigrate the Punjabi royals in any particular way. Rather, the point is simply that there is more complexity to this story than we are perhaps used to hearing, and that raising new and critical questions about dominant narratives, or the internal dynamics of our primary sources, is just as vitally important when writing the history of the Sikh Empire as it is for any other period or event from the past. It enables us to learn so much more about the world of this kingdom, and also to better appreciate and investigate what its politics, culture and society did or did not share with its contemporaries. Royal culture was a lively force in this period; and royal elites, for better or worse, could not be scrubbed out overnight. On the contrary, the Sukerchakia dynasty is arguably a rather valuable example of a monarchy taking several severe knocks, but still somehow remaining standing and even somewhat popular, whilst adapting to continually shifting cultural and political environments.

In looking at these circumstances, I want us to concentrate not on trying yet again to 'solve' what led to the fall of the Empire or its dynasty, but instead to come at this period from an entirely different angle: to actually consider how Ranjit Singh's family managed to stay on the throne of Lahore for another ten years, despite the increasingly challenging circumstances that they faced. For really no one could have predicted that the ruling dynasty would have been deposed by 1849, nor that the entire Empire would have been swallowed up into the British one—no matter how self-assuredly certain Company politicians might have blustered that the 'unruly Sikhs' would easily be 'set right' by the superior might and wisdom of the British. In fact, perhaps in contrast to immediate appearances here, even Henry Lawrence was a fan of Ranjit Singh, and acted as a passionate advocate for keeping the Sikh Empire intact and its royal family on the throne.

As we shall see further in the next chapter, Lawrence's writings were not necessarily intended as an attack on the Punjabi rulers, but as a plan for 'reforming' them and their monarchy, so as to enable them to legitimately stay in power and meet the newer standards of behaviour and governance that the Company was increasingly demanding of its Indian royal allies. The Resident at Lahore was not alone in imposing such demands and ideas on the Punjabi monarchy, and these were not without their problems. As we will see in this chapter, the royals faced similar pressures from within their own *durbar* and from their subjects, in a way that would gradually and substantially alter the nature of their authority.

By flipping our focus in this manner, we can start to see with fresh eyes how the world of the Punjabi royals was transformed in this crucial period. We will discover in the next chapter the consequences of this for the wider region's evolving political culture and power relations, and for the last guardians of Sikh power in the Punjab—Jind Kaur and Duleep Singh—but for now let us lay the path to that final confrontation. Let's go back to the accession of Kharak Singh.

A Dynasty Divided: The Battle for Control of Lahore

If we are to see royal deaths as crucial turning points, then the untimely loss of Maharajahs Kharak Singh and Nau Nihal Singh within just five days of each other in November 1840 was at least as devastating as the demise of Ranjit Singh, if not more so. We can get an impression of the sadness and confusion that their deaths caused from this evocative passage by Suri, which we looked at earlier in Chapter 2:

> At that sad moment there was not a single eye which had not become fraught with disgust and sorrow. The ashes of the father and son [Kharak Singh and Nau Nihal Singh] were made to depart by the way leading out of the gate under the city wall ... and such a huge crowd of the people residing in Lahore was witnessed there at that time that the people, having closed the shops in the town, were weeping and crying ... In seventeen months [after the first Maharajah's death], not a single trace was left of his dynasty, which was a decoration for the kingdom ... [and] an imparter of comfort and convenience to the world and its people...[20]

The double death of the second and third Maharajahs was indeed a source of great disruption, for their successions had gone rather smoothly after Ranjit Singh's demise on 27 June 1839. Despite the speculations of many British officers that a power struggle would erupt between the Maharajah's eldest sons, Kharak Singh and Sher Singh, the order of succession was widely considered as settled within the Punjab itself. Kharak Singh had first been marked as his father's successor back in 1816. This decision was re-affirmed while Ranjit Singh was on his deathbed. For a very short while, Sher Singh seemed as though he might be moving to stir up a rebellion, but he quickly dropped these intentions and rather easily fell into line behind his brother and nephew. Kharak Singh and Nau Nihal Singh in turn made a concerted effort to treat Sher Singh with ample generosity, to ensure that he would have no cause for complaint against them.[21]

Thus, contrary to British colonial expectations, there was no great princely battle for power in 1839 as there had been for generations of Mughal princes in the Punjab; and, ironically, the Sikh succession followed a model of primogeniture similar to that of the British royals. It was therefore accepted that the royal stewardship of the Empire was a fixed matter, and it was hoped that it would pass without incident from Ranjit Singh to Kharak Singh, and from

Kharak Singh to Nau Nihal Singh. For this reason, the two heirs' early—and particularly in Nau Nihal Singh's case—startlingly sudden deaths turned upside-down the relative sense of stability and continuity that their successions had previously provided.

There has since been a lot of conjecture about the untimely ends of the two new Maharajahs. As we know, even if there was no succession struggle between Kharak Singh and Sher Singh, a major clash did occur between the second Maharajah and his son—although, again, we can't fully be sure of the reasons why. Was the 'weak-minded' Kharak Singh really a bad ruler who needed to be stopped in his tracks? Was Nau Nihal Singh therefore a brave and wise prince, or just a very power-hungry son? These are some of the theories that past biographers have toyed with, but these are the basic facts that we know for certain: Kharak Singh only ruled as Maharajah for just under a year and a half, during which time he lost the majority of his power to Nau Nihal Singh and Ranjit Singh's former *vazir* (prime minister), Rajah Dhyan Singh, after the prince and the minister brutally assassinated Kharak Singh's own chosen *vazir* and friend, Chet Singh Bajwa, in front of his very eyes. Why this murderous event took place, and how badly it impacted both the father–son relationship and Lahore courtly politics, has long been a matter of debate.

Our understanding of Nau Nihal Singh's story is all the more complicated by the fact that strangely he too would die, on the very day of his father's funeral. The short-lived third Maharajah was hit by crumbling chunks of falling masonry while passing through a gate on his return to his palace within the Lahore Fort. This accident left him unconscious and bleeding from the head. The young Maharajah subsequently died from his injuries, but there has been intense speculation over whether the blow that he suffered at the gate was really sufficient to have caused his death, or whether Dhyan Singh—who had quickly taken control of Nau Nihal Singh's care, being the first man on the spot—had seized the incident as an opportunity to kill off his new master and strengthen his own power within the kingdom.[22] All of this has led to critical questions being raised about the political intentions of Dhyan Singh and his family, Hindu Dogra Rajputs from Jammu who had rapidly ascended the political ladder under the earlier favour of Ranjit Singh. Was Dhyan Singh really a loyal minister who did everything he could to preserve the safety and security of his late master's kingdom? Or was he a dangerous upstart who secretly hoped to replace the Maharajah's family with his own on the Lahore throne?

This dramatic episode in the Sikh Empire's fortunes has long been debated. Both contemporaries of the Punjabi ruling elite and later historians have sought to uncover explanations not only of how and why the two new Maharajahs died, but additionally whether any conspiracies behind their deaths could point to the existence of deeper political problems lurking at the heart of the Sikh imperial state.[23] I don't have any new answers to give on this question and it remains to be seen whether anyone will be able to prove what 'really happened'. Instead I think we need to look at the deaths of Ranjit Singh's son and grandson in a different light. Perhaps the somewhat obsessive search for answers about what went wrong with Kharak Singh and Nau Nihal Singh speaks of a lingering sense of trauma from the violent disruption their deaths brought to the royal succession, and so to the settled order of Punjabi elite society. We can see from Suri's writing that he, at least, believed the royal dynasty established by Ranjit Singh to have effectively ended with the death of Nau Nihal Singh. The court historian was certainly not alone in thinking that Kharak Singh and Nau Nihal Singh were the only princes truly in the direct line of succession, and he seems to have actively disregarded the claims of other princes to be recognised as Ranjit Singh's children and successors, especially Sher Singh and his 'twin' Tara Singh.

Regardless of these contentions, and indeed the deaths of the second and third Maharajahs, the Punjabi monarchy was kept in place after 1840. Its position front and centre in the governance of the Sikh Empire had become entrenched, and apparently all that was needed was for a new ruler to be placed on the throne. The institution itself was not seriously in doubt; rather, the question of who this successor should be was what really caused havoc, opening up a whole lot of issues about how a legitimate succession should be defined. This is the key matter that we must look into much more closely. For, together with the up-ending of Ranjit Singh's royal succession plan, a whole new variety of people were able to push themselves into this debate and claim a stake in the mounting power struggle at the heart of the Lahore government: junior royals, the recently ennobled aristocrats of the late Ranjit Singh's *durbar*, the Khalsa Army, and eventually the East India Company too. But how did these new players manage to justify their interventions in the Sikh Empire's politics, both at the time and in subsequent histories of these events? And what was their ultimate impact?

* * *

In November 1840, at the critical juncture following the deaths of Ranjit Singh's two key heirs, it was actually a woman who immediately took charge of the government. Maharani Chand Kaur, the seniormost wife of Kharak Singh and mother of Nau Nihal Singh, sat herself on the family throne at Lahore. However, the Maharani did not seek to rule in her own name. One of Nau Nihal Singh's wives, Rani Sahib Kaur, had fallen pregnant shortly before her husband's death, and so Chand Kaur asserted her right to rule as Queen-Regent until the child was born and had attained an age of maturity, at which point he (for it was assumed that the junior queen would give birth to a son) would be able to rule independently. Chand Kaur was following in the footsteps of the many Sikh *sardarnis* who had gone before her, including Raj Kaur and Sada Kaur (Ranjit Singh's mother and mother-in-law), who had previously taken over the running of their respective *misls* after their husbands passed away, if their children were too young to take leading roles in their own right. In assuming control of the Lahore government, the Maharani also called on the support of a group of leading male courtiers, including Fakir Azizuddin, Ranjit Singh's skilled diplomat; former prime minister Dhyan Singh's equally influential brother, Gulab Singh; and other experienced former ministers of the first Maharajah's court, who offered to act as her advisory 'council'.[24]

Despite the strictures of the Sikh faith about men and women being societal equals, such ideas had not sufficiently penetrated into the political sphere to enable Sikh queens to rule as independent sovereigns—but there was definitely enough of a precedent to justify Chand Kaur's legitimate assumption of power as Regent. Crucially, too, her rights were initially upheld against the rival claims of Sher Singh, who—despite any disregard for his disputed bloodline—had long been treated as a prince with a similar level of responsibility and recognition to those of Kharak Singh and Nau Nihal Singh.

How Sher Singh managed to turn the tables on his 'sister-in-law' is worth careful attention. In his *Umdat-ut-tawarikh*, Suri gives a very interesting account of how the prince attempted to strengthen his own case whilst tearing down Chand Kaur's authority. Suri describes how, soon after the funerals of the two late Maharajahs, Sher Singh took Dhyan Singh aside to press upon him the dangers of female involvement in government, and urged him to consider an alternative:

> The enforcement of the affairs of kingdom and kingship ... is quite impossible for ladies to cope with and carry on. Since the olden times wherever they have been rulers in the end the pages of the book of the kingdom were scattered. You are a man of great wisdom and intelligence by the grace of Immortal God. Therefore you must think of some wise and suitable plan by reason of which the garden of kingship ... and the rule and sovereignty of the deceased Noble Sarkar [Ranjit Singh] may begin to flourish and prosper ...[25]

In other words, the prince resorted to blatant misogyny in order to support his own claim—conveniently overlooking the role that his own grandmother, Sada Kaur, had originally played in supporting the rise of Ranjit Singh to power as Maharajah. In this context, we see a conflict arising that was not simply about princely self-interest, but which dragged into it competing arguments about the proper way of determining a legitimate succession: on the grounds of gender, versus those of lineage and blood. It is also telling that Sher Singh tried to present himself as acting out of loyalty to his father's memory, and to ensure the future prosperity of the kingdom established by the first Maharajah. This shows how, as early as 1840, Ranjit Singh's name and memory had become a central and authoritative symbol that all of the ruling elite were expected to honour and respect. This is somewhat different from the way in which British officials were turning the late Maharajah into a particular style of icon to set against his own heirs; but there is nevertheless a parallel here in which the ghost of the 'great man' could be evoked in a disciplinary way, to impose certain norms or agendas on individual Punjabi figures—in this case, working to freeze out the claims of royal women to wield power.

Whether Sher Singh knew it or not, this marked a major break from the dynamics of a pivotal conversation that Dhyan Singh had been involved in over a year before. At that time, he had just been formally confirmed by the dying Ranjit Singh as the ongoing *vazir* or chief minister of the Sikh Empire, simultaneously to the Maharajah's confirmation that Kharak Singh would be the heir to the throne. However, there was a keen awareness amongst key figures in the Empire that this relationship could quickly break down. Whether out of genuine grief or as an act of provocation, after Ranjit Singh died Dhyan Singh started to make known that that he wished to join the late Maharajah's Hindu wives in committing *sati* on his funeral pyre, claiming that he could not face life in a world without the security of his former master's presence.

One day, he went so far as to make this striking assertion in the apartments of Rani Katochan, one of the Hindu queens who was actually about to commit *sati*, whom he had been visiting together with the new Maharajah. Kharak Singh was greatly perturbed to hear his prime minister say such a thing, and appears to have panicked. He immediately tried to reassure the *vazir* of his good intentions towards him, and apparently even 'put his head upon [Dhyan Singh's] feet and said that he could never show any kind of deviation or opposition to his orders[,] and [that he] would always look upon him as a substitute of the Sarkar [i.e. Ranjit Singh]'. The Rani, however, was much less impressed by Dhyan Singh's words and clearly felt that he was putting on an act. She may well have thought that his statements were deeply disrespectful to the sacrifice that she and the other Hindu queens were preparing to make. The proud Rajput Rani derided the *vazir* and said that, by joining her on her husband's funeral pyre, he would only prove how false his promises had been to 'always remain with the stirrup of the Sarkar [the reigning Maharajah]'.

Rani Katochan's stinging retort mirrors Sher Singh's reference to the 'Noble Sarkar'. This incident shows even more clearly how Ranjit Singh's memory had quickly (within just a few days of his death, no less) become a potent tool for extracting loyalty and conformity amongst the Punjabi ruling elite—though of course here the first Maharajah's name was used to support the power of a queen, rather than to weaken it. For the Rani did not stop there. She went on to demand that Dhyan Singh make a similar oath of loyalty to the one that Kharak Singh had just sworn to him. Urging him to take the *Bhagavad Gita* (a sacred Hindu text) into his hands, Rani Katochan pushed Dhyan Singh to 'swear that he would not create any dispute or bring about any deception to estrange the father and son [Kharak and Nau Nihal], and that in rendering services and in proving loyal and obedient [as a governing minister] he would never make the elder Kanwar [Kharak Singh] do anything that might be a source of trouble and sorrow to the younger Kanwar [Nau Nihal, or perhaps even Sher Singh].'[26]

Rani Katochan apparently saw in Dhyan Singh's threat to commit *sati* a worrying attempt to extract political concessions from Kharak Singh; she evidently felt that the minister could pose a threat to the political stability of her dynasty's kingdom. During the course of his reign, Ranjit Singh had promoted to high office a whole variety of talented men like Dhyan Singh and his brothers, who had had relatively humble origins, as another way of cementing the pre-eminent standing of his own family at the head of the new imperial state—over and above his erstwhile allies and rivals, the chiefs of the other Sikh *misls*. After Ranjit Singh's death, several of the leading families at the Lahore *durbar* began jockeying anew for more power and influence—with something of a divide forming between the Sikh elites who shared ties of kinship and religion with the Maharajah's heirs, and the new 'parvenu' class of courtiers and ministers whom Ranjit Singh had raised to prominence, foremost among them the Hindu Dogra family headed by Dhyan Singh.[27] We can see echoes of this split in the power struggle that emerged soon after for the *vazir*-ship between Dhyan Singh, the first Maharajah's man, and Chet Singh Bajwa, Kharak Singh's friend and kinsman, who would be assassinated by Dhyan Singh and Nau Nihal Singh.

Rani Katochan's verbal challenge to Dhyan Singh demonstrates not only her concerns about a potential threat to her dynasty, but equally her confidence in her own legitimacy and right to take active steps to try and mitigate this risk. The relative privacy of her *zenana* seems to have been the ideal location for dealing with such a critical problem. She was also clearly determined to uphold what she perceived as the sanctity of certain royal and religious rituals, and was not prepared to allow Dhyan Singh to subvert these in any way. If anything, her upcoming self-sacrifice seems to have lent further moral authority to her demands. Indeed, the fulfilment of the wishes of a widow about to commit *sati* were widely viewed by her contemporaries as a sacred duty to be respected by those who would live on after her death, and so Dhyan Singh would not easily have been able to directly reject her command. At the time of Ranjit Singh's passing, then, the influence and authority of a Punjabi queen—whether she was living or dead—was no insignificant thing.

We can't know whether this tricky conversation returned to Dhyan Singh's mind when Sher Singh came to him and complained about the quality of female rule. However, the *vazir* apparently did not take much convincing to side with the prince against Chand Kaur. Suri's chronicle goes on to tell us how Dhyan Singh approached the Maharani to advise that Sher Singh should be appointed as Maharajah—although with the added caveats, perhaps to soften the blow to her pride, that Sher Singh should present himself to her twice daily and that he should seek her advice on all matters of governance. Chand Kaur complained against this proposal with great bitterness, seeing it as a breach of loyalty and a painful blow after the deaths of the rightful rulers, her late husband and son. Thereafter, she signalled her determination to rule independently, effectively prompting the outbreak of a civil war between her supporters and those of Sher Singh. The Lahore *durbar* and the elite chiefs of the Punjab split into two factions behind the Maharani and the prince. Representatives of two powerful Sikh families joined Chand Kaur's council (including Lehna Singh Majithia, the eventual owner of the Sanskrit astronomy manuscript, and Attar Singh Sandhawalia, a kinsman of Ranjit Singh), whilst the powerful Dogra brothers, the Rajahs Dhyan Singh and Gulab Singh, opportunistically split up and stationed themselves on either side of the conflict.[28]

It is important to recognise in this which side Suri himself was on. We know that he had been a loyal supporter of Kharak Singh's lineage, but it is worth noting that the chronicler's more fervent backing for Chand Kaur's claims over Sher Singh's may well have been further influenced by the fact that he and his family had also been directly employed by the second Maharajah's household, meaning that they had a direct, vested interest in its success. Suri, of course, had been a longstanding and prominent *vakil* (clerk) at Ranjit Singh's *durbar*; but his nephew had also served the late Nau Nihal Singh in the same capacity, and apparently continued in the employ of the Maharani, who gave him the hugely important responsibility of bringing the influential Rajah Gulab Singh from Jammu to Lahore, so that he could support her cause against Prince Sher Singh.[29] In short, Suri was not just a court historian duly documenting events for posterity; he had skin in the game.

We can find a much more critical account of the Maharani's short-lived reign in the writings of the famous Punjabi poet Shah Muhammad. If we compare Suri's testimony with Shah Muhammad's epic *Jangnama*, the underlying gender politics of the clash between Chand Kaur and Sher Singh come out even more starkly. This poem appears to have been written after the civil war, some time in 1846, and was primarily reflecting on the disastrous losses of the Khalsa Army that had just occurred in the First Anglo-Sikh War. However, Shah Muhammad also shares his thoughts on the tumult and tragedies that befell Ranjit Singh's heirs after his death, particularly the untimely deaths of his son and grandson. As such, although this poem has typically been studied with a view to its richly detailed narrative on the causes and impact of the war with the British, it actually contains some very interesting ideas about the royal succession struggle of 1843 as well:

> Someone conveyed to Sher Singh this black news,
> Who had lost his brother and nephew in this manner.
> Post-haste he shot forth from Batala,
> Caring little for rain or shine; night or day.
> And as he entered the city of Lahore
> He lost all restraint, weeping like a child.
> O Shah Mohammed! The kinsmen console one another in such an hour,
> But not Chand Kaur, so vindictive had she turned.
>
> Secretly she had stationed four armed men with orders:
> 'If ever Sher Singh enters the fort,
> Unload your deadly carbines on him

So that he falls dead that very moment.'
But the Raja [Dhyan Singh] had sent a message to Sher Singh:
'You do not enter the portals of the dead.
O Shah Mohammed! You are not so strong at this time.
Wait for the moment when I invite you.'

Chand Kaur was not clean in her conscience.
'Twas treachery and treachery all the way.
Sher Singh immediately left Lahore
And went to Mukerian to set himself up there.
In the meanwhile, Chand Kaur ascended the throne,
Egged on by her courtiers and sycophants:
O Shah Mohammed! 'Another prince won't be born.
The forts, the cities and the people are all yours.'[30]

The Maharani's reported lack of grief over her husband's death provides the opening for Shah Muhammad's critique of the abnormality of female rule. Her greed for power is presented here as corrupting the affections that should naturally arise from kinship ties, turning them instead from sympathy to murderous enmity. The poet later describes how God delivered the throne up to Sher Singh after the prince laid siege to the Lahore Fort.[31] The implication is that Chand Kaur's ambitions were but a perversion of the moral order of society. Her reign was thus one that could only be sustained by underhand means, and inevitably would result in unnecessary turmoil and bloodshed.

This entire poem is tinged throughout with a palpable misogynistic strain. Not only Chand Kaur but women in general are blamed in later stanzas for the moral disarray and the destruction of otherwise brilliant male rulers throughout history.[32] The *Jangnama* is actually best known for its trenchant critique of Maharani Jind Kaur, the woman who would eventually become the last queen of the Sikh Empire (though Shah Muhammad himself did not know it at the time). It firmly placed the blame for the outbreak of the 1845–6 war with the Company on her shoulders—an event that led to the destruction of the Khalsa Army and the loss of a great deal of the Punjab's independence (see Chapter 5). This negative attitude towards women and female power may actually have something to do with the very genre of poetic form that Shah Muhammad selected for his work. Although the poem is popularly known as a *jangnama*, the historian Jeevan Deol has pointed out that its structure and themes demonstrate how its composition is actually an interesting mixture of genres, suggesting that the poem is somewhere between a *var* and a *qissa*—leaning more towards the latter, which commonly had misogynistic undertones.

Whatever the artistic influences on Shah Muhammad's work, we cannot overlook the similarity in the nature and tone of his words about female leadership with the kinds of sweeping assertions that Sher Singh himself had made about the problems that always seemed to arise when 'ladies' were expected to 'cope and carry on' with the affairs of government. Though written a few years after Sher Singh's own death, this poem's characterisations of the two protagonists reveals implicitly that Shah Muhammad had been a staunch supporter of the prince's right to the Lahore throne. Mirroring Suri's connections with the household and lineage of Kharak Singh (now of course vested in Chand Kaur, the protector/regent of Nau Nihal Singh's unborn child), some of Shah Muhammad's distinguished relatives had themselves served as clerks, gunners and military commanders within Sher Singh's court and camp. The poet himself had been born in the town of Batala, which had been part of Maharani Mehtab Kaur's estate before passing to her son Sher Singh, and which Shah Muhammad continued to frequent throughout his life.[33] All of this probably encouraged the poet to be loyal to Sher Singh's cause and, above all, provided him with access to valuable information and ideas from the perspective of the prince and his supporters.

On the other hand, Suri's account takes the side of the Maharani and reflects such grave concerns of misrule and cruelty on to Sher Singh instead. He records how 'mischievous Singhs' raised as troops for the prince's cause wreaked havoc on Lahore after capturing the fort in January 1841, setting out to plunder the bazaars and properties of the local people, and paying no heed to the orders of the new Maharajah or the *durbar*'s officials.[34] Above all, in perhaps the most scathing criticism offered by the otherwise subtle chronicler, Suri records with horror how Sher Singh secretly ordered for 'hot medicines' to be administered to Nau Nihal Singh's widows, to ensure that they miscarried any pregnancies:

> After finishing with the establishment of his sway in Lahore, Shahzada Sher Singh began to behave in a very improper manner in the case of his dealings with the ladies of the deceased Kanwarji—in such a way that the tongue of the pen finds itself incompetent and bleeds with respect to their description. What should be written about it? When such kind of treatment and dealings take place with respect to the ladies of such great dignitaries ... what can be the nature of the treatment and situation of the other poor men?[35]

In this shocking passage, we gain evidence of the attempt made by Sher Singh to annihilate the chance of any other female contender coming forward against him. By forcibly terminating the widows' pregnancies, he could cut off their source of power and legitimacy as potential queen-regents. This would in turn enable him to establish his own lineage as the new rulers of the Empire—indeed, as soon as the fourth Maharajah was settled into power, he quickly involved his eldest son, Prince Partap Singh, in diplomatic activities with the British, continuing the forms of princely education and dynastic diplomacy that had marked his own childhood.[36]

Above all, however, what both this passage and Shah Muhammad's verses about Chand Kaur's power grab show is that passions at court were beginning to run undeniably high. Of course, we can make rough judgements about how each of the two writers was influenced to take sides in the succession struggle, and it is perhaps fair enough to suggest that their accounts are just as coloured by political biases and rivalries as the British colonial narratives that we saw earlier in this chapter. Yet, despite and beyond this, both sources amply demonstrate the emergence of a bigger problem: a significant disagreement that had arisen within the Punjab about the ability of women to continue playing a political role in the Empire. In particular, the rights and treatment of royal women had flared up as a major issue at the heart of a deeply contentious debate about who could claim to be the legitimate ruler. Perhaps this was an exacerbation of tensions that had been in existence for some time—maybe at least since Ranjit Singh had himself sought to restrict the powers of his female kin and other Punjabi *sardarnis*, notably setting aside his mother-in-law Sada Kaur—but any such endeavours had certainly been less strident and less overtly misogynistic than the new attacks on female power that emerged in 1840.

Both Sohan Lal Suri and Shah Muhammad portray the issue of women's roles as a 'high stakes' matter and, each in their own way, lament in deeply emotive terms how the respective Maharajah and Maharani were imperilling the moral order of society, by acting in ways that were perceived to violently overturn accepted gender norms for men or women. The two writers did not portray the infighting within the royal dynasty as simply mindless 'family drama' or 'court intrigue', but were clearly very fearful about the likely impact that either ruler could have on the safety and security of the lives of ordinary people. They even seem to partially echo the poignant and powerful critique made centuries before by Guru Nanak in his *Baburvani*, in which he too had portrayed how the mistreatment of elite women—usually the most protected and highly respected group of people in society—likely spelled disaster for the rest of the populace.

Soon after seizing control of the Sikh capital and terminating the pregnancies of his nephew's wives, Sher Singh had taken the final step in protecting himself against a renewed challenge for power, by secretly ordering the assassination of Chand Kaur. Rajah Dhyan Singh, the re-instated *vazir*, supposedly arranged for the Maharani's servant girls to beat their own mistress to death.[37] With this ugly episode, the newly forceful ideas about the limitations of women's role or ability as leaders became a definitive and powerful fact of life at court in Lahore, and in Sikh politics.

All of these important gendered shifts in the political world of this period have been entirely missed by commentators and scholars thus far, who—perhaps swept up in the increasingly dramatic turn of events within the Lahore *durbar* elite—have shown relatively little interest in the political role of women and the evolving culture surrounding the Punjabi monarchy. This oversight is particularly surprising because these very changes to royal and political culture had a considerable impact on how the government would run in the remaining years of the Sikh Empire's existence, with a major snowball effect on the positions of its last two rulers: the boy-king Maharajah Duleep Singh and his queen-regent mother, Maharani Jind Kaur.

The Royals versus the Rebel Army

Mother and son would come to the Lahore throne in 1843, for Sher Singh himself would not survive long as Maharajah. The Sandhawalia *sardars*, relatives of the unfortunate Chand Kaur, were under no illusions about who was behind her death. The *sardars* bided their time and slowly worked their way into Sher Singh's trust, only to turn the Lahore *durbar* upside down in the bloodiest manner one September day: killing off not only the Maharajah, but also his young son Prince Partap Singh and the minister Dhyan Singh, in a stunning *coup d'état*.

It was at this point that the 5-year-old Duleep Singh, Ranjit Singh's youngest son, was selected by the Sandhawalia *sardars* to be the next Maharajah. The fact that he was chosen by leading Sikh chiefs, rather than having seized or inherited the throne, in itself shows the major transformation that had taken place in the standing of the Punjabi monarchy in the three turbulent years since the 'double death' of Kharak Singh and Nau Nihal Singh. The boy was chosen over and above his older half-brothers: Sher Singh's own 'twin', Tara Singh, and his other adult siblings, Peshaura Singh, Kashmira Singh and Multana Singh. With this fresh outburst of violence, the authority of the imperial dynasty had been weakened even further, and the power to control the monarchical succession slipped entirely from royal hands.

This is not to say, however, that any of the *sardars* or other leading courtiers really managed to achieve a dominant sway over the throne either. Dhyan Singh's son, Rajah Hira Singh, managed to avenge his father's murder within a day, after swiftly issuing a rallying cry to a body of Sikh troops to support him in punishing the 'treacherous' Sandhawalia *sardars*. The soldiers backed Hira Singh at this pivotal moment, knowing that Maharajah Ranjit Singh himself had treated him much like a son. On this basis, the young Rajah (who was barely in his twenties) was able to take over as *vazir*—perhaps fulfilling his father's dream of becoming the most powerful man in the Empire, given that the new Maharajah whom he now 'served' as chief minister was but a child. At this point in time, Maharani Jind Kaur (unlike her predecessor, Chand Kaur) had little direct say in the affairs of her son's government and appears not to have been given room to act as Queen-Regent. But, in contrast with his father's long service at Ranjit Singh's and Nau Nihal Singh's side, Hira Singh's time in the sun would end rather quickly, even if his control of events was not quite as short-lived as the Sandhawalia *sardars*' had been. After being placed in charge, the new *vazir* set about trying to regain mastery over the state's finances. This endeavour would swiftly put him at odds with his erstwhile supporters: the soldiers he had hired to attack the Sandhawalia *sardars* and their followers.

As we saw in Chapter 3, Ranjit Singh had hired talented foreign mercenary generals from Europe and beyond to completely reshape the nature of the war bands that had previously fought for the *misls* and the united army of the Khalsa. The first Maharajah had kept the name of the *Fauj-i-Khalsa* ('Army of the Khalsa') for these remodelled military forces, in deference to the wider Sikh ethos of egalitarianism and in keeping with the humble naming of his government as the *Sarkar-i-Khalsa*. However, as we have already seen, this army was put to use in growing and defending a kingdom that would become increasingly dynastic and imperial in nature, overshadowing the authority of other Sikh elites and coming to act as a competitive player against other major regional powers, the Company and the Afghans.

In the first three decades of the nineteenth century, Ranjit Singh had achieved these goals by diversifying the nature of his armed forces: recruiting European generals to build new infantry and artillery units, but equally employing larger numbers of non-Sikh troops, particularly to work as foot-soldiers within these new regiments. It was only in the 1830s that more Sikhs began joining the army again, with their numbers amongst the infantry regiments finally beginning to rise. These regiments had previously been unpopular amongst Sikh men who had placed greater value on the cavalry, which was much more akin to the older style of hand-to-hand fighting on horseback adopted by previous generations of Sikh warriors, during the guerrilla wars fought in the era of Guru Gobind Singh and the *misls*.[38] In any case, although, ideally, more research needs to be done into the internal views of the Sikh Empire's army, there is a common understanding that the soldiers of the Khalsa Army as a whole were deeply loyal to Maharajah Ranjit

Singh, and were generally quite willing to follow his orders and policies, so long as they could be assured that they would definitely receive good pay and other rewards. The personal attention and pride Ranjit Singh gave to his armed forces was no small factor in creating this sense of loyalty.[39]

However, in the increasingly turbulent period of the early 1840s, the troops of this state army became a dangerous force to be reckoned with. With each successive power struggle that had erupted since the 'double death' of 1840, the soldiers had demanded ever higher sums in bribes from the various factions seeking to gain their assistance. This rapidly turned the Khalsa Army into a massive drain on the royal coffers. The monthly pay of a soldier rose from its 1839 level of Rs. 9.9 to Rs. 14 by 1843–4. The number of troops on the state payroll also increased, from around 35,000 men to over 51,000.[40] We saw in Suri's account of the Chand Kaur/Sher Singh civil war his great fear and dismay at the unchecked manner in which the so-called 'mischievous Singhs' had been able to loot and ransack the city of Lahore, after they had broken through Chand Kaur's garrison of the main fort. Three years later, by 1843, the Khalsa Army was effectively able to act as kingmaker within the imperial state. As such, they could dictate terms to the Lahore *durbar* about what their pay and orders should be, rather than accepting commands from the royals or their ministers.

In this context, it is not surprising that, as the Empire's leading minister, Hira Singh would have tried to curb such expenditure and wrest back control over the reins of government. However, by the time of his coup, another fairly momentous change had taken place in the internal workings of the Army: most critically, the soldiery had begun to throw off the more 'foreign' style of military discipline imposed upon them from the early years of Ranjit Singh's reign, and had instead adopted their own form of self-management. By 1843–4 they had begun asserting a more actively political 'Khalsa' identity, against both their generals and the Lahore *durbar*. They seized the much more tangible 'kingmaking' authority that they had been able to gain through the court elite's repeated bribery since the clash between Sher Singh and Chand Kaur, and swiftly conducted an internal revolution of power within their own ranks. The troops replaced the formal system of military discipline that had been imposed by Ranjit Singh and his generals, instead instituting a *panchayat* system of self-governance. Soldiers would gather together within their regiments and elect leaders from amongst themselves, who would then represent them at the highest level, deciding on matters for the Army as a whole and delivering its demands to the government.

These political gatherings amongst the military were similar to the kind of local-government-via-village-council that the *panchayat* had traditionally embodied within Indian society, but also harked back to the foundation of the Khalsa *panth* (holy community) by Guru Gobind Singh.[41] As we saw in Chapter 1, the last Guru had anointed five Sikhs as the first members of the new, sovereign order, who were then to 'baptise' him as a Khalsa too. These five Sikhs became known as the Guru's *Panj Pyare* ('Five Beloved Ones') and gave rise to the idea that, wherever five true Sikhs gathered, they could form a sovereign spiritual council amongst themselves, guided by the teachings of the *Guru Granth Sahib*.[42] This new Sikh concept carried echoes of a north Indian phrase common in Jatt society: '*pānch panch parmeswara*', meaning that 'five *panches* or council-members are like five gods' or 'where five *panches* are sitting there is God'.[43] It also marked a partial return to, or an echo of, the old-style *gurmata* assembly system from the earliest days of the post-Guru *misls*.

All of these startling changes within the Khalsa Army were observed closely by the intelligence officers of the East India Company's political affairs department. Whilst several British officials seem to have been aware of the history of the Khalsa and the notion of *pānch panch parmeswara*, it is interesting to note how British magazines and journals at the time consistently conflated the Army's increasing self-assertion with a shift towards republicanism, with the rebellious Sikh soldiers repeatedly likened to the Praetorian Guard of the Roman Republic.[44] We do not have exact details for how and when this shift in the internal self-governance of the Army was first precipitated, nor we do know what individual soldiers themselves thought of the changes, nor the extent to which they all participated in the new political situation. But it is fundamentally clear that power had passed out of the hands of the Lahore *durbar* and into that of the military as a whole, a detachment of which stationed itself permanently in the capital city to ensure that this remained the case.

And so, when Hira Singh attempted to cut down on the pay and privileges of the Khalsa Army, it was no surprise that such a move cut little ice with the soldiers. Added to this inflammatory situation was the fact that the young *vazir* had also managed to make an enemy of Jind Kaur, or Rani Jindan as she was popularly known. The Maharani was equally the subject of Hira Singh's austerity plans, to her bitter resentment. The final straw appears to have been when the minister reprimanded her for spending large sums of money on alms for Brahmin mendicants.[45] In December 1844, Jind Kaur went to the *panchayat* of the Khalsa Army and complained angrily about Hira Singh's disrespect towards her, demanding that the soldiers respect her honour as the widow of Ranjit Singh and remove the *vazir* from his post. One source even goes so far as claiming that Hira Singh and his former tutor, Pandit Jallah, 'had been in the habit of sending for the Ranee at night, and by threats of ill treatment compelling her to allow of criminal intercourse with her.'[46] Whatever the case, Jindan's complaints were enough to move the Army to action: they swiftly descended upon Hira Singh and Jallah and took their lives.

From this point onward, the Maharani was able to take direct charge of affairs at Lahore. Jind Kaur was the youngest and most junior of all Ranjit Singh's wives. Though a Sikh, she had not come from an elite *misl* family, but was the daughter of one of the court kennel keepers.[47] It is thought that Jindan was married to the Maharajah through a *chadar dalni* ceremony of 'protection through marriage', and it is clear that she only gained a more prominent position when she bore Ranjit Singh a son in the last year of his life. Even then, no one had expected Duleep to get anywhere near the throne—at the time of his father's death, he was at the bottom end of the princely pecking order; seemingly in recognition of this fact, he and his mother had lived a rather quiet existence in one of Dhyan Singh's *havelis* in Jammu, until their very sudden rise to power in 1843.

Most likely because of this background, Jindan appears to have been much less politically experienced than her female predecessors at the outset of her reign. On being made Regent by the Khalsa Army in December 1844, she swiftly passed her governing responsibilities to the men in her life: her brother, Rajah Jawahir Singh, and her former bodyguard (and reputed lover) Rajah Lal Singh; as well as the ministers of the *durbar*, including men such as Diwan Dina Nath, Bhai Ram Singh and the Fakirs Nuruddin and Azizuddin, who had held office since Ranjit Singh's reign and had provided the Lahore government with a basic element of stability and continuity despite the clashes over the succession. Despite this bank of experienced advisors, the challenges facing the Maharani's new government were no different from what Hira Singh had been grappling with. The Army still needed to be reined in politically, and the overspending on their wages required urgent control if the treasury was not to be completely depleted.

The government's grip on the wider reaches of the Empire had also weakened as a result of these events. During Kharak Singh's reign (June 1839 to November 1840), the Lahore *durbar* had managed to fulfil its friendship treaty obligations to the Company during the ongoing war with the Afghans, and had even added new territory to the Empire, through the conquest of land up to Ladakh under the aegis of Rajah Gulab Singh (Dhyan Singh's brother) and the talented Sikh general Zorawar Singh. Even in Sher Singh's reign (18 January 1841 to 15 September 1843), the regional administration of the interior seems to have gone on reasonably well. However, a growing problem that first emerged during his time in power had become a major issue by the time Jindan became Queen-Regent at the end of 1844: a number of the leading nobles of the Lahore *durbar* were increasingly spending time away from the troubled royal court, in order to concentrate their efforts on consolidating their personal control over their landed estates. This would ensure that they could maintain their own wealth and status no matter what happened to the central government. The most notorious exemplar of this kind of behaviour was Rajah Gulab Singh.

Unlike his brother Dhyan, who apparently was greatly desirous of maintaining a powerful position at the heart of the Lahore *durbar*, Gulab Singh was much more wary of becoming implicated in its increasingly treacherous political vortex. To some extent, he was justified in feeling this way, since he had seen it take four lives in his family: his brother Dhyan Singh, his nephew Hira Singh, and another brother and nephew along the way.[48] All evidence points to Gulab Singh quietly working to transform the Dogra family's extensive estates in Jammu and Kashmir into an independent powerbase. He kept carefully aloof of all demands to get involved in the Lahore government and aimed, as far as possible, to get away with not paying revenues to the state. Gulab Singh's actions, and those of other like-minded members of the Punjabi aristocracy, effectively echoed the behaviour of the Mughal nobility in the declining stages of that Empire; they also suggested a return to the power struggles that had once put Ranjit Singh's Sukerchakia *misl* in power. Now, that same dynamic between *misls* and kingdoms was threatening to play out against the royal dynasty, unless they could find a way to re-establish their authority.

These problems were compounded by the fact that the Army, though claiming to represent the Khalsa *panth*, was also apparently doing little to help with maintaining law and order throughout the Empire. Admittedly, the only sources we have to go on about the activities of the 'mutinous' soldiery are written from the perspective of either the Punjabi elite or British colonial officers, and obviously neither group was going to look on the Army's political manoeuvring with a kindly eye. From this material, all we can see is that the Sikh soldiers were increasingly telling family members in their home villages to turn a blind eye to the demands of the *kardars* (state revenue officials) and instead, for more young men to come and join the Army, where they could enjoy high salaries.[49] This created a vicious circle that proved increasingly impossible for the Lahore *durbar* to undo, since it reduced the amount of revenue that they could draw upon to meet the demands of the Army's representatives, whilst simultaneously augmenting the cost of military wages that they were expected to pay out.

The only figure who managed to have some semblance of influence over the Army at this point was Jind Kaur herself. Though she had handed over practical, day-to-day responsibility for the governance of the Empire to her appointed ministers, with her brother acting as her *vazir*, the Maharani maintained a direct relationship with the *panchayat* of the Khalsa Army, which appears to have been integral to providing a modicum of stability in relations between the *durbar* and the soldiers for the first year or so after Hira Singh's removal.

In formal courtly gatherings, the young Maharajah would typically be seated at the front with his mother behind him, screened from public view by a curtain. However, Jind Kaur was flexible with her maintenance of *purdah* in such situations; when she felt there was a need, she wilfully chose to confront the Army directly. At times, she would reportedly harangue the soldiers with harsh, emasculating words from behind her curtain, to humiliate them into doing what they were told. At other times, she would cast the *purdah* aside with electrifying effect: 'on one occasion, when the Durbar was terrified by a crowd of drunken and disorderly soldiers, she came out from behind her curtain, threw aside her veil, and addressed the people. The men were delighted, for she was young and handsome.'[50] Jindan is known to have independently addressed up to 2,000 armed men in such a manner—apparently against the wishes of her male ministers.

She may well have had less direct political experience than her female predecessors when she first came to power, but Jindan would surely have been well aware of the precedent for female authority that had existed within the Punjab since the days of the *misls*, which had equally involved Sikh women in managing armed forces. She also supposedly admired and sought to emulate a character we met in the previous chapter: Begum Samru of Sardhana, an Indian woman of relatively humble origin who had married a European mercenary, but who was widowed at a young age and thereafter managed to turn her deceased husband's estate into a small but mighty kingdom, which she had ruled with great alacrity until her own death in 1836.[51] Jindan's behaviour with the Army and at court demonstrates how aware she was of the symbolic authority she wielded as the widow of Ranjit Singh and the mother of the Maharajah. More interestingly, though, it also suggests that after becoming Queen-Regent she grew in confidence, developing her own personal style of politics, which ably manipulated gender conventions to exert control over the men who surrounded her. In particular, her manipulation of the observation or discarding of *purdah* would become a signature political tool, enabling her to include or exclude different people at will. This subverts the standard Orientalist idea of Indian women being 'imprisoned' by *purdah*, with Jindan's example highlighting how, in certain circumstances, it could actually be very useful for creatively asserting female agency and even enhancing a queen's power.

However, Jind Kaur was only able to keep the army in check for so long. By 1845, the volatility of its demands was increasing again, coupled with growing threats against both the Maharani and the young Maharajah, to replace them with two of the remaining princes, Peshaura Singh and Kashmira Singh, unless the mother and son delivered up higher wages and emoluments. The Army thus fell back upon its kingmaker card in order to wrench back control from the stabilising Lahore *durbar*. Jawahir Singh, Jindan's brother and *vazir*, reacted rashly to this ultimatum, and secretly ordered for the two princes to be captured and murdered. On receiving the news that Peshaura Singh had been killed, Jawahir Singh reportedly began celebrating in his palace apartments, in the premature belief that he had managed to get the best of the tricky situation with the Army. The Maharani's brother had gained a particularly notorious reputation in British intelligence reports and government correspondence for his 'debauched' and self-indulgent behaviour. Such colonial records painted him as an entirely unruly and immoral influence on Jindan's government, and British officials were most concerned by his volatile shifts in decision-making: alarmingly, the minister would threaten on a whim to send the Army into war with the British, so that they could loot British-Indian territories instead of ransacking the state treasury; but then he suddenly hit upon the drastic plan of killing off the Army's princely leverage.[52]

The latter decision would cost Jawahir Singh his life, for the Khalsa Army's senior representatives were incensed when they heard about Peshaura Singh's murder. Again, on the pretext that the killing of one of Ranjit Singh's sons was a treasonous act, Jawahir Singh was summoned into the camp of the Army *panchayat* for punishment. The petrified *vazir* took his young nephew, the Maharajah, with him on his own elephant, in the hope that this would save his life, but the Sikh soldiery were not willing to take prisoners and set upon him in droves, throwing Duleep Singh into the arms of his mother, who watched on helplessly as her brother was slain.

The murder of Jawahir Singh even became a widely discussed, near-infamous incident in press coverage within Britain. A cartoon depicting the *vazir* being dragged off his elephant by a snarling bunch of sword-wielding Sikhs appeared on the front page of the popular new magazine the *Illustrated London News*, in the same month as war broke out in the Punjab—effectively painting life at Lahore as being dictated by dangerous savages.[53] Indeed, leaving aside the Orientalist tint of this view, the minister's brutal murder has long been regarded as the pivotal event that supposedly led to the eventual outbreak of war between the Sikh Army and the East India Company, rupturing the relationship that had been the cornerstone of the Lahore government's foreign policy for decades. Maharani Jind Kaur is the central figure in this version of events, which was popularised throughout the Punjab in the stirring verses of Shah Muhammad. As the story goes, Jindan was so bitter and distraught at the loss of her brother that she vowed to get her revenge by destroying the Khalsa Army:

> For nothing do they [the soldiers] demand rewards and twelve rupees.
> If I am a Jat's daughter then I shall have the whole Punjab widowed.
> Desolation shall reign supreme over this entire land.
> They shall not be left honourable enough to enter Lahore—
> Not just the officers, but also the subalterns.
> Their corpses shall rot in the foreign lands,
> O Shah Mohammed! So thoroughly shall
> I have this *Desh* [country] destroyed![54]

In Shah Muhammad's telling, the Maharani planned to deliberately incite the Khalsa Army into war with the Company, in full hope that they would be massacred by the British—thus satisfying her burning desire for revenge. It is for this reason that the poet talks of the soldiers' 'corpses dying in a foreign land' (or being 'trampled on', to translate his words as directly as possible): in order to provoke a war with the Company, the Sikh Army would need to be ordered to cross the River Sutlej and thereby break with one of the core principles of the 1809 friendship pact that Ranjit Singh had signed with Sir Charles Metcalfe, prohibiting either side from encroaching on the other's territories.

However, the day-to-day intelligence records of the British political department in India, as well as the one surviving account written by a member of the Lahore *durbar* itself, present a starkly more complicated picture of events. As we know, the Company authorities had long kept a close eye on the political affairs of the Punjab;

but as the scene grew ever more violent and volatile, the intensity of their surveillance had also increased. The military leaders of the Company's armed forces were particularly concerned about the rapidly inflating size of the Khalsa Army: not solely because of the threat that this could pose to British-Indian territories, but also, for a long time, out of fear that knowledge of the Sikh troops' considerably higher wages could provoke desertion attempts on the part of the Company's own sepoys, who could be tempted to flee and join the Sikh soldiers or, even worse, launch a mutiny if they decided to make militant demands for similar pay increases.[55]

Under the new Governor-General of India, Sir Henry Hardinge (1844–8), steps were gradually taken to build up the British-Punjabi frontier with military reinforcements, and a bridge of boats was even carefully prepared, to enable Company troops to easily cross the Sutlej themselves, should the British be switched into a directly aggressive policy against the Sikhs.[56] This enhanced military presence on the border greatly perturbed both the Lahore *durbar* and the soldiers of the Khalsa Army.[57] The suspicion of the British was mirrored on the other side of the Sutlej, perhaps even more so because the Punjabis had just witnessed the Company annex the formerly semi-independent states of the Amirs of Sindh. By the winter of 1845, these developments had given rise to significant concern in the Punjab—bordering on panic—that Hardinge and his generals had a similar fate in mind for the Sikh Empire, not least after Company troops occupied the disputed border town of Ferozepore, which Ranjit Singh himself had claimed as part of his own territory.

The rarely cited memoir of a Lahore courtier, Diwan Ajudhia Parshad, provides us with fascinating alternative insights into Jind Kaur's position at this point in time. In this account, the Maharani was certainly greatly traumatised and enraged by the cold-blooded murder of her brother, but calmed down within a few days or weeks, and managed to reconcile herself with her loss. Far from baying for blood, Jindan supposedly tried her hardest to find a peaceable solution whereby she could avoid the onset of a war with the British and tame the Khalsa Army. According to Ajudhia Parshad, the two problems had fused into one, since the Army itself had begun demanding that the *durbar* support it in making war on the

Company, so that the Sikh troops could give a fitting answer to the provocations made by the British, and also have the enjoyment of looting their territories in India.[58]

This version of events is credibly backed up by the testimony of British intelligence records. These show that the Sikh soldiers did not blame Jind Kaur for Peshaura Singh's assassination, but sought to punish the men around her instead. Despite this, they were determined to remain in control of the Maharani. They agreed to keep her in power so long as she 'would move into their camp, and let them see her unveiled whenever they thought proper.' They also reportedly separated her by force from her new *vazir*, Lal Singh, whom the British records at least portrayed as being her lover. According to these documents, the Sikh soldiers protested against her 'open co-habitation' with her Hindu minister, who had formerly acted as bodyguard to her and young Duleep; as a punishment, the Army placed him in irons for dishonouring 'the mother of all the Sikhs'. Intriguingly, they supposedly recommended that the Maharani 'take a husband as she seems to dislike solitude', but restricted her choice to a 'Sirdar, Akalee or wise man'.[59]

Although Jindan managed to avoid having her marriage arranged for her by her soldiers, she was nevertheless trapped in a highly sensitive situation. Her ability to assert herself politically had proven short-lived and, if anything, had created something of a backlash against her. The legacy of animosity towards female power that had crept in so significantly during the ousting of Chand Kaur was beginning to make itself felt once again, leaving Jind Kaur with rapidly decreasing room for manoeuvre.

All of this information was compiled through the intelligence network that had initially been established by Claude Martin Wade, but which would be extended further in the 1840s by the Company's new Political Agent on the Northwestern Frontier, Major George Broadfoot. Unlike Wade or even Henry Lawrence, Broadfoot was no friend to the Sikhs; he was actively hoping for a war in the Punjab. His letters and reports reveal in further detail how and why the Maharani completely lost control over events in her own kingdom.

As we know, Rajah Gulab Singh had been doing his best to evade lending a hand to the Lahore government, and dodging demands that he pay his dues to the state coffers. The *durbar* had been forced to send troops repeatedly to his enclave in Jammu in order to bring him to task, but on each occasion he had managed to bribe the soldiers into leniency, so that he could hold on to his extensive wealth and territories. The Rajah appears to have been wise enough to know that this tactic would only carry him so far. He therefore secretly made overtures to Broadfoot and Hardinge throughout 1845, seeking to cut a deal with them that could safeguard his interests in Jammu and Kashmir once and for all. In August of that year, he promised to provide an army of at least 40,000 men to fight the Sikhs and claimed that he could induce 'nearly every chiefship in the hills from our frontier to Affghanistan and Tartary, including Cashmere...to revolt against the Sikhs and submit to the British'; thus dividing 'the Durbar, the Country and the army...and [leaving] the Capital open to the British, who would not have to fire a shot.'[60]

The Dogra Rajah was apparently under the impression that the British government had limited the Company's power, meaning that it could not outrightly annex the Punjab, and that if their two armies did go to war, the worst that could happen was that the Khalsa troops would be disbanded and a Resident and British force stationed at Lahore, perhaps adding Duleep Singh's Empire to the Sikh states already under British protection. This situation would have been perfect for Gulab Singh and the chiefs supporting him, because it would safeguard their own positions, while removing the threat to their lives posed by the mutinous Army. All that remained was to push the Sikhs into crossing the Sutlej, so that the Company would have a legitimate pretext for attacking and destroying them.

To this very end, Gulab Singh had been bribing the Khalsa soldiers since April 1845, gradually bringing them round to his favour.[61] They seem to have been willing to go along with him, as having a male leader would have appeared less complicated than the continuance of their frustrations with Jind Kaur and her refusal to live and act in the meek manner that they desired. On the eve of the outbreak of war in December 1845, Gulab Singh's influence over the Army had reached such a peak that the *panchayat* issued a declaration to the Maharani, threatening that if she did not raise their pay, they would replace her with the Dogra Rajah as Regent and *vazir* for the remainder of Duleep Singh's minority. Only two weeks prior to this, Jindan had just about managed to preserve her position against another deposition attempt: during a trip to the treasury in Amritsar to withdraw funds for the payment of the Army, she had been forced to return rapidly to Lahore on hearing that the Khalsa was claiming that she had absconded with Duleep to his Cis-Sutlej territories. They had then attempted to replace the young Maharajah with one of Sher Singh's sons, Shahzadah Shiv Deo, and Jindan as effective ruler with Gulab Singh in the position of *vazir*.[62]

These events convinced Jindan that she had lost all authority. Whereas immediately after her brother's death in October, she still commanded enough loyalty to warrant her being maintained in power, by December she could no longer rely on this. Instead she faced threats of imprisonment or death if she opposed the Army's appointment of Gulab Singh as *vazir* in place of her own minister Lal Singh. At no time was she given any indication by her government's erstwhile ally, Governor-General Hardinge, of the kinds of treasonous activity that Gulab Singh had been orchestrating behind her back. It seems entirely fair, then, to argue that the war began at the end of 1845 not because the Maharani lost control of her emotions after her brother's murder and lashed out, but because her political rivals managed to get the best of her. In both British colonial documents and the testimony of the courtier Ajudhia Parshad, Jindan is described as being powerless and confused about how to address the threatening British presence at Ferozepur. The charge levelled against her that she wished to avenge her brother's death does not stand up at all in light of the evidence present in these records. As Lahore became increasingly lawless, with funds in the state treasury running dry and their lives very much on the line, Jind Kaur and Duleep really had no choice but to sanction the invasion of Company territory.

These circumstances have not been given the attention they deserve in histories of the deteriorating situation both within the Sikh Empire and in its relations with the British. I have here tried to stitch together a partially revisionist narrative of this critical turning point in the Empire's history, drawing on the richer expanse of source material available on the day-by-day events leading up to the war of 1845–6. However, this is not just a new, 'more authentic' narrative of 'what caused the war'. There is a lot to reflect on in all of this. Firstly, there is the obvious—if somewhat incredible—fact that, despite the heightened tensions between the Sikh Army and the royal government, there was no apparent desire on the part of the former to take over from the latter or to dispose of the monarchy entirely. The presence of so many remaining princes certainly gave the Army valuable leverage against the Maharani's regency, which perhaps rendered it is unnecessary for the Army *panchayat* to bother with assuming complete control. Nevertheless, it is fascinating to see how the relationship between the royals and the rebellious soldiers and ministers was gradually reset in these few years, forcing the monarchy and its more loyalist courtiers to effectively act as the servants of the 'Khalsa Army'.

In the midst of all this, it is unmistakable how gendered the evolving conversation about royal power became. It is somewhat ironic that Maharani Jind Kaur should today be the most famous of all the Punjab's queens, since she had started out as the least well-known and most junior of Ranjit Singh's many wives. Her fame, however, is not entirely positive: as we'll see more clearly in the next chapter, the array of popular narratives that have been spun about her role in the two Anglo-Sikh Wars as well as her private life have given her an entirely divided reputation. Jindan is either a self-centred slave to her passions, or a noble queen and model mother. There is no doubt that the political circumstances in which Jindan and Duleep found themselves between September 1843 and November 1845 were of unprecedented difficulty and danger, incomparable with the less serious challenges to Punjabi royals who had come before them. The intense political drama of their lives makes it unsurprising that they should be the subject of popular interest, not least because their reigns marked the fateful climax of the Sikh Empire's fortunes. But what we should object to is any narrative that seeks to treat Jindan and Duleep—a young Queen-Regent and an even younger Maharajah—as somehow 'exceptional' for having ruled as a woman or as a child.

As we have seen throughout this book, within both the Sukerchakia *misl* and the imperial dynasty that emerged from it, *sardarnis*, queens and princes were repeatedly pushed to take on responsibility in complex and challenging political circumstances, which they managed to juggle with great success on multiple occasions. Only by placing Jindan and Duleep into this broader cultural and political story can we begin to understand the terms on which they came into power, and the true nature of the opportunities and challenges that they were faced with by the mid-1840s. Alongside this, we must recognise that the gendered dynamics of the internal dynastic struggle for the throne were but one facet of a renewed, overall struggle for power that emerged in the Punjab during this period, one that involved not only royals but also scheming courtiers and rebellious soldiers. This tussle over who had legitimate authority to decide the Sikh Empire's fate was arguably interconnected with the origins of Sikh politics, and not just precipitated by Ranjit Singh's departure from the scene. The sequence of events outlined over the last few pages presents compelling evidence that the reign of Jindan and Duleep suffered not from new problems arising out of their own incompetence as a 'mere' woman and boy, but rather from a flaring up of key political contentions dating to the early stages of Sukerchakia power, further complicating the Maharani's ability to rule.

In the opportunistic, self-preserving activities of figures like Gulab Singh, we can see parallels with the ambitious manner in which the *sardars* of the eighteenth century had endeavoured to consolidate their own powerbases and to project themselves into a new tier of royalty—for the Rajah did succeed in leveraging his secret deal with Hardinge and Broadfoot, becoming the new Maharajah of Jammu and Kashmir by March 1846. Similarly, in the Army's activities we may able to perceive a throwback to the short-lived era of rule by *gurmata* assembly—perhaps as an endeavour to impose a particular understanding of Khalsa norms on an increasingly cosmopolitan ruling elite, and to restore power to the *panth* rather than letting it remain in the hands of the increasingly centralised imperial state. One question beyond the scope of this book, which could do with further research, is this: when the soldiers told their family members to avoid paying taxes to the Empire's revenue collectors, and instead to join their ranks, were they echoing the actions of their forefathers and seeking to establish a form of *Khalsa raj* alternative to the self-styled *Sarkar-i-Khalsa* ruling from Lahore? Or was this really an army that had descended into nothing more than 'mob rule', invoking the Khalsa identity in name only, and seizing the opportunity of stripping wealth and power from its weakened leaders?

Taken together, the struggles with the Army, the land grabs and secret 'backstage' deals by ambitious *sardars* and ministers, and the internal battles within the royal dynasty were all ways in which the new political struggle of the 1840s played out 'live' in the Punjab. However, looking beyond this, and returning to the points that I raised at the very outset of this chapter, we equally need to acknowledge that this was a struggle unfolding in a discursive way, within the pages of the new 'histories' being written by various interested individuals at the time of, or hot on the heels of, events themselves. Perhaps most explicitly in this chapter, we have been able to witness the increasingly direct interplay between words, events and lived experiences, and how this real-time writing of history shaped the evolving fortunes of the Punjabi kingdom after Ranjit Singh's death in 1839.

The impact of the written word on live politics will come out even more vividly in the next chapter. For, although the Khalsa Army proved to be a much more formidable enemy in the field than Hardinge and his generals had planned for, it was eventually beaten down by the Company—thanks in a large part to the treachery of the Sikhs' own commanders, the notorious Lal Singh and Tej Singh. In March 1846, the British were able to enter the gates of Lahore for the first time not as invited guests, but as conquerors, with bold plans to rewrite the future of the Punjab.

5

THE BOY-KING, THE REBEL QUEEN AND THE BRITISH EMPIRE

At the Battle of Sobraon on 10 February 1846, the Khalsa Army suffered a bitter defeat. The East India Company's Governor-General, Henry Hardinge, knew that the opportunity to take over the entire Sikh Empire was now in his grasp. Thousands of the Punjab's finest soldiers had lost their lives in the battle, which was one of the fiercest fought by British officers and Company sepoys anywhere in India. There was no way that Khalsa forces would be able to regroup quickly enough to mount a renewed challenge against British arms. Yet, within ten days of this battle, the Governor-General had declared peace in the Punjab and had formally re-instated the young Maharajah Duleep Singh on his throne in the Lahore fort.

What prompted Hardinge to pursue such a course of action, especially having allied with the double-dealing Rajah Gulab Singh to purposefully bring on the war in the first place? It appears from the Governor-General's private documents that, though he had been keen to decimate the Khalsa Army, he was very wary of the considerable risk and expense of embarking on a wholesale annexation of the Punjab. The territories of the Sikh Empire were vast, spreading out from the River Sutlej to the border with Afghanistan in the northwest, and those with Tibet and Nepal in the northeast. To add to the complications weighing on Hardinge's government, the Company's finances were in a bad way. It could in no way contemplate scaling up its own army to the extent that would be required to mount and sustain the total occupation of Duleep Singh's entire kingdom. It therefore seems wholly fair to judge Hardinge's policy in fighting the First Anglo-Sikh War as a very intriguing example of a carefully calculated risk. By going to war, he evidently sought to neutralise the threat of the Khalsa Army and a hostile government at Lahore, averting any risk that they could invade and occupy British territory in India; but he, equally, endeavoured to end the fighting as quickly and cheaply as possible, cutting deals with any players who could be bought for the Company's benefit, so that affairs within the Punjab could be brought under more effective (though still indirect) British control.

Certainly, behind the defeat of the Khalsa Army there lies the infamous 'treachery' of three key figures from the Punjabi ruling elite. Sardar Tej Singh, the army's unpopular Commander-in-Chief, passed intelligence to the Company's generals and enabled his own troops to be massacred at the Battle of Sobraon. He ordered a hasty retreat across the River Sutlej, whilst allegedly allowing the Khalsa Army's bridge of boats to be damaged, so that around 20,000 fleeing Sikh soldiers were tragically left to drown or be killed by the Company sepoys firing at their backs. Rajah Lal Singh, Jind Kaur's *vazir*, also passed military intelligence to a British officer, with a view to securing his own safety against the Army that had earlier threatened to depose and kill him. Whether the Maharani herself knew about this has been a matter of inconclusive debate amongst historians, who have noted that Lal Singh used her name in his secret dealings with British military officers, but it is unclear if he did this with her knowledge or consent.[1] And, last but not least, Rajah Gulab Singh of course played a leading role in orchestrating the entire conflict. He was subsequently 'rewarded' with his own kingdom in Jammu and Kashmir, as part of the peace treaty forced on the Lahore government by him (as acting *vazir*) and Hardinge in March 1846. None of these men acted in concert with one another, as they were all very much looking out for themselves. They would go on to take leading political offices after the war ended, but the rivalries and tensions that their earlier activities gave rise to would cause immense problems for Jind Kaur's regency government going forward.

Altogether, we can see that going to war on such terms had been an incredibly risky gamble for Hardinge and the Company, but one that paid off handsomely when they emerged as victors after the

Battle of Sobraon. In this chapter we will see what happened next: how and why Hardinge and his deputies in the Punjab chose to continue supporting the royal family at Lahore after beating their Army in the field. This policy went hand-in-hand with plans to 'reform' the nature of the Sikh monarchy and its royal culture in a way that was intended to make Punjabi politics a more stabilised affair. This suited British interests in the region, but created complications over time, particularly by unravelling further the gendered dynamics underlying the rule of Ranjit Singh's dynasty—culminating in disaster for the Sikh Empire as a whole by 1848–9.

The treaty negotiations carried out in March 1846 set in train Hardinge's policy to restore the Punjabi royal government on a test basis. His aim was to see whether the state of affairs within the Sikh Empire could be re-organised for the kingdom to act once again as a useful buffer between British India and the rest of South and Central Asia. The volatility of the Khalsa Army and the inability of Jind Kaur's government to handle the situation had certainly shaken up the Company's leading men, especially after they witnessed the strength of the Sikh soldiery on the battlefield. Leveraging the support of the ambitious Rajah Gulab Singh, a peace treaty was designed to make sure that no future threat could emerge from within the kingdom itself against Company territories. The initial Treaty of Lahore mandated that around two thirds of Duleep Singh's Empire would be annexed by the Company. The fertile and lucrative region of Jalandhar Doab, to the east of the Maharajah's kingdom, was put directly under British colonial rule, extending the boundary of the Company's Indian territory up from the River Sutlej to the River Beas. The provinces of Jammu and Kashmir were also removed from Sikh control and given to Gulab Singh and his heirs in perpetuity to form their own new kingdom, as a 'reward' for his services in arranging the treaty.

This new independent state under Maharajah Gulab Singh and the advanced British frontier, now encircled the remaining rump of Ranjit Singh's former Empire. The British were now only a very short march away from the capital of Lahore—if the Khalsa Army or Duleep Singh's government were to turn hostile again in the future, Company forces backed by the troops of Gulab Singh would be able to attack the Punjab from two fronts. It was a deal that would infuriate Maharani Jind Kaur and many of the Khalsa soldiery, when they learnt that Gulab Singh was going to profit from their wartime defeat. From a completely different and more modern perspective, however, it is also striking how eerily close the new borders imposed by the 1846 division of Punjabi territory came to foreshadowing the boundary lines drawn up a century later by the British lawyer, Cyril Radcliffe, when he partitioned the Punjab between independent India and Pakistan, leaving the princely state of Jammu and Kashmir to decide its own fate in the midst of the deeply troubled region.

The Treaty of Lahore's other two major requirements were the payment of a heavy war indemnity and, most critically, for the power of the Khalsa Army to be neutralised. Hardinge demanded that the number of soldiers in the Army's core regiments be dramatically reduced; that any guns that had been pointed at Company troops be surrendered into British control; and that the pay of the remaining military force be cut to the level that had been paid in Ranjit Singh's day.[2] All of these clauses were part of the attempt to protect British India from any further possible Sikh insurrections. It was an especially clever strategy on the Governor-General's part to leave this onerous responsibility at the door of the Lahore *durbar*. Reining in the Khalsa Army was a mammoth task that would make anyone who endeavoured to accomplish it deeply unpopular—as had been shown time and again in the run-up to the war. Hardinge remained consistently averse to getting British hands dirty by directly implicating the Company in such work, which would have been necessary had formal indirect rule or an annexation been imposed on the Sikh Empire at this time.[3] On the basis of such calculations, he instead set in train a 'watch and wait' policy, to see how Jind Kaur and her government would fare with the job. This would allow deliberation over a longer period as to whether greater British intervention in the Punjab would be worthwhile.

This policy of Hardinge differed from that followed by his predecessors towards other troubled Indian states. Typically, following a breakdown in relations between the Company and an Indian ruler (usually after a trading alliance ended in war or the near-bankruptcy of a kingdom's finances), the Company would set up what was known as a 'subsidiary alliance' with a dependent royal government.

The specific agreements of such treaties could vary from state to state, but the key purpose of a subsidiary alliance was essentially to enable the Company to impose 'indirect rule' over a kingdom: by preventing its rulers from having an independent foreign or military policy, and forcing them to fire any Europeans in their employment, as well as banning them from hiring anyone apart from British officials approved by the Company. The Indian ruler was typically enabled (or made) to have a 'Resident' British officer based at their capital together with a British garrison, which—at the local ruler's expense—would protect the local government from any internal or external aggression.

This arrangement enabled the Company to exert considerable formal and direct interference in the administration of an Indian kingdom, in contrast with the role of a Political Agent like Claude Martin Wade, which tended to be focused more on diplomacy and information-gathering. Essentially, the Indian ruler locked into a 'subsidiary alliance' would have control over their own internal administration, but little else, and would have to acknowledge the British as the 'paramount power' in India.[4] All of these conditions were applied to the Sikh Empire in the Treaty of Lahore by Hardinge, with one all-important exception: the imposition of a British Resident and garrison. This omission signalled that the Governor-General was wary of wading too deeply into the choppy waters of the Sikh Empire's politics.

Hardinge was certainly determined that the Punjab would never again be entirely independent, but nevertheless declared privately to his leading deputy in the region, the Political Agent Henry Montgomery Lawrence, that its government should ideally be either 'Sikh or British'. By this, Hardinge meant that either the Company would have to take over the region entirely, or that Duleep Singh's government should control the region with as little drama as possible—nothing in between.[5] The latter option was the ideal way for the Company to maintain the security of its north-western frontier, and it was Hardinge's preferred outcome—no doubt influenced by the multiple ways in which the Company had been burnt before, during attempts to intervene more aggressively in the politics of Asian countries such as Afghanistan, Burma and Nepal.[6] However, the initial Treaty of Lahore's incredibly challenging demands on the weakened imperial state left Jind Kaur and her ministers in a very complex situation. They needed to pay off the war indemnity and cut down the Khalsa Army in order to safeguard the future independence of the kingdom; but they all knew that, even after the Army had been defeated in battle, it would be an exceedingly difficult task to peaceably dismantle and demobilise a body of men who had hitherto been so militant in their political activity.

Such circumstances forced the Maharani to ask Henry Lawrence and Frederick Currie, the Governor-General's Secretary, to stay on at Lahore with the British garrison. If the royal government were to have any hope of fulfilling the terms of the Treaty, a military force was desperately needed to help not only with managing an orderly re-organisation of the Khalsa Army, but also with keeping the peace in the capital and enforcing revenue collection throughout the remaining lands of the Sikh kingdom. Within two days of the original Treaty being ratified, Currie swiftly negotiated and knocked together an additional set of 'Articles of Agreement', which were signed by Duleep Singh and his key courtiers on 11 March 1846. This granted the support of the British garrison at Lahore until December, but set a deadline: by that time, all of the obligations of the first Treaty should have been met. The Maharajah's government would also have to foot the additional bill for the cost of the Company troops.[7] The post of Resident was still not added at this stage, however, so Lawrence and his assistants were only meant to play a supporting and supervisory role in the internal administration of the Sikh Empire.

As could be expected, though, Hardinge was quick to instruct Lawrence to send him detailed reports on all happenings at Lahore:

> I should be glad to receive in Demi-official letters to Mr Currie as much information as you can give of the Court—the Ranee's mode of life, the parties at Court, those in the Provinces likely to be troublesome, the temper of the inhabitants of Lahore, that of the S[ikh] Troops—& even of our own Troops.[8]

All of this information would help the Governor-General to ascertain whether or not to adjust his plans for the re-establishment of a Sikh royal government, as well as providing useful material with which to justify his decision to his own superiors in London—the Company's Board of Directors and Parliament. The experiment had begun, though with a strict deadline by which miracles were expected to be achieved.

The intelligence records and reports sent by Lawrence to Hardinge, together with the ever-helpful chronicle of Sohan Lal Suri, shed valuable light on life at Lahore during this critical period, as Jind Kaur, her *vazir* Lal Singh and the rest of the royal court endeavoured to meet the stringent demands of the new treaties. The matters that needed to be addressed most urgently were the reduction of the troops and the payment of the indemnity. These issues required austerity measures that were deeply unpopular, since they struck at the landed and financial privileges of the very groups that had hitherto dominated the state: the soldiers, and the wealthy *sardars* and landholding courtiers. The problem was further compounded by the loss of large chunks of valuable territory to the British and Gulab Singh, which meant that not only would many of the Punjab's landed elite have to relinquish substantial sums of personal wealth in order to help pay off the indemnity bill; but the royals and the court would either have to significantly curb their own expenditure too, or else rapidly find new sources of revenue.

Jind Kaur and Duleep Singh held a daily *durbar* together every morning, at which all of these problems were tackled bit by bit. The Maharani would typically consult with the appointed ministers and courtiers and transact state business on behalf of, but in the presence of, her young son.[9] Lawrence's news-writers reported that she made regular complaints about the delays of the *kardars* (the *durbar*'s local tax-collectors) in sending grain and revenue payments, and promptly sent fresh orders in every direction to bring them into line.[10] There is also a mention of 200 boy-soldiers from the Maharajah's so-called 'Lilliputian Regiment' being discharged, as part of the courtly retrenchments and the overall project of military demobilisation.[11] Duleep Singh, now 8 years old, had previously held 'reviews' of these 'troops' at his *durbars*, on which occasions he had 'inspected' their drills and appearance—much as his father and older half-brothers had in the past. The formation of a specific regiment of young boys for Duleep to supervise was most likely part of his military training, and perhaps also a valuable way for a new generation of soldiers to form a personal bond with the Maharajah. However, the drastic austerity measures that his mother was having to force through clearly cut short this interesting project.

This is not to say that the Maharani completely abandoned a sense of creativity in governance at this time. One project of hers that has gone completely unnoticed by historians until now is the new town that she ordered to be built in the heart of the kingdom, named Duleepgurh. While we know of a settlement of the same name that was established by a British military officer in or around Bannu in December 1847,[12] it is not entirely clear what happened to Jind Kaur's Duleepgurh. Suri's chronicle contains a note about how the Queen-Regent and the Maharajah carried out a personal inspection of the site on 23 December 1846, as a midway stop during a trip to the Golden Temple in Amritsar. Their camp was pitched 'near Dogaich',[13] which suggests that the royal establishment of Duleepgurh must have been located somewhere nearby, on the road between the two main Punjabi cities of Lahore and Amritsar. It would seem too that the project had been initiated as early as 1843, and initially managed by Jind Kaur's brothers, Jawahir Singh and Hira Singh (no relation to the assassinated *vazir*).[14]

Lawrence's *akhbars* (Persian intelligence/news reports) note that, in late March 1846, as the peace was concluded, the Maharani's 'favourite slave girl' had been given charge of Duleepgurh as a *jagir* and dispatched there 'in order to see what condition it was in'. This right-hand woman, called Mangla, was handed turbans and shawls to present to the local *zamindars* and headmen as *khi'lats*—ceremonial gifts that would honorifically bind them as the Maharajah's loyal and respected subjects—and she was instructed to 'transact the affairs of all that part of the country'.[15] Within a few days, Mangla sent an inspection report back to the *durbar*, urging that 'unless the Bankers and men of wealth now in the city of Umritsir [Amritsar] choose to go and live in Duleepgurh it is impossible that it can ever thrive.' Jind Kaur responded swiftly to this and 'directed that orders should be sent to the Bankers of Umritsir to build themselves houses in Duleep Gurh and set trade and commerce afloat.'[16] The fact that she sent her 'favourite slave girl' to carry out such work, rather than a *sardar* or another male courtier, is intrigu-

Fig. 15: Two men look through a telescope in the *Sarvasiddhantattvacudamani*, the Sanskrit astronomy manuscript commissioned by Kharak Singh in 1839.

Fig. 16: Signs of the Zodiac in the astronomy manuscript, which originally contained a horoscope for Kharak Singh's son and heir, Nau Nihal Singh.

Fig. 17: Maharajah Nau Nihal Singh as a prince (r. 1839–40): he took power from his father only to perish on the day of Kharak Singh's funeral. Pahari, early nineteenth century.

Fig. 18: Nau Nihal Singh's mansion in Lahore: intricate decoration around a west-side window. In Sikh Empire design, natural imagery represented the fertility and prosperity of both the royal dynasty and the land they ruled.

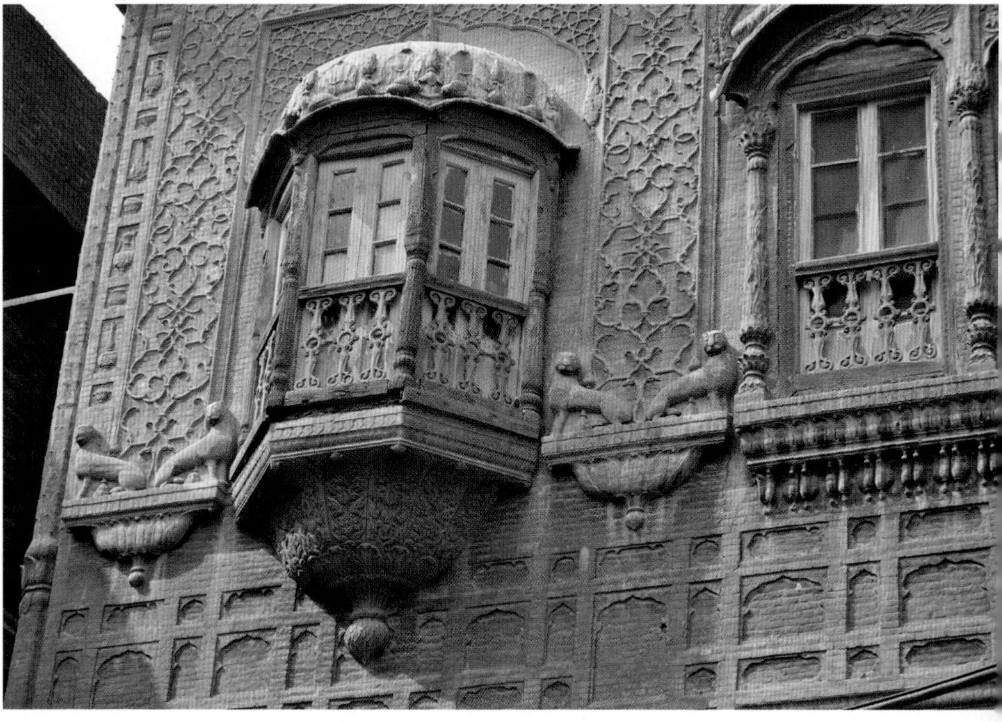

Fig. 19: Proud lions flank a window on the southeast side of the mansion.

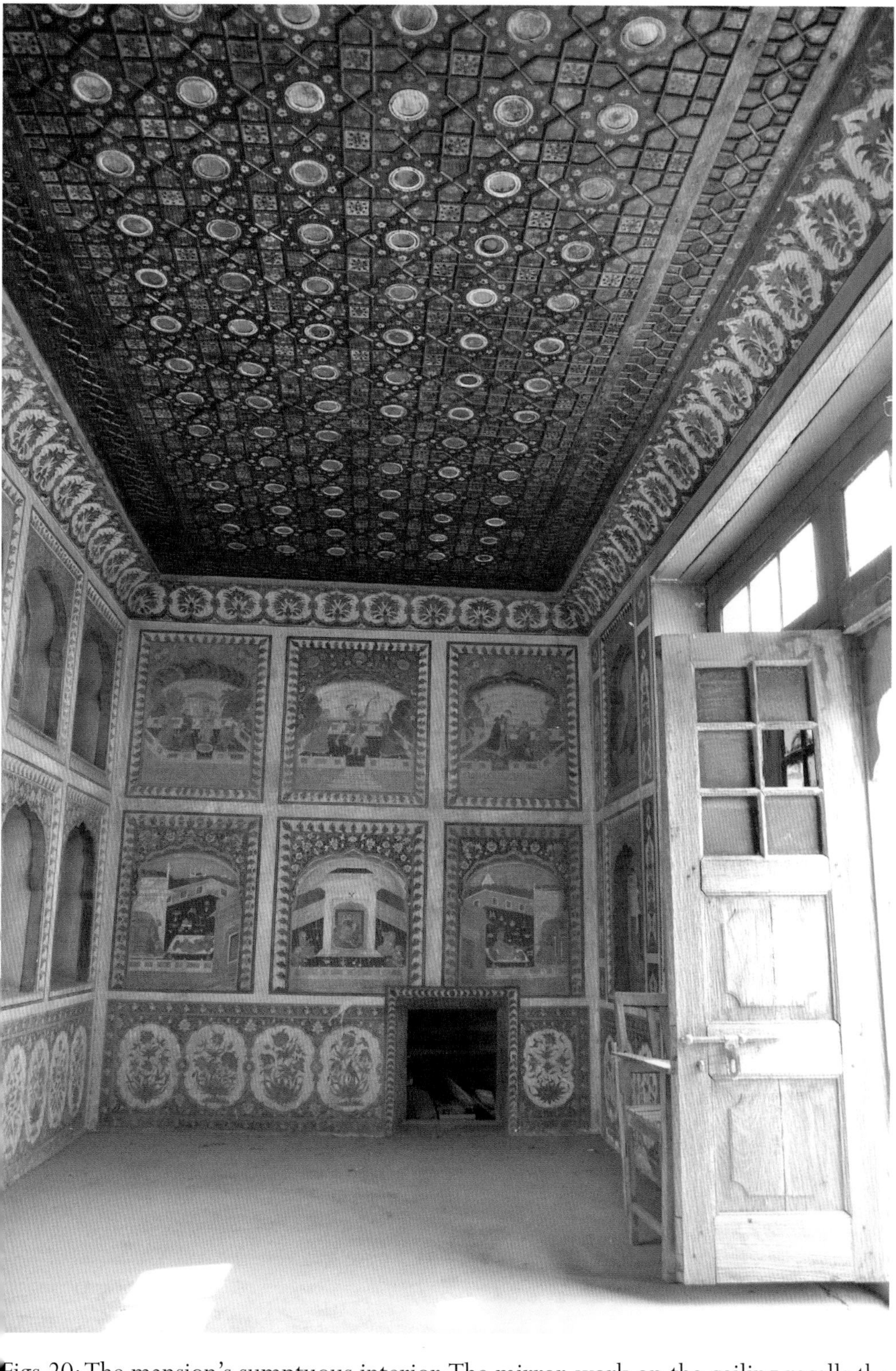

Figs 20: The mansion's sumptuous interior. The mirror-work on the ceiling recalls the grand design of the Mughal royal apartments in the Lahore Fort, which Ranjit Singh himself occupied.

Fig. 21: Maharani Chand Kaur (r. 1840–1), mother of Nau Nihal Singh, whose claim of her rights as Queen-Regent saw her assassinated. This is Company artwork. Watercolour, c. 1865.

Fig. 22: Maharajah Sher Singh (r. 1841–3), son of Ranjit Singh, who waged a violent and misogynistic war for the throne. Pahari, c. 1841.

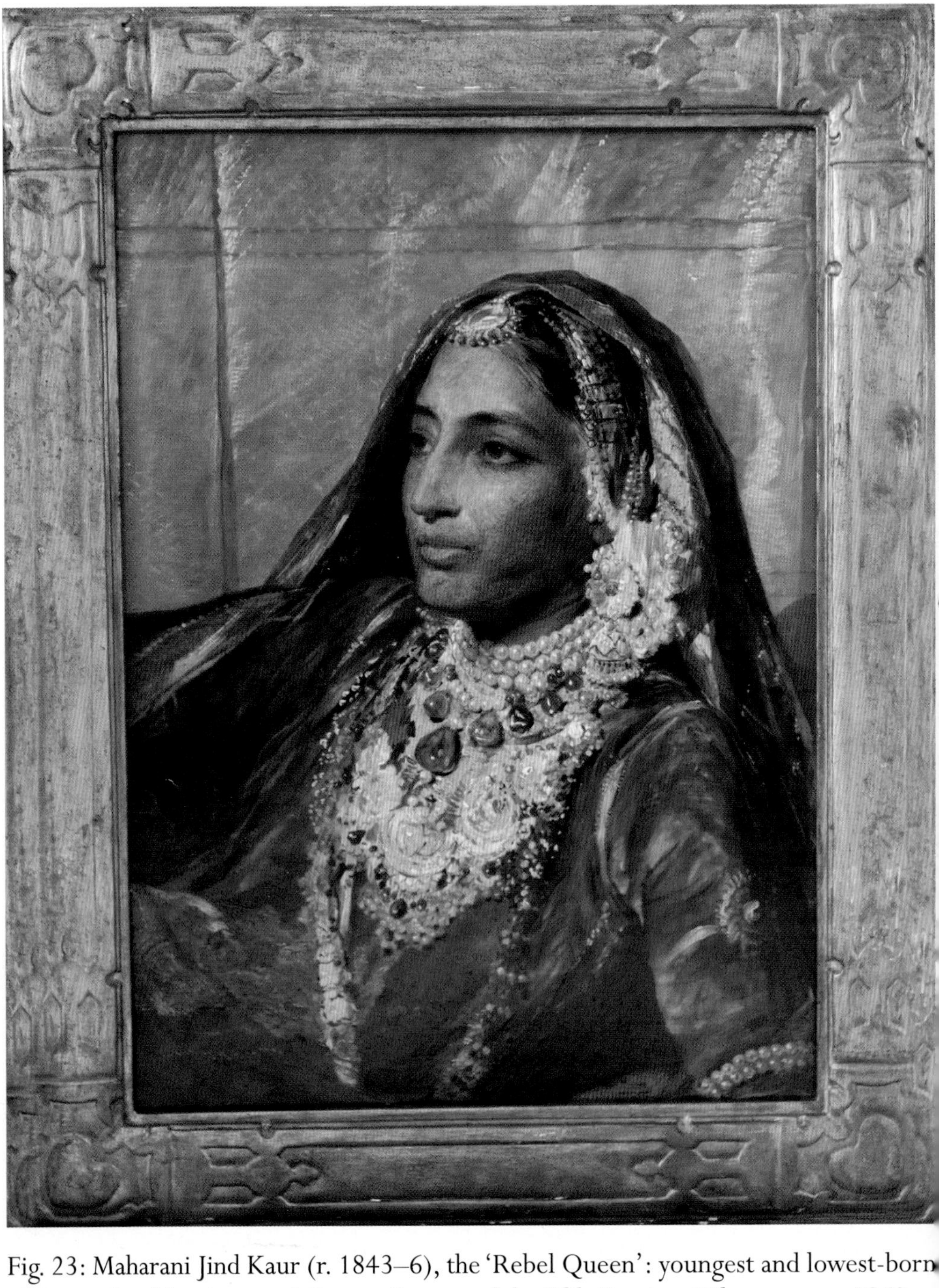

Fig. 23: Maharani Jind Kaur (r. 1843–6), the 'Rebel Queen': youngest and lowest-born of Ranjit Singh's wives, and Queen-Regent of the Sikh Empire. Oil on canvas, 1860s.

Fig. 24: Maharajah Duleep Singh (r. 1843–9), the boy-king and last Maharajah, shown here at court. Lahore, c. 1843.

Fig. 25: Rajah Dhyan Singh, who also notably arranged the assassinations of both Kharak Singh's own minister and Chand Kaur. Kangra or Lahore, c. 1840.

Fig. 26: Rajah Gulab Singh, his brother, whose rebellion against Jind Kaur and connivance with the British saw him crowned Maharajah of Jammu & Kashmir. Lahore c. 1845.

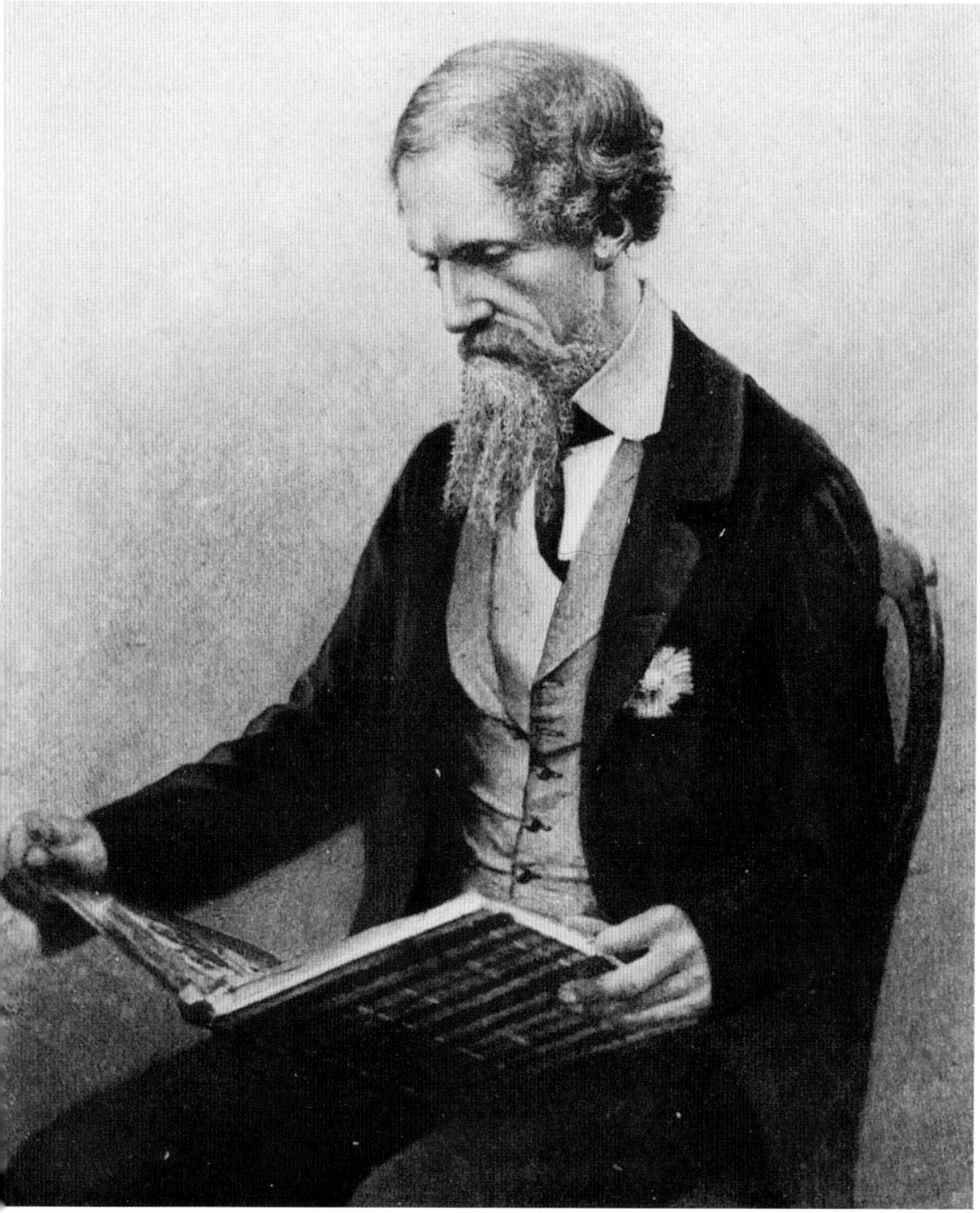

Fig. 27: Sir Henry Lawrence, the East India Company's Political Agent in the Punjab, who defeated Jind Kaur's forces in the field but kept Duleep Singh on the throne. c. 1857.

Fig. 28: Duleep Singh (depicted smaller than his ministers) signs the Treaty of Lahore. With this settlement, the last Maharajah lost most of his Empire to the British East India Company. Painted on paper, 1846.

ing. It perhaps suggests that the Maharani was keen above all to maintain direct control over the estate and was only prepared to send someone she personally trusted.

Of course, such enterprising endeavours on Jind Kaur's part mirror the style of 'dynastic colonialism' that had been a central feature of empire-building for Ranjit Singh and his family nearly forty years earlier. As we have seen, in that period, several of the Maharajah's female relations personally occupied important forts and strategic posts in the Punjabi countryside, including Sada Kaur and Mai Nakain. His eldest son and grandson, Kharak Singh and Nau Nihal Singh, had also established new forts on the fringes of the Empire to mark and protect its expanding borders, including at Dera Ismail Khan and Peshawar. Other newborn princes were even named after recently conquered territories, including Kashmira Singh, Peshaura Singh and Multana Singh (relating of course to the conquests of Kashmir, Peshawar and Multan). Unfortunately, I have not been able to find any modern records of the continued existence of a town known as 'Duleepgurh' located between Lahore and Amritsar, which likely suggests that Jind Kaur's project was not as successful over the long term as those of her predecessors.[17] Yet this does not detract from the fact that the Maharani evidently attempted to administer her dynasty's imperial territories in a similar fashion to the *sardarnis* and queens who had gone before her, whose own positions and endeavours significantly transgressed the boundaries between what Victorian-era British officials believed to be appropriate 'male' and 'female' spheres of activity. It certainly highlights the determined and inventive manner in which Jind Kaur tried to build and tap into new revenue streams in order to pay off the heavy financial burden weighing on the freedom of her son's kingdom.

Despite these heroic efforts, the Maharani and the *durbar* were unable to meet all of the demands of the Treaty by December 1846. As early as September, Jind Kaur had confessed her worries about the likelihood of failure to Henry Lawrence's brother John, who normally held the charge of settling the Company's newly conquered territory in the Jalandhar Doab, but who was filling in as the Political Agent and head of the garrison at Lahore for a few months while his brother was away on sick leave. Hardinge had been prepared for the possibility of failure on Jind Kaur's part, and had actively encouraged the younger Lawrence to sound out the Maharani and other key members of the *durbar* on their preparedness for the withdrawal of the British garrison at the end of the year. He had also ordered Lawrence to make it clear to the Punjabi elite that he was serious about removing the Company troops, so that there was no chance that they could feel any sense of complacency.

It was under this duress that Jind Kaur told John Lawrence of her fear that the Maharajah's government would collapse if the British troops left Lahore, and that her and Duleep's lives would once again be under threat from the Khalsa Army. She was therefore keen for the British garrison to stay on, but only wanted it to remain on the terms of the Treaty of Lahore. While there is little indication in the available sources from this period that the Maharani or the *durbar* were directly facing any major threats from the Khalsa troops, she may well have been driven by a lingering sense of fear and insecurity following her much more frightening experiences the year before. Many of the Lahore *durbar*'s leading *sardars* expressed similar concerns for their own and the government's security; however, they seem to have been even more averse to the Maharani and Lal Singh retaining control over the Empire, a state of affairs that they perceived as inimical to their own landed interests. In a private conversation with Runjore Singh Majithia, John Lawrence discreetly took on board a suggestion that the Maharani should be removed from power altogether and that a British regent should be appointed in her stead. Runjore Singh apparently indicated that he and many of the other *sardars* would be more willing to work with a Resident than to continue taking orders from the Maharani and Lal Singh. This idea greatly appealed to the Acting Agent and was duly forwarded to Hardinge, who was equally pleased to hear it.[18]

These conversations were taking place only half a year after the settlement had begun. Why were Hardinge and his deputies now so keen to get rid of the Maharani and Lal Singh? With the *vazir* in particular, there was great suspicion that his only reason for pursuing a ministerial career was to line his own pockets as much as he could. Lal Singh was a 'parvenu' chief, a former client of the Hindu Dogra family of Dhyan Singh and Gulab Singh, who rose rapidly up the ranks within courtly circles at Lahore during the tumults of the 1840s. His appointment as the guard of the Maharani's private apartments provided him with close personal access to Jind Kaur, from which time he was taken completely into her confidence. As a *vazir*, however, he was widely unpopular with the Lahore elite and the British alike, both before and after the war with the Company.

Henry Lawrence supposedly felt that Lal Singh showed potential as a greatly talented minister, but was displeased by the way in which the *vazir* jealously guarded his power and bristled at any attempt by Lawrence to interfere in his affairs.[19] This might have been understandable: after the war, both the Maharani and her chief minister were keen to restore the Punjab to an independent footing as soon as possible. However, in private correspondence and reports, the Lawrence brothers shared evidence of the *vazir*'s corruption, claiming that Lal Singh was using the imposition of austerity measures to confiscate the *jagirs* of old landed families and to deduct pay from the soldiers, redistributing this wealth to himself, his family members and his favourites. Henry Lawrence himself warned the *vazir* to discontinue such impolitic activities, but does not seem to have been able to take any stronger action, since he was technically not allowed to intervene directly in the affairs of the Lahore *durbar*.[20]

The desired opportunity finally came in the autumn of 1846, when it emerged that Lal Singh had been plotting to block the transfer of Kashmir to Gulab Singh. The previous Lahore-appointed governor of the province, Sheikh Imamuddin, revealed to Lawrence that he had received letters from the *vazir*, urging him to resist Gulab Singh's attempts to take over the country. It seems highly likely that the Maharani was equally behind the plot to stop Gulab Singh from becoming Maharajah of Kashmir, since it was undoubtedly a cause of great bitterness to lose such a valuable territory, especially after the Rajah's betrayal and at a time when the Lahore government needed whatever resources it could get to throw off the financial burden of the March Treaty.[21] However, as with the earlier clash between the Khalsa Army and the Maharani's government in November 1845, Jind Kaur herself would not be punished at this stage—it was her *vazir* who was treated as the culprit, especially since only his name and hand could be seen in the incriminating evidence. In a startling turn of events, at the start of December, Sir Frederick Currie returned to the Punjab and, together with the

Lawrence brothers, took control over the *durbar* at Lahore. It was turned into a tribunal, at which Lal Singh was put on trial for 'treason'. Since British colonial law could not be used against him, the text of the Lahore Treaty was taken as the basis upon which he could be judged and punished. He was swiftly found guilty, stripped of his personal treasure and 2,000 Afghan bodyguards, and sent into exile by 13 December.

Jind Kaur was reportedly devastated at the banishment of Lal Singh, but also extremely perturbed about likely British intentions towards her rule following this development. She quickly endeavoured to raise support for the immediate reinstatement of an independent Sikh government under her authority, but Hardinge and Henry Lawrence were swift to stop this movement from gaining ground. The Maharani had made herself unpopular by refusing for several years to let go of Lal Singh and, whether it was true or not, her attachment to him had made it easy for successive British officers to portray the relationship as a sexual affair. The intelligence reports sent by Lawrence to Hardinge were replete with suggestive mentions about the private liaisons between the Maharani and her *vazir*—also implicating her trusted servant, Mangla, who was accused of being Jind Kaur's accomplice in her supposedly notorious 'debaucheries'. After Lal Singh's exile, such reports switched to gossiping about the Maharani's heartache over his absence and her desire to avenge her loss. These representations fuelled the idea spread about by Lawrence that the Queen-Regent's personal and political acts were motivated by 'passion and not patriotism', and that she could not be trusted to rule in an effective and disinterested manner.[22]

In making such assertions, Henry Lawrence was in fact following closely in the footsteps of his predecessor: the Company's Political Agent to the North-West Frontier, Major George Broadfoot. Prior to the war, Broadfoot had similarly filled his intelligence reports and private correspondence with condemnatory descriptions of the Sikh queen's government, which he had characterised as running more like a 'brothel' than anything else. The following excerpt of a letter he wrote to Hardinge's secretary, Currie, is fairly typical of the manner in which Broadfoot portrayed affairs at Lahore:

> The state of parties is seriously changed but the cause is the Ranee's mind having been seriously affected by her excesses.

> Messalina picked big men, and Catherine [the Great of Russia] liked variety, but what do you think, in addition to all of this, of four young fellows changed as they cease to give satisfaction passing every night with the Ranee.
>
> She has become stupid instead of clever and lively, is sometimes for days in a state bordering on fatuity…she takes but little concern in the public business compared with what she used to do and then is chiefly guided by her low paramours and servants.[23]

Broadfoot was the first person to claim that the Maharani was having an affair with Lal Singh, but as we can see here, he generally characterised her as being such a sex addict that she could barely bring herself to concentrate on her responsibilities as a mother and a ruler—a hugely significant indictment of her character in both British and Sikh culture. Hardinge had regularly fed back these types of comments to his superiors in London throughout the autumn and winter of 1845. They had proven invaluable in backing up his radical decision to break with the longstanding policy of amity towards the Lahore *durbar*, instead declaring war on the Sikhs. Most importantly, selections of such licentious anecdotes about the Maharani's personal affairs were published in the 'Blue Book' on the First Anglo-Sikh War: the set of documents presented to Parliament by the Company, giving its official narrative on the causes, management and peace settlement of the recent war.[24]

It is crucial to acknowledge that these entirely negative characterisations of Jind Kaur were publicly challenged by another British officer, Joseph Davey Cunningham. Cunningham, a former political assistant at Ludhiana, not only had a personal rivalry with Broadfoot (who had beaten him to taking over Wade's job), but also strongly disagreed with the Political Agent's more abrasive style of handling relations with Lahore, which he argued was partially to blame for the First Anglo-Sikh War.[25] Cunningham's *History of the Sikhs* was published in 1849. It directly criticised Hardinge and Broadfoot for the unnecessarily confrontational and interventionist policy that they had adopted towards the Lahore *durbar*. Cunningham particularly disparaged the manner in which the papers printed in the Blue Book (specifically the correspondence from Broadfoot that Hardinge cited in his letters to London) excessively referred to the 'amours of the Muharanee', in order to 'heighten the folly and worthlessness of the Lahore court':

> the Muharanee may have attempted little concealment of her debaucheries, but decency was seldom violated in public; and the essential forms of a court were preserved to the last, especially when strangers were present ... Further, the proneness of newsmongers to enlarge upon such personal failings is sufficiently notorious; and the diplomatic service of India has been often reproached for dwelling pruriently or maliciously on such matters.[26]

There are echoes here of the problematic British narratives we encountered in the last chapter about the Sikh princes. Here, a Company man says it himself: for Cunningham, the accusations of debauchery and misrule levelled at Jind Kaur were part of a newly emerging colonial discourse, and not simply an accurate and natural reflection of changing morals or temperaments seated on the Lahore throne. As with the British views of Ranjit Singh's successors—both the Maharajahs and Chand Kaur—we can see here that the new colonial outlook in the Jind Kaur era was internally contested by British officials, let alone Punjabis themselves. We must remember that the same types of Company newsletters that carried such scandalous bits of gossip about the Maharani's personal life also included the information we've learnt about her more constructive efforts to manage her kingdom. However, as Cunningham powerfully highlighted, any such evidence that could act in the credit of Jind Kaur and the *durbar* was purposefully overlooked by Hardinge in his letters to London and in the selection of documents to be published in the 'Blue Books'.

By the time that Cunningham's own book was published in 1849, the attitude of the Company's leading political authorities towards the Punjabi royal family had shifted decisively away from the comparably equitable and friendly policy that had been advocated by Cunningham's former boss, Claude Martin Wade, a decade before. After his book's bold critique became public knowledge, Cunningham himself was swiftly made persona non grata in British-Indian governing circles. He was punished for airing his criticism of Company policy so publicly, being immediately removed from his post as Resident at the court of the Begum of Bhopal.[27] The disciplining force of the Company's official party line could thus be made to fall with strength not only upon the heads of its colonised subjects, but equally upon those of its own 'wayward' servants.

What we can perceive in all of this is a clear gendered bias against the rule of Indian women amongst a number of Company officials—a prejudice that, in many ways, both mirrored and fed into the political misogyny that had emerged within the Punjab itself since the clash between Maharani Chand Kaur and Prince Sher Singh. In fact, Henry Lawrence's views on that earlier queen (and Punjabi women in general) were considerably more hostile even than those of Shah Muhammad. He actually seems to have believed that Chand Kaur even had a hand in the murder of her own husband:

> Mai Chund Kour ... a bold, bad woman, who had instigated, or at least encouraged, the atrocities against her husband Khuruk Singh, exerted herself to form a party [to lay claim to the Lahore throne]. She was, like most Seikh and Jaut women, and especially all Seikh widows left under no restraint, of very dissolute habits, and soon gathered round her a strong party, of which her paramour, the notorious Ajeet Singh Sindawala [one of the *sardar* kinsmen who later avenged Chand Kaur's murder, not shown to be her lover in any Punjabi historiography], was one of the chiefs.
>
> ... It may be here stated, that the Seikh law recognises the claims of females to inheritance; and Mai (now Ranee) Chund Kour, while she shewed how many ladies had succeeded to the estates of their husbands on both sides of the Sutlej, urged the further argument that, when England was ruled by a queen, surely the Punjab might be by a Ranee. And we have little doubt that had Chund Kour gone quietly and prudently to work, she would at this moment be at the head of the Government, and that all the Seikh blood that had been lately shed, would have been spared; but ... she gave way to her passions, and before her authority was established, she both gave cause for every scandal, and forgot that she owed her position to the troops, who found that they not only did not receive the donatives and indulgences they had expected, but that they were denied their positive rights.[28]

The Indian, especially the Sikh, queen and her paramour(s) are a staple feature of Henry Lawrence's extensive published writings on the subjects of Indian history, politics and culture. In his view, the rule of a woman produced nothing more than corruption, debauchery and petty, self-interested feuds. Prominent female leaders such as the Marathi queen Tarabai Bhonsle, Baiza Bai of Gwalior or indeed Maharani Chand Kaur were, to Lawrence, 'the strumpetocracy of India'.[29] In this particular passage, he deftly manages to avoid conflating the British queen, Victoria, with such negative gendered representations, by playing up the racial aspect of his argument: emphasising the inability of the Sikh queen to control her lust and greed, and thereby making a mockery of her attempt to rule in the style of a British monarch.

On the other hand, Lawrence was prepared to be much more forgiving of Maharajah Ranjit Singh, whom he greatly admired—despite also characterising him as being prone to habitual debauchery:

> Runjeet Singh's lustful propensities were his most odious vices; but we do not hear of his having, as other monarchs European and Asiatic have done, torn wives and virgins from their families. No; his was rather systematic and methodical beastliness, performed without shame and without any feeling of impropriety. It injured himself; but it affected no innocent families; and shameless as he was, he may be favourably contrasted with any contemporary monarch of Asia; and it may be added, with some of Europe. While we execrate such acts in a half civilised Asiatic, let us remember the conduct of many Kings of France; of Augustus of Saxony; of the great Catherine and the greater Peter—indeed, of our own Henry and Charles.[30]

Essentially, in Lawrence's view, it was fine for a man to behave in less-than-exemplary fashion, but not for a woman. Even more intriguingly, he was prepared to doubly excuse Ranjit Singh's behaviour because he considered the Maharajah to have been an 'oriental despot' and a 'half civilised Asiatic'. This logic is particularly nonsensical on Lawrence's part, because here he explains Ranjit Singh's behaviour with the very same ideas that he uses to condemn Chand Kaur's: the Maharajah, it seems, cannot truly be blamed for his degenerate ways, for he is an Asian man—but Chand Kaur, we may remember, was condemned precisely for being 'like most Seikh and Jaut women ... very dissolute'.

Such opinions aligned with a particular school of thought amongst British colonial officers, which today we would identify as Orientalist: the idea that, while development of the Indian people and their political and cultural 'civilisation' was a few steps behind that of the 'modern' world of the West, there was still much to appreciate about Indian society in a romantic sense.[31] However, portraying Indian culture as 'charming' and 'quaint' though 'backward' was no less derogatory or devoid of power politics than an outright assault on Indian morals. It entrenched a one-dimensional perspective of the subcontinent's cultures and stripped Indians themselves of agency, particularly those who deviated from the dominant colonial view of how local society was supposed to work.[32]

Such ideas powerfully informed the political strategy that Hardinge and Lawrence were keen to establish within the Punjab. Henry Lawrence's writings vividly attest to his deep interest, bordering on obsession, in Punjabi affairs—above all highlighting his great desire to remodel the internal life of the Sikh Empire and its royal government to meet his own very particular understanding of how an ideal Indian monarchy should operate.[33] He and Hardinge shared the view that it was worthwhile maintaining good relations with Indian rulers, in order to be able to manage the British Empire on the cheap and to lessen reliance on a large standing army in India, which Lawrence, in particular, was convinced was an expensive and risky policy.[34] But if they were going to collaborate with Indian royal allies, Hardinge and Lawrence were clearly only prepared to deal with Indian men. At the war's end in early 1846, the two had chosen to keep the Sikh Empire running with a pair of safe royal hands at the helm, but the prospect of working more closely with Maharani Jind Kaur was anathema to them, whilst the idea that she could actually be a good or capable ruler was an impossibility in their minds.

In other words, there was no way that Hardinge or Lawrence were going to allow Jind Kaur to run the Sikh Empire independently on behalf of her son, with or without a British garrison at Lahore. Immediately on Henry Lawrence's return to the Punjab after his period of convalescence leave, and following the trial of Lal Singh, Hardinge counselled his deputy on the importance of weakening the Maharani's campaign. He encouraged Lawrence to find additional ways to undercut her claims that she was the authoritative representative of the ruling dynasty—having come to recognise that Punjabi political culture otherwise entirely legitimised her right to act as Queen-Regent. The Governor-General now wished to set up a government at Lahore controlled by Henry Lawrence as British Resident, taking over from Jind Kaur as Duleep Singh's guardian and Regent—but Hardinge wanted the *sardars* to make the request, rather than embarking on an act of overt imperial fiat.

The key tactic that he recommended to Henry Lawrence was to win over the Attariwala family,[35] with whose daughter Jind Kaur had arranged Duleep's betrothal in July 1845, in order to provide further support for her own regency government.[36] Chattar and Sher Singh Attariwala, father and son, were two of the most prominent *sardars* in Punjabi politics and high society by the mid-1840s, and their backing carried a great deal of weight in the *durbar*. By leveraging the Attariwalas' kinship ties with the young Maharajah, Hardinge and Lawrence thought they could passably justify their removal of his mother from power. Much of this echoed the style of competitive inter-clan politics that had abounded in Ranjit Singh's early years at the head of the Sukerchakia *misl*. Indeed, by backing the rising star of Henry Lawrence against the Maharani, Sher Singh Attariwala showed himself to be a very ambitious *sardar*, happy to act ruthlessly to further his own and his family's interests. And once he had agreed to the ousting of Jind Kaur, it did not take long for the rest of the Lahore government's leading ministers to sign up to the plan: they would give the Maharani a large pension and push her out of power.

The result of all of this political manoeuvring was a new treaty. This installed Henry Lawrence as Duleep Singh's guardian and Regent of his government, and committed Company forces to maintaining the peace and stability of the Maharajah's kingdom until he came of age at 16 on 4 September 1854. Thereafter he was to be allowed to rule independently once more—so long as the Punjab could be settled according to British wishes, of course.

The 'Second Ranjit Singh' versus the 'Rebel Queen'

Soon after the agreement was reached between Henry Lawrence and the *sardars*, a request was sent to Duleep Singh to travel to

Bhyrowal, in order to meet with Hardinge and formally sign the new treaty at the end of December 1846. This notification reached the Maharajah while he was on his tour of Amritsar and Duleepgurh with his mother, which led Jind Kaur to ask whether or not she should accompany him too. A senior Lahore minister, Diwan Dina Nath, discussed the matter with Lawrence and suggested that the Maharani should be allowed to attend the meeting, since the Maharajah was only 'a boy of small years'. However, Lawrence strictly ordered that the Maharani must remain at Amritsar throughout, letting Duleep go ahead alone.[37] From this point on, the separation of mother and son would become a central feature of the new Resident's policy for training and educating the boy-king—combined with a new, steadily growing paternalist view that juxtaposed British guardianship of the Maharajah with the critical, gendered narratives of Jind Kaur's personal and political flaws.

This shift towards a firmly patriarchal form of government and politics was clearly in evidence at the *durbars* held to mark the signing of the Bhyrowal treaty and creation of the new Residency at Lahore. We can see this in Suri's chronicles. At one such event in early January 1847, the assembled *sardars* flatteringly beseeched Hardinge to act as a benevolent patron towards their young Maharajah, to which the Governor-General replied, 'for that very purpose the Big Sahib [Henry Lawrence] had been appointed', since 'he considered him [Duleep] as his son'.[38] At the next *durbar*, the symbolic adoption of Duleep Singh was taken one step further:

> The Lord Sahib [Hardinge] held the hand of [the] Maharaja with his own hand and put it in the hand of the Big Sahib, who placed his own hand upon the Maharaja's head. It was declared that all the chieftains should give advice and instruction regarding the administration and affairs of the state, and should remain obedient and loyal to the Maharaja ... and not show any kind of deviation from the instructions [that] had been given to them in writing by Currie Sahib [Sir Frederick Currie, Secretary to the Governor-General, Hardinge].[39]

It is fascinating to see here how closely Hardinge and Lawrence are mirroring the earlier courtly deportment of Ranjit Singh, ritually embracing his youngest son—Lawrence even appears to bless

Duleep Singh by putting his own hand on the Maharajah's head. To an extent, such gestures were a continuation of the formerly dynastic style of Anglo-Punjabi diplomacy that we saw in Chapter 3, but they were now providing a way for the new British elite at Lahore to embed themselves as the dominant and superior figures in the kingdom—occupying the place of Ranjit Singh, yet subtly altering what this place, or his memory, would represent. Such encounters gave rise to a colonial reinterpretation of Punjabi royal culture: not only was it increasingly patriarchal in nature, but it was ultimately intended to enable the Company authorities to tighten their hold over the young Maharajah and his diminished Empire.

For Henry Lawrence, this was a moment of great delight, since he was finally able to live his dream of becoming 'a second Runjeet Singh' to the Punjab. In his novel, *Adventures of an Officer in the Service of Runjeet Singh*, he had constructed his protagonist, Bellasis, as the fictional ideal of a manly, energetic and bold 'soldier-administrator': the type of man and political officer he saw as best suited to operating successfully in the world of 'intrigue', 'warfare' and 'ambition' that was, to Lawrence, an Indian kingdom. Bellasis' character was supposedly based loosely on the European officers who had been in the employ of Ranjit Singh's Khalsa Army.[40] However, given the extensive nature of Lawrence's wider writings on the Punjab, and his great enthusiasm for the role of Resident, I think we can plausibly see his novel as at least partially embodying some of his own dreams, and his aspirations to one day have a powerful say in the running of the Sikh Empire. As we have seen, Lawrence's novel highlighted his low opinion of the majority of Ranjit Singh's sons; by the end of the story, he had the Maharajah himself proclaiming Bellasis' virtues as 'the pearl of the age, the one honest man in his kingdom'. The adventurous British officer manages to win the Maharajah's favour to such a great extent that Lawrence's own hero, Ranjit Singh, is characterised as desperately wishing for Bellasis to accept the charge of running the country of Kashmir (displacing the Dogra family of Rajah Dhyan Singh), where he could take his rightful place as a 'ruler over princes'.[41]

On becoming Resident and head of the Lahore government, Lawrence certainly began acting much like a Maharajah. He formally opened his Residency headquarters at Anarkali's Tomb in

Lahore and immediately set about appointing his own set of political assistants throughout the Punjab: junior officers of the Company's Army, whom Lawrence would rely upon—as the fictional Ranjit Singh relied upon Bellasis—to establish law and order, win over the local people and gain thorough control over revenue collection. Lawrence presided over the *durbar* himself, in kingly fashion, and began scrutinising the conduct and characters of the court's leading ministers more closely than before, deciding which figures would be most amenable and useful in supporting his rule. He quickly identified the rivalry between Sardar Tej Singh, the Khalsa Army's former treacherous commander at Sobraon, and Sher Singh Attariwala, Duleep Singh's prospective brother-in-law; he chose to favour the former over the latter, despite the help of the Attariwala *sardar* in the establishment of his regency. Most significantly, Lawrence would increasingly host *durbars* at the Residency rather than the Lahore Fort, dispensing with Duleep Singh's presence on several occasions and instead himself monopolising the Maharajah's position.[42]

The new Resident's kinship ties played an important role in creating his new administration. As we know, his younger brother, John Lawrence, was already in charge of settling the recently conquered Jalandhar Doab; but the Resident would also appoint their older brother, George, to supervise the affairs of the Punjabi-Afghan frontier from Peshawar. The strategic spread of the Lawrences was yet another parallel with the dynastic model of governance that Ranjit Singh and his immediate relations established by the 1830s. Such a rise to power was in itself striking evidence of how the fortunes of British families could be dramatically transformed through a combination of sheer determination, careful use of kinship networks and the opportunities created by the fluid political situation of early nineteenth-century India.[43] These families were often of middle-class status, hailing from the fringes of the British Isles and seeking a 'step up' on the subcontinent—the Lawrences originated from Ireland. No less than it had been for Ranjit Singh's dynasty, the 'culture of relatedness' was vital in embedding British colonial control over the Punjab.[44] This certainly cohered with the idiom of local political culture, and brought an element of stability through the semblance of continuity, particularly enhanced by the fact that John Lawrence would stand in for his brother during his two of his periods of sick leave.

On the other hand, the role of the Mrs Lawrences was entirely different from that of Mai Nakain, Chand Kaur and their ilk: Honoria Lawrence, the Resident's wife, wrote in the *Calcutta Review* that 'the soldierly woman' was nothing more than a 'most offensive hybrid', who had laid aside 'all that is becoming and delicate in her own sex', without possibly being able to gain any 'masculine qualities'.[45] These words, though targeted at the British wives of Company soldiers rather than elite Indian women, nevertheless carried within them the ideology that informed her husband's approach in isolating and cutting off Jind Kaur's remaining sources of power. The 'corrupting influence of the *zenana*' was another key trope of British colonial writing on Indian society. As the nineteenth century progressed, under the British Raj, it became exceedingly common for princes or minor Maharajahs to be separated from their mothers and removed from *zenana* apartments, in order for them to be given a more 'masculine' and 'healthy' education along the lines set out by British Residents or appointed tutors.[46]

Of course, as we've seen repeatedly throughout this book, the lives of royal women within the Punjab were certainly not restricted to a *zenana* or *harem* environment. The ideas of the Sikh Gurus about equality for men and women, combined with the more generally fluid social and political circumstances across post-Mughal northern India, had enabled a diverse variety of women to take up positions of power and authority in the array of newly independent states that emerged at that time. This had included women of very different walks of life within the Punjab, from the elite *sardarni* Sada Kaur to the former dancing girl Gul Begum, and from all over India, including such formidable queens as the Begums of Bhopal, or Begum Samru of Sardhana and Begum Hazrat Mahal in Awadh. These women posed a striking challenge to the gender norms conformed to by Henry and Honoria Lawrence. Many lived their whole lives in the precise manner of the 'soldierly woman' Honoria so despised, whilst also taking a very active role in training their children how to run their kingdoms, within but equally outside of their *zenanas*.

After Henry Lawrence took over as Resident, everything changed. Historians may not have appreciated the dramatic nature of the shift, but Jind Kaur was actually pushed into a restricted *zenana* environment by Lawrence, against her will. Within six months, the Maharani was reduced from a ruler deeply involved in all aspects of her kingdom's administration—indeed, even openly addressing her troops without *purdah* and personally inspecting neighbouring regions—to a life of powerlessness and incarceration within the apartments of her own palace. As Resident, Henry Lawrence increasingly exploited the misogynistic bent within Punjabi politics that had emerged during the early 1840s, to encourage the pro-British *sardars* of the *durbar* to support him in imposing draconian restrictions on the 'debauched' and 'unruly' Maharani. His political diaries show that a close watch was kept on Jind Kaur's activities and on any visitors to her apartments. Despite having been removed from her formal role as Regent, it is abundantly clear that the Maharani was determined to remain informed about what was happening with her son's government and to influence matters wherever she could—much to Lawrence's annoyance. He tried to stopped her from meeting with individual *durbar* officials in her private apartments, by taking a leaf out of Broadfoot's book and raising concerns about how she was corrupting them with sexualised 'manipulation'; however, the Maharani simply resorted to holding larger meetings, with up to fifteen *sardars* at a time.[47] Lawrence also became increasingly suspicious and disparaging of her reception of large numbers of Brahmin mendicants, to whom she regularly presented alms or whose feet she washed as penitence.

By the summer of 1847, the Resident decided it was time to put a stop to such activity, which he felt was designed somehow to undermine his authority. He directed a stern letter to the Maharani, invoking her late husband's memory in an attempt to shame her into comporting herself in a more 'appropriate' manner:

> Entertaining, as I do, a sincere wish to maintain the dignity and honor of the family of the late Maharajah Runjeet Sing, and to establish good government in every department ... it is right that I should, in time, and with all due respect and delicacy, point out to Her Highness wherein her present and future interests really consist.
>
> I now, therefore, write to say that the conduct of Her Highness ... is quite without precedent, and altogether unnecessary and out of place. It is, moreover, a breach of decorum and royal etiquette.

> The regard I have for Her Highness' honor and reputation, obliges me, therefore, to beg that she will, in future, regulate her private life in strict conformity with the treaty alluded to [Bhyrowal], permitting no one, whatever his rank may be, to have access to her, but her own servants and confidential followers.
>
> If the Maharanee wishes to give alms to the poor, and to feed religious men, let her do so on the first of each month ... in short, let her follow the example of Maharajah Runjeet Sing.
>
> And with respect to visits of ceremony, or polite inquiry, from the Sirdars, it seems to me much more decorous that five or six should call together, once a month, and that, even then, Her Highness should sit behind the screen, as do the Princesses of other courts, such as Jodhpore, Jyepore, and Nepal.[48]

The Maharani's withering riposte powerfully conveys how incensed she was to have received such a letter from Lawrence:

> ... So long as the Maharajah is sovereign of his own kingdom, it is the same as if I was sovereign myself. But if the new treaty has devised some better plan for securing the State's welfare, why, I am content ...
>
> Referring to the part of your memorandum wherein you express your anxious regard for the honour of Maharajah Runjeet Sing's family, the good government of the kingdom, and the shielding of my honor and reputation, I am much obliged to the British Government for taking such care of my fair fame. But you institute a comparison between me and the Princesses of Jodhpore, Jyepore and Nepal. It is easy for them to keep themselves aloof behind their purdahs, since there are in those States wise and faithful ministers, who watch over the interests of those to whom they owe allegiance. Here, you need not be told what sort of ministers there are! Rely on one thing, however, that I have never been in the habit of admitting strangers to my private apartments; and never mean to.
>
> ... It is a subject of deep congratulation to me that both the Maharajah and myself are now reaping the benefits of the friendship which Maharajah Runjeet Sing sowed with the Company.[49]

This exchange vividly illuminates just how far life at Lahore had changed since the days of Ranjit Singh, despite Lawrence's invocation of his reign and behaviour as an exemplary model to back his arguments. It equally highlights the extent of the Resident's new-found power and audacity. He had free rein to try and impose his ideas about 'authentic' Indian royal decorum on the Punjabi elite, drawing on his understanding of how a particular vision of Rajasthani princely culture should provide a benchmark of Indian courtly etiquette.[50] The Maharani, on the other hand, argued from a viewpoint that considered largely unguarded female political activity to be normal, if not necessary, in the circumstances faced by her child. The two visions were completely irreconcilable, and it was abundantly clear that Jind Kaur was not going to go out without a fight. Lawrence was now compelled to recognise that, if British influence over Duleep Singh's education and government were to be firmly and permanently established, he would have to remove the Maharani from the scene altogether, regardless of how close she and Duleep were to one another.[51]

Just as he had had to bide his time to find a plausible excuse to get rid of the *vazir* Lal Singh, Lawrence was now forced to wait until August 1847 until he was provided with an appropriate opportunity to justify exiling Jind Kaur from Lahore. He had planned an extravagant *durbar*, at which he intended to reward those ministers who had been most energetic and supportive in establishing his regency council and setting its plans afoot. Several men were to be promoted with new titles, including Tej Singh and Sher Singh Attariwala, who were to be made Rajahs. However, Lawrence consulted neither the Maharajah nor the Maharani on these promotions, though he expected Duleep Singh to perform the ceremonial role of touching every *khi'lat* and presenting them to each *sardar*. Such blatant usurpation of the royal prerogative greatly angered Jind Kaur. She decided to hit back at Lawrence and the *sardars* with a plan to disrupt the ceremony, secretly instructing her son to refuse to touch the *khi'lat* of Tej Singh or mark his forehead with a *tikka* when called upon to do so by the Resident. In obedience to his mother's words, the 9-year-old Maharajah stood with his hands firmly behind his back in the *durbar* and refused to yield to Lawrence's urgent persuasion, much to the embarrassment of the Resident and Tej Singh.

With great anger and mortification, Lawrence reported the day's events to the Governor-General's council—piecing together a deeply conspiratorial picture of the Maharani's motivations by linking the *durbar* incident with the revelations of the recently uncovered 'Preyma plot'. This plot to assassinate Tej Singh and the Resident was named after the shady man who had organised it with several associates from Lahore and Jammu, allegedly including the Maharani's *munshi* (secretary), Buta Singh. It had been easily exposed six months earlier, and at the time Lawrence had not been inclined to take it very seriously.[52] However, after the '*tikka* incident', which he quickly found had been instigated by the Maharani, he urged Hardinge to consider Jind Kaur a 'dangerous and bitter enemy', and 'the main source of all difficulty'. He argued that she must have had a hand in the Preyma plot, even though no evidence could be found to directly implicate her. On these grounds, he urged that she be removed from Lahore and separated from Duleep Singh as soon as possible, as otherwise she would exploit 'the mischievous influence she possesses over her son, [and] would devote her leisure to the shortsighted task of widening the breach between him and his ministers.'[53]

It is in such accusations that we finally see the Punjabi *zenana* emerge as a site of secretive intrigue, one that was apparently capable of exerting malevolent and corrupting force over the young Maharajah. It is fair to say that this was at least partially a monster of Lawrence's own making, born from his limited and negative perception of Indian royal women's political role and reinforced by the repressive policy that he had imposed on Jind Kaur. The Maharani may not have been a blameless character, but it is not surprising that she should have been galled by the manner in which her powers and freedom were increasingly circumscribed, as well as seeing her little boy, the reigning king, being trained to act and think in ways that broke radically with the education and culture of past Sikh princes.

It did not take much convincing for Hardinge to fall in with the views of his leading man on the ground. However, we should scrutinise a little more closely the justification that the two men devised for the Maharani's proposed exile from Lahore. The Governor-General was keen to ensure that the *durbar* should be fully on board with the planned removal and that the explanation to be offered publicly for her sudden exile be as 'broad' and 'general' as possible, to avoid any cause for widespread complaint—whether from Punjabi subjects or his superiors in London.[54] Despite Jind Kaur's reputation, she was still the Maharajah's mother and Ranjit Singh's widow, and this carried weight within Sikh society, particularly the Khalsa Army. Hardinge sought to co-opt this feeling by transferring the legitimacy of Ranjit Singh from the Maharani to the Company: the eventual proclamation issued on 20 August 1847 was more explicit than any other British document or act in assuming the first Maharajah's glorified mantle, and enforcing a new patriarchal norm on the Punjab:

> The Right Honorable the Governor-General of India, taking into consideration the friendly relations subsisting between the Lahore and British Governments, and the tender age of Maharajah Duleep Sing, feels the interest of a father in the education, and guardianship, of the young Prince.
>
> With this end in view, it appeared to the Governor-General to have become absolutely necessary to separate the Maharajah from the Maharanee, his mother; an opinion in which the Durbar perfectly coincided...

The announcement went on to accuse Jind Kaur of consistently attempting to 'embarrass and impede the public business', and setting a pernicious example to her son and others by enabling 'strangers to visit her without restriction' and by acting as a fount of inspiration to 'every seditious intriguer who was displeased with the present order of things'.[55] Partly as a sop to those who were perturbed by the Maharani's removal, it was decided to send her to Sheikhupura. Her imprisonment at the Fort as a political exile could not have been a more marked reversal of the lifestyle that Mai Nakain had led there as a powerful queen.

Fighting for the Future of the Punjab

And so it was that Lawrence, with the full support of the leading courtiers at Lahore and Governor-General Hardinge, took the drastic step of forcibly separating Jind Kaur from her son. Once the Maharani was removed from court, control over the Maharajah's education fell completely into the Resident's hands. Until that point, Duleep Singh had mainly been tutored by the sons of the esteemed diplomat Fakir Azizuddin, and the boy was noted as having become particularly proficient in painting and Persian studies.[56] However, John Lawrence (Acting Resident again during a second period of convalescence leave for his brother) now managed to supplement this schooling with a much more demanding programme. British political officers were appointed to work with the 9-year-old Maharajah daily, teaching him English and initiating him into an approved curriculum of historical and scientific studies.[57] For the most part, it appears that the royal family's involvement in the Maharajah's training was completely stripped away, and that Duleep Singh was pushed into predominantly cerebral, scholarly pursuits. Where previously he had at least accompanied his mother on tours of inspection, or to worship at gurdwaras and shrines, Duleep's ability to learn about rulership through direct participation in administrative and military affairs was dramatically curtailed after the signing of the Bhyrowal Treaty—even his 'Lilliputian' boys' regiment had mostly been disbanded with the demobilisation of the majority of the Khalsa Army. The young Maharajah was taken on occasional hunting trips and regularly went on riding excursions, but it would seem otherwise that he was kept at all times within the bounds of the countryside immediately surrounding Lahore.

From all this, we can see the new kind of role that Duleep Singh was intended to play. He was to be a liberally educated figure, who would rely on a body of specialist administrative officers (most likely Punjabis) to run his state for him, along guidelines provided and closely supervised by British authorities through ongoing political monitoring. By 1848, the extent of personal authority that he would be able to wield on attaining his majority, in terms of shaping or directing the internal workings and development of his own kingdom, had not been clarified, and would most likely have become a significant matter of debate had the Second Anglo-Sikh War not broken out. Nevertheless, it was certainly clear that the Maharajah's role would continue to be important in a diplomatic and ceremonial sense, not only regionally, but within the wider imperial politics of the Indian subcontinent too. After all, the Bhyrowal Treaty had stipulated that Duleep Singh was to be allowed to rule his Empire independently once he reached the age of 16, in 1854. It seems fair to assert that Hardinge and the Lawrence brothers were setting up the young Maharajah for the same handy role that Ranjit Singh had played as a controlling buffer on the Company's northwestern frontier—though they were clearly educating Duleep to be an enhanced and modernised version of his father.

This Punjabi royal experiment was also part of broader developments in this period, a significant precursor to the British policy adopted towards the Indian princely states in the second half of the century. After the 1857 Revolt, the East India Company itself was abolished, and all power for ruling India was assumed by the British Crown and its government in London. With the issuing of Queen Victoria's Royal Proclamation in 1858, annexationist policy against the remaining Indian kingdoms was suspended and the loyalty of the subcontinent's remaining Maharajahs became a vital pillar for securing the shaken foundations of the British Raj. These rulers' education and administrative training was closely monitored by British Residents and political officers in order to engrain loyalty to the Raj from a young age. Arguably, Duleep Singh's case tells us that such endeavours truly began well before the ending of Company rule, and that he was among the first of a new coterie of Indian princes to be educated under predominantly British auspices. The curriculum that he was exposed to would subsequently evolve in later-nineteenth-century royal schoolrooms across India, but there will have been many essential similarities in the ethos and goals behind his training and that of later Indian Maharajahs living under the British Raj.[58] Such a project, however, could only really make progress under relatively peaceful and stable conditions, and with the backing of a Governor-General who was keen to maintain a relationship with a local Indian ruler. Neither of these two conditions would remain intact for long in late 1840s Punjab.

In April 1848, a rebellion broke out in Multan, one of the key strategic cities within the Sikh Empire. Multan was originally conquered in 1818 under the banner of Prince Kharak Singh, after months of effort had been poured into a protracted siege of Multan's main fortress; the prince had been heavily supported by the Khalsa Army's most talented generals and his mother, Mai Nakain. The governance of the surrounding province had thereafter remained with the family of Diwan Sawan Mal. By 1848 however, Sawan Mal's son, Mulraj, was about to be removed from the post of Governor (*nazim*), since the British-controlled Lahore government was unhappy at what they perceived as his growing insubordination and low revenue payments. A body of Sikh troops was dispatched to Multan, led by Mulraj's newly appointed replacement, Kahan Singh Man, and accompanied by two political officers from the Company, a lieutenant and his assistant. However, on arrival at the citadel, the Sikh soldiers turned on all of their officers and later killed the two Company men. They seized control of the fort and subsequently proclaimed a rebellion throughout the entire province against the Residency government.

This dramatic turn of events sparked great unease and confusion throughout the Punjab. It was unclear at the time whether the murderous outbreak at Multan was an isolated incident or part of a deeply laid conspiracy; but a crisis suddenly erupted when Mulraj (willingly or unwillingly) assumed leadership of the soldiers and with them issued an appeal for the remainder of the Khalsa Army to rally behind Maharajah Duleep Singh and his mother. The soldiers' proclamation described the boy-king and Jind Kaur as being 'in sorrow and affliction' after the Maharani's forced exile from Lahore the previous year, and encouraged all of their loyal followers to fight to establish the Maharajah 'firmly' in his government, by ousting the British.[59] Once again, Jind Kaur was being recognised as the 'Mother of all the Sikhs.'[60] From this moment on, she began to be characterised as the symbolic icon of both heroic Punjabi resistance and victimised motherhood, and is still revered as such today in popular Sikh history—a far cry from the way she had been perceived and treated by the Khalsa Army on the eve of the First Anglo-Sikh War. In November and December 1845, according to British colonial records at least, the Sikh soldiers had used that same title in a much more moralising manner, to justify their attempts to curb the Maharani's freedom of association with Lal Singh—much as Henry Lawrence had invoked her motherhood in his attempts to control her *zenana*-based activities before he eventually had her exiled.

Unsurprisingly, there was grave concern that the soldiers' revolt and the killing of the British officers marked a resurgence of the Khalsa Army's revolutionary bent. Above all, the naming of Jind

Kaur within the Multan proclamation led many in the British government to suspect that the Maharani must have been implicated in the mutiny somehow, despite her being locked up at Sheikhupura.[61] She was swiftly and forcibly exiled from the Punjab altogether as the crisis unfolded, being moved first to Benares and then to Chunar, where she was held effectively as a state prisoner in a jail-like fort, with a constant watch placed on her and her servants, over 700 miles from her son. In a complete reversal of all normal forms of decorum for the treatment of an Indian queen, the Maharani and her servant girls even had their baggage and their persons subjected to searches, to check for any incriminating evidence they might have on them.[62] Nothing was immediately found to connect Jind Kaur or her people with the Multan rebellion, but these measures marked the increasingly brutal manner in which the British colonial authorities were prepared to crack down on any remaining shreds of the Maharani's personal autonomy.

The reaction of the British and Punjabi ruling elite to the April 1848 uprising was very uneven, which in itself triggered a downward spiral of political antagonism. There was great suspicion within British ranks about which Punjabi *sardars* and courtiers could now be trusted, and this in turn prompted fear and consternation amongst the latter about the sincerity of the Company's intentions towards them. Chattar Singh Attariwala, Duleep Singh's prospective father-in-law, had only recently been trying to get the then Acting Resident, Sir Frederick Currie (Henry Lawrence was again away for a prolonged convalescence period), to confirm a date for the betrothal of his daughter to the young Maharajah and to ensure that the marriage alliance originally arranged with Jind Kaur would still go ahead. Currie coldly replied that arranging Duleep Singh's marriage was not a 'line of policy which the government may consider it right to pursue now or at any future time in respect to the administration of the Punjab.'[63] Coming as this did around the time that the Maharani had had her pension slashed and was forced into exile in Benares, the chilling tone of Currie's response sparked concern that the Maharajah himself might not be safe on the throne for much longer. The Attariwala *sardars* had of course been key allies to Henry Lawrence in orchestrating the ousting of Jind Kaur from Lahore, but they had never anticipated that either they or the royal family as a whole could be rendered so easily disposable by the British government.

Chattar Singh Attariwala was to receive an even more painfully rude shock when James Abbott, the British political agent stationed in the province he governed, raised a levy of local Muslim tribes and launched an attack on the Attariwala fort at Haripur in early September. For reasons known only to Abbott, he suspected the *sardar*'s loyalty, and went so far as to take over the Attariwala *jagirs* and suspend the blameless Chattar Singh from his position as Governor of Hazara. Currie did attempt to intervene and rebuke Abbott, but it was all too late. Chattar Singh took his combined treatment by Currie and Abbott as the gravest of insults and threats, and decided to throw his weight behind the mounting rebellion. It did not take long for his son Sher, an important courtier at Lahore, to join him, becoming similarly disgusted and fearful at this shocking turn of events by October. Chattar Singh even took the radical step of reaching out to Dost Muhammad Khan of Afghanistan, to try to forge a pact for ousting the British from the region altogether.

A full-scale war was on the verge of breaking out in the Punjab. Yet this could have been averted with relative ease and speed. Crucial to this deeply precarious situation were the terms of the 1846 Bhyrowal Treaty, under which the British Resident at Lahore (Currie at this time) wielded the power to mobilise whatever military force he needed to put down any rebellion against the government, which he himself controlled as the Maharajah's Regent. The Resident's actions were only subject to the approval of the Governor-General. Had Hardinge still been in post when these events unfolded, there might have been a diffusion of tensions at the point of this check and balance. However, when the Multan rebellion erupted, Hardinge was no longer the Company's leading man in India. He had retired from the post and had been replaced from the beginning of January 1848 by a rampantly pro-annexationist successor: James Broun-Ramsay, Marquis of Dalhousie.

Dalhousie had no patience for Hardinge and Lawrence's experimental policy of 'watching and waiting' to determine whether the Lahore monarchy could serve British interests. Currie too had switched to favouring annexation and appeared to have been eager to deploy Company forces to quell the rebellion as soon as possible, stuck as he was in Lahore. There was one problem, however: although a military intervention could be justified under such conditions, the takeover of Duleep Singh's entire kingdom could not—since neither the Maharajah nor any of his ministers at Lahore had themselves rebelled. Currie was therefore ordered by his new boss to carry out an adapted version of Hardinge's 'wait and see' approach: this time, to hold fast on deploying the Residency government's full military powers until the cold weather season, and meanwhile to watch on as the rebellion worsened into a major conflict, so that a 'Second Anglo-Sikh War' and a subsequent annexation could be justified.

In strikingly candid terms, Dalhousie had confided privately to a friend in August that 'The result cannot be doubted, as a military operation. But after that will come the settling, and it will be a crooked affair.'[64] When Rajah Sher Singh Attariwala joined the Multan rebellion two months later, Dalhousie was delighted:

> They have been and done it now. Raja Shere Sing, the [prospective] brother-in-law of the Maharaja, has joined Moolraj with his whole army, and issues proclamations in the name of the Maharaja calling on all true Sikhs to join him, pithily adding, 'Murder all Feringees [= foreigners].'
>
> This is short and sweet and decides the question. I have ordered the army to be augmented, [with] troops from Madras and from Bombay, and have written for 3 regiments from home [i.e. Britain] which Hardinge sent away in January! I have told the C.-in-C. that the whole business must be done this cold weather, if possible...
>
> ... since they will force war on me, I have drawn the sword, and this time thrown away the scabbard. If the Sikhs, after this is over, rise again, they shall intrench themselves behind a dunghill, and fight with their finger-nails, for if I live 12 months they shall have nothing else left to fight with.[65]

Currie was made to wait until the winter of 1848–9 for these extra reinforcements to arrive in the Punjab, along with Dalhousie himself, who was stationed at Government House in Calcutta and had moved to the Ludhiana frontier post at the start of the winter. In the meantime, the Acting Resident had no choice but to put the strongest defences he could around the capital, where he was forced to pretend that he was governing the Sikh Empire as the loyal minister of the Maharajah until the war's end on 11 March 1849.

By the end of 1848, Henry Lawrence himself had also returned to the Punjab, but was only able to resume his beloved job as Resident for a short while longer. It was then that Dalhousie began to unveil the true extent of his revisionist policy for the Punjab's future. Not only did he intend to take direct control of the remaining independent Sikh Empire, but he was also determined to wipe out the entire Punjabi aristocracy, stripping them of all their power and wealth by depriving them of their *jagirs*. For the Punjab of 1849, this would represent a root-and-branch destruction of the ruling elite culture, as Lawrence recognised—even after the destabilising overthrow of Maharani Jind Kaur, one of the main causes of the Multan rebellion's outbreak, more damage could still be done.

In what we now know were the dying days of the Sikh Empire, Lawrence wrote a series of private letters desperately urging Dalhousie not to annex the Punjab. He even tried to get the Governor-General to consider that it would be wiser policy for neither the blameless Maharajah nor the rebellious *sardars* to be too harshly punished, and argued that peace in the Punjab could be restored if those men who had stood with the British Residency were rewarded with additional *jagirs* and titles for their loyalty.[66] As Sada Kaur had once guided her teenage son-in-law Ranjit Singh after his own taking of Lahore, so Lawrence attempted to instruct his new boss in the regional etiquette of acting as a noble conqueror:

> Ours is the only Government that has ever, in India, restricted itself to resuming jagheers. The Delhi Kings & Hindoo Princes were very arbitrary but what they took from one they gave to another. The Government of the day, therefore always had some friends among the influential & military classes. I fear that, beyond our army, there are few that willingly lift a finger for us. It is therefore that, while I do remember our financial difficulties, I advocate liberality to Jagheerdars.[67]

This advice fell on deaf ears; in Dalhousie's mind, not even 'loyal' *sardars* should be entitled to rewards.[68] He in fact intended for the *jagirdar* class as a whole to be phased out within a generation or two,[69] and, most ominously, would not even lay out a plan of financial provision for any future children of Duleep Singh.[70] The rupturing impulses of the colonising reforms imposed by Hardinge and the Lawrences had been turned into a full-blown revolution by the new Governor-General, destroying the power of Ranjit Singh's dynasty forever.

* * *

Thus ended the Sikh Empire. Little Duleep Singh, the 10-year-old Maharajah, was compelled to sign a punitive annexation treaty in March 1849, through which he lost his ancestral Empire, almost all of his dynasty's wealth and property, and—most importantly of all—his personal freedom. Within nine months, he was transported out of his former kingdom as a political exile, just as his mother had been two years earlier. His new home in Fatehgarh was then ransacked by Indian rebels in the 1857 Revolt, and he decided to settle in England. Tragically, neither Jind Kaur nor Duleep Singh would ever set foot on Punjabi soil again. They would only be reunited in 1861, Duleep travelling to Calcutta after thirteen years of painful separation to bring his ailing mother back to England with him. But, given the heights from which mother and son had fallen, the enormous physical distance that had been placed between them, and the increasing might of the British in India, this was an extraordinary reunion against the odds.

By the time of Duleep Singh's fall and exile, Jind Kaur had pulled off an incredible feat: she had managed to escape from Chunar Fort, disguised as her seamstress. It finally emerged in 1849 that she had been behind the Multan insurrection all along. Whilst imprisoned at Sheikhupura, she had secretly hatched a plan for Kahan Singh Man and his troops to launch a rebellion upon their arrival at Mulraj's fort. It was only when one of her priests was captured at Lahore that evidence incriminating the Maharani finally fell into British hands, in the form of incendiary letters that had been cleverly sealed inside of a pair of innocent-looking amulets.[71] The rebel queen had been powerless to lead the uprising once she had been removed from the Punjab, but had never given up the fight. Whilst at Benares, she had even hired her own British lawyer to push back against the slanderous representations of her in the Anglo-Indian press,[72] and was preparing to pay him to take her case to the British Parliament when Dalhousie cracked down on her plans by blocking any further lawyer visits to her prison quarters.[73] At that point, the Maharani realised that only by escaping from British custody could she have any hope of restoring her son to the throne and resurrecting the independence of Punjab. So, with an astonishingly indefatigable spirit, she slipped out of jail and trekked all the way to Nepal, to seek a sanctuary from which she could keep alive her hopes of seeing her son again, and continuing the struggle for the Punjab.

To the very end, then, the tale of the last Maharani and Maharajah of the Sikh Empire is also a story of survival and ingenuity. This was something they shared with all the queens and princes of their family who had come before them—the very people who had built the Sikh Empire to begin with. Whatever their mistakes and losses, the royal family deserve to be remembered in all of their rich complexity: as shrewdly creative individuals who crafted and ran a kingdom beyond their ancestors' wildest dreams; and who never quite admitted defeat.

CONCLUSION

For many Punjabi families, this little couplet has long been a folk favourite:

Ik si rajah, ik si rani,

Dono margeh, khatham kahaani!

Translated into English, this means: 'Once there was a King and Queen, they both died, end of story!' It's an irreverent quip that most likely stems from the folktales about fictional royalty that have been passed down between generations throughout India over the course of many centuries. My own dad never tired of repeating this joke to my brother and me while we were growing up—though it does get more annoying when you're a bit older and trying to write an actual book about royalty! There is no doubt that we have seen a lot of kings, queens and princes dying during the course of this book, some under especially brutal and unforgettable circumstances. Just as Guru Nanak preached, not even the most powerful and wealthy kings can cheat death. But their deaths only ended their own stories: what the preceding pages have taught us is that, contrary to what has been assumed for so long, royal deaths alone did not end the Sikh Empire—not even that of the Lion of Punjab, Ranjit Singh.

As a kingdom, the Sikh Empire was wiped off the map 170 years ago, but it left behind a significant legacy: not only in terms of shaping politics and culture in the region of Punjab, but also as a lasting imprint on popular memory, which of course has its most prominent resonance in Ranjit Singh's role as a national hero for many Sikhs and Punjabis to this day. Yet only by equally resurrecting the story of both the 'Rajah' and the 'Rani'—or more accurately, the many Ranis—can we truly and deeply understand the inner world of the Sikh Empire. It has been an exciting challenge to ask new, critical questions and explore alternative sources about this extraordinary period and region, and to open up new perspectives on how the men, women and children of the Punjabi royal elite went about constructing a new kingdom in the late eighteenth and nineteenth centuries—whether it was Sada Kaur helping out Ranjit Singh on the battlefield, Kharak Singh 'hugging' the British in a diplomatic gesture, Mai Nakain commissioning works of art for her royal apartments, or Nau Nihal Singh getting married and having children, to mention just a few aspects of their busy and colourful lives. The historical footprints left behind by Ranjit Singh's parents, uncles, aunts, in-laws, wives, children and grandchildren deserve to take their place in history. That history should not be limited to the story of one 'great man' alone, no matter how talented he might have been.

Beyond these leading figures of Ranjit Singh's dynasty, we have also uncovered the evolving dynamics of the wider 'royal' world around them: particularly how perceptions of individual monarchs, as well as ideas about kingship more generally, ebbed and flowed with each passing generation of subjects. Even when entire monarchies or dynasties are removed from the scene, the influence and symbolic power of royal culture still linger on, taking new forms in accordance with changing circumstances and interests. Across several centuries of Punjabi history, we have encountered in this book all sorts of debates and reformulations around who could legitimately rule and what it meant to be royal—from the revolutionary royalism of the Khalsa founded by Guru Gobind Singh in 1699; to Chand Kaur's battles with Sher Singh over the rights of women to rule in 1840; and then again, in the new style of colonial government and ceremonial royal culture forced upon Jind Kaur and Duleep Singh by the British after 1846.

The process of looking anew and with more curiosity at these characters and ideas in turn compels us to come to a very different understanding and appreciation of history-writing itself, whether on the subject of the Sikh Empire, or on the evolving role and status of royalty more generally. We may never have all the answers about lingering questions or controversies in the history; and, of course, our reflections on the past will always be coloured by our own contemporary concerns and biases. However, by at least questioning the hagiography, misogyny and Orientalism that have infused the dominant narratives about this fascinating kingdom and its society, and by unravelling how these have coloured our perceptions, I think it's fair to say that we not only reach a richer, more insightful understanding of what really contributed to the rise and fall of the Sikh Empire; but also, in a broader sense, we can more fully appreciate what this history has meant to generations of people interested in its fate, and the continual evolution of the narratives constructed around it by political, cultural and scholarly observers to this day.

The rise and fall of the Sikh Empire was never really a self-contained or isolated affair. We cannot overlook the fact that its story is embedded in the wider world of the nineteenth century, a time when the powers and privileges of royal elites across the globe were subject to great challenge and change. As we know today, by the end of the 1800s, many monarchs would be much less powerful than before, if they even had a throne to continue sitting on, but of course many of them hadn't known that this would happen when their reigns began. Indeed, the first half of the century was still an era of great vibrancy and political fluidity for royalism; even of huge opportunity for all sorts of men and women to make a grab for power. Ranjit Singh's own ancestors had been peasant farmers to begin with; and, although by the time he came to take over his *misl* he was a third-generation *sardar*, we cannot forget that his dynasty only succeeded in further growing its power by incorporating a wide range of people from many different backgrounds—with his last and ultimately most influential queen being Jind Kaur, the daughter of a kennel-keeper.

The royal power of this particular dynasty was uprooted in a formal sense in 1849, when the Sikh Empire was dismantled and annexed by the East India Company. This pattern followed for many other royal houses across India and Pakistan as a whole, into the second half of the twentieth century. Yet it is important to remember that this British takeover was very much a piecemeal process; in fact, India's remaining royal families only lost their right to 'privy purses' in 1971. Even today, when both nations are republics, the trappings of regional royal culture continue to live on in many ways, as they imbue the performance of state ceremonial and popular politics. Dynasticism still remains a dynamic force within the corridors of power in modern South Asia too. Whilst there appear not to be any direct descendants of Ranjit Singh around in the Punjab today, it is significant that the Indian state's Chief Minister at the time of writing is Captain Amarinder Singh, a man whose father was the last Maharajah of Patiala—a neighbouring Sikh state to Ranjit Singh's kingdom, becoming the most influential Punjabi princely state after the Company annexed the former Sikh Empire in 1849.

Since the Cis-Sutlej states had previously entered into the Company's protection, and as they remained pacific during its wars with the Sikh Empire and later came to British aid during the 1858 Revolt, they and other similarly acting Indian kingdoms were kept intact and treated as important allies for the remainder of the British Raj, in a reversion to the old style of princely diplomacy advocated by the likes of Claude Wade and Henry Lawrence in the 1830s and 1840s. In many cases, the royal rulers of such states went on to wield great influence in post-independence India and Pakistan, alongside the rising star of several new, non-royal dynasties, including the Nehru-Gandhis in India and the Bhuttos in Pakistan.

On the other hand, for the Sikhs in particular, the question of their own sovereignty remains a deeply complex one, over seventy years after their homeland was split down the middle and divided between two different, increasingly antagonistic nation-states. The legacy of the Sikh Empire loomed large in the calls of many Sikhs for political redress during the 1947 'transfer of power' negotiations. However, with Sikh populations scattered throughout the vast region of pre-Partition Punjab, and with Sikh political opinion on the matter internally conflicted, any demands for the (re)creation of a Sikh-dominated state were dismissed. In many ways, that period of contestation, as the British withdrew from the subcontinent, mirrored the much earlier uncertainties and tensions within the *panth* following the death of Guru Gobind Singh in 1708, when the Sikhs grappled with difficult decisions over how to organise their self-governance as a sovereign people. Despite all this, the Gurus' spirit and ideas about revolutionary royalty continue to live on: every time a Sikh visits their local gurdwara and bows to make an offering or say a prayer before a *Guru Granth Sahib*, that holy book is covered with an ornate canopy, behind which a priest stands to carefully wave a fly-whisk, ensuring that not a speck of dust touches its surface. In every such moment, the ancient royal culture of the Indian subcontinent that was first refashioned by the Gurus is re-enacted again and again.

That said, one thing is for sure: despite Punjabis' and Sikhs' ongoing fascination, pride and debates about the legacy of the Sikh Empire and its royal family, there is no popular desire today for a restoration of Sikh monarchy—indeed, there has not been any such call since the 1880s, when Duleep Singh launched a desperate bid to reclaim his kingdom and declare war on the British Empire. At this point in his life, the Maharajah-in-exile proudly proclaimed his Sikh identity. However, this was a recent change in him. At the age of 14 he had become a baptised Christian, and then as a young adult, Duleep Singh wholeheartedly embraced life as an Anglicised country gentleman. In his new life in England, he was accorded a warm welcome in the family circle of Queen Victoria—enjoying a lot more grandeur and respect than he could expect in India under Dalhousie's regime. In an ironic way, by becoming so friendly with the British Crown, Duleep Singh also managed to fulfil the ambitious dreams of his father Ranjit Singh, forging a close bond with the British royals. Dalhousie was deeply unhappy at the 'special treatment' accorded to the young Maharajah in Britain; but all concerned with the stability of the British Raj seemed to agree that there was less chance of trouble being stirred up in the Punjab if he remained away from India and his mother.

Even that plan failed, however, for Duleep managed to find discreet ways to contact Jind Kaur in her free exile in Kathmandu. By 1861, after the 'Indian Mutiny' had been quelled, mother and son were begrudgingly granted permission to meet in Calcutta. Thereafter, it was decided by India's first Viceroy, Lord Canning, that it would be probably be safer after all for them both to be settled in England, rather than separated again—forcibly or otherwise.[1] Relatively modern Sikh/Punjabi oral tradition has often had it that, in the two years they spent living with one another before the Maharani died in 1863, the blind but still feisty Jind Kaur stoked in her son a burning desire for rebellion.[2] While there is certainly plenty of evidence that the Maharani did push Duleep to fight for his lost kingdom, her words clearly did not have any real immediate impact on him, since he wouldn't actually move to launch his vengeance mission against the British imperial government for another twenty-five years.

It was Duleep Singh's newfound radical scheme in the 1880s that led him to reconnect with the remainder of his family and his former servants at Lahore, hoping to gain their support for his bold political plans. His key supporters within the Punjab were his Sandhawalia cousins—the family that had put him on the throne in the first place when he was a boy of five. Continuing the family's rebellious streak (they were also, after all, the ones who had attempted to avenge Chand Kaur's murder), Thakur Singh acted as the new prime minister of Duleep's ill-fated 'provisional government-in-exile'. As for the figures we've come to know over this book, unfortunately, we only have scraps of information from colonial pension records and scattered letters amongst the last Maharajah's papers to guess at what happened to the overlooked descendants of Duleep Singh's older half-brothers, the Sikh princes; or to the wives of the late Ranjit Singh, Kharak Singh, Sher Singh and Nau Nihal Singh, as well as their adopted children and servants.

From such sources, we can at least glean that Gul Begum seems to have become the seniormost queen in the pension rankings after Jind Kaur's enforced exile.[3] It seems that, in the end, of all Ranjit Singh's wives, it was the dancing-girl and the kennel-keeper's daughter who had the last laugh. Gul Begum and the other remaining royal women, together with the descendants of the various princes, lived out the rest of their lives on their scattered estates in Lahore and elsewhere across the Punjab, funded by dwindling stipends that were paid to them by the colonial state out of the dynasty's former treasury revenues. Another intriguing find in the pension lists is the possibility that Kharak Singh's second queen had been involved in the Khalsa Army mutiny at Multan: Khem Kaur Kalalwali had her lucrative estate confiscated—it had been worth Rs. 12,000 a year—and her pension slashed to Rs. 2,400 as punishment for supporting the rebellion, though it's not clear whether she had collaborated with Jind Kaur.

It is unclear how far Duleep Singh himself had wished or managed to keep in touch with his extended family in the years after he was deposed and forced to leave Lahore as a boy, but as an adult, it seems for the most part—rather tragically, one could say—that his interest in their fate and fortunes became increasingly connected with finding out how he could lay claim to their stipends after they died. He was concerned to secure the financial future of his own growing family in England, especially after it became clear that Dalhousie and his colleagues had made no plans for the support of his heirs. Duleep Singh would have six children with his first wife, Bamba Muller, and a further two with his mistress, whom he married after Bamba's death. Arguably, the real tipping-point into rebellion against the Raj was Duleep's powerlessness to ensure that his newly built home in the Suffolk countryside would pass to his eldest son and heir, Victor—named after his godmother, Queen Victoria. That endeavour too would fail, and the last Maharajah of the Sikh Empire eventually died a broken-spirited man, alone in a Paris hotel room in 1893.[4]

Despite this desolate end, the names of Duleep Singh and Jind Kaur continue to live on in the popular memory of the Punjab, almost as famously as that of Ranjit Singh. But they, along with the other queens and princes we have come to know in this book, are forever associated with the tragedy and scandal that surrounded the fall of the Sikh Empire, whereas the first Maharajah so often takes all the glory for its rise. Perhaps the world will yet come to recognise and remember these young men and women not as the weak, dissolute figures of British colonial accounts, but as the dynamic, ambitious players that they were, battling for power in a world and era of great change.

APPENDICES

QUEENS OF THE SIKH EMPIRE

Appendix I. A Marriage Map

Below is a map showing the geographical (and familial) origins of the first four Maharajahs' royal wives, giving an insight into the Sukerchakia dynasty's strategic use of marriage alliances to strengthen its empire-building project. The wives of the first Maharajah, Ranjit Singh, are represented by stars; those of his two eldest sons, Kharak Singh and Sher Singh, are shown as circles and hexagons respectively; the wives of his grandson, Nau Nihal Singh, are marked as triangles.

I first created a version of this map for my PhD thesis, kindly reworked here by Sebastian Ballard. The data used to populate it derives partly from the mentions of Punjabi royal women in Persian courtly histories from Ranjit's reign, including Suri's *Umdat-ut-tawarikh* and the *Zafarnama-i-Ranjit Singh*; and also from the India Office Records in the British Library, which contain lists of the stipendiary pensions provided to members of the 'Lahore Royal Family' after the annexation of the Sikh Empire in 1849. These sources collectively provide information on the names and origins of a range of Punjabi, Kashmiri and Pathan women, as well as the dates of their marriage or presentation as concubines. The exact style of marriage ceremonies carried out by the Maharajahs is unknown, but we can see here the initial formation of kinship ties with close-by *misls*, as well as those with other neighbouring powers, from the Hindu hill-states close to the Himalayas and the independent Sikh kingdoms across the River Sutlej, to the Afghan frontier region and the Hindu Rajput states to their east.

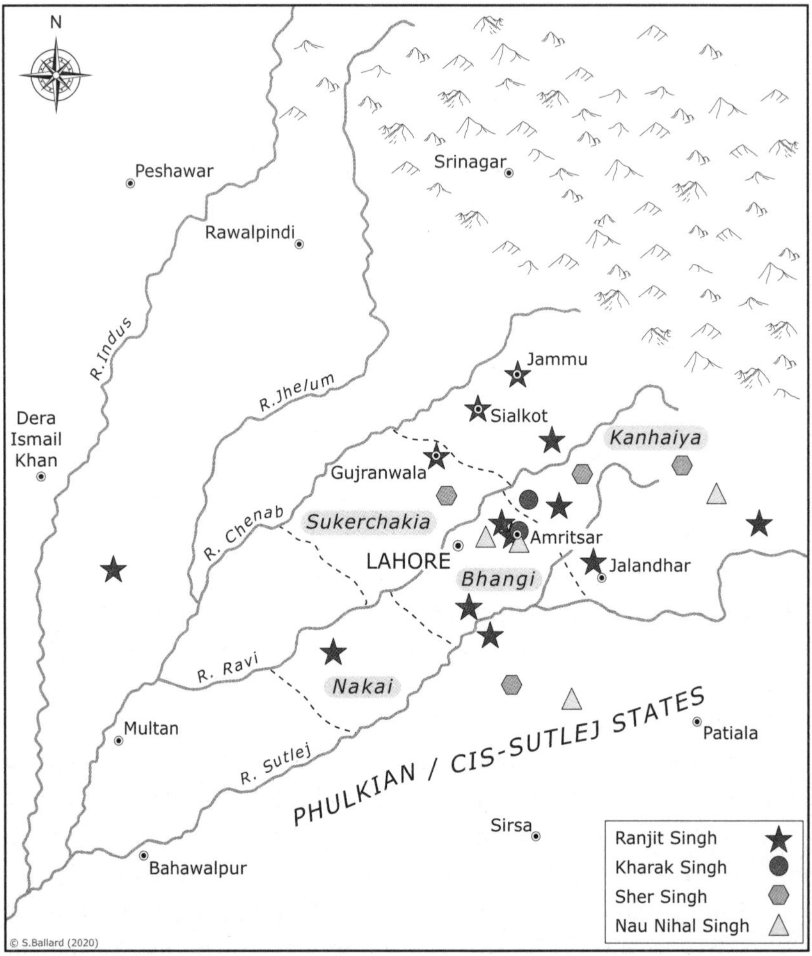

Map 3: Geographical origins of Sukerchakia wives and concubines, 1795–1842.

Appendix II. List of All Known Queens of the Empire

The information provided here is the closest I could get to producing a full, tabulated list of all the *ranis* of Ranjit Singh's dynasty. The pension values given in the tables are those documented in British colonial records: after 1849, these 'stipends' were paid to the wives/widows of Ranjit Singh and his sons, out of the Punjab government revenues. To my knowledge, these tables constitute the greatest amount of data ever published about these forgotten women.

Ranjit Singh's wives:

Name of Rani	*Background*	*Date married*	*Date of death*	*Pension value*	*Other property*	*Dependants/heirs*
Mehtab Kaur	Daughter of Kanhaiya *misl*	1789	1813	–	Batala *jagir*	Maharajah Sher Singh and Prince Tara Singh
Mai Nakain (Datar Kaur)	Daughter of Nakai *misl*	1797	1838	–	Sheikhupura *jagir*	Maharajah Kharak Singh
Moran	Dancing girl from Amritsar	1802	1839?	Unknown	Multiple houses, garden and public buildings in Lahore	–
Rattan Kaur	Widow of Sahib Singh Bhangi	1811	?	Rs. 1,000	–	Prince Multana Singh (supposedly procured from one of Mai Nakain's Muslim slave girls?)
Daya Kaur	Widow of Sahib Singh Bhangi (Rattan Kaur's sister)	1811	?	Unknown	–	Princes Kashmira & Peshaura Singh. Mai Raj Kaur (mother of Rattan and Daya Kaur) received a British pension of Rs.400 until she died on 23 February 1852.
Unknown	Zamindar's daughter from Vainiki	1812	?	Unknown	–	–
Roop Kaur	Daughter of Jai Singh, Kot Said Mehmood	1815	?	Rs. 1,980	–	Adopted her nephew's son.

Jumrul Beebee	Daughter of a shawl weaver, presented to Ranjit by Governor of Kashmir	1816	?	Rs. 1,800	–	–
Luchmee Kaur Vudpuggun	Adopted daughter of *sardar* of Kartarpur	1820	?	Rs. 11,200	–	Looked after Duleep when Jind Kaur was exiled. Adopted a girl, Ram Kaur.
Jind Kulan	Daughter of a Pathan from Mankera	1824	?	Rs. 1,800	–	–
Jind Kaur	Daughter of Manna Singh Aulakh (kennel-keeper at Lahore)	1825?	1863	Rs. 30,000	Duleepgarh, jewellery	Maharajah Duleep Singh
Doulee Khoond	Daughter of Rajputs from Jammu	1826	?	Rs. 1,563	–	–
Chund Kaur	Daughter of Jatt *zamindars* of Duska, Sialkot	1827	?	Rs. 2,520 (cut to Rs. 1,260 after she eloped in 1852!)	Residence in Sialkot	–
Dukhno	Daughter of a Rajput family from Kangra	1827	?	Rs. 1,908	Residence in Kangra	–
Katochan (Mehtab Devi/ Guddan)	Daughter of Rajah Sansar Chand of Kangra	1829	1839 (by *sati*)	–	–	–
Raj Banso	Daughter of Rajah Sansar Chand of Kangra	1829	1830s (suicide)	–	–	–
Medno	Daughter of Suleria	1829	?	Rs. 7,291	–	–

	zamindar, 'Oochul Singh' from Gurdaspura					
Mehtab Kaur (2)	Daughter of Soojana Singh, Jatt *zamindar* from Sialkot	1829	?	Rs. 1,930	–	–
Zebo	Presented to Ranjit Singh by Governor of Kashmir (possibly Sher Singh: also later his concubine?)	1830	1855?	Rs. 1,620	–	May have raised a boy, Buksheesh Singh: son of a Kashmiri pundit adopted by Sher Singh while he was Governor of Kashmir (the child received a pension of Rs. 1,974 after Zebo's death).
Gul Begum	Dancing girl from Amritsar	1830	1863?	Rs. 12,380	*Jagir* (in Ranjit Singh's lifetime), plus *haveli*, mosque and garden in Lahore	Adopted a Muslim boy.
Bhooree	Daughter of Goojur family from Mandi	1831	?	Rs. 10,096	–	Adopted Bhoop Singh, child of a slave-girl.
Deokee Khoord	Former slave girl from Jusrota	1832	?	Rs. 2,465	Residence in Jammu(?), where she moved.	–
Suman Kaur	Daughter of Jatt *zamindar* from Ferozpur	1832	?	Rs. 1,440	Residence in Ferozpur(?), where she moved back home.	–

Chainpurwala	Unknown	?	?	Unknown	–	Rs. 360 given to her sister-in-law, Rajim, at Chainpur?
Hardavi	Daughter of Bavee & Singhasno, from Utulgarh, *zillah* Gurdaspura	?	1839 (by *sati*)	–	–	Parents received Rs. 925 pension as she was a *sati*.
Deokee Kulan	Unknown	?	1854	Unknown	–	–
Doulee Kulan	Former slave-girl of Rani Kishno(?)	?	1859	Rs. 3,015	–	–
Durooptee	From Nurpur	?	29 Dec 1852	Rs. 1,782	–	–
Gulab Kaur	From Sialkot	?	July 1856 (aged 47)	Rs. 1,620	–	–

Kharak Singh's wives:

Name of Rani	*Background*	*Date married*	*Date of death*	*Pension value*	*Other property*	*Dependents/ heirs*
Chand Kaur	Daughter of Jaimal Singh Kanhaiya	1811	1842 (murdered)	–	–	Maharajah Nau Nihal Singh
Khem Kaur Kalalwali	Daughter of Jodh Singh Kalalwala	3 July 1815?	?	Rs. 2,400	*Jagir* worth Rs. 12,000 confiscated after she was caught colluding in the Multan rebellion	Adopted cousin's son, Bhagwan Singh.
Kishan Kaur (AKA Subhrawali)	Daughter of Jatt *zamindar* from Gurdaspur	1815	?	Rs. 2,324	–	–

Nau Nihal Singh's wives:

Name of Rani	*Background*	*Date married*	*Date of death*	*Pension value*	*Other property*	*Dependents/ heirs*
Nanki Kaur	Daughter of Sham Singh Attariwala	1837	November 1856	Rs. 4,600	–	–
Sahib Kaur	Daughter of Gurdit Singh Gilwaliwala of Amritsar	?	1841	–	–	–
Bhadauran Kaur	Daughter of a *sardar* of Bhadaur	?	1840 (reputedly by *sati*)	–	–	–
Katochan Kaur	Daughter of Mian Rai Singh of Lambagraon	?	1840 (reputedly by *sati*)	–	–	–

Sher Singh's wives:

Name of Rani	*Background*	*Date married*	*Date of death*	*Pension value*	*Other property*	*Dependents/heirs*
Prem Kaur	Daughter of Hari Singh, Jatt *zamindar* of Mouza Luddhewala, Gujranwalla	1822	?	Rs. 7,200	–	Prince Partap Singh (murdered in 1843). Adopted a son, Narain Singh, after annexation in 1849.
Partap Kaur	Daughter of *sardar* Jugut Singh of Kot Kapoora	1825	August 1857	Rs. 5,400	–	Adopted cousin's son, Thakoor Singh, in 1847. He was 14 & was awarded Rs. 1,800 cash pension from 1848. Studied at Lahore High School & married to daughter of Jatt *zamindar* of Nabha territory.

Golee	Formerly a 'prostitute' from Gurdaspur	1832	?	Rs. 3,600	–	–
Kundo	Daughter of Jatt *zamindar* of a village near Kangra. Sent as slave-girl in 1829 from Kangra.	1841	?	Rs. 1,260	Residence in Kangra?	–
Dukhno	Daughter of a Chang *zamindar*, reputedly presented to Sher Singh by a *kardar* at Kangra	1842	?	Rs. 9,000	Residence in Benares, where she lived from July 1856	Prince Shiv Deo Singh (received a *jagir* worth Rs. 10,000 for land outside the Punjab after 1849).
*Dhurm Kaur Rundhavee	Unknown	1841?	Rs. 7,200	–	–	Adopted son?
*Chund Kaur	Unknown	1842?	?	–	–	Dewa Singh: reputed illegitimate son of Sher Singh, born 1838.

*According to the British pension records, these two women were supposedly the wives of Tara Singh, Sher Singh's brother; however, they are mentioned as having joined Sher Singh's *zenana* once he became Maharajah. Dhurm Kaur Rundhavee is noted as having originally married Tara Singh in 1823. These same records also imply that Tara Singh was 'impotent' and an 'imbecile', and that he died by 1861.

Peshaura Singh's wives:

Name of Rani	*Background*	*Date married*	*Date of death*	*Pension value*	*Other property*	*Dependents/heirs*
Jeevun Kaur	Unknown	?	?	Rs. 1,800	–	Juggut Singh (received a *jagir* from the British based outside the Punjab, worth Rs. 5,000)
Sada Kaur	Unknown	?	?	Rs. 720	–	–
Utur Kaur	Unknown	?	?	Rs. 720	–	–

Kashmira Singh's wives:

Name of Rani	*Background*	*Date married*	*Date of death*	*Pension value*	*Other property*	*Dependents/heirs*
Chund Kaur	Unknown	?	?	Rs. 1,800	–	Futteh Singh (received a *jagir* worth Rs. 5,000 outside of Punjab from the British)
Jind Kaur	Unknown	?	?	Rs. 720	–	–

Multana Singh's wives:

Name of Rani	*Background*	*Date married*	*Date of death*	*Pension value*	*Other property*	*Dependents/heirs*
Chund Kaur	–	?	?	Rs. 1,000	Residence in Amritsar?	Keshun & Kesra Singh
Man Kaur	Formerly wife of Boodhoo Munshi, Muslim from Lahore? (So likely a concubine)	1857?	?	–	–	Arjan Singh, who received pension of Rs. 1,030 and was married to a daughter of a Hindu Jatt *zamindar* from Amritsar.

NOTES

INTRODUCTION

1. On Punjabi wedding customs, see Kristina Myrvold, 'Wedding Ceremonies in Punjab', *Journal of Punjab Studies*, vol. 11, no. 2 (2004), pp. 155–70; and Shinder Thandi, 'What is Sikh in a "Sikh Wedding"? Text, Ritual and Performance in Diaspora Marriage Practices', *Journal of Punjab Studies*, vol. 23, no. 1/2 (Spring–Fall 2016). On dowry and gender inequality, see Ranjana Sheel, *The Political Economy of Dowry: Institutionalization and Expansion in North India* (New Delhi: Manohar, 1999); and Werner Menski (ed.), *South Asians and the Dowry Problem* (London: Trentham, 1998).
2. Sohan Lal Suri, trans. V.S. Suri, *Umdat-ut-tawarikh*. Daftar III [Parts I–III] (Amritsar: Guru Nanak Dev University, 2002), p. 438.
3. I have used the term 'Sikh Empire' throughout this book, since in modern parlance that is the most widely recognised name used for the kingdom of Ranjit Singh's dynasty. It is not exactly how the state/kingdom was described by its contemporaries, but as I explain in Chapter 1, within the Punjab itself, the government of the Empire as a whole was known in Punjabi as the *Sarkar-i-Khalsa* ('the government of the Khalsa')—a title maintained by Ranjit Singh and his successors in deference to the sovereign body/community of the Khalsa, as established by the last of the ten Sikh Gurus, Guru Gobind Singh. Interestingly, British and European contemporaries of the Punjabi royals referred to the state as the 'kingdom of Lahore' and to Ranjit's dynasty as the 'Lahore royal family'. The term 'Sikh Empire' seems to have entered into more popular usage during the twentieth century, perhaps as an adaptation of the '*Sarkar-i-Khalsa*' title into English, though with a clearer recognition of the imperial nature of the territorial kingdom established by Ranjit Singh's Sukerchakia *misl* and his successors.
4. I am here building upon groundbreaking work on the gender history of the Sikhs and nineteenth-century Punjab, produced by scholars such as Jakobsh and Nesbitt. See especially Doris R. Jakobsh, *Relocating Gender in Sikh History: Transformation, Meaning and Identity* (New Delhi: OUP, 2003); and, more recently, Eleanor Nesbitt, '"Woman Seems to Be Given Her

Proper Place": Western Women's Encounter with Sikh Women 1809–2012', *Religions*, vol. 10, no. 9 (2019).
5. See Ruby Lal, *Domesticity and Power in the Early Mughal World* (Cambridge: CUP, 2005); and Munis D. Faruqui, *The Princes of the Mughal Empire, 1504–1719* (Cambridge: CUP, 2012).
6. See Purnima Dhavan, *When Sparrows Became Hawks: The Making of the Sikh Warrior Tradition, 1699–1799* (New York: OUP, 2011); Louis E. Fenech, *The Darbar of the Sikh Gurus: The Court of God in the World of Men* (New Delhi: OUP, 2008); and Louis E. Fenech, 'Ranjit Singh, the Shawl, and the *Kaukab-i Iqbal-i Punjab*', *Sikh Formations*, vol. 11, nos 1–2 (2015), pp. 1–25; plus the multiple works by J.S. Grewal on Sikh politics in general and on Ranjit Singh's rulership in particular, especially *The Reign of Maharaja Ranjit Singh: Structure of Power, Economy and Society* (Patiala: Punjabi University, 1981).
7. Not least in returning to the efforts of committed Punjabi scholars of the twentieth century, who initiated the work of translating, studying and interpreting the Persian records of the Sikh Empire, a large number of which still reside in the Punjab Government Archives, housed at Anarkali's Tomb in Lahore, or are otherwise scattered across libraries (or even the cupboards of family homes) throughout Indian Punjab. This includes not only the richly detailed research of J.S. Grewal and Indu Banga on the regional history of the Punjab's society, economy and politics (e.g. *Early Nineteenth Century Panjab: From Ganesh Das' Char Bagh-i-Panjab* (London: Routledge India, 2015); or *Civil and Military Affairs of Maharaja Ranjit Singh*, (Amritsar: Guru Nanak Dev University, 1987)), but also the pioneering works of early twentieth-century historians—especially Sita Ram Kohli, Hari Ram Gupta and Ganda Singh, who translated, compiled and published multiple volumes of courtly records and private correspondence relating to the world of the Sikh Empire and the eventual Anglo-Sikh Wars. I am indebted to the incredible hard work carried out by this generation of scholars, whose publications provided a deeply useful and accessible foundation for my own research.

1. TO BE A SIKH KING

1. Sohan Lal Suri, trans. V.S. Suri, *Umdat-ut-tawarikh*. Daftar II (Amritsar: Guru Nanak Dev University, 2002), p. 1.
2. This was a key finding of my doctoral research: see Rajpreet Atwal, *Between the Courts of Lahore and Windsor: Anglo-Indian relations and the re-making of royalty in the nineteenth century* (unpublished DPhil thesis: University of Oxford, 2017), pp. 15–17.
3. A fact that has increasingly been recognised and studied anew by historians of Sikh politics, at least since the 1970s/80s. See, for example: Bhagat

Singh, *Sikh Polity in the Eighteenth and Nineteenth Centuries* (New Delhi: Oriental Publishers and Distributors, 1978), especially pp. 137–215; Fauja Singh, *Some Aspects of State and Society under Ranjit Singh* (New Delhi: Master Publishers, 1982), pp. 17–50; and J.S. Grewal, *Sikh Ideology, Polity and Social Order: From Guru Nanak to Maharaja Ranjit Singh* (New Delhi: Manohar, 2007), pp. 174–222, 258–77.

4. I am here citing the translation and analysis of Nikky-Guninder Kaur Singh: 'Babarvani and the call for gender justice', *Sikh Formations*, vol. 13, nos 1–2, p. 7 (2017).
5. Ibid., p. 11.
6. Ibid., p. 6.
7. Rattan Singh Bhangu, trans. Kulwant Singh, *Sri Guru Panth Prakash*, vol. II (Chandigarh: Institute of Sikh Studies, 2008), p. 271.
8. Ibid., pp. 253–79.
9. Ibid., pp. 7, 11–15.
10. Words such as *jan* or *banda* are descriptors repeatedly used with this meaning throughout the *Guru Granth Sahib*.
11. Pashaura Singh, *Life and Work of Guru Arjan: History, memory and biography in the Sikh tradition* (New Delhi: OUP, 2006), pp. 105–8.
12. I take on board here Pashaura Singh's insightful analysis of the 'disarming humility' of Guru Arjan. Ibid., p. 122.
13. Guru Arjan, 'Siri Ragu' 2, *Adi Granth*, p. 74, cited by Pashaura Singh, ibid., p. 121.
14. Pashaura Singh, *Life and Work of Guru Arjan*, p. 115.
15. Abu'l-Fazl's *Akbarnama*, cited by ibid., p. 19.
16. Pashaura Singh, *Life and Work of Guru Arjan*, pp. 193–8.
17. Ibid., p. 88.
18. A. Azfar Moin has explored the concepts of 'sacred kingship' and 'sainthood' in Islam, through the expressions of sovereignty of the Mughal-Timurid and Safavid dynasties during the early modern era. See *The Millennial Sovereign: Sacred Kingship and Sainthood in Islam* (New York: Columbia University Press, 2012), pp. 1–6.
19. Pashaura Singh, *Life and Work of Guru Arjan*, p. 19.
20. This argument about the significance of Guru Hargobind's changes to the nature of the guruship, and of Sikh sovereignty as a whole, is derived from the work of Hardip Singh Syan, *Sikh Militancy in the Seventeenth Century: Religious Violence in Mughal and Early Modern India* (London: Bloomsbury, 2013), particularly Chapter 2.
21. Louis E. Fenech, 'Ranjit Singh, the Shawl, and the *Kaukab-i Iqbāl-i Punjāb*', *Sikh Formations*, vol. 11, nos 1–2, p. 89 (2015).
22. See for example Pashaura Singh's *Life and Work of Guru Arjan*, pp. 65–8, for details of the fifth Guru's wide-ranging education in scriptural tradi-

tion, music, poetry and philosophy across the Gurmukhi, Hindi and Persian languages. Additionally, for further evidence of the interest shown by Guru Gobind Singh and Maharajah Ranjit Singh in Islamic/Persianate and ancient Indic literature on courtly ethics, see Fenech, 'Ranjit Singh, the Shawl and the *Kaukab-i Iqbāl-i Punjāb*'; and Louis E. Fenech, *The Sikh Zafar-namah of Guru Gobind Singh: A Discursive Blade in the Heart of the Mughal Empire* (New York: OUP, 2013).

23. For a detailed study of the emergence of these gendered courtly norms during the reign of Akbar, see Rosalind O'Hanlon's important article, 'Kingdom, Household and Body History, Gender and Imperial Service under Akbar', *Modern Asian Studies*, vol. 41, no. 5 (2007), pp. 889–923.
24. Syan, *Sikh Militancy*, p. 49.
25. I here utilise Louis Fenech's translation of the Guru's Persian letter from *The Sikh Zafar-namah*, p. 85.
26. I have again drawn here on Fenech's rich and highly insightful analysis of the *Zafarnamah* as a 'Sikh Shahnameh'. *The Sikh Zafar-namah*, in particular Chapters 1, 3 and 5.
27. Again, Fenech's new arguments about the formation of the Khalsa as a fascinating form of continuation, or even extension, of the nascent style of a rebelliously humble courtly culture under the Sikh Gurus are a fascinating contribution to our understanding of Sikh history for this watershed period. Representing the inauguration of the Khalsa as a moment of collective 'coronation', rooted in Guru Gobind Singh's re-interpretation of notions of Indo-Persian 'sacred kingship' (which seems to have enabled him to recognise both the sovereignty and divinity of the *panth*) is an incredibly powerful idea, and really does seem to demonstrate that other arguments around the Khalsa representing a form of religious 'republicanism' are rather too simplistic, and do not entirely convey the depth of the manner in which the Guru was trying to empower his people. Louis E. Fenech, *The Cherished Five in Sikh History* (New York: OUP, forthcoming).
28. Khushwant Singh, *Ranjit Singh: Maharaja of Punjab* (Mumbai: Penguin Random House India, 2008), p. 36.
29. Ibid., p. 37.
30. Patwant Singh & Jyoti M. Rai, *Empire of the Sikhs: The Life and Times of Maharaja Ranjit Singh* (London: Peter Owen, 2008), pp. 202–3.
31. Purnima Dhavan, *When Sparrows Became Hawks: The Making of the Sikh Warrior Tradition, 1699–1799* (New York: OUP, 2011), p. 57.
32. Ibid., pp. 84, 97.
33. Muzaffar Alam, *The Crisis of Empire in Mughal North India: Awadh and the Punjab, 1707–48* (New Delhi: OUP, 2013), Chapter 4.
34. This chapter does not include much original research of my own, but

instead draws on the rich scholarship about Sikh political/intellectual history produced in recent years by scholars such as Nikky-Guninder Kaur Singh, Louis Fenech, Purnima Dhavan, J.S. Grewal and others. It is intended to provide a context for the rest of my book, with respect to outlining the social, religious and political dynamics of the Punjab, for the period leading up to the emergence of the 'Sikh Empire'.

35. Kapur Singh, ed. Piar Singh and Madanjit Kaur, *Parasaraprasna:The* Baisakh *of Guru Gobind Singh* (Amritsar: Guru Nanak Dev University, 1959), p. 41.
36. Ibid. See particularly the chapter 'The Sikh Raj'. As can be seen in the footnotes of Patwant Singh & Rai, *Empire of the Sikhs*, p. 281.
37. Interestingly overlooking the more standard Sikh-Mughal binary in this instance. For Kapur Singh, it was a 'Hindu' royal elite, together with the 'Brahman priesthood', that had deliberately suppressed an older, more progressive Indic tradition of republicanism throughout the centuries leading up to the era of the Sikh Gurus.
38. Kapur Singh, ed. Piar Singh and Madanjit Kaur, *Parasaraprasna:The* Baisakh *of Guru Gobind Singh*, 4th edition (Amritsar: Guru Nanak Dev University, 2017), pp. 202–50.
39. Kapur Singh was not alone in some of the criticisms that he levelled at the Sikh Empire. Teja Singh, another Sikh historian and approximate contemporary of Kapur Singh, is also somewhat critical of the impact and style of Ranjit Singh's rule: he too represents it as deviating away from the earlier 'pristine purity' of Sikh life and governance under the direct aegis of the Khalsa. He characterises the Maharajah's reign as a time when 'kingship became a thing of jewels and clothes, [and] Sikhism too, with the higher classes, became a mere fashion of the beard and turban.' (*Essays in Sikhism* (Lahore: Sikh University Press, 1944, p. 118.) Although these are speculative comments at this stage, it seems that the works of both scholars share common goals. Firstly, they fervently argue that the Sikh faith and community was entirely distinct from that of Hindus, thus following in the footsteps of the late-nineteenth-century Tat Khalsa movement of Sikh revivalists, who aimed to re-assert more exclusive and strictly defined notions of 'Sikh' identity and practice. Although their two texts were published on either side of Indian independence—Teja Singh's in 1944 and Kapur Singh in 1959—it is possible to infer that the same core concerns inform both scholars' reflections on the career of Ranjit Singh and criticisms about the neglect/abolition of the *gurmata/ Sarbat Khalsa*. These were nothing short of ensuring that Sikh demands and political representations were amply respected in the plans for an independent India following the ending of the British Raj; but equally that the Sikh *panth* could not be opportunistically absorbed into or dom-

inated by the larger Hindu population—similarly to the fears of Muhammad Ali Jinnah and the Muslim League, regarding the respective 'minority' of Muslims in relation to the larger Hindu population in the subcontinent, which led to Partition and the creation of Pakistan.

40. Dhavan, *When Sparrows Became Hawks*, p. 42.
41. *Rahitnama* attributed to Desa Singh, cited in ibid., p. 80.
42. Dhavan, *When Sparrows Become Hawks*, Chapter 4.
43. Khatris were a Hindu caste, who predominantly worked as mercantile traders and civil administrators in Mughal Punjab.
44. McLeod discusses these issues of authorship and dating in detail, in the introduction to his translation of Randhir Singh's version of the *Prem Sumarag Granth*. W.H. McLeod, *Prem Sumarag: The Testimony of a Sanatan Sikh* (New Delhi: OUP, 2006), pp. 1–9.
45. Ibid., p. 91.
46. Ibid., pp. 99–100, 102–3.
47. Ibid., p. 90.
48. Milinda Banerjee's book, *The Mortal God*, provides valuable insights into comparable examples of martial–peasant understandings of collective and internalised sovereign–royal status, spread across a body of lower-class/-caste people. His case studies are rooted in nineteenth- and twentieth-century Bengal and Tripura, highlighting the wide-ranging presence of these ideas of 'subaltern' royalty and sovereignty: cropping up across the Indian subcontinent and continuing on even in the 'postcolonial'/'postmodern' world. See especially Chapters 4 and 5 in *The Mortal God: Imagining the Sovereign in Colonial India* (Cambridge: CUP, 2018). On the successor states created by 'lapsed' Mughal nobles, there is a growing body of literature, including (but not limited to) the following works: Alam, *The Crisis of Empire*; Richard B. Barnett, *North India Between Empires: Awadh, the Mughals, and the British, 1720–1801* (Berkeley, CA: University of California Press, 1980); Munis D. Faruqui, 'At Empire's End: The Nizam, Hyderabad and Eighteenth-Century India', *Modern Asian Studies*, vol. 43, no. 1 (2009), pp. 5–43.
49. Interestingly, this is despite the fact that the *Prem Sumarag Granth* advocated the maintenance of such a system, though founded on an entirely meritocratic principle: one in which any talented individual could be made a noble, rather than drawing upon an existing pool of recognised elites. See McLeod, *Prem Sumarag*, pp. 100–1, 103.
50. I take this point from Fenech's valuable analysis in his *Sikh Formations* article on 'Ranjit Singh, the Shawl and the *Kaukab-i Iqbāl-i Punjāb*'.
51. Khushwant Singh, *Ranjit Singh*, p. 36.
52. Available to view online via the Victoria & Albert Museum website: 'Maharaja Ranjit Singh's throne', http://collections.vam.ac.uk/item/

O18891/maharaja-ranjit-singhs-throne-throne-chair-hafiz-muhammad-multani/ (accessed on 12 July 2019).

53. Fenech, 'Ranjit Singh, the Shawl, and the *Kaukab-i Iqbāl-i Punjāb*', p. 91.

2. NEW DYNASTY, NEW EMPIRE

1. J.S. Grewal, *The Reign of Maharaja Ranjit Singh: Structure of Power, Economy and Society* (Patiala: Punjab Historical Studies Dept, Punjabi University, 1981), p. 2.
2. *Ibid.*, p. 2.
3. Grewal describes how the administrative structure established by the Sukerchakia *sardars* mostly drew on pre-existing local practices; they were evidently not keen on disturbing their new subjects too much. The *sardars* kept the posts of *thanedar* (superintendent) and *faujdar* (military commander) as maintained by other Sikh chiefs, and simply replaced men with their own capable supporters. Additionally, they emulated Mughal financial hierarchies by appointing a *kardar* for the collection of revenue (in coin or kind) at the local level, with a *diwan* (advisor) looking after financial affairs overall, to manage the payment of soldiers.
4. I borrow this useful term from the work of Susan Broomhall and Jacqueline Van Gent, historians of the early modern princely house of Orange-Nassau. They describe 'dynastic colonialism' as being 'the House's domination of land and spaces in material and cultural ways that engendered political consequences: namely, to extend its sphere of influence politically and geographically'. They discuss how engagement with material culture (e.g. collecting objects, engaging in gift exchange, or experimenting with the designs of their homes and gardens) enabled the men and women of the Orange-Nassau family to represent their dynastic identity collectively and to project their growing power in Europe and across their colonies. Broomhall and Van Gent, *Dynastic Colonialism: Gender, materiality and the early modern house of Orange-Nassau* (Abingdon: Routledge, 2016), p. 2. This is a very helpful study of the ways in which dynastic power and self-fashioning can be culturally performed, and I would argue that the activities of the Orange-Nassau family have strong parallels with the case of Ranjit Singh's kin, as they shifted away from being seen as the leaders of one *misl* among many to becoming the ambassadors of a new imperial kingdom and royal lineage.
5. Jeroen Duindam, *Dynasties: A Global History of Power, 1300–1800* (Cambridge: CUP, 2016), p. 301.
6. Hari Ram Gupta, *History of the Sikhs*, vol. IV (New Delhi: Munshiram Manoharlal, 1982) p. 232.

7. Sohan Lal Suri, trans. V.S. Suri, *Umdat-ut-tawarikh*, Daftar II (Amritsar: Guru Nanak Dev University, 2002), p. 14.
8. Gupta, *History of the Sikhs*, vol. IV, p. 264.
9. Suri, *Umdat-ut-tawarikh*, Daftar II, p. 35.
10. Mai Nakain's given name was Raj Kaur, but to avoid confusion with Ranjit Singh's mother she was later renamed Datar Kaur; Mai Nakain is the name by which she is popularly known.
11. Suri, *Umdat-ut-tawarikh*, Daftar II, pp. 36–7.
12. As Dhavan has argued. Purnima Dhavan, *When Sparrows Became Hawks: The Making of the Sikh Warrior Tradition, 1699–1799* (New York: OUP, 2011), pp. 145–6.
13. Suri, *Umdat-ut-tawarikh*, Daftar II, pp. 40–1.
14. Indeed, the boldness of Ranjit Singh's treatment of Jaimal Singh Kanhaiya is evinced in an entry of the *Umdat-ut-tawarikh* from 1807, where Suri notes: 'the Sarkar stayed at the town of Shaharmal in the fief of Jaimal Singh Kanhia, father-in-law of prince Kharak Singh. The place was brought under control. Dewan Harbhaj Rai was placed under arrest and was charged Rs. 25,000 as tribute. The Sarkar crossed from the point of Bolaki Chak, plundered the dominions of Jaimal Singh, charged the due and hurriedly arrived at Amritsar.' Daftar II, p. 59.
15. In this group, I have included the wives of Ranjit Singh and of Princes Kharak Singh, Nau Nihal Singh and Sher Singh. These were the only princes treated explicitly as potential heirs to the throne during Ranjit Singh's lifetime and who succeeded as Maharajahs after his death (Duleep Singh ruled as a minor). I have taken the dates of their marriage from the pension lists for the 'Lahore Royal Family' held in the British Library (IOR/L/PS/6/525, Coll. 42/1: Provision for Members of the Lahore Royal Family, 8 May 1861). These lists also include the names and pensions of the wives of other, minor Sikh princes who were the sons of Ranjit Singh's wives (Peshaura Singh, Kashmira Singh and Multana Singh), but do not mention the dates on which these princes were married. The three junior princes married a total of six women, and Multana Singh kept one additional concubine.
16. Gupta, *A History of the Sikhs*, vol. IV, pp. 250–1.
17. The Ranis Gulab Kaur, Medno, Chund Kaur and another Mehtab Kaur hailed from Sialkot and Gurdaspura in the north; Lachmi Kaur Vadpaggan, Roop Kaur and one unnamed woman came respectively from Kartarpur and the villages around Amritsar (Kot Said Mehmood and Vainiki), in the Sikh heartlands of the Punjab plains; and finally, Suman Kaur originated from Ferozpur, the southernmost point of Ranjit Singh's empire bordering the Cis-Sutlej states. For more details about the backgrounds of Gulab Kaur, Medno, Chund Kaur (the second), Mehtab Kaur, Lachmi Kaur

Vadpaggan, Roop Kaur and Suman Kaur, see BL IOR/L/PS/6/525, Coll. 42/1: 'Statement of the Members of the Lahore Royal Family, receiving provision from Government'.

18. Suri notes, for example, a marriage between the Maharajah and a woman from Vainiki after the death of the local *thanadar* (superintendent), Jit Singh, whose land Ranjit Singh took possession of. *Umdat-ut-tawarikh*, Daftar II, p. 133.
19. Jind Kaur's father, Manna Singh Aulakh, supposedly pressed the Maharajah to take his daughter as a wife. Anita Anand, *Sophia: Princess, Suffragette, Revolutionary* (London: Bloomsbury, 2015), p. 14.
20. Suri, *Umdat-ut-tawarikh*, Daftar III (Parts I–III), pp. 31–2.
21. BL, 'Statement of the Members of the Lahore Royal Family'.
22. Suri, *Umdat-ut-tawarikh*, Daftar III (Parts I-III), p. 216.
23. Terms that also appear repeatedly in the *Umdat-ut-tawarikh*.
24. Amar Nath, trans. Kirpal Singh, *Zafarnama-e-Ranjit Singh* (Patiala: Punjabi University, 1995), p. 196.
25. Ibid., p. 196.
26. From email correspondence with Arundeep Singh Sarkaria, May 2015.
27. Ruby Lal, *Domesticity and Power in the Early Mughal World* (Cambridge: CUP, 2005), p. 167.
28. Fakir Syed Waheeduddin, *The Real Ranjit Singh* (Patiala: Punjabi University, 2001), p. 129.
29. Patwant Singh & Jyoti M. Rai, *Empire of the Sikhs: The Life and Times of Maharaja Ranjit Singh* (London: Peter Owen, 2008), pp. 156–7.
30. John Pemble (ed.), *Miss Fane in India* (Gloucester: Alan Sutton, 1985), pp. 209–10.
31. Khushwant Singh, *Ranjit Singh: Maharaja of Punjab* (Mumbai: Penguin Random House India, 2008), pp. 6–8.
32. Salma Sultana, 'Architecture of Sheikhupura Fort in Historical Perspective', *South Asian Studies*, vol. 5 (1989), p. 116.
33. Nadhra Khan notes how mangoes carried connotations of female fertility in Maharani Gul Begum's pavilion/tomb and apartments, suggesting that this was a well-known artistic device amongst elite Punjabi women: 'The Secular Sikh Maharaja and his Muslim Wife', in Mahesh Sharma & Padma Kaimal (eds), *Indian Painting: Themes, Histories, Interpretations. Essays in Honour of B. N. Goswamy*, (Ahmedabad: Mapin, 2013), pp. 256–8.
34. RAS Persian 89: Sohan Lal Suri, *Umdat-ut-tawarikh*, ff.312.
35. Depictions of the Gurus were also included in the *samadhi* (mausoleums) of Ranjit Singh, Kharak Singh and Nau Nihal Singh. The visual association between the Sikh Gurus and the imperial dynasty may or may not have been linked to the apocryphal tale of a blessing given by a Guru to one of Ranjit Singh's early ancestors. This episode opens the second vol-

ume of Suri's *Umdat-ut-tawarikh*, in which he outlines the rise to power of the Sukerchakia *misl* (Daftar II, pp. 1–3). The origins of this tale are not known, but such legends were a common feature of Sikh *misl* histories of the eighteenth century, and were used to legitimise the claims of a *sardar*'s family to conquered territory and royal status. Purnima Dhavan, 'Redemptive Pasts and Imperiled Futures: the Writing of a Sikh History', *Sikh Formations*, vol. 3, no. 2 (December 2007), pp. 122–3.

36. In popular Sikh tradition, Guru Gobind Singh is referred to by the title of *Kalgidhar*, which translates as 'wearer of a *kalgi*' (a turban ornament in the shape of a plume or feather). A *kalgi* was part of the royal accoutrement of Rajput and Mughal kings, and so the last Guru's adorning of his own turban in this style was yet another way in which he subverted the social hierarchies of his day, as well as laying claim to sovereignty (*patshahi*) in both a spiritual and temporal sense. Whilst early portraits of Ranjit Singh certainly depict him wearing jewels in the folds of his turban, they do not show him sporting a *kalgi*, as can be seen in the oldest known portraits of the Maharajah, in the British Museum (1936, 0411, 0.1) or as published in Davinder Toor's catalogue, *In Pursuit of Empire: Treasures from the Toor Collection of Sikh Art* (London: Kashi House, 2017), pp. 46–7. However, it would seem that as the Maharajah grew older and his reign became more established, his court artists (and perhaps Ranjit himself) became more active in representing him in more overtly regal style. In a portrait produced in the very last year or so of the Maharajah's life, his likeness is delicately painted with full Mughal-style regalia included: featuring a *chattri* (parasol), *shamsa* (halo/sunburst) and a golden *kalgi* on his otherwise simple turban (Victoria & Albert Museum: IS.111–1953).
37. Suri, *Umdat-ut-tawarikh*, Daftar II, p. 469.
38. Aruti Nayar, 'Moran, the mystery woman', *The Tribune*, 24 August 2008, http://www.tribuneindia.com/2008/20080824/spectrum/main3.htm (accessed 30 October 2016).
39. Khan, 'Secular Sikh Maharaja', pp. 256–7.
40. J.S. Grewal & Indu Banga, *Civil Athe Military Mamle* (Amritsar: Guru Nanak Dev University, 2001), p. 119.
41. Jean-Marie Lafont's work on Ranjit Singh's Empire provides ample evidence of such shared celebrations (*Maharaja Ranjit Singh: Lord of the Five Rivers* (New Delhi: OUP, 2002), pp. 68–83). See also Harjot Oberoi, 'From the Ritual to the Counter-Ritual: Re-thinking the Hindu-Sikh Question, 1884–1915', in Joseph T. O'Connell, Milton Israel & Willard G. Oxtoby (eds), *Sikh History and Religion in the Twentieth Century* (Toronto: University of Toronto Press, 1988), pp. 137, 156.

42. Peter Bance, *Sovereign, Squire and Rebel: Maharajah Duleep Singh* (London: Coronet House, 2009), p. 47.
43. Radha Sharma, 'General Preface', in Suri, *Umdat-ut-tawarikh*, Daftar II.
44. Suri, *Umdat-ut-tawarikh*, Daftar II, p. 40.
45. Ibid., p. 54.
46. Ibid., pp. 15–16; for drawings of the birth horoscopes for Ranjit Singh and Kharak Singh, see RAS Persian 89: *Umdat-ut-tawarikh*, ff.194 & 234–5.
47. A. Azfar Moin, *The Millennial Sovereign: Sacred Kingship and Sainthood in Islam* (New York: Columbia University Press, 2012), p. 11.
48. From his account of Duleep Singh's birth in 1838, Suri seems to have been harbouring a hope that the Maharajah would commission him to produce a horoscope for the newborn prince, but nobody seems to have asked him, possibly because there is a hint that the zodiacal signs for his birth might not have been that positive. Suri, *Umdat-ut-tawarikh*, Daftar III (Parts IV–V), pp. 253–4.
49. Suri, *Umdat-ut-tawarikh*, Daftar IV, pp. 138–9.
50. Sohan Lal Suri, trans. Gurbaksh Singh [Punjabi language], *Umdat-ut-tawarikh*, Daftar IV (Amritsar: Guru Nanak Dev University), p. 130.
51. Suri, trans. V.S. Suri, *Umdat-ut-tawarikh*, Daftar II, p. 96. All references to the chronicle hereafter in the form 'Suri, *Umdat-ut-tawarikh*' are to this English-language edition.
52. RAS Persian 89: *Umdat-ut-tawarikh*, ff.294.
53. Ibid., ff.295.
54. Suri, *Umdat-ut-tawarikh*, Daftar II, p. 98.
55. Waheeduddin, *Real Ranjit Singh*, p. 102.
56. Suri, *Umdat-ut-tawarikh*, Daftar II, p. 87.
57. Munis D. Faruqui, *The Princes of the Mughal Empire, 1504–1719* (Cambridge: CUP, 2012), pp. 6–13.
58. Suri, *Umdat-ut-tawarikh*, Daftar III, Part IV, p. 227.
59. Rosalind O'Hanlon, 'Kingdom, Household and Body History, Gender and Imperial Service under Akbar', *Modern Asian Studies*, vol. 41, no. 5 (2007), p. 903.
60. Lafont, *Maharaja Ranjit Singh*, pp. 74–5.
61. Suri, *Umdat-ut-tawarikh*, Daftar II, pp. 25–6.
62. Ibid., p. 23.
63. O'Hanlon, 'Kingdom, Household and Body History'; Rosalind O'Hanlon, 'Masculinity and the Bangash Nawabs of Farrukhabad', in Tony Ballantyne & Antoinette Burton (eds), *Bodies in Contact: Rethinking Colonial Encounters in World History* (Durham, NC: Duke University Press, 2005), p. 22.
64. O'Hanlon, 'Masculinity and the Bangash Nawabs', p. 22.
65. British Library Or.5259, *Sarvasiddhantattvacudamani*. Details of the com-

mission and contents were found in Cecil Bendall, *Catalogue of the Sanskrit Manuscripts in the British Museum* (London: Gilbert & Rivington, 1902), p. 208.

66. Suri, *Umdat-ut-tawarikh*, Daftar II, p. 238.
67. Mian Pir Muhammad, ed. Harnam Singh Shan, *Chattian Di Var* (Chandigarh: Punjab University, 1970), stanza 10. For a fascinating analysis of this poem, see Jeevan Deol, '"To Hell with War": Literature of Political Resistance in Early Nineteenth-Century Punjab', *South Asia Research*, vol. 17, no. 2 (Autumn 1997), pp. 197–202.
68. George Carmichael Smyth, *A History of the Reigning Family of Lahore* (Calcutta: W. Thacker & Co., 1847), pp. 13–14.

3. ALL THE WORLD'S A STAGE

1. Alexander Burnes, 'On the Political State of Cabool', 26 November 1837, in *Reports and Papers, Political, Geographical and Commercial Submitted to Government by Sir Alexander Burnes, Lt Leech, Dr Lord and Lt Wood, Employed on Missions in the Years 1835–36–37 in Scinde, Affghanisthan and Adjacent Countries* (Calcutta: G.H. Huttmann, Bengal Military Orphan Press, 1839).
2. Sohan Lal Suri, trans. V.S. Suri, *Umdat-ut-tawarikh*, Daftar III (Amritsar: Guru Nanak Dev University, 2002), Part IV, p. 223.
3. Two important examples highlighted by Suri are the grandson of the Rajah of the neighbouring Sikh kingdom of Kapurthala, who visited in mid-August, and Rajah Ajit Singh Ladwa of the smaller state of Thanesar, who made arrangements to travel to Lahore in person by November. Suri, *Umdat ut-tawarikh*, Daftar III, Part IV, p. 247; and Suri, *Umdat ut-tawarikh*, Part V, p. 259.
4. Ram Sukh Rao, ed. Joginder Kaur, *Sri Fateh Singh Partap Prabhakar* (Patiala: J. Kaur, 1980), p. 543.
5. The families of lesser *sardars* were not treated quite so gently by the Maharajah on occasions when they lost the head of their household. Such families, who were perhaps lower in the pecking order of Punjabi society, or without claims to exemption on religious grounds as the Bedis enjoyed, perhaps only received consolatory visits from state officials—accompanied by demands for tribute, or even the annexation of portions of land inherited by heirs. Nevertheless, as Dhavan has explained, such demands had to be couched in terms that did not hurt the *izzat* (honour or self-respect) of the family in question, as Sikh rulers had to be seen to be charitable (particularly to Khalsa families) and to guarantee the continued livelihood and dignity of the individuals now brought metaphorically under their 'protection'. Purnima Dhavan, *When Sparrows Became Hawks: The*

Making of the Sikh Warrior Tradition, 1699–1799 (New York: OUP, 2011), pp. 145–6.

6. Michael H. Fisher, 'Diplomacy in India, 1526–1858', in H.V. Bowen, Elizabeth Mancke & John G. Reid, *Britain's Oceanic Empire, Atlantic and Indian Ocean Worlds, c. 1550–1850* (Cambridge: CUP, 2012), pp. 253, 258–60.
7. Suri, *Umdat-ut-tawarikh*, Daftar III, Part IV, pp. 242–4.
8. Ibid., pp. 248–9.
9. Ibid., p. 249.
10. Patwant Singh & Jyoti M. Rai, *Empire of the Sikhs: The Life and Times of Maharaja Ranjit Singh* (London: Peter Owen, 2008), pp. 135–52; Khushwant Singh, *Ranjit Singh: Maharaja of Punjab* (Mumbai: Penguin Random House India, 2008); Fauja Singh, *Some Aspects of State and Society under Ranjit Singh* (New Delhi: Master Publishers, 1982), p. 326.
11. Dhavan, *When Sparrows Became Hawks*, p. 97.
12. For some useful comparative case studies, see the following works: Rosalind O'Hanlon, 'Masculinity and the Bangash Nawabs of Farrukhabad', in Tony Ballantyne and Antoinette Burton (eds), *Bodies in Contact: Rethinking Colonial Encounters in World History* (Durham, NC: Duke University Press, 2005); Hannah L. Archambault, 'Becoming Mughal in the Nineteenth Century: The Case of the Bhopal Princely State', *South Asia: Journal of South Asian Studies*, vol. 36, no. 4 (2013), pp. 479–95; and Munis D. Faruqui, 'At Empire's End: The Nizam, Hyderabad and Eighteenth-Century India', *Modern Asian Studies*, vol. 43, no. 1 (2009), pp. 5–43.
13. Dhavan, *When Sparrows Became Hawks*, p. 144.
14. Charles Joseph Hall Jr, *The Maharaja's Account Books: State and Society under the Sikhs, 1799–1849*, (unpublished PhD thesis: University of Chicago-Illinois, 1981), pp. 120–1.
15. Indrani Chatterjee, 'Introduction', in Indrani Chatterjee (ed.), *Unfamiliar Relations: Family and History in South Asia* (New Brunswick: Rutgers University Press, 2004), p. 20.
16. Michael H. Fisher, 'Becoming and Making "Family" in Hindustan', in Chatterjee, *Unfamiliar Relations*, p. 95. The Begum actually accompanied a British diplomatic party to an important meeting with the Maharajah; but, on the orders of the Governor General, the ambitious lady was prevented from leaving the camp or meeting Ranjit Singh. Suri, *Umdat-ut-tawarikh*, Daftar III, Parts I–III, p. 112; M.L. Ahluwalia, *Maharani Jind Kaur, 1816–1863*, Amritsar: Singh Bros, 2001, p. 31.
17. Khushwant Singh, *Ranjit Singh*, pp. 52–7.
18. Suri, *Umdat-ut-tawarikh*, Daftar II, p. 109.
19. Ibid., p. 69.

20. John William Kaye, *The Life and Correspondence of Charles, Lord Metcalfe*, vol. 1 (London: Smith, Elder & Co., 1858), pp. 186–8.
21. Ibid., p. 168; Patwant Singh & Rai, *Empire of the Sikhs*, pp. 105–6.
22. Suri, *Umdat-ut-tawarikh*, Daftar II, pp. 74–5.
23. Ibid., pp. 229–30.
24. Ibid., p. 89. Ranjit Singh would send two *munshis* (secretaries) from Lahore to act as his representatives at this time: Baba Meher Bux Bedi and Hafiz Umar Daroga, who were tasked with accompanying the British-appointed *vakil* back to his station. Ibid., p. 95.
25. A detailed biography of Fakir Azizuddin has been written by his descendant, Fakir Syed Aijazuddin, which thoroughly documents his considerable success as a diplomat and political figure serving at the Lahore *durbar*: Fakir S. Aijazuddin, *The Resourceful Fakirs: Three Muslims Brothers at the Sikh Court of Lahore* (New Delhi: Three Rivers, 2014).
26. Suri, *Umdat-ut-tawarikh*, Daftar II, pp. 421–2.
27. Suri, *Umdat-ut-tawarikh*, Daftar III, Part I, p. 36.
28. Suri, *Umdat-ut-tawarikh*, Daftar II, p. 176.
29. Patwant Singh & Rai, *Empire of the Sikhs*, pp. 141–2.
30. Suri, *Umdat-ut-tawarikh*, Daftar III, Parts I–III, p. 76.
31. Ibid., p. 78.
32. Suri, *Umdat-ut-tawarikh*, Daftar III, Part V, pp. 314–15.
33. Henry Thoby Prinsep, *Origins of the Sikh Power in the Punjab* (Lahore, 1897), pp. 120–1.
34. Louis E. Fenech, 'Ranjit Singh, the Shawl, and the *Kaukab-i Iqbāl-i Punjāb*', *Sikh Formations*, vol. 11, nos 1–2, (2015) pp. 96–101.
35. Suri, *Umdat-ut-tawarikh*, Daftar III, Part IV, pp. 38–41.
36. Ibid., Part V, p. 311.
37. Singh & Rai, *Empire of the Sikhs*, p. 161.
38. Emily Eden, *Up the country: Letters written to her sister from the upper provinces of India*, vol. 1 (London: R. Bentley, 1866), pp. 297–8; W.G. Osborne, *The Court and Camp of Runjeet Sing* (London: Henry Colburn, 1840), pp. 84–90, 95–8.
39. Osborne, *Court and Camp*, pp. 189–91.
40. Osborne, it would seem, appreciated the performances of Ranjit Singh's Kashmiri dancing girls better than the style of singing showcased by his female musicians. However, as Kapuria's work on these female artists demonstrates, the performances and sartorial codes of Punjabi dancing girls and musicians together formed a crucial component of representing the Sikh Empire's martial glory and cultural grandeur to European dignitaries. Radha Kapuria, 'Of Music and the Maharaja: Gender, affect, and power in Ranjit Singh's Lahore', *Modern Asian Studies*, vol. 54, no. 2 (March 2020), pp. 1–37.

41. Suri, *Umdat-ut-tawarikh*, Daftar III, Parts I–III, p. 76.
42. Ibid., p. 73.
43. RAS Persian 212: Muhammad Fazil, 'A Treatise in Horticulture'.
44. RAS Persian 212: Hamishah Bahar. Wade's accompanying letter is in the inside cover of the manuscript.
45. Garden imagery was very extensively used by one of Emperor Shah Jahan's most celebrated Hindu secretaries, Chandar Bhan, who himself originated from Lahore. His best-known work, the *Chahar Chaman* ('The Four Gardens'), used the metaphor of the garden as a context for imaginatively describing the greatness and inner culture of his courtly world. This text would later be used by generations of courtiers, and then East India Company officials, to gain an understanding of the sociopolitical decorum of the Mughal *durbar*. See Rajeev Kinra's book on Chandar Bhan's writings and career: *Writing Self, Writing Empire: Chandar Bhan Brahman and the Cultural World of the Indo-Persian State Secretary* (Oakland, CA: University of California Press, 2015), p. 67 (and thanks to one of my anonymous reviewers for recommending this fascinating monograph to me!). It would be highly surprising if figures such as Sohan Lal Suri or Fakir Azizuddin had not been aware of Chandar Bhan and his work, though I have not thus far found any direct evidence of them reading or speaking about it.
46. Suri, *Umdat-ut-tawarikh*, Daftar III, Parts I–III, p. 101.
47. Ibid., Part V, pp. 352, 354.
48. Suri, *Umdat-ut-tawarikh*, Daftar III, Parts I–III, p. 81.
49. Suri, *Umdat-ut-tawarikh*, Daftar II, pp. 115–16.
50. Ibid., pp. 114–15.
51. Ibid., p. 117.
52. RAS Persian 89: Sohan Lal Suri, *Umdat-ut-tawarikh*, ff.311.
53. Khushwant Singh, *Ranjit Singh*, pp. 262–3.
54. Suri, *Umdat-ut-tawarikh*, Daftar II, p. 118.
55. Suri, *Umdat-ut-tawarikh*, Daftar III, Part IV, p. 12.
56. The work was originally begun as early as 1771 by Ganpat Rai, Suri's father, who had started recording the events of the day under the aegis of *Sardars* Charat Singh and Maha Singh Sukerchakia. Radha Sharma, 'Preface', in Suri, *Umdat-ut-tawarikh*, Daftar II.
57. Suri, *Umdat-ut-tawarikh*, Daftar III, Part I–III, p. 38.
58. Ibid., pp. 430–1.
59. Ibid., pp. 432–4.
60. Ibid., p. 436.
61. Ranjit Singh's female relations may well have contributed to earlier royal weddings, but as Suri deliberately kept his record of the 1811 *tambol* gifts short, no comparable evidence of their involvement is available. For the

1837 wedding, many of Ranjit Singh's wives are specifically named in the list, including Gul Begum, Katochan, Deoki, Gulab Devi, Dooli, Halewali and Rabeli.

62. This also matched the sum presented by the Rajah of Nabha. Suri, *Umdat-ut-tawarikh*, Daftar III, Part I–III, p. 441.
63. Ibid., Part III, p. 439.
64. Ibid., p. 446.
65. O'Hanlon, 'Masculinity and the Bangash Nawabs', pp. 30–1.
66. Suri, *Umdat-ut-tawarikh*, Daftar III, Part IV, p. 9.
67. Osborne's account makes repeated reference to the Maharajah's deeply inquisitive nature and the rapid-fire approach with which he shot questions at British representatives during official audiences at his *durbar*. See, for example, *Court and Camp*, pp. 176–7.
68. Fauja Singh Bajwa, *Military System of the Sikhs During the Period 1799–1849* (Delhi: Motilal Banarsidass, 1964), pp. 1–107.
69. Singh & Rai, *Empire of the Sikhs*, p. 168.
70. Suri, *Umdat-ut-tawarikh*, Daftar III, Part IV, p. 8.
71. Ibid., pp. 10–11.

4. AFTER THE LION: WRITING THE STORY OF RANJIT SINGH'S HEIRS

1. British Library, Or 5259: *Sarvasiddhantattvacudamani*.
2. See details about the manuscript and its mysterious history in Cecil Bendall, *Catalogue of the Sanskrit Manuscripts in the British Museum* (London: Gilbert & Rivington, 1902), p. 208; and Jerry Losty, *The Art of the Book in India* (London: British Library, 1982), pp. 154–5.
3. BL Or 5259: *Sarvasiddhantattvacudamani*, available at http://www.bl.uk/onlinegallery/onlineex/apac/other/033ori000005259u00009000.html (accessed 30 March 2020).
4. George Carmichael Smyth, *A History of the Reigning Family of Lahore* (Calcutta: W. Thacker & Co., 1847), pp. 32–3.
5. See for example, Patwant Singh & Jyoti M. Rai, *Empire of the Sikhs: The Life and Times of Maharaja Ranjit Singh* (London: Peter Owen, 2008), p. 210.
6. Sohan Lal Suri, trans. V.S. Suri, *Umdat-ut-tawarikh*, Daftar III (Amritsar: Guru Nanak Dev University, 2002), Part V, p. 404.
7. Alexander Burnes, *Cabool: A Personal Narrative of a Journey to, and Residence in that City, in the Years 1836, 7, and 8* (Philadelphia, PA: Carey & Hart, 1843), p. 47.
8. Andrew Halliday, 'Happy Idiots,' *Nineteenth-Century Disability: Cultures & Contexts*, http://www.nineteenthcenturydisability.org/items/show/3 (accessed 21 January 2017).
9. Alexander Burnes, 'On the Political State of Cabool', 26 November 1837,

in *Reports and Papers, Political, Geographical and Commercial Submitted to Government by Sir Alexander Burnes, Lt Leech, Dr Lord and Lt Wood, Employed on Missions in the Years 1835–36–37 in Scinde, Affghanisthan and Adjacent Countries* (Calcutta: G.H. Huttmann, Bengal Military Orphan Press, 1839), p. 22.

10. Among the first such high-profile Company figures to write political histories of the Punjab pointing to the likely instability of the ruling elite after Ranjit Singh's death was Henry Thoby Prinsep, a member of the Governor-General secretariat and later a Company director from 1850. His views on Ranjit Singh as a 'great man' unlikely to be matched by his eldest son were published in the last chapter of his popular work, *Origin of the Sikh Power in the Punjab and Political Life of Muha-Raja Runjeet Singh* (Calcutta: G.H. Huttmann, 1834).
11. Burnes, 'On the Political State of Cabool'.
12. Such views were propounded in the preface of Smyth, *Reigning Family of Lahore*, in which he argued that the Company should have moved to annex the entire Sikh Empire after the deaths of Maharajahs Kharak Singh and Nau Nihal Singh in 1840.
13. Wade to Macnaghten, 1 January 1838, in Fauja Singh (ed.), *Maharajah Kharak Singh: select records preserved in the National Archives of India* (Patiala: Dept of Punjab Historical Studies, Punjabi University, 1977), pp. 12–13.
14. That the princes themselves recognised the value of having British support for their future succession is evident in the fact that, during the 1830s, both Kharak Singh and Sher Singh courted Company officials individually to try to win them over, and also sent personal letters to Wade, to put out feelers for a deal to be struck between them and the Company in the event that they might have to fight for the throne. Wade was ordered by his bosses to keep these overtures on ice, but nevertheless, it highlights how he himself was not exactly inclined to exploit these underlying rivalries. See Fauja Singh (ed.), *Maharajah Kharak Singh*, pp. 5–8. It seemed to be enough for him that he was on generally good personal terms with Kharak Singh, as he had been with his father, and that the prince was committed towards upholding Ranjit Singh's policy of an amicable Anglo-Punjabi alliance. Kharak Singh apparently remained steadfast in his support for Wade, despite the eagerness of Nau Nihal Singh and many of other Sikh chiefs to take a more bold and potentially antagonistic stance towards the British, which eventually led to the removal of Wade from his post as the Political Agent at Ludhiana. R.R. Sethi, *The Lahore Darbar (in the light of the Correspondence of Sir C.M. Wade, 1823–1840)* (Delhi: Keeper of Records, Government of Punjab, 1950), pp. 268, 275–6.
15. The reasons for this are unclear, but it may have something to do with

the greater political instability that developed during the rapid successions between the reigns of Maharajahs Kharak Singh and Duleep Singh, in the years 1839–43. See Fauja Singh (ed.), *Maharajah Kharak Singh*, p. xi.

16. H.M.L. Lawrence, *Adventures Of An Officer In The Service of Runjeet Singh*, vol. 2 (reprinted edition, 1975), pp. 216–17.
17. British Library, MSS Eur F85/30/2a, f.217: H.M.L. Lawrence to F. Currie, 16 January 1847.
18. Lawrence, *Adventures*, vol. 1, p. xxiii.
19. See the 2017 Indian TV drama serial, *Sher-e-Punjab: Maharaja Ranjit Singh*; or equally the feature-length 2017 movie, *The Black Prince* (dir. Kavi Raz), about the life and rebellion of Maharajah Duleep Singh, which was released internationally in the same year and which has since been launched on Netflix.
20. Suri, *Umdat-ut-tawarikh*, Daftar IV, pp. 138–9.
21. Ibid., pp. 11, 14, 62.
22. See in particular the conspiracy theories of Smyth in *Reigning Family of Lahore*, particularly Chapter 1, 'Secret History of the Lahore Durbar'.
23. See Patwant Singh & Rai, *Empire of the Sikhs*, Chapters 8 & 9; and Bawa Satinder Singh, *The Jammu Fox: A Biography of Maharaja Gulab Singh of Kashmir, 1792–1857* (Carbondale, IL: Southern Illinois University Press, 1974), Chapter 3.
24. Suri, *Umdat-ut-tawarikh*, Daftar IV, p. 143.
25. Ibid., p. 140.
26. Ibid., p. 486.
27. Andrew J. Major, *Return to Empire: Punjab under the Sikhs and the British in the Mid-Nineteenth Century* (New Delhi: Sterling, 1996), pp. 43–4.
28. Suri, *Umdat-ut-tawarikh*, Daftar IV, p. 143.
29. Ibid., pp. 141–2.
30. Shah Muhammad, 'Jangnama' in P.K. Nijhawan (ed.), *The First Punjab War* (Amritsar: Singh Brothers, 2001), stanzas 12–14, pp. 77–81.
31. Ibid., stanza 19, p. 91.
32. See J. Deol, '"To Hell with War": Literature of Political Resistance in Early Nineteenth-Century Punjab', *South Asia Research*, vol. 17, no. 2 (Autumn 1997), pp. 190–5.
33. Piara Singh Padam (ed.), *Jangnama Singhan Te Firangian* (Amritsar: Singh Brothers, 2006) p. 12.
34. Suri, *Umdat-ut-tawarikh*, Daftar IV, pp. 162–3.
35. Ibid., pp. 164–5.
36. Prince Partap Singh had been involved in diplomatic receptions for Claude Martin Wade and George Clerk with his father since 1838 (Suri, *Umdat-ut-tawarikh*, Daftar III, Part I, p. 149), and would be sent to meet for-

mally with the Governor-General alongside Fakir Azizuddin at the start of January 1843, the first major diplomatic occasion after Sher Singh took the throne (Suri, *Umdat-ut-tawarikh*, Daftar IV, pp. 217–19).

37. Singh & Rai, *Empire of the Sikhs*, p. 219.
38. Fauja Singh Bajwa, *Military System of the Sikhs During the Period 1799–1849* (Delhi: Motilal Banarsidass, 1964), Chapters 4, 5.
39. Ibid., pp. 45–7.
40. M.L. Ahluwalia, *Maharani Jind Kaur, 1816–1863* (Amritsar: Singh Bros, 2001), p. 25.
41. Ibid., p. 100.
42. Louis E. Fenech, *Guru Gobind Singh and the Khalsa* (forthcoming), p. 26.
43. M.C. Pradhan, *The Political System of the Jats of Northern India* (Bombay: OUP, 1966), p. ix. The equivalent phrase in Punjabi was '*panch mein Parmesar*'.
44. See, for example, 'The Punjab', *The Foreign Quarterly Review*, vols 33–4 (October 1844), p. 46; 'The Dynasty of the Lions', *Ainsworth's Magazine*, vol. 7 (1845), p. 351; and W.L. McGregor, 'The Sikhs', *The New Monthly Review* vol. 79 (January 1846), p. 135.
45. Suri, *Umdat-ut-tawarikh*, Daftar IV, pp. 308–9.
46. Smyth, *Reigning Family of Lahore*, p. 127.
47. Ahluwalia, *Maharani Jind Kaur*, p. 13.
48. Dhyan Singh's younger son (and Gulab Singh's nephew), Mian Udham Singh, was actually walking alongside Maharajah Nau Nihal Singh on the day of his father's funeral, and was also hit by the falling rubble at the gate of the Lahore Fort. Udham Singh appears to have died on the spot, to the great shock and distress of his father, who (in Suri's account at least) cried out that his son had sacrificed his life for the Maharajah (Suri, *Umdat-ut-tawarikh*, Daftar IV, pp. 124–5). Additionally, Dhyan Singh and Gulab Singh's younger brother, Rajah Suchet Singh, died fighting against his nephew, Hira Singh, for control of the *vazir*-ship; see Bawa Satinder Singh, *Jammu Fox*, pp. 63–4.
49. Ajudhia Parshad, 'Waqai Jang-i-Pheroshahr', in Vidya Sagar Suri (ed.), *Some Original Sources of Panjab History* (Lahore: Punjab University Historical Society, 1956), pp. 54–5; see also Major, *Return to Empire*, pp. 54–5.
50. William Broadfoot, *The Career of Major George Broadfoot in Afghanistan and the Punjab* (London: John Murray, 1888).
51. Ahluwalia, *Maharani Jind Kaur*, p. 31.
52. See, for example, British Library, India Secret Consultations (5 September–29 November 1845): Broadfoot to Currie, 20 September 1845.
53. 'Death of the Wuzeer of Lahore', *The Illustrated London News*, no. 87 (29 November 1845), p. 1.
54. Shah Muhammad, 'Jangnama', p. 45.

55. British Library, Secret Letters from Bengal & India, f.532: Hardinge to Secret Committee, 2 December 1845.
56. Broadfoot, *Major George Broadfoot in Afghanistan and the Punjab*, pp. 283–4.
57. Hardinge himself was aware of the disquiet his troop movements had caused at Lahore, but was quick to dismiss this as a valid reason for Sikh hostility: Governor-General to the Secret Committee, 2 December 1845—in *Despatches of Viscount Hardinge, General Lord Gough and Major General Sir Harry Smith and other documents, comprising the engagements of Moodkee, Ferozeshah, Aliwal and Sobraon* (London: John Ollivier, 1846), p. 3.
58. Parshad, 'Waqai Jang-i-Pheroshahr', pp. 59–60.
59. BL, India Secret Consultations: Major George Broadfoot to Sir Frederick Currie, 1 October 1845.
60. BL, India Secret Consulations: Major George Broadfoot to Sir Frederick Currie, 25 August 1845.
61. British Library, 'Secret Letters from Bengal & India', f.182: Hardinge to Secret Committee, 22 April 1845.
62. British Library, 'Secret & Political Letters from Bengal and India', 2nd series, vol. 2 (1844–5), f.517: Sir Henry Hardinge to Secret Committee, 18 November 1845.

5. THE BOY-KING, THE REBEL QUEEN AND THE BRITISH EMPIRE

1. On the roles of Tej Singh and Lal Singh, see Patwant Singh & Jyoti M. Rai, *Empire of the Sikhs: The Life and Times of Maharaja Ranjit Singh* (London: Peter Owen, 2008), chapters 8–9; and M.L. Ahluwalia & Kirpal Singh, *The Punjab's Pioneer Freedom Fighters* (Bombay: Orient Longmans, 1963), pp. 81–4. There is direct evidence of Lal Singh having reached an agreement with a British officer named P. Nicholson, to pass on secret information and even induce his own troops to march in a manner conducive to helping a British attack, in the correspondence between Major George Broadfoot and his successor as Agent, Henry Montgomery Lawrence (British Library, MSS EUR F85/42d, f.457: P. Nicholson to Broadfoot, 18 December 1845). However, there is no mention in this document of any involvement of Jind Kaur; her *vazir* appeared to be looking out for his own personal interests in striking this deal.
2. *Treaty between the British Government and the State of Lahore—1846*, 9 March 1846, available at http://www.anglosikhwars.com/treaty-of-lahore-1846/#jp-carousel-2195 (accessed on 14 September 2019).
3. Indeed, when it came to deposing Jind Kaur in the autumn of 1847, Hardinge reflected with some satisfaction on his success in having had the

Maharani deal with the initial load of the austerity cuts. See British Library, MSS EUR/F85/48 f.81: Hardinge to Henry Lawrence, 30 May 1847.

4. Charles Tupper, *Our Indian Protectorate: An introduction to the study of the relations between the British government and its Indian feudatories* (London: Longmans, 1893) pp. 39–41.
5. British Library, MSS EUR/F85/48, ff.116–117: Lord Hardinge to H.M. Lawrence, 23 October 1847
6. Michael H. Fisher, *Indirect Rule in India: Residents and the Residency System, 1764–1858* (Delhi: OUP, 1991) pp. 123–268.
7. *Articles of Agreement concluded between the British Government and the Lahore Durbar on the 11th March 1846*, available at http://www.anglosikhwars.com/treaty-of-lahore-1846/#jp-carousel-2575 (accessed on 14 September 2019).
8. British Library, MSS EUR/F85/48, f.15: Sir Henry Hardinge to H.M. Lawrence, 29 March 1846.
9. Copies of intelligence reports in the British Library's Henry Montgomery Lawrence Papers (HMLP) provide ample examples of such *durbars*, e.g. British Library, MSS Eur F85/29a (HMLP), ff.139–41: Punjab Intelligence, 22 March 1846.
10. Ibid., ff.160–1: Punjab Intelligence, 27 March 1846.
11. Ibid., ff.139–41: Punjab Intelligence, 22 March 1846.
12. Herbert Edwardes, *A Year on the Punjab Frontier in 1848–9*, vol. 1 (London: R. Bentley, 1851), p. 158.
13. Sohan Lal Suri, trans. V.S. Suri, *Umdat-ut-tawarikh*, Daftar V (Amritsar: Guru Nanak Dev University, 2002), p. 37.
14. Henry Montgomery Lawrence, *Political Diaries of the Agent to the Governor-General, North-West Frontier and Resident at Lahore* (Allahabad: Pioneer Press, 1909) p. 258.
15. British Library, MSS Eur F85/29a, ff.143–8: Punjab Intelligence, 23 March 1846.
16. Ibid., ff.143–50: Punjab Intelligence, 23 & 25 March 1846.
17. All that I have so far been able to trace about Duleepgarh's fate is that, in August 1847, Lawrence's regency council seized control of the settlement's administration from Hira Singh, Jind Kaur's younger brother (no relation to the murdered *vazir*), due to accusations of mismanagement—though, significantly, this took place just days before his sister, the Maharani, was suddenly banished from Lahore. Lawrence, *Political Diaries*, pp. 257–61.
18. The details of these pivotal conversations between Hardinge, Lawrence, Jind Kaur and the *sardars* were brought to light by the insightful research of Harold Lee, published in his biographical work on Henry and John

Lawrence: *Brothers in the Raj: The Lives of Henry and John Lawrence* (Oxford: OUP, 2004), pp. 178–85.

19. Ibid., p. 166.
20. Andrew J. Major, *Return to Empire: Punjab under the Sikhs and the British in the Mid-Nineteenth Century* (New Delhi: Sterling, 1996), pp. 82–4.
21. Suri's chronicles show that, at first (during 3–5 March, 1846), Jind Kaur appeared to agree to the proposal granting Kashmir to Gulab Singh (as well as his Jammu territories) in order to settle part of the war indemnity; but within a day or two, when she was presented with formal documents to sign so that the transfer could be confirmed, she and her courtly advisers dodged the matter. The Maharani finally ratified the agreement at the end of March, under significant pressure from the British officers at Lahore. Suri, *Umdat-ut-tawarikh*, Daftar V, pp. 3–4.
22. British Library, MSS Eur F85/30/2a (HMLP), f.2167: H.M. Lawrence to F. Currie, 16 January 1847.
23. British Library, IOR/P/SEC/IND/119 (India Secret Consultations): Broadfoot to Currie, 20 September 1845 (entry for 6 August 1845).
24. *Papers relating to the Articles of Agreement concluded between the British Government and the Lahore Durbar, on the 16th of December, 1846, for the administration of the Lahore State during the minority of the Maharajah Duleep Sing* (London: Houses of Parliament, 1847).
25. G. Khurana, *British Historiography on the Sikh Power in the Punjab* (London: Mansell, 1985), pp. 117–18.
26. Joseph Davey Cunningham, *A History of the Sikhs: From the Origin of the Nation to the Battles of the Sutlej* (London: John Murray, 1849), p. 299.
27. Khurana, *British Historiography*, p. 112. During Cunningham's time at Bhopal, he had worked on amicably productive terms with Sikandar Begum, the reigning queen, who now petitioned Dalhousie (without success) for Cunningham to be reinstated.
28. H.M. Lawrence, 'Recent History of the Punjab', *Calcutta Review*, vol. 1, no. 2 (August 1844), pp. 481–2.
29. Henry Lawrence and Honoria Lawrence, 'Romance and Reality of Indian Life', *Calcutta Review*, vol. 2, no. 2 (December 1844) pp. 427–8.
30. Lawrence, 'Recent History of the Punjab', pp. 502–3.
31. Douglas M. Peers, 'Soldiers, Scholars, and the Scottish Enlightenment: Militarism in Early Nineteenth-Century India', *The International History Review*, vol. 16, no. 3 (August 1994), p. 442.
32. As was powerfully argued in Edward Said's groundbreaking work, *Orientalism* (London: Routledge & Kegan Paul, 1978). See especially the introduction and first chapter.
33. Rajpreet Atwal, *Between the Courts of Lahore and Windsor: Anglo-Indian rela-*

tions and the re-making of royalty in the nineteenth century (unpublished DPhil thesis: University of Oxford, 2017), Chapter 3.

34. H.M.L. Lawrence, *Adventures Of An Officer In The Service of Runjeet Singh*, vol. 2, reprinted edition (Karachi: OUP, 1975), pp. 135–6.
35. Lee, *Brothers in the Raj*, pp. 185–6.
36. Suri, *Umdat-ut-tawarikh*, Daftar IV, p. 359.
37. Suri, *Umdat-ut-tawarikh*, Daftar V, pp. 38–9.
38. Ibid., p. 45.
39. Ibid., pp. 45–8.
40. Khushwant Singh, 'Introduction' to Lawrence, *Adventures*, p. ix.
41. Lawrence, *Adventures*, vol. 2, pp. 216–17.
42. See Lawrence, *Political Diaries*, p. 163 (8 June 1847) for a description of one of Henry Lawrence's *durbars*. Duleep Singh's presence at the *durbar* was only reinstated as a formal requirement by John Lawrence in December 1847, after Jind Kaur had been removed from Lahore; a new protocol and schedule were also drawn up by him at this time and forced on the Maharajah and his courtly officers, in order to regularise their daily activities. Ibid., p. 373).
43. Margot Finn, 'Family formations: Anglo India and the familial proto-state', in David Feldman & Jon Lawrence (eds), *Structures and Transformations in Modern British History: Essays for Gareth Stedman Jones* (Cambridge: CUP, 2011), pp. 102–3.
44. The fortunes of the Scottish Logins were also made in political service in India, particularly in connection with the Punjabi royal dynasty. John Spencer Login, a Company doctor, was a close friend of Henry Lawrence, and was appointed as guardian and tutor to Duleep Singh once the annexation of the Punjab was finally announced in 1849. Login's younger brother, James, was the only other Residency surgeon in India at the time and was able to secure an appointment to the Kathmandu court, where Jind Kaur fled after escaping from the British jail at Chunar Fort. Thus the two Login brothers were charged with supervising and separating Jind Kaur and Duleep in 1850, whilst the process of annexation was completed and the Maharajah was exiled from his kingdom. Lena Login, *Sir John Login and Duleep Singh* (London: W.H. Allen & Co., 1890), pp. 4–10, 159–61.
45. Honoria Lawrence, 'English Women in Hindustan', *Calcutta Review*, vol. 4 (September 1845), p. 108.
46. Satadru Sen, 'The Politics of Deracination: Empire, Education and Elite Children in Colonial India', *Studies in History*, vol. 19, no. 1 (2003), pp. 23–5.
47. Lawrence, *Political Diaries*, p. 118.
48. 'Roobukaree sent by the Resident at Lahore to the Lahore durbar, for

their perusal, and the information of the Ranee' in *Papers relating to the Punjab: 1847–1849. Presented to both Houses of Parliament by command of Her Majesty, May 1849* (London: Harrison & Son, 1849), p. 26.

49. Maharani Jind Kaur to Resident at Lahore, no date, in *Papers Relating to the Punjab*, pp. 26–7.
50. Atwal, *Between the Courts of Lahore and Windsor*, chapter 3.
51. BL: Lawrence to Currie, 16 January 1847.
52. Lawrence, *Political Diaries*, p. 21.
53. British Library, MSS EUR F85/30/2a, ff.470–8: H.M. Lawrence to H.M. Elliott (Secretary to Governor-General), 9 August 1847.
54. British Library, MSS EUR F85/48 (HMLP), ff.104–8: Viscount Hardinge to H.M. Lawrence, 12 August 1847.
55. 'A General Proclamation, for the information of the Chiefs of the Lahore Durbar, the Priests, Elders, and People of the Countries belonging to Maharajah Duleep Singh', 20 August 1847, in *Papers Relating to the Punjab*, p. 53.
56. Lawrence, *Political Diaries*, p. 211.
57. Ibid., pp. 354, 372–3.
58. Sen, 'The Politics of Deracination', pp. 19–39.
59. 'Proclamation of the Sikh Army', 22 April 1848, cited in Khushwant Singh, *A History of the Sikhs, 1839–2004*, vol. II (New Delhi: OUP, 2009), p. 69.
60. Hardinge had used the nickname when discussing plans for where to put the Maharani after her immediate removal from Lahore: 'Her Highness' seclusion at Shiekhupoora, is in my view preferable to a more distant banishment. It avoids the national affront of parading the Mother of all the Sikhs through Hindostan, & will reconcile the Sikh people to the step, and as we cannot publish all we know of her misconduct, but must justify the step on the expediency of the separation, the less any of the measures taken have the appearance of punishment the better.' British Library, MSS EUR/F85/48, f.108: Hardinge to Henry Lawrence, 24 August 1847.
61. 'The Governor-General in Council to the Secret Committee', 3 June 1848, in *Papers Relating to the Punjab*, p. 145.
62. 'The Resident at Lahore to the Secretary of the Governor-General', 30 June 1848, in *Papers Relating to the Punjab*, p. 235.
63. This was Currie's reply to Herbert Edwardes, the British Political Agent at Bannu, whom Chattar Singh Attariwala had approached to seek lobbying support for fixing his daughter's marriage. Cited in Lee, *Brothers in the Raj*, p. 229.
64. Dalhousie to Sir George Couper, 4 August 1848, in J.G.A Baird (ed.),

Private Letters of the Marquess of Dalhousie (Edinburgh/London: W. Blackwood & Sons, 1910), p. 29.

65. Dalhousie to Couper, 8 October 1848, in Baird (ed.), *Private Letters*, p. 34.
66. National Records of Scotland, GD45/6/97 (Dalhousie Papers): H.M. Lawrence to Lord Dalhousie; letters dated 3 and 9 October 1848, and 15 January 1849.
67. Ibid.: H.M. Lawrence to Lord Dalhousie, 1 March 1849.
68. NRS: GD45/6/97 (Dalhousie Papers): Lord Dalhousie to H.M. Lawrence, 28 February 1849.
69. Royal Archives, VIC/MAIN/N/14/78: Lord Dalhousie to Queen Victoria, 6 February 1855.
70. Atwal, *Between the Courts of Lahore and Windsor*, Chapter 6.
71. 'Memorandum by the Resident at Lahore (and enclosures of statements and confiscated correspondence)', in *Papers Relating to the Punjab*, pp. 492–5.
72. Mr Newmarch to Lord Dalhousie, *The Englishman*, vol. x, no. 352 (Calcutta, 21 December 1848).
73. 'The Secretary with the Governor-General to Major Macgregor', 23 January 1849, in *Papers Relating to the Punjab*, p. 580.

CONCLUSION

1. Rajpreet Atwal, *Between the Courts of Lahore and Windsor: Anglo-Indian relations and the re-making of royalty in the nineteenth century* (unpublished DPhil thesis: University of Oxford, 2017), Chapter 6.
2. In particular, this is the version of events given in the epic Punjabi ballad of Sohan Singh Seetal, *Dukhiye Maa Putt* (1969).
3. These are the same pension lists used for Map 3 showing the Sukerchakia marriage alliances. See Appendix.
4. Atwal, *Between the Courts of Lahore and Windsor*, Chapter 6.

BIBLIOGRAPHY

Primary manuscript sources

British Library, London (BL):

Devidas, *Rajniti Buddhi-Baridh*: Mss Hindi D13b
Durgashankar Pathak, *Sarvasiddhantattvacudamani*: BL Or.5259
Henry Montgomery Lawrence Papers (HMLP): MSS Eur F85/30—55
India Secret Consultations: IOR/P/SEC/IND/119
Secret Letters from Bengal & India (1845): IOR/L/PS/5/51
Provision for Members of the Lahore Royal Family: IOR/L/PS/6/525, Coll. 42/1

Royal Asiatic Society Library, London (RAS):

Sohan Lal Suri, *Umdat-ut-tawarikh*: RAS Persian 89
Muhammad Fazil, *Hamishah Bahar*: RAS Persian 212

Royal Archives, Windsor (RA):

VIC/MAIN/N/14 (from Queen Victoria's India Papers)

National Records of Scotland:

Papers of the 10th Earl and 1st Marquis of Dalhousie as Governor-General of India: GD45/6

Primary published sources in Punjabi

Grewal, J.S. and Banga, Indu (eds), *Maharajah Ranjit Singh: Civil Athe Military Mamle* (Amritsar: Guru Nanak Dev University, 2001).
Muhammad, Mian Pir, ed. Harnam Singh Shan, *Chattian Di Var* (Chandigarh: Punjab University, 1970).
Muhammad, Shah, 'Jangnama' in P.K. Nijhawan (ed.), *The First Punjab War* (Amritsar: Singh Brothers, 2001).
Nath, Amar, trans. Kirpal Singh, *Zafarnama-e-Ranjit Singh* (Patiala: Punjabi University, 1995).

Padam, Piara Singh (ed.), *Jangnama Singhan Te Firangian* (Amritsar: Singh Brothers, 2006).

Rao, Ram Sukh, *Sri Fateh Singh Partap Prabhakar*, ed. Joginder Kaur (Patiala: J. Kaur, 1980).

Suri, Sohan Lal, trans. Gurbaksh Singh, *Umdat-ut-tawarikh*, 6 vols (Daftars) (Amritsar: Guru Nanak Dev University, 2002).

Primary published sources in English

Despatches of Viscount Hardinge, General Lord Gough and Major General Sir Harry Smith and other documents, comprising the engagements of Moodkee, Ferozeshah, Aliwal and Sobraon (London: John Ollivier, 1846).

Papers respecting the late hostilities on the North-Western Frontier of India: presented to Parliament by command of Her Majesty (London: Harrison & Son, 1846).

Papers relating to the Articles of Agreement concluded between the British Government and the Lahore Durbar, on the 16th of December, 1846, for the administration of the Lahore State during the minority of the Maharajah Duleep Sing (London: Houses of Parliament, 1847).

Papers relating to the Punjab, 1847–1849. Presented to both Houses of Parliament by command of Her Majesty, May 1849 (London: Harrison & Son, 1849).

The War in India: despatches of Lt.-Gen. Viscount Hardinge, Governor-General of India, General Lord Gough, Commander-in-Chief, Majr.-Gen. Sir Harry Smith, and other documents, comprising the engagements of Moodkee, Ferozeshah, Aliwal, and Sobraon (London: John Ollivier, 1846).

Baird, J.G.A. (ed.), *Private Letters of the Marquess of Dalhousie* (Edinburgh/London: Blackwood & Sons, 1910).

Bhangu, Rattan Singh, trans. Kulwant Singh, *Sri Guru Panth Prakash* (Chandigarh: Institute of Sikh Studies, 2008), 2 vols.

Broadfoot, William, *The Career of Major George Broadfoot in Afghanistan and the Punjab* (London: John Murray, 1888).

Burnes, Alexander, *Cabool: A Personal Narrative of a Journey to, and Residence in that City, in the Years 1836, 7, and 8* (Philadelphia, PA: Carey & Hart, 1843).

Carmichael-Smyth, George, *A History of the Reigning Family of Lahore* (Calcutta: W. Thacker & Co., 1847).

Cunningham, Joseph Davey, *A History of the Sikhs: From the Origins of the Nation to the Battles of the Sutlej* (London: John Murray, 1849).

Eden, Emily, *Up the country: Letters written to her sister from the upper provinces of India*, vol. 1 (London: R. Bentley, 1866).

Edwardes, Herbert, *A Year on the Punjab Frontier, in 1848–9* (London: R. Bentley, 1851), 2 vols.

Kaye, John William, *The Life and Correspondence of Charles, Lord Metcalfe*, vol. 1 (London: Smith, Elder & Co., 1858).

Lawrence, Henry and Lawrence, Honoria, 'Romance and Reality of Indian Life', *Calcutta Review*, vol. 2, no. 2 (December 1844), pp. 377–443.

Lawrence, H.M., *Adventures Of An Officer In The Service of Runjeet Singh*, reprinted edition (Karachi: OUP, 1975), 2 vols.

——— 'Recent History of the Punjab', *Calcutta Review*, vol. 1, no. 2 (August 1844), pp. 449–507.

Lawrence, Henry Montgomery, *Political Diaries of the Agent to the Governor-General, North-West Frontier and Resident at Lahore* (Allahabad: Pioneer Press, 1909).

Lawrence, Honoria, 'English Women in Hindustan', *Calcutta Review*, vol. 4 (September 1845), pp. 96–107.

Login, Lena, *Sir John Login and Duleep Singh* (London: W.H. Allen & Co., 1890).

Osborne, W.G., *The Court and Camp of Runjeet Sing* (London: Henry Colburn, 1840).

Pemble, John (ed.), *Miss Fane in India* (Gloucester: Alan Sutton, 1985).

Prinsep, Henry Thoby, *Origins of the Sikh Power in the Punjab* (Lahore, 1897).

Singh, Fauja (ed.), *Maharajah Kharak Singh: select records preserved in the National Archives of India* (Patiala: Dept of Punjab Historical Studies, Punjabi University, 1977).

Singh, Ganda (ed.), *Private Correspondence Relating to the Anglo-Sikh Wars: Being private letters of Lord Ellenborough, Hardinge, Dalhousie and Gough and political assistants addressed to Sir Fredric Currie, the British resident at Lahore* (Amritsar: Sikh History Society, 1955).

——— *Maharaja Duleep Singh Correspondence* (Patiala: Punjabi University, 1977).

Singh, Kirpal (ed.), *Hardinge Papers Relating to the Punjab* (Patiala: Punjabi University, 2002).

Suri, Sohan Lal, trans. V.S. Suri, *Umdat-ut-tawarikh*, 5 vols (Daftars) (Amritsar: Guru Nanak Dev University, 2002).

Suri, Vidya Sagar (ed.), *Some Original Sources of Panjab History* (Lahore: Punjab University Historical Society, 1956).

Newspapers / magazines

Ainsworth's Magazine
Illustrated London News
The Englishman
The Foreign Quarterly Review
The New Monthly Review

Correspondence with author

Emails exchanged with Arundeep Singh Sarkaria, May 2015.

Secondary literature in Punjabi

Seetal, Sohan Singh, *Dukhiye Maa Putt* (1969).
——— *Sikh Raj Kiveh Giah?*, 6th edn (Ludhiana, 2012).

Secondary literature in English

Ahluwalia, M.L., *Maharani Jind Kaur, 1816–1863* (Amritsar: Singh Bros, 2001).
Ahluwalia, M.L. and Singh, Kirpal, *The Punjab's Pioneer Freedom Fighters* (Bombay: Orient Longmans, 1963).
Aijazuddin, Fakir S., *Sikh portraits by European artists* (London: Sotheby Parke-Bernet, 1979).
——— *The Resourceful Fakirs: Three Muslims Brothers at the Sikh Court of Lahore* (New Delhi: Three Rivers, 2014).
Alam, Muzaffar, *The Crisis of Empire in Mughal North India: Awadh and the Punjab, 1707–48* (New Delhi: OUP, 2013).
Ali, Daud, *Courtly Culture and Political Life in Early Medieval India* (Cambridge: CUP, 2004).
Anand, Anita, *Sophia: Princess, Suffragette, Revolutionary* (London: Bloomsbury, 2015).
Archambault, Hannah L., 'Becoming Mughal in the Nineteenth Century: The Case of the Bhopal Princely State', *South Asia: Journal of South Asian Studies*, vol. 36, no. 4 (2013), pp. 479–95.
Archer, W.G., *Indian Paintings from the Punjab Hills: A Survey and History of Pahari Miniature Paintings* (London/New York: Sotheby Parke-Bernet, 1973).
Bajwa, Fauja Singh, *Military System of the Sikhs During the Period 1799–1849* (Delhi: Motilal Banarsidass, 1964).
Bal, Surjit Singh, *British Policy towards the Panjab, 1844–49* (Calcutta: J.N. Sinha Roy, 1971).

Ballantyne, Tony, *Between Colonialism and Diaspora: Sikh Cultural Formations in an Imperial World* (New Delhi: Permanent Black, 2007).

Balzani, Marzia, *Modern Indian Kingship: Tradition, Legitimacy and Power in Rajasthan* (Oxford: James Currey, 2003).

Bance, Peter, *Sovereign, Squire and Rebel: Maharajah Duleep Singh* (London: Coronet House, 2009).

Banerjee, Milinda, *The Mortal God: Imagining the Sovereign in Colonial India* (Cambridge: CUP, 2018).

Barnett, Richard B., *North India Between Empires: Awadh, the Mughals, and the British, 1720–1801* (Berkeley, CA: University of California Press, 1980).

Bayly, Christopher, *Indian Society and the Making of the British Empire* (Cambridge: CUP, 1988).

Bendall, Cecil, *Catalogue of the Sanskrit Manuscripts in the British Museum* (London: Gilbert & Rivington, 1902).

Bhagavan, Manu, *Sovereign Spheres: Princes, Education and Empire in Colonial India* (New Delhi: OUP, 2003).

Broomhall, Susan and van Gent, J.J.M., *Dynastic Colonialism: Gender, Materiality and the Early Modern House of Orange-Nassau* (Abingdon: Routledge, 2016).

Buckler, F.W., 'The Political Theory of the Indian Mutiny', in M.N. Pearson (ed.), *Legitimacy and Symbols: The South Asian Writings of F.W. Buckler* (Ann Arbor, MI: Center for South and Southeast Asian Studies, University of Michigan, 1985).

Chatterjee, Indrani (ed.), *Unfamiliar Relations: Family and History in South Asia* (New Brunswick: Rutgers University Press, 2004).

Chaudhry, Nazir Ahmad, *Lahore Fort: A Witness to History* (Lahore: Sang-e-Meel, 1999).

Dalrymple, William, *Return of a King: The Battle for Afghanistan* (London: Bloomsbury, 2014).

Deol, Jeevan, '"To Hell with War": Literature of Political Resistance in Early Nineteenth-Century Punjab', *South Asia Research*, vol. 17, no. 2 (Autumn 1997), pp. 178–209.

Dhavan, Purnima, *When Sparrows Became Hawks: The Making of the Sikh Warrior Tradition, 1699–1799* (New York: OUP, 2011).

——— 'Redemptive Pasts and Imperiled Futures: the Writing of a Sikh History', *Sikh Formations*, vol. 3, no. 2 (December 2007), pp. 111–24.

Duindam, Jeroen, *Dynasties: A Global History of Power, 1300–1800* (Cambridge: CUP, 2016).

Ernst, Waltraud and Pati, Biswamoy, 'People, Princes and Colonialism' in Ernst, Waltraud and Pati, Biswamoy (eds), *India's Princely States* (Abingdon: Routledge, 2007).

Faruqui, Munis D., 'At Empire's End: The Nizam, Hyderabad and Eighteenth-Century India', *Modern Asian Studies*, vol. 43, no. 1 (2009), pp. 5–43.

——— *Princes of the Mughal Empire, 1504–1719* (Cambridge: CUP, 2012).

Fenech, Louis E., *The Darbar of the Sikh Gurus: The Court of God in the World of Men* (New Delhi: OUP, 2008).

——— *The Sikh Zafar-Namah of Guru Gobind Singh: a discursive blade in the heart of the Mughal Empire* (New York: OUP, 2013).

——— 'Ranjit Singh, the Shawl, and the *Kaukab-i Iqbal-i Punjab*', *Sikh Formations* (2015), vol. 11, nos 1–2, pp. 1–25.

——— *The Cherished Five in Sikh History* (New York: OUP, forthcoming).

Finn, Margot 'Family formations: Anglo India and the familial proto-state', in David Feldman and Jon Lawrence (eds), *Structures and Transformations in Modern British History: Essays for Gareth Stedman Jones* (Cambridge: CUP, 2011).

Fisher, Michael H., *Indirect Rule in India: Residents and the Residency System, 1764–1858* (Delhi: OUP, 1991).

——— 'Diplomacy in India, 1526–1858', in H.V. Bowen, Elizabeth Mancke and John G. Reid, *Britain's Oceanic Empire, Atlantic and Indian Ocean Worlds, c.1550–1850* (Cambridge: CUP, 2012).

Goodyear, Sara Suleri, *The Rhetoric of English India* (Chicago, IL: University of Chicago Press, 1992).

Grewal, J.S., *The Reign of Maharaja Ranjit Singh: Structure of Power, Economy and Society* (Patiala: Punjabi University, 1981).

——— *Sikh Ideology, Polity and Social Order: From Guru Nanak to Maharaja Ranjit Singh* (New Delhi: Manohar, 2007).

Grewal, J.S. and Banga, Indu, *Early Nineteenth Century Punjab: from Ganesh Das' Char Bagh-i Panjab* (London: Routledge India, 2015).

——— *Civil and Military Affairs of Maharaja Ranjit Singh: A study of 450 orders in Persian* (Amritsar: Guru Nanak Dev University, 1987).

Gupta, Hari Ram, *History of the Sikhs* (New Delhi: Munshiram Manoharlal, 1982), vol. IV

Hambly, Gavin R.G. (ed.), *Women in the Medieval Islamic World: Power, Patronage and Piety* (Basingstoke: Palgrave Macmillan, 1998).

Jakobsh, Doris R., *Relocating Gender in Sikh History: Transformation, Meaning and Identity* (New Delhi: OUP, 2003).

Jhala, Angma Dey, *Courtly Indian Women in Late Imperial India* (London: Pickering & Chatto, 2008).

Kapuria, Radha, 'Of Music and the Maharaja: Gender, affect, and power in Ranjit Singh's Lahore', *Modern Asian Studies*, vol. 54, no. 2 (2019), pp. 1–37.

Kaur Singh, Nikky-Guninder, 'Babarvani and the call for gender justice', *Sikh Formations*, vol. 13, no. 1–2 (2017), pp. 5–19.

Khan, Nadhra, 'The Secular Sikh Maharaja and his Muslim Wife', in Mahesh Sharma and Padma Kaimal (eds), *Indian Painting: Themes, Histories, Interpretations. Essays in Honour of B. N. Goswamy*, (Ahmedabad: Mapin, 2013).

Khan, Shaharyar M., *The Begums of Bhopal: A Dynasty of Women Rulers in Raj India* (London: I.B. Tauris, 2000).

Khurana, G., *British Historiography on the Sikh Power in the Punjab* (London: Mansell, 1985).

Kinra, Rajeev, *Writing Self, Writing Empire: Chandar Bhan Brahman and the Cultural World of the Indo-Persian State Secretary* (Oakland, CA: University of California Press, 2015).

Kohli, Sita Ram, *Catalogue of Khalsa Darbar Records* (Lahore: Government Printing, Punjab, 1919–27), 2 vols.

——— *Sunset of the Sikh Empire*, ed. Khushwant Singh (New Delhi: Orient Longmans, 1967).

Lafont, Jean-Marie, *Maharaja Ranjit Singh: Lord of the Five Rivers* (New Delhi: OUP, 2002).

Lal, Ruby, *Domesticity and Power in the Early Mughal World* (Cambridge: CUP, 2005).

Latif, Syed Muhammad, ed. S.P. Gulati, *The Successors of Maharaja Ranjit Singh* (Delhi: National Book Shop, 2001).

Lebra-Chapman, Joyce, *The Rani of Jhansi: A Study in Female Heroism in India* (Honolulu, HA: University of Hawaii Press, 1986).

Lee, Harold, *Brothers in the Raj: The Lives of John and Henry Lawrence* (Oxford: OUP, 2004).

Majeed, Javed, *Ungoverned Imaginings: James Mill's 'The History of British India and Orientalism'* (Oxford: Clarendon Press, 1992)

Major, Andrew J., *Return to Empire: Punjab under the Sikhs and British in the Mid-Nineteenth Century* (New Delhi: Sterling, 1996).

McLeod, W.H. (ed.), *Prem Sumarag: The Testimony of a Sanatan Sikh* (New Delhi: OUP, 2006).

Menski, Werner (ed.), *South Asians and the Dowry Problem* (London: Trentham, 1998).

Metcalf, Barbara, 'Islam and Power in Colonial India: The Making and Unmaking of a Muslim Princess', *The American Historical Review*, vol. 116, no. 1 (February 2011), pp. 1–30.

Moin, A. Azfar, *The Millennial Sovereign: Sacred Kingship and Sainthood in Islam* (New York: Columbia University Press, 2012).

Myrvold, Kristina, 'Wedding Ceremonies in Punjab', *Journal of Punjab Studies*, vol. 11, no. 2 (2004), pp. 155–70.

Nesbitt, Eleanor, '"Woman Seems to Be Given Her Proper Place": Western Women's Encounter with Sikh Women 1809–2012', *Religions*, vol. 10, no. 9 (2019).

O'Hanlon, Rosalind, 'Masculinity and the Bangash Nawabs of Farrukhabad', in Tony Ballantyne and Antoinette Burton (eds), *Bodies in Contact: Rethinking Colonial Encounters in World History* (Durham, NC: Duke University Press, 2005).

——— 'Kingdom, Household and Body History, Gender and Imperial Service under Akbar', *Modern Asian Studies*, vol. 41, no. 5 (2007), pp. 889–923.

Oberoi, Harjot, 'From the Ritual to the Counter-Ritual: Re-thinking the Hindu-Sikh Question, 1884–1915', in Joseph T. O'Connell, Milton Israel and Willard G. Oxtoby (eds), *Sikh History and Religion in the Twentieth Century* (Toronto: University of Toronto Press, 1988).

Peers, Douglas M., 'Soldiers, Scholars, and the Scottish Enlightenment: Militarism in Early Nineteenth-Century India', *The International History Review*, vol. 16, no. 3 (August 1994), pp. 441–65.

Peirce, Leslie P., *The Imperial Harem: Women and Sovereignty in the Ottoman Empire* (New York: OUP, 1993).

Pradhan, M.C., *The Political System of the Jats of Northern India* (Bombay: OUP, 1966).

Price, Pamela G., *Kingship and Political Practice in Colonial India* (Cambridge: CUP, 1996).

Richards, John F. (ed.), *Kingship and Authority in South Asia* (Delhi: OUP, 1983).

Said, Edward, *Orientalism* (London: Routledge, 1978).

Seetal, Sohan Singh, *The Sikh Empire and Maharaja Ranjeet Singh*, 2nd edn (Ludhiana: Lahore Book Shop, 2013).

Sethi, R.R., *The Lahore Darbar (In the Light of the Correspondence of Sir C.M. Wade, 1823–1840)*, (Delhi, 1950)

Sen, Satadru, 'The Politics of Deracination: Empire, Education and Elite Children in Colonial India', *Studies in History*, vol. 19, no. 1 (2003), pp. 19–39.

——— *Migrant races: Empire, identity and K.S. Ranjitsinhji* (Manchester: Manchester University Press, 2004).

Sen, Sudipta, *A Distant Sovereignty: National Imperialism and the Origins of British India* (New York: Routledge, 2002).

Sharma, Radha, *The Lahore Darbar* (Amritsar: Guru Nanak Dev University, 2001).

Sheel, Ranjana, *The Political Economy of Dowry: Institutionalization and Expansion in North India* (New Delhi: Manohar, 1999).

Sidhu, Amarpal, *The First Anglo-Sikh War* (Stroud: Amberley, 2010).

——— *The Second Anglo-Sikh War* (Stroud: Amberley, 2016).

Singh, Amarinder, *The Last Sunset: The Rise and Fall of the Lahore Durbar* (New Delhi: Roli Books, 2010).

Singh, Bawa Satinder, *The Jammu Fox: A Biography of Maharaja Gulab Singh of Kashmir, 1792–1857* (Carbondale, IL: Southern Illinois University Press, 1974).

Singh, Bhagat, *Sikh Polity in the Eighteenth and Nineteenth Centuries* (New Delhi: Oriental Publishers and Distributors, 1978).

Singh, Fauja, *Some Aspects of State and Society under Ranjit Singh* (New Delhi: Master Publishers, 1982).

Singh, Kapur, eds Piar Singh and Madanjit Kaur, *Parasaraprasna: The Baisakhi of Guru Gobind Singh*, 4th edition (Amritsar: Guru Nanak Dev University, 2017).

Singh, Kavita (ed.), *New insights Into Sikh Art* (Mumbai: Marg Foundation, 2003)

Singh, Khushwant, *Ranjit Singh: Maharaja of Punjab* (Mumbai: Penguin Random House India, 2008).

Singh, Pashaura, *Life and Work of Guru Arjan: History, memory and biography in the Sikh tradition* (New Delhi: OUP, 2006).

Singh, Patwant and Rai, Jyoti M., *Empire of the Sikhs: The Life and Times of Maharaja Ranjit Singh* (London: Peter Owen, 2008).

Singh, Teja, *Essays in Sikhism* (Lahore: Sikh University Press, 1944).

Stronge, Susan (ed.), *The Arts of the Sikh Kingdoms* (London: V&A Publications, 1999).

Subrahmanyam, Sanjay, *Courtly Encounters: Translating Courtliness and Violence in Early Modern Eurasia* (London: Harvard University Press, 2012).

Sultana, Salma, 'Architecture of Sheikhupura Fort in Historical Perspective', *South Asian Studies*, vol. 5 (1989), pp. 103–17.

Syan, Hardip Singh, *Sikh Militancy in the Seventeenth Century: Religious Violence in Mughal and Early Modern India* (London: Bloomsbury, 2013).

Thandi, Shinder, 'What is Sikh in a "Sikh Wedding"? Text, Ritual and Performance in Diaspora Marriage Practices', *Journal of Punjab Studies*, vol. 23, no. 1/2 (Spring–Fall 2016).

Toor, Davinder, *In Pursuit of Empire: Treasures from the Toor Collection of Sikh Art* (London: Kashi House, 2017).

Tupper, Charles, *Our Indian Protectorate: An Introduction to the Study of the Relations between the British Government and its Indian Feudatories* (London: Longmans, 1893).

Waheeduddin, Fakir Syed, *The Real Ranjit Singh* (Patiala: Punjabi University, 2001).

Washbrook, David, 'India, 1818–1860: The Two Faces of Colonialism', in A.N. Porter and William Roger Louis (eds), *The Oxford History of the British Empire*, Volume III (Oxford: OUP, 1998).

Unpublished theses

Atwal, Rajpreet, *Politics Behind the Purdah: Maharani Jind Kaur and Anglo-Sikh Relations, 1843–1849* (unpublished undergraduate thesis: University of Oxford, 2011).

Atwal, Rajpreet, *Between the Courts of Lahore and Windsor: Anglo-Indian Relations and the Re-making of Royalty in the Nineteenth Century* (unpublished DPhil thesis: University of Oxford, 2017).

Hall Jr, Charles Joseph, *The Maharaja's Account Books: State and Society under the Sikhs, 1799–1849* (unpublished PhD thesis: University of Chicago-Illinois, 1981).

Kapuria, Radha, *A Social History of Music in Colonial Punjab* (unpublished PhD thesis: King's College London, 2018).

Web resources

'About: The Black Prince', accessed 11 February 2017, at: http://www.theblackprince.com/about/

'Court Circular' of *The Times*, issue 21156 (1 July 1852) p. 5, accessed via *Times* Digital Archive, 22 February 2015.

'Eurindia—Virtual library', accessed 17 January 2017, at: http://www.e-corpus.org/eng/virtualcollections/eurindia/notices/70210-Shahnama-of-Firdusi-.html

Nayar, Aruti, 'Moran, the mystery woman', *The Tribune*, 24 August 2008, accessed 30 October 2016, at: http://www.tribuneindia.com/2008/20080824/spectrum/main3.htm

Terms granted to, and accepted by, Maharajah Duleep Singh—1849, available at *The Anglo-Sikh Treaties Project*, accessed 12 January 2017, at: http://www.sikhmuseum.org.uk/portfolio/the-anglo-sikh-treaties-1806-1846/#jp-carousel-454

Halliday, Andrew, 'Happy Idiots,' *Nineteenth-Century Disability: Cultures & Contexts*, accessed 21 January 2017, at: http://www.nineteenthcenturydisability.org/items/show/3

Singh, Parminder, 'Satinder Sartaaj to play Maharaja Dalip Singh in multi-million *The Black Prince* movie', *Sikh Siyasat News*, 14 July 2014, accessed 10 August 2016, at http://sikhsiyasat.net/2014/07/14/satinder-sartaj-to-play-maharaja-dalip-singh-in-multi-million-hollywood-movie/

INDEX

Abbott, James, 202
Adinanagar, 100
Afghan-Sikh Wars, 12, 30, 31, 44, 129
  First (1751–65), 32
  Second (1766–99), 47
  Third (1800–37), 50, 55, 61, 76
Afghanistan; Afghans 1, 2, 35, 36, 45, 57, 96, 98, 102, 154, 171
  Chatar Singh Attariwala, relations with, 202
  blindness and, 79
  British Wars, *see* Anglo-Afghan Wars
  dharamyudh and 36
  kin networks and, 57
  peasant brotherhoods, 80
  Sikh Wars, *see* Afghan-Sikh Wars
  Tripartite Treaty (1838), 85–6, 88, 90, 102, 122–3, 130, 131
aftabgir, 63
Ahluwalias, 94, 101
Ain-i-Akbari (Abu'l Fazl), 78
Akal Takht, Amritsar, 23, 58
Akalgarh, 50
Akalis, 58
Akbar, Mughal Emperor, 21, 22, 41, 57, 64, 76–8, 80
Akbarnama (Abu'l Fazl), 78
alcohol, 108
Ali, Aown, 61
Amar Das, Sikh Guru, 23
Amritsar, 18, 19, 20
  Akal Takht, 23, 58
  Akalis, 58
  founding of, 18
  gurmata meetings 30, 32
  Guru Arjan's development of, 18, 19, 20–21, 23
  Guru Hargobind's development of, 23
  halemi raj, 20
  Harmandir Sahib, 19, 20–21, 41, 58, 178
  Kharak Singh's wedding (1811), 114–15
  low-caste groups in, 21, 35
  Nau Nihal's wedding (1837), 1–4, 6, 10, 45, 54, 60, 112, 113, 116–24
  Ranjit Singh and, 53
  Wade's visit (1826–7), 100
Anandpur Sahib, 18, 26, 27
Anarkali's Tomb, Lahore, 190–91
Angad, Sikh Guru, 23

Anglo-Afghan Wars
First (1839–42), 85–6, 88, 122, 158, 175
Anglo-Sikh Wars
First (1845–6), 7, 133, 135–6, 148–9, 165–9, 171–3, 183
Second (1848–9), 6, 7, 136, 198, 203–4
Arjan, Sikh Guru, 17, 18, 19–22, 26
Akbar, relations with, 21
Amritsar, development of, 18, 19, 20–21, 23
execution (1606), 17, 22, 24, 26
Guru Granth Sahib, compilation of, 19, 26
halemi raj, 20, 21, 27, 41
Hargobindpur, founding of, 18
Harmandir Sahib, building of, 19, 20–21
Jahangir, relations with, 17, 21, 22
Arjuna, 115
asceticism, 37
astrology, 70–71
astronomy, 70, 80–81, 125–6, 127–8, 134, 147
Attari, 117
Attariwala family, 188, 201–2, 203
Chattar Singh, 188, 201
Sham Singh, 113, 117, 119–20
Sher Singh, 188, 191, 195, 202, 203
Attock, 76
Auckland, George Eden, 1st Earl
Lahore *durbar* (1838), 102, 104, 105–7, 108, 112
Mai Nakain's funeral (1838), 88
Nau Nihal Singh's wedding (1837), 122
Order of the Bright Star, 105
Punjab tour (1838–9), 108, 121
Aurangzeb, Mughal Emperor, 17, 26–7, 76–8
austerity, 157, 177, 178, 181
Awadh, 192
Azizuddin, Fakir
Chand Kaur, service of, 143
Duleep Singh, service of, 198
Jind Kaur, service of, 158
Ranjit Singh, service of, 88, 99, 100, 101, 111, 116, 122

Babur, Mughal Emperor, 15–18
Baburvani, 15–16
Badshahi Masjid, Lahore 48
Bahadur Shah, Mughal Emperor, 27
Baherwal, 74
Baiza Bai, Queen of Gwalior 186
Bajwa, Chet Singh, 141, 146
Balkh, 128
Ballard, Sebastian, 215
Bannu, 178
Batala, 60, 150
Battle of Sobraon (1846), 171, 172, 191
Beas river, 173
Bedis, 52, 74, 87
Sahib Singh, 52, 74, 87
Belgium, 13
Benares, 81, 125, 126, 201, 205
Bengal, 106

Bentinck, William Cavendish-Bentinck, Lord, 102, 103, 107
Bhadaur, 54
Bhag Singh, Rajah of Jind, 93–7, 98, 114
Bhagavad Gita, 146
Bhangi *misl*, 47–9, 50, 52–3
  Chet Singh, 48, 49
  Gujar Singh, 47
  Mohar Singh, 48, 49
  Sahib Singh, 50, 52, 53
Bhangi, Chet Singh, 48, 49
Bhangu, Rattan Singh, 16–18
Bhonsle, Tarabai, 186
Bhopal, 184, 192
Bhutto family, 210
biradari, 91, 113
blindness, 79
Blue Book, 183
Bollywood, 1, 137
Brahmin mendicants, 157, 193
Brazil, 13
British India (1757–1947)
  Anglo-Afghan War, First (1839–42), 85–6, 88, 122, 158, 175
  Anglo-Sikh War, First (1845–6), 7, 133, 135–6, 148–9, 165–9, 171–3, 183
  Anglo-Sikh War, Second (1848–9), 6, 7, 136, 198, 203–4
  Begum Samru, relations with, 92
  Bengal annexation (1765), 106
  Bhangu on, 17–18
  diplomacy, 85–90, 93–124, 151
  durbar attendance, 102, 103–4, 105–8, 111, 112
  Gulab Singh, relations with, 165, 166, 168, 171, 172, 173
  indirect rule, 175
  intelligence gathering, 17, 121, 156, 162, 164, 175, 182
  Jawahir Singh, murder of (1845), 161–2
  Jind Kaur, relations with, 5–6, 7, 161–4, 171–97
  Lal Singh, relations with, 180–82
  Kharak Singh, narratives on, 81, 127–33, 134, 135
  Mai Nakain's funeral (1838), 86–9, 102
  Marathas, relations with, 94, 122
  Mughal Empire, relations with, 2, 8–9, 17–18, 76, 88, 93, 106
  Multan rebellion (1848), 199–201, 203, 204
  Partition (1947) 1, 34, 136, 174
  princely states and 13, 199
  Ranjit Singh, narratives on, 8–9, 80–81, 83, 130, 137, 144
  Ranjit Singh, relations with, 85–90, 93–124
  Revolt (1857–8), 199, 205, 210
  Sikh Empire, annexation of (1849), 7, 40, 72, 136, 139, 205, 209

subsidiary alliances, 174–5
'transfer of power' negotiations (1947), 210
Treaty of Lahore (1846), 172–6, 179–82
Treaty of Bhyrowal (1846), 188–9, 194, 198, 202
Tripartite Treaty (1838), 85–6, 88, 90, 102, 122–3, 130, 131
British Library, 125–6, 215
Broadfoot, George, 164, 165, 168, 182–3, 193
Broun-Ramsay, James, Marquis of Dalhousie, 202–5, 206, 211, 213
Bulgaria, 13
Burma, 175
Burnes, Alexander, 137
Hazuri Bagh visit (1831), 103, 108–9, 112
horses, transportation of, 105
Kharak Singh, description of, 128–30, 135, 137
Sikh collapse predictions, 130
Tripartite Treaty (1838), 130, 131

Calcutta, 203, 205, 211
Calcutta Review, 192
Canning, Charles, 1st Earl, 211
caste, 21
Catherine II, 'the Great', Empress of Russia, 183
Central Asia, 72, 86, 96, 102, 173
chadar dalni, 52–3, 57, 157
Chand, Mohkam, 73
Chand Kaur, Sikh Maharani
assassination (1842), 152, 153, 212
British narratives on, 184, 185
Civil War (1840–41), 147–52, 155, 185, 208
Jangnama on, 148–9
Kharak Singh, death of (1840), 72, 143, 185
Kharak, engagement to, 51, 72
Kharak, wedding to (1811), 62, 113, 114–16
Nau Nihal Singh's wedding (1837), 118
Regency (1840–41), 143–4, 147–52, 164
Charat Singh, Sukerchakia Chief, 4, 31, 32, 43, 44, 46, 47, 69
Chattha clan, 83
chattri, 63
chauri, 19–20, 63, 210–11
Christianity, 211
Chunar, 201, 205
Chunian, 73
Cis-Sutlej states, 57, 95–6, 114, 116, 166, 210
Clerk, George, 98, 104, 105–6
Clive, Robert, 1st Baron, 106
cocktails, 108
coins, minting of, 29, 40
courtesans, 55, 64
courtly culture, 81, 84, 90–91
astrology, 70, 80–81
chauri, 19–20
gurus and, 19, 21, 27, 36
femininity, 64, 80, 81
Khalsa and, 80
'private' vs 'public' areas, 112
Ranjit Singh and, 29, 40, 80, 111

culture of relatedness, 91, 92, 191
Cunningham, Joseph, 183–4
Currie, Frederick, 176, 181–2, 189, 201–3

Dal Khalsa, 32
Singh, Dal, 50
Dalhousie, James Broun-Ramsay, Marquis, 202–5, 206, 211, 213
dancing girls, 37, 55, 57–9, 62, 64, 107–8, 192, 212
Daya Kaur, Sikh Maharani, 52
Delhi Gazette, 135
Delhi Sultanate (1206–1526), 14, 15–16
Delhi, 93, 97–8
Deol, Jeevan, 150
Dera Ismail Khan, 132, 179
Dharam Kaur, 50
dharamyudh, 36
Dhavan, Purnima, 9, 36–7
Dhyan Singh, Dogra Rajah, 141–7, 149, 152, 153, 158, 190
Nath, Diwan Dina, 158, 189
Dipalpur, 73
divankhana, 61
Dogra Rajputs, 141, 146, 158–9, 165, 180, 190
Dost Muhammad Khan, Emir of Afghanistan, 85, 88, 202
Duleep Singh, Sikh Maharajah, 5, 7, 8, 40, 54, 66, 72, 139, 152–3, 159, 208
  accession (1843), 5, 66, 153, 157
  Anglo-Sikh War, First (1845–6), 165, 171
  betrothal (1845), 188, 201
  British annexation (1849), 72, 205
  British narratives on, 134
  Christianity, conversion to, 211
  Dalhousie, relationship with, 205, 211
  death (1893), 213
  durbars, 177, 195–6
  education of, 195, 197–8
  England, life in, 205, 211
  exile (1849), 205
  exile of mother (1847), 197
  government in exile, 212
  Jawahir Singh, murder of (1845), 161
  Lawrence, relationship with, 136, 195, 196, 197–9
  Lilliputian Regiment, 177–8, 198
  Multan rebellion (1848), 200
  pension book, 68
  restoration, calls for (1880s), 211
  reunion with mother (1861), 205, 211
  screen depictions of, 137
  Treaty of Bhyrowal (1846), 188–9, 194, 198–9, 202
  Treaty of Lahore (1846), 173, 175, 176, 177, 179–80
  troop reviews, 177
Duleepgurh, 178
durbars, 57, 102, 103–4, 105–7
  Lahore (1838), 104, 105–7, 111, 112
  Lahore (1847), 195

Rupar (1831), 102, 103–4, 108–9
dynastic colonialism, 45, 59, 73, 179
dynastic diplomacy, 88, 92, 132, 151

East India Company
Anglo-Afghan War, First (1839–42), 85–6, 88, 122, 158, 175
Anglo-Sikh War, First (1845–6), 7, 133, 135–6, 148–9, 165–9, 171–3, 183
Anglo-Sikh War, Second (1848–9), 6, 7, 136, 198, 203–4
Begum Samru, relations with, 92
Bengal annexation (1765), 106
Bhangu on, 17–18
diplomacy, 85–90, 93–124, 151
Duleep Singh, narratives on, 134
durbar attendance, 102, 103–4, 105–8, 111, 112
Gulab Singh, relations with, 165, 166, 168, 171, 172
indirect rule, 175
intelligence gathering, 17, 121, 156, 162, 164, 175, 182
Jawahir Singh, murder of (1845), 161–2
Jind Kaur, relations with, 5–6, 7, 161–4, 171–97
Kharak Singh, narratives on, 81, 127–33, 134, 135
Lal Singh, relations with, 180–82
Mai Nakain's funeral (1838), 86–9, 102
Marathas, relations with, 94, 122
Mughal Empire, relations with, 2, 8–9, 17–18, 76, 88, 93, 106
Multan rebellion (1848), 199–201, 203, 204
Ranjit Singh, narratives on, 8–9, 80–81, 83, 130, 137, 144
Ranjit Singh, relations with, 85–90, 93–124
Revolt (1857–8), 199, 205, 210
sepoys, 121, 163, 171, 172
Sikh Empire, annexation of (1849), 7, 40, 72, 136, 139, 205, 209
subsidiary alliances, 174–5
'transfer of power' negotiations (1947), 210
Treaty of Lahore (1846), 172–6, 179–82
Treaty of Bhyrowal (1846), 188–9, 194, 198, 202
Tripartite Treaty (1838), 85–6, 88, 90, 102, 122–3, 130, 131
Eden, Emily, 112
Eden, George, 1st Earl of Auckland, *see* Auckland, George Eden
egalitarianism
Khalsa and, 80, 90–91

Sikhism and, 3, 12, 20, 21, 29, 35, 154
elephants, 78, 114, 115, 119

family and state, 91
famines, 21
Fane, Henry Edward, 121
Fane, Henry, 60, 116, 118, 119–23
Fane, Isabella, 59–60, 112
fanning, 19–20
Faruqui, Munis, 9
Fateh Singh Ahluwalia, Rajah of Kapurthala, 94, 101
Fatehgarh, 115, 205
Fazil, Muhammad, 110
Fazl, Abu'l, 64, 78
femininity, 64, 80, 81, 110, 133, 179
Fenech, Louis, 9, 25, 42
Ferozepur, 163, 166
festivals, 65
fly-whisks, 20, 63, 210–11
foot washing, 56, 59, 193
France, 95, 105
Francis I, King of France, 102
Friendship Treaty
1806: 94
1809: 96, 97, 102, 162

Ganges river, 93
Ganpat Rai, 69
gardens, 109–12
Hazuri Bagh, 103, 108–9, 112
Shalabagh, 109–10, 112, 116
George IV, King of the United Kingdom, 90
gifts, 96–7, 105, 111
wedding, 114, 118, 119
Gobind Jas, Rai 98, 122
Gobind Singh, Sikh Guru, 19, 25–8
Anandpur Sahib, fortification of 18, 26
assassination (1708), 11, 30, 35, 39, 210
Aurangzeb, relations with, 26–7
guerrilla warfare, 154
Guru Granth Sahib, compilation of, 26
halemi raj, 27
human Gurus, ending of, 27–8, 29, 35
Khalsa, creation of, 17, 26–9, 32–5, 156, 208
misls and, 31
portraits of, 63, 125
Prem Sumarag Granth and, 37
Zafarnamah (1705), 27
Golden Temple, Amritsar *see* Harmandir Sahib
gopi, 62
Governor-General of India, 85, 88, 101, 102, 103, 106
Auckland (1836–42), 88, 102, 104–8, 112, 121–2
Bentinck (1828–35), 102, 103, 107, 108
Dalhousie (1848–56), 202–5, 206, 211
Hardinge (1844–48), *see* Hardinge, Henry
Governor-General of Punjab, 94, 97
Greece, 13

Grewal, Jagtar Singh, 9, 43, 44
Grey, Charles 2nd Earl, 103
Gujranwala, 2, 31, 43, 78–9
Gul Begum, Sikh Maharani, 55, 56, 64–5, 192, 212
Gulab Singh, Dogra Rajah, 143, 158–9, 164–6, 168, 171, 172, 173
  Anglo-Sikh War, First (1845–6), 171, 172
  British, deal with (1845), 165, 166, 168, 171
  Civil War (1840–41), 147, 148
  Treaty of Lahore (1846), 168, 172, 173–4, 181
gurdwaras, 19, 20–21, 198, 210
  Harmandir Sahib, 19, 20–21, 41, 58
  Kartarpur Sahib, 18
Gurkha Kingdom (1559–1768), 102
gurmata, 30–31, 32, 37, 39, 156, 168, 229
Guru Granth Sahib, 19, 36, 156, 210
  Baburvani, 15–16, 152
  chauri and 19–20, 210–11
  God, figure of, 11–12
  gurmata, 30
  Guru Arjan and, 19, 26
  Guru Gobind Singh and, 26
  Khalsa and, 34
  monarchy in, 19
Gwalior, 24, 186

haldi, 118
halemi raj, 20, 21, 25, 27, 41
Hamishah Bahar, 109–10
Har Rai, Sikh Guru, 12
Hardinge, Henry, 163, 169, 171–3, 175, 187
  Anglo-Sikh War, First (1845–6), 169, 171–3
  Blue Book and, 184
  Cunningham's criticism, 183
  Duleep Singh, relations with, 197, 199
  frontier reinforcement (1844–5), 163
  Gulab Singh, deal with (1845), 165, 166, 168, 171
  intelligence gathering, 176–7, 183, 184
  Jind Kaur, relations with, 179, 182, 184, 187–8, 196, 197
  Lal Singh's banishment (1846), 182, 187
  retirement (1848), 202
  Treaty of Lahore (1846), 172–3, 174, 175, 179, 180
  Treaty of Bhyrowal (1846), 189
  'watch and wait' policy, 174, 202, 203
Hardwar, 93
harems, *see zenanas*
Hargobind, Sikh Guru, 18, 22–5, 26
  Akal Takht, building of, 23
  Hargobindpur, founding of, 18
  Jahangir, relations with, 24–5
  militarism 23, 24, 25, 26
  Prithi Chand dynasty and, 23–4
  as 'warrior prince', 22, 24, 25, 26

Hargobindpur, 18
Haripur, 202
Harmandir Sahib, Amritsar, 19, 20–21, 41, 58, 178
havelis, 59, 61–4, 65, 89, 157
Hazara, 202
Hazrat Mahal, Begum of Awadh, 192
Hazuri Bagh, Lahore, 103, 108–9, 112
Henry VIII, King of England, 102
Hinduism; Hindus, 11, 12, 22, 26, 28, 29, 30
  Bhagavad Gita, 146
  festivals, 65
  marriage, 55
  Nanak and 11
  Rajah Janak, 22
  Rajputs, *see* Rajputs
  Ranjit Singh and 33, 81
  Rathayatra festival, 115
  sati, 145
Hindustan, 15–17
Hindustani language, 103
Hira Singh, 56, 178
Hira Singh, Dogra Rajah, 5, 153–4, 155, 157, 158, 159
History of the Sikhs (Cunningham), 183
horoscopes, 70–71, 126
horses, 105
hunting, 24, 61, 64
Hyderabad, 88

Illustrated London News, 161
Imamuddin, Sheikh, 181
indirect rule, 175
Indo-Persian culture, 25, 40, 91
  Arjan and, 21
  astrology, 70
  Gobind Singh and, 27
  Ranjit Singh and, 29, 40, 80, 109
Ireland, 191
Islam; Muslims, 18, 21, 27
  dancing girls, 55, 58
  Gul Begum and, 65
  jizya, 21
  dharamyudh and, 36
  festivals, 65
  madrasas, 64
  marriage, 55
  Moran and, 64
  mosques, 64, 65
  Sufism, 11
Italy, 13
izzat, 49, 53, 57, 91

Jagannath temple, Puri, 115
jagirs, 56, 60, 73, 118, 204
  Attariwala, 202
  Bhag Singh, 94, 96
  Gul Begum, 56, 65
  Jawahir Singh, 56
  Kahan Singh, 73–5
  Hira Singh, 56
  Lal Singh, 181
  Mangla, 178
  Mehtab Kaur, 60
  Mai Nakain, 60, 65, 86
Jahangir, Mughal Emperor, 17, 21, 22, 24–5, 41, 61
Jalandhar Doab, 173, 179, 191
Jallah, Pandit, 157
Jammu, 148, 157, 159, 165, 168, 172–4, 196

Dogra Rajputs, 141, 146, 158–9, 165, 180
Partition (1947), 174
Preyma plot (1847), 196
Treaty of Lahore (1846), 168, 172, 173–4
Jamrud, 85
Janak, Rajah, 22
Jangnama (Shah Muhammad), 148–50
Jasrota, 114
Jaswant Singh, Rajah of Nabha, 114
Jatts, 21, 35, 52, 80, 91, 156, 162
Jawahir Singh, 56, 157, 159, 161, 166, 178
Jind Kaur, Sikh Maharani, 5–6, 7, 8, 54, 139, 152–69, 208
accession (1843), 5, 66, 153, 157
Anglo-Sikh War (1848–9), 6, 7, 165–9, 172
austerity, 157, 177, 178, 181
Begum Samru, influence of, 92
Benares, life in, 201, 205–6
Brahmin mendicants and, 157, 193
death (1863), 212
Duleepgurh project, 178
durbars, 177, 195–6
exile (1847), 197, 201, 204
'heroine'/'whore' reputation, 6, 167
Hira Singh, relationship with, 157
imprisonment (1847–8), 6
Khalsa and, 157, 158–69, 197, 200
Jangnama on, 149–50
Jawahir Singh, murder of (1845), 161–2, 166, 181
Lal Singh, relationship with, 164, 180–83, 200
Lawrence, relations with, 5–6, 180, 187–8, 192–7
Lilliputian Regiment, 177–8, 198
Multan rebellion (1848), 200–201, 205
Nepal, life in, 206, 211
Peshaura Singh, murder of (1845), 161, 164
Preyma plot (1847), 196
purdah, 159–60, 193
Regency appointment (1844), 157
reunion with Duleep (1861), 205, 211
Sheikhupura, life in, 197, 201, 205
Treaty of Lahore (1846), 173, 174, 176, 177, 179–82
Treaty of Bhyrowal (1846), 189, 194
wedding to Ranjit Singh (1835), 54
zenana, life in, 192, 196, 200
Jind Kulan, 55
Jind, 93, 95, 96
jizya, 21
Jowai, Allah 57–8
Jumna river, 93, 96

Kabul, 110
Kahan Singh Man, 205
Kahan Singh Nakai, 73–4, 82, 129

kalgi, 63
Kanhaiya *misl*, 47, 48, 50, 52, 60, 75, 83
kanwar, 67
Kapurthala, 94
kardars, 54, 159, 168, 177
karma, 38
Kartarpur, 94, 101
Kartarpur Sahib, 18
Kashmir
  Bhangi *misl* in, 47
  concubines from, 55, 108
  flora of, 110
  Gulab Singh, rule of, 159, 165, 168, 172, 173–4, 181
  Lawrence on, 190
  Partition (1947), 174
  Sikh expansion in, 55
  Sher Singh's governorship, 55, 76
  Treaty of Lahore (1846), 168, 172, 173–4, 181
Kashmira Singh, Sikh Prince, 71, 76, 153, 161, 179
Kasur, 73, 74
Kathmandu, Nepal, 211
Katochan, Rajput Queen, 55, 145–7
Kaukab-i-Iqbal-i-Punjab, 105
Kaur, 28, 34
Khalistan, 33, 137
Khalsa, 17, 26, 27–8, 29, 35–7, 39, 80, 154–69, 208
  Anglo-Sikh War, First (1845–6), 148, 149, 165–9, 171–3
  aristocracy and, 32–3
  Civil War (1840–41), 155
  creation of (1699), 17, 26–9, 32–5, 156, 208
  dharam, 36
  demobilisation, 176–7, 198
  egalitarianism, 80, 90–91
  Fauj-i-Khalsa, 154
  Gulab Singh and, 165
  gurmata and, 30, 32, 156, 168
  Guru Granth Sahib and, 34
  Hira Singh and, 155, 157, 158
  Jind Kaur and, 157, 158–69, 197, 200
  martial ethos, 80, 81
  mercenary generals, 122, 154
  military strength, 121, 122
  misls and, 31, 36–7
  Multan rebellion (1848), 200
  non-Sikh troops, 154
  panchayat, 156, 157, 159, 161, 165, 167
  princes and, 67
  rahit, 36
  remodeling of, 122, 154
  republicanism and, 28–35, 36, 156
  Sarkar-i-Khalsa, 29, 39, 45, 96, 154, 168
  Treaty of Lahore (1846), 173, 174
  wages, 155, 157, 158, 159, 163, 165, 174, 181
Khan, Abdul Nabi, 98
khandan, 72
Kharak Singh, Sikh Maharajah, 6, 29, 51–2, 66, 67, 158
  Afghan War (1939–40), 158
  Azizuddin, relationship with, 99
  birth (1801), 29, 51, 68, 69–70, 72

British narratives on, 81, 127–33, 134, 135
Chand Kaur, engagement to, 51–2, 72
Chand Kaur, wedding to (1811), 62, 113, 114–16
character, 81, 127–33, 134, 135, 141
death (1840), 71–2, 139–43, 147, 148, 155, 185
death of mother (1838), 87, 89
Dhyan Singh, relationship with, 145–7
diplomacy, 101, 103–4, 106–7, 112
durbars, 103–4, 106–7
education, 81–2
empire building, 76, 179
heir apparent accession (1816), 68, 140
intellect, 81, 127–33, 134, 135, 141
jagirs, 60, 73–4, 75
Multan annexation (1818), 61, 82, 199
Nakai estates seizure (1811), 73–4, 82, 129
Nau Nihal's wedding (1837), 117, 118, 119
painting of, 62
Sarvasiddhantattvacudamani and, 80–81, 126, 127–8, 134
Sheikhupura annexation (1808), 60, 75, 79
succession, 126–7, 129, 130, 132, 140–41
Wade, relationship with, 101, 103–4

Khatris, 37
Khem Kaur Kalalwali, Sikh Maharani, 212
khi'lat, 50, 91, 96, 104, 110, 178, 195
Khushal Singh, 56
Khusrau, Mirza, 22
Khwabgah, Lahore Fort, 112
kinship
  British and, 191
  culture of relatedness, 91, 92
  marriage alliances, 1, 45–59, 91, 107, 113
Koh-i-Noor diamond, 115
Kot Kamalia, 82
Kot Said Mehmood, 56
Kotli Loharan, 43
Krishna, 62
Kumbh Mela, 93

Ladakh, 2, 158
Lahore, 2, 5, 29
  Anarkali's Tomb, 190–91
  durbar (1838), 102, 104, 105–7, 108, 111, 112
  durbar (1847), 195–6
  Fort, *see* Lahore Fort
  Gul Begum's *haveli*, 65
  Hazuri Bagh, 103, 108–9, 112
  horse trade, 105
  Kharak Singh, birth of (1801), 69–70
  Kharak, wedding of (1811), 62, 113, 114–16
  kitab-khana, 40
  Lawrence's residency, 135–6, 176–7, 188–99, 204
  Mai Nakain's funeral (1838), 86–9, 123

Nau Nihal Singh's wedding (1837), 1–4, 6, 10, 45, 54, 60, 112, 113, 116–24
Preyma plot (1847), 196
Ranjit Singh's capture of (1799), 47–50, 93, 204, 208
Shalabagh, 109–10, 112
Siege (1799), 48
Siege (1840–41), 149
throne, 29, 40, 41, 112
Tripartite Treaty (1838), 85–6, 88, 90, 102, 122–3, 130, 131
zenana, 52–3, 55, 59, 112, 146
Lahore Fort, 41, 74, 103, 109, 141
doorkeeper, 106
kennels, 54, 157, 209, 212
Khwabgah, 112
Maharanis in, 59
Mussumun Burj, 112, 116
Nau Nihal, death of (1840), 141
Octagonal Tower, 116
Siege (1799), 48
Siege (1840–41), 149
Takhtgah, 112
throne, 41
Wade's visit (1838), 88, 112
Lake, Gerard, 1st Viscount, 94, 97
Lal Singh, Rajah, 158, 166, 169, 172, 177
Jind Kaur, relationship with, 164, 180–83, 200
trial and exile (1846), 181–3, 187
Lal, Ruby, 9
Lawrence, George, 191
Lawrence, Henry, 5–6, 135–6, 139, 175, 187, 210
Adventures of an Officer, The, 135, 190
Chand Kaur, views on, 185
Dalhousie, relationship with, 204
Duleep, relationship with, 136, 195, 196, 197–8
durbar (1847), 195–6
Jind Kaur, relations with, 5–6, 180, 187–8, 192–7, 201, 204
Lahore residency, 135–6, 176–7, 188–99, 204
Lal Singh, relations with, 181–2, 187
Preyma plot (1847), 196
Ranjit Singh, views on, 139, 186
Treaty of Bhyrowal (1846), 188–9
women, views on, 185–6, 193
Lawrence, Honoria, 192
Lawrence, John, 179–80, 182, 191, 198, 199
Légion d'honneur, 105
Lilliputian Regiment, 177–8, 198
literacy, 39, 110
Lodi dynasty (1451–1526), 14, 15–16
lotus flower, 20–21, 41
Ludhiana, 85, 88, 98, 100, 104, 110, 183, 203

Macnaghten, William, 131

madrasas, 64
Maha Singh, Sukerchakia Chief, 4, 43, 46
administrative system, 44
Afghan wars, 32
chronicling of life, 69
death (1790), 46, 78–9
mother, death of, 83
Maharanis, 59–65, 216–23
diplomacy, 112
havelis, 59, 61–5
jagirs, 56, 60, 65, 86
martiality, 61, 82
purdah, 55–6, 59, 82, 159–60, 193
princely education, 81–2
Mai Desan, 46, 47
Mai Lachmi, 53
Mai Nakain, Sikh Maharani, 6–7, 51, 60–64, 68
death (1838), 83, 86–9, 102, 123
haveli, 9, 61–4
jagirs, 9, 61–4, 86
Kharak Singh, birth of (1801), 51, 68
Kharak Singh, education of, 81–2
Kharak Singh, wedding of (1811), 115
Multan annexation (1818), 61, 82, 199
Nau Nihal's wedding (1837), 6, 118
paintings, 9, 61–4
Sada Kaur, rivalry with, 51, 68
Sheikhupura, life in, 9, 60–64, 75, 86, 109, 197
wedding (1798), 48, 52
Majithia family
Lehna Singh, 98, 126, 147
Runjore Singh, 180
Mal, Diwan Sawan, 200
Mangla, 178–9, 182
Mankera, 55
mansabdari system, 41
Maratha Confederacy (1645–1818), 80, 94, 102, 122, 186
Mardana, Bhai, 63
marriage, 1, 45–59, 91, 107, 215–16
chadar dalni, 52–3, 57, 157
index of power and, 57
map of, 215–16
polygamy, 46
sarkarat, 55
sati, 145
widowhood, 52–3, 57, 68, 150
weddings, 1, 45, 54, 113–24
'martial masculinity', 77–80, 81
masculinity, 77–80, 81, 192
massage, 56, 118
matchlocks, 43, 46
McGregor, W.L., 106
meditation, 12
Mehtab Kaur, Sikh Maharani, 47, 51, 52, 60, 68
death (1813), 60, 74–5
illegitimate children, 68
jagirs, 60, 150
Sada Kaur, rivalry with, 51, 68, 75
Sher Singh, birth of (1807), 68, 70
mercenaries, 122, 154, 160
Metcalfe, Charles, 94, 95, 97, 114, 162

Mexico, 13
misls, 3–4, 14, 17, 31–2, 34, 39, 49, 67
  Bhangi, 47–9, 50, 52–3
  Dal Khalsa, 32
  guerrilla warfare, 154
  jagirs, 73
  Jatts in, 35
  Kanhaiya, 47, 48, 50, 52, 60, 75, 83
  Khalsa and, 31, 36–7
  marriage alliances 46–53, 55, 57
  martial skills, 79
  Nakai, 48, 50, 52, 61, 73–4, 82, 129
  rakhi, 31
  Ramgarhia, 50
  Ranjit Singh, death of (1839), 146
  religious and, 91, 92
  royal symbolism, 91
  succession rules, 73
  Sukerchakia, see Sukerchakia *misl*
  surrender protocol, 49–50
misogyny, 144, 149–50, 152, 185–6, 193
monarchies, 13, 137, 209
Moran, Muslim Queen, 55, 58, 64
morchal, 63
mosques, 64, 65
Muazzam, *see* Bahadur Shah
Mughal Empire (1526–1857) 2, 8–9, 10, 11–30, 39, 138
  Arjan, relations with, 17, 21, 22, 24, 26
  Begum Samru, relations with, 92
  Bengal, ceding of (1765), 106
  British, relations with, 2, 8–9, 17–18, 76, 88, 93, 106
  dharamyudh and, 36
  Gobind Singh, relations with, 11, 26
  Hargobind, relations with, 24–5
  Hindustan, conquest of, 15–17
  Indo-Persian culture, 25, 40, 111
  jizya, 21
  khi'lat, 50, 91
  mansabdari system, 41
  marriage alliances, 57
  'martial masculinity', 77–8, 80
  misls and, 35
  Nanak, relations with, 15–18
  paintings, 64
  princes, 76–8, 80, 140, 159
  'sacred kingship', 22, 25, 35, 41, 70
  Shahnameh and, 27
  surrender protocol, 50
Muhammad, Pir, 83
Muhammad, Prophet of Islam, 16
Mukerian, 75, 101
Muller, Bamba, 213
Mulraj, 200, 205
Multan, 48, 76, 114, 117
  annexation (1818), 61, 82, 199
  rebellion (1848), 199–201, 203, 204, 205, 212
Multana Singh, Prince, 71, 153, 179
musammat, 55

Mussumun Burj, Lahore Fort, 112, 116

Nabha, 95
Nakai *misl*, 48, 50, 52, 61, 73–4, 82, 129
Kahan Singh, 73–4, 82, 129
Nanak, Sikh Guru, 11, 15–17, 18, 23, 24, 207
  Babur, meeting with, 15–17, 18
  Baburvani, 15–16, 152
  Kartarpur Sahib, founding of, 17
  portraits of, 63, 125
  succession, 23
Napoleon I, Emperor of the French, 105
Nath, Diwan Amar, 56, 59
Nath, Diwan Dina, 158, 189
Nau Nihal Singh, Sikh Maharajah, 55, 66, 67
  death (1840), 71–2, 139–43, 147, 148, 155
  Dhyan Singh, relationship with, 146
  diplomacy, 101, 103
  empire building, 179
  forts, 179
  Hindu brides, 55
  Peshawar campaign (1834), 76
  Sarvasiddhantattvacudamani and, 126
  succession, 126–7, 132, 140–41
  wedding (1837), 1–4, 6, 10, 45, 54, 60, 112, 113, 116–24
nautch, *see* dancing girls
nazarana, 110
Nehru-Gandhi family, 210
Nepal, 102, 171, 175, 194, 206, 211
North-Western Frontier, 85, 98, 131, 132, 164, 182, 199
Nurpur, 114
Nuruddin, Fakir, 158

Ochterlony, David, 98, 114, 116
Octagonal Tower, Lahore Fort, 116
Old Delhi, 94
Order of the Bright Star, 105
Orientalism, 133, 162, 187
  and 'decadence', 108
  and 'despotism', 9, 186
  and femininity, 133
  and princely conflict, 76, 81
  and women, 59, 82, 160
Osborne, W.G., 108
Ottoman Empire (1299–1922), 79

paintings, 9, 61–4, 198
Pakistan, 1, 137, 174, 210
pāncha panch parmeswara, 156
panchayat, 156, 157, 159, 161, 165, 167
Panj Pyare, 28, 156
panth, 32, 33, 35, 37, 39, 210
  gurmata and, 30, 31, 156
  Guru Granth Sahib, 36
  Hargobind and, 23, 24
  Khalsa and, 39, 156, 159, 168
Parshad, Ajudhia 163, 166
Partap Singh, Prince, 151, 153

Partition of India (1947), 1, 34, 136, 174
Pathak, Durgashankar, 126
Pathans, 11, 44, 55, 215
Patiala, 95, 210
pensions, 54, 60, 68, 188, 201, 212
Persia
  astrology in, 70
  British, relations with, 102
  Islam in, 64
  royal culture, *see* Indo-Persian philosophy
Persian language, 64, 75, 98, 103, 109, 198
  khalisa, 34
  khandan, 72
  navoseh, 73
  sahibzadah, 67
  Umdat-ut-tawarikh, 62
Peshaura Singh, Prince, 71, 76, 153, 161, 164, 179
Peshawar, 76, 85, 117, 128, 129, 179, 191
Phagwara, 101
Phillaur, 101
Phulkian *sardars*, 95–6
Pind Dadan Khan, 43
poetry
  Chattha clan, 83
  Guru Arjan, 20
  Guru Gobind Singh, 26
  Guru Nanak, 11, 15
  Mughal, 111
  Shah Muhammad, 148–50
  Suri, 62
polygamy, 46
Portugal, 13
Praetorian Guard, 156
Prem Sumarag Granth, 37–9
Preyma plot (1847), 196
primogeniture, 23, 140
princely states, 13, 199
princes, 66–82
  horoscopes, 70–71
  education, 75–82, 151
  empire building, 61, 76, 82
  jagirs, 73–5
  'legitimacy' of 68, 71–2
  marriages, 1–3, 6, 10, 51–2, 54, 60, 62, 72, 113–24
  sahibzadah, 67
  succession, 8, 81, 126–52
  weaponisation, 72
Prithi Chand, 23
private vs public areas, 112
privy purses, 209
Punjab, 1, 2
  Mughal rule, 11–28, 29, 30, 31, 39
  Partition (1947) 1, 136, 174
  weddings in 1
Punjabi language, 103
purdah, 55–6, 59, 82, 159–60, 193

qissa, 150

rabab, 63
Radcliffe, Cyril, 136, 174
rahitnameh, 36
Rai, Diwan Hakim, 73
Raj Banso, Rajput Queen, 55, 58
Raj Kaur, Sukerchakia Chief, 45, 46, 53, 55, 83, 143
Rajputs, 34, 50, 58, 91, 145

Dogras, 141, 146, 158–9, 165, 180, 190
rakhi, 31
Ram, Dya, 47
Ram Bagh, 100
Ram Das, Sikh Guru, 18, 19, 23
Ram Singh, Bhai, 89, 117, 158
Ram Singh, Bhaya, 82
Ramdaspur, 18, 19
Ranjit Singh, Sikh Maharajah
Akalis, relations with, 58
Azizuddin, relationship with, 99
Bhag Singh, relationship with, 93–7
Bhangis, relations with, 47–9, 50, 52–3
British narratives on, 8–9, 80–81, 83, 130, 137, 144
childhood, 78–9
chronicling of life, *see Umdat-ut-tawarikh*
coins, minting of, 29, 40
daughters, 68
death (1839), 7, 126–7, 133, 136, 145
death of father (1790), 78–9
death of mother, 83
diplomacy, 85–90, 93–124
durbars, 57, 102, 103–4, 105–8, 111, 112
dynastic colonialism, 45, 59, 74
dynastic diplomacy, 92, 98
elephant incident, 78
empire building, 43–4, 47, 68, 76
eye, loss of, 79
'feminine' courtliness, 64, 80, 81, 110
foreign policy, 85–90, 93–113
gardens, 109–12
gift giving, 96–7, 105, 111
Gul Begum, wedding to (1832), 55, 56, 59
gurmata and, 30–31, 32
halemi raj, 41
Harmandir Sahib, development of, 41
Hinduism and, 33, 81
horses, love of, 105
illiteracy 39, 110
Indo-Persian culture, 29, 40, 80, 109
intellect, 80–81
intelligence network, 121–2
Khalsa, leadership of, 122, 154–5
Kharak Singh, birth of, 29, 51, 68, 69–70, 72
Kharak Singh, marriage of, 51–2, 62, 72, 113, 114–16
Kharak Singh, succession of, 126–7, 129, 130
kinship relations and, 51–9, 91–2, 107, 113–23
kitab-khana, 40
Lahore, capture of (1799), 47–50, 93, 204, 208
leadership, narratives on, 8, 81, 127, 138, 144–5, 193–5, 207
as 'Lion of Punjab', 1, 6, 25, 28, 133, 207
'love marriages', 55
Maharajah, proclaimed as (1801), 52, 67

Mai Nakain's funeral (1838), 86–9
Marathas, relations with, 94, 122
marriage alliances, 51–9, 91–2, 107, 113–23, 215, 209
'martial masculinity', 77–80, 81
Moran, wedding to (1802), 55, 58
Nau Nihal, marriage of (1837), 1–4, 6, 10, 45, 54, 60, 112, 113, 116–24
Nau Nihal, succession of, 126–7
nautch parties, 107–8
Order of the Bright Star, 105
philosophies of kingship, 40
portraits of, 63–4
princely education, 77–82, 135
republicanism and, 28–35
sacralisation and, 41
Sada Kaur, relationship with, 47–52, 72, 75, 83, 151
Sahib Singh Bhangi's death (1811), 52–3
Sarkar-i-Khalsa, 29, 39, 45, 96, 154
screen depictions of, 137
Sheikhupura *thanedar* imprisonment, 64
Sher Singh, birth of (1807), 68, 70
Sohadara siege (1790), 78–9
succession, 126–7, 130, 132
Sukerchakia *misl*, *see* Sukerchakia *misl*
throne, 9, 29, 40, 41
Tripartite Treaty (1838), 85–6, 88, 90, 102, 122–3, 130, 131
Umdat-ut-tawarikh, 6, 40, 48, 53–4, 62, 64, 67
ras-lila, 62
Rasulnagar, 83
ratha, 115
Rathayatra festival, 115
Rattan Kaur, Sikh Maharani, 52
republicanism, 28–36, 156
Roman Republic (509–27 BCE), 156
Roop Kaur, Sikh Maharani, 56
Royal Asiatic Society, 110, 115
Runjore Singh Majithia, 180
Rupar *durbar* (1831), 102, 103–4, 108
Russian Empire, 95, 102, 183

Sacha Padishah, 12, 16, 20
Sada Kaur, Kanhaiya Chief, 45, 47–52, 55, 57, 60, 82–3, 143, 144
Bhangi conflict, 47–9, 50
British, relations with, 83
finances 50–51
forts, 179
house arrest, 83
jagirs, 75, 82–3
Kanhaiya *misl*, 47, 48, 50, 52, 60, 75, 83, 113
Lahore, capture of (1799), 47–50, 93, 204, 208
Mehtab, rivalry with, 51, 68, 75
sidelining of, 51–2, 72, 75, 83, 151

Safavid dynasty (1501–1736), 70
Sahib Kaur
  death of Nau Nihal (1840), 143
  wedding (1837), 1–4, 6, 10, 45, 54, 60, 112, 113, 116–24
Sahib Singh Bedi, Baba, 52, 74, 87
Sahib Singh Bhangi, 50, 52, 53
sahibzadah, 67
Sahiwal, 75
salt mines, 43
samadhi, 64–5
Samru, Begum of Sardhana, 10, 92, 160, 192
Sandhawalia, 147, 153–4, 212
  Attar Singh, 147
Sanskrit, 80, 115
sardarni, 55
sardars, 3–4, 14, 31, 32, 36, 37, 49, 67
  gurmata and, 32
  Khalsa and, 36–7
  marriage alliances and, 54
  martial skills, 79
  surrender protocol, 49–50
  wealth of, 43
Sardhana, 92, 160, 192
Sarkar-i-Khalsa, 29, 39, 45, 96, 154, 168
sarkarat, 55
Sarkaria, 56
Sarvasiddhantattvacudamani, 80–81, 125–6, 127–8, 134, 147
Satgarha, 73
sati, 145
sepoys, 121, 163, 171, 172
servants, 55
Shah Jahan, Mughal Emperor, 22, 41, 77, 109, 110
Shah Muhammad, 148–50, 162
Shah Shuja, Durrani Emir, 85, 88, 122
Shahjahanabad, 94
Shahnameh, 27
shahzada, 67
Shiv Deo, Shahzadah, 166
Shalabagh, Lahore, 109–10, 112, 116
Sheikhupura, 6, 79
  Jind Kaur in, 197, 201, 205
  Mai Nakain in, 9, 60–64, 75, 86, 109, 197
Sher Singh, Sikh Maharajah, 66, 67, 68, 158
  Azizuddin, relationship with, 99
  birth (1807), 70
  Civil War (1840–41), 147–52, 155, 185, 208
  Dhyan Singh, relationship with, 144–5, 146, 147
  diplomacy, 100–101
  empire building, 68, 76
  as 'illegitimate', 68, 71
  jagirs, 75, 82–3
  Kashmir governorship, 55, 76
  marriages 54, 55
  succession, 132, 140, 141, 142, 143–4
  Wade's visit (1826–7), 100
Sikhism, 3, 11–42
  Akalis, 58
  Baburvani, 15–16
  dharamyudh and, 36

egalitarianism, 3, 12, 20, 21, 29, 35, 154
gender equality, 192
God, figure of, 11–12
gurdwaras, 18, 19, 20–21, 41, 198, 210
gurmata, 30–31, 32, 37, 39, 156, 168, 229
Guru Granth Sahib, see *Guru Granth Sahib*
gurus, 11–28, 29, 35, 39
halemi raj, 20, 21, 25, 27, 41
meditation, 12
monarchy and 3, 13–42
Mughal Empire and, 11–28
pacifism, 24
Prem Sumarag Granth, 37–9
primogeniture and, 23
rahitnameh, 36
republicanism and, 28–32, 36
Sacha Padishah, 12, 16, 20
sardars, 3–4, 14
temptations and, 12, 15, 20, 37
Sindh, 76, 163
Singh, Amarinder, 210
Singh, Buta, 196
Singh, Dal, 50
Singh, Kapur, 33–4, 36
Singh, Khushwant, 28, 29
Singh, Patwant, 28, 29, 33
Singh, Tej, 169, 172, 191, 195, 196
Singh, Thakur, 212
Singh, Zorawar, 158
slaves, 55, 68, 178–9
smallpox, 79
Sobraon, 171, 172, 191
Sodhis, 101
Kesra Singh, 50
soft power, 45
Sohadara, 78
Spain, 13
Subhadra, 115
subsidiary alliances, 174–5
Sufism, 11
Sukerchak, Gujranwala, 31
Sukerchakia *misl*, 3, 4, 31, 36, 43–59, 75, 84, 137, 159, 188
administrative system, 44
Bhangi conflict, 47–9, 50, 78–9
Chattha conflict, 83
chronicling of history, 69
as dynasty, 45, 71–2, 137
empire building, 75, 76, 90
marriage alliances, 45–60, 62, 63, 65, 67, 91, 113, 215
princely education, 78–9
Suri, Sohan Lal, 40, 68–9, 133, 138
on astrology, 70
on Bhag Singh, 97
on Civil War (1840–41), 148, 150, 155
on elephant incident, 78
on European diplomats, 101, 103, 105–6
on Hardinge, 189
on Jind Kaur, 177
on Kharak Singh, 67, 69, 71–2, 114, 115, 140
on Lahore conquest (1799), 48
on 'legitimacy' 68, 71
on Mai Nakain, 6–7, 62, 64, 115
on marriages, 53–4

on Nau Nihal, 71–2, 116–20, 140, 142
on princes 69–72, 75, 78–9
on queens, 6, 69
on Shalabagh, 109
on Sher Singh, 67, 144, 150–51
on women's roles, 152
on 'veil of chastity', 6, 69
Sutlej river, 57, 74, 93, 97, 162, 171, 172, 173

Takhtgah, Lahore Fort, 112
tambol, 114, 118, 119
Tanda, 101
Tara Singh, Prince, 153
character, 134
horoscope, lack of, 71
as 'illegitimate', 68, 70, 71
jagirs, 75, 82–3
succession, 142
tawaif, 64
taxation, 54, 159, 168, 177, 200
Tegh Bahadur, Sikh Guru, 17, 26
temptations, 12, 15, 20, 37
thanedar, 64
Tibet, 2, 171
tigers, 24
tikka, 195
Tipu Sultan, Sultan of Mysore, 10
transfer of power negotiations (1947), 210
treaties
Bhyrowal Treaty (1846), 188–9, 194, 198, 202
Friendship Treaty (1806), 94
Friendship Treaty (1809), 96, 97, 102, 162
Lahore Treaty (1846), 172–6, 179–82
Tripartite Treaty (1838), 85–6, 88, 90, 102, 122–3, 131
tribute, 31, 54, 60, 73, 110
Tripartite Treaty (1838), 85–6, 88, 90, 122–3
turbans, 23, 63, 91

Umdat-ut-tawarikh (Suri), 40, 68–9, 133, 138, 165
on astrology, 70–71
on Bhag Singh, 97
on Civil War (1840–41), 148, 150, 155
on elephant incident, 78
on European diplomats, 101, 103, 105–6
on Hardinge, 189
on Jind Kaur, 177
on Kharak Singh, 67, 69, 71–2, 114, 115, 140
on Lahore conquest (1799), 48
on 'legitimacy' 68, 71
on Mai Nakain, 6–7, 62, 64, 115
on marriages, 53–4
on Nau Nihal Singh, 71–2, 116–20, 140, 142
on princes 69–72, 75, 78–9
on queens, 6, 69
on Shalabagh, 109
on Sher Singh, 67, 144, 150–51
on 'veil of chastity', 6, 69
Una, 87

Vainiki, 49

Vaisakhi festival, 27
vakils, 69, 86, 87, 97–9, 100, 113, 117, 148
var, 150
vatna, 118
vazirs
  Dhyan Singh, 141–7, 149, 152, 153
  Gulab Singh, 166, 172
  Hira Singh, 5, 153–4, 155, 157, 158, 159
  Jawahir Singh, 56, 157, 159, 161, 178
  Lal Singh, *see* Lal Singh
veiling, 55–6, 59
Victor Singh, Sikh Prince, 213
Victoria, Queen of the United Kingdom, 90, 107, 186, 199, 211, 213

Wade, Claude Martin, 85–6, 92, 97, 98, 99, 102, 137, 184, 210
  Adinanagar visit (1831), 101
  Hamishah Bahar gift, 109–10
  Hazuri Bagh visit (1831), 103, 108–9
  intelligence network, 164, 175
  Kharak Singh, description of, 131–2, 137
  Lahore *durbar* (1838), 111
  Lahore visit (1826–7), 100
  Mai Nakain's funeral (1838), 86–9, 102, 123
  Nau Nihal Singh's wedding (1837), 122–3
  Order of the Bright Star, 105
  river navigation, 105
  Shalabagh visit (1831), 109
  Tripartite Treaty (1838), 85–6, 102, 122–3, 131
Wazir Khan, Nawab of Sirhind, 26
weddings, 1, 45, 113–23
  cost of, 115
  gifts, 114, 118, 119
  Kharak Singh (1811), 62, 113–16
  Nau Nihal Singh (1837), 1–4, 6, 10, 45, 54, 60, 112, 113, 116–24
  vatna ceremony, 118
widowhood, 52–3, 57, 68, 150
William IV, King of the United Kingdom, 103, 111
women, 7
  British, 192
  chadar dalni, 52–3, 57, 157
  femininity, 64, 80, 81, 110, 133, 179
  leadership, 144, 147–69, 179, 192, 208
  Maharanis, 59–65
  marriage alliances, 45–59
  martiality, 61, 82
  misogyny, 144, 149–50, 152, 185–6, 193
  mistreatment of, 15, 152
  musammat, 55
  political activity, 82–4
  princely education, 81–2
  princesses, 68
  purdah, 55–6, 59, 82, 159–60, 193
  sardarni, 55
  sati, 145
  widowhood, 52–3, 57, 68, 150
  zenanas, see *zenanas*

Yashwant Rao Holkar, Maratha Maharajah, 94, 122

Zafarnama-i-Ranjit Singh (Amar Nath), 215
Zafarnamah (Guru Gobind Singh), 27
zamindars, 53, 178
Zebo, 55
zenanas, 52–3, 55, 57, 59, 80, 82, 192, 196
  chadar dalni, 52–3
  Fane's visit, 59, 112
  intrigue in, 82, 196
  Jind Kaur in, 192, 196, 200
  Katochan in, 146
zenankhana, 61